ACCESS TO EVIDENCE IN CIVIL PROCEDURE

ELGAR LITIGATION SERIES

The Elgar Litigation Series is a library of works by leading practitioners and scholars covering the broad area of dispute resolution. The titles in the series are analytical in approach, highlighting and unpicking the legal issues that are most critical and relevant to practice. Designed to be detailed, focussed reference works, the books in this series aim to offer an authoritative statement on law and procedure. The series will include texts covering specific civil courts and procedural rules, as well as key topics such as appeals, damages and remedies, disclosure, evidence and injunctions.

For a full list of Edward Elgar published titles, including the titles in this series, visit our website at www.e-elgar.com.

ACCESS TO EVIDENCE IN CIVIL PROCEDURE

European Law and Practice

Edited by

FERNANDO GASCÓN INCHAUSTI
Professor and Chair in Procedural Law, Complutense University of Madrid, Spain

ASTRID STADLER
Professor and Chair of Private Law, Civil Procedure Law, Private International Law and Comparative Law, University of Konstanz, Germany

MAGNE STRANDBERG
Professor and Vice Dean, Faculty of Law, University of Bergen, Norway

ELGAR LITIGATION SERIES

Edward Elgar PUBLISHING

Cheltenham, UK · Northampton, MA, USA

Published by

Edward Elgar Publishing Limited
The Lypiatts
15 Lansdown Road
Cheltenham
Glos GL50 2JA
UK

Edward Elgar Publishing, Inc.
William Pratt House
9 Dewey Court
Northampton
Massachusetts 01060
USA

Authorised representative in the EU for GPSR queries only: Easy Access System Europe – Mustamäe tee 50, 10621 Tallinn, Estonia, gpsr.requests@easproject.com

A catalogue record for this book is available from the British Library

Library of Congress Control Number: 2025951121

This book is available electronically in the Elgaronline
Law subject collection
https://doi.org/10.4337/9781035336135

MIX
Paper | Supporting responsible forestry
FSC® C013604

ISBN 978 1 0353 3612 8 (cased)
ISBN 978 1 0353 3613 5 (eBook)
ISBN 978 1 0353 9245 2 (ePub)

Printed and bound by CPI Group (UK) Ltd, Croydon, CR0 4YY

CONTENTS

EXTENDED CONTENTS

LIST OF CONTRIBUTORS

Fernando Gascón Inchausti is Full Professor of Procedural Law at the Complutense University of Madrid, Spain. His main fields of interest are civil and criminal procedure, both from a European and comparative perspective. He is currently Secretary General of the International Association of Procedural Law and Co-Editor in Chief of the International Journal of Procedural Law. He has published several books on European and international civil procedure law.

Emmanuel Jeuland is Law Professor at the University of Paris 1 Panthéon-Sorbonne, France, where he also completed his Master of Law. He holds an LL.M from King's College (London). His PhD on the law of obligations focused on the procedural law relating to the substitution of persons in contractual and procedural matters. He has been the Director of the Sorbonne Institute of Legal Research and now, within that Institute, he is the Director of the Department "Sorbonne Justice et procès". He is also currently the Director of the Master's Program on Justice and Litigation at the University of Paris 1Panthéon-Sorbonne. He has published textbooks and essays on procedural law and legal theory.

Bart Krans is Full Professor of Civil Law and Civil Procedure Law at Leiden Law School, the Netherlands.

Johannes Landbrecht (*Privatdozent*, Dr. iur, LL.B.) practices international arbitration in Geneva as German *Rechtsanwalt*, Swiss *avocat*, and English barrister, with a focus on energy and IP-related disputes. He is also a lecturer at the universities of Konstanz, Münster, and Zurich. His main research interests lie in the fields of civil procedure, arbitration, conflict of laws, and law and language.

Elisabetta Silvestri was until October 2020 Associate Professor of Italian Civil Procedure and Comparative Civil Procedure at the Department of Law, University of Pavia, Italy. She received her legal education at the University of Pavia, where she earned her LL.B., and Cornell Law School, where she obtained her LL.M. She was also visiting Scholar at Yale Law School and the London School of Economics. She continues lecturing today as an invited speaker at Italian and other European universities on a variety of subjects in the field of civil procedure and related matters as well as publishing extensively in Italy and abroad.

John Sorabji is teaching at University College London, UK, where he runs courses on civil justice and alternative dispute resolution. As a visiting professor he regularly teaches at the University of Paris II. He is a practising barrister and acted as the Principal Legal Advisor to the Lord Chief Justice and the Master of the Rolls. He is a council member of the International Association of Procedural Law.

Astrid Stadler (Dr. iur, Dr. h.c.) is a Professor of Law at the University of Konstanz, Germany, and holds a chair on civil law, civil procedure law, comparative law and private international law. Her areas of research are German, European and international civil procedure law, property law and contract law. A main area of her research is mass litigation where she has published numerous articles and books. Since 2022 she has been the president of the German Association of Civil Proceduralists and she is also co-editor of one of the leading legal periodicals in Germany: *Juristenzeitung (JZ)*.

Magne Strandberg is Professor at the Faculty of Law at the University of Bergen, Norway. Civil procedure law and tort law are his main fields of teaching and research, and he has a special interest for the law on evidence on which he wrote his doctoral thesis. He is member of several national and international associations of procedural and comparative law.

Michael Stürner (Dr. iur, M.Juris, Oxford) is Professor of Civil Law, Private International Law and Comparative Law at the University of Konstanz, Germany, since 2012. He also serves as a judge at the Higher Regional Court (Oberlandesgericht) in Karlsruhe, Germany, with a special responsibility for the recognition and enforcement of foreign titles and arbitral awards. Moreover, he has served as Vice-Rector for teaching at the University of Konstanz (Prorektor für Lehre, 2019-2024). His main research interests lie in the fields of cross-border dispute resolution, comparative law, conflict of laws, and European private law.

Nicolò Trocker is emeritus Professor of Civil Pocedure at the University of Florence, Italy. He is also a Member of the International Association of Procedural Law and has been a Visiting Professor at the University of Munich, Germany, at the University of Nagoya, Japan, at the University of California at Berkeley and on numerous occasions at the University of Miami, School of Law, USA, teaching International Civil Litigation.

Niek Zondag is PhD fellow at Leiden Law School, Institute of Private Law, the Netherlands. He is preparing a thesis in the field of evidence law.

TABLE OF CASES

AUSTRIA

DENMARK

EUROPEAN COURT OF HUMAN RIGHTS

EUROPEAN COURT OF JUSTICE

FRANCE

GERMANY

ITALY

THE NETHERLANDS

NORWAY

SPAIN

SWEDEN

SWITZERLAND

UNITED KINGDOM

UNITED STATES

TABLE OF LEGISLATION

AUSTRIA

DENMARK

ESTONIA

EUREOPEAN LEGILATION

REGULATION

GREECE

HUNGARY

ITALY

KOREA

LATVIA

LITHUANIA

THE NETHERLANDS

NORWAY

PORTUGAL

PRIVATE/NON-STATE RULES

SPAIN

SWEDEN

SWITZERLAND

UNITED KINGDOM

UNITED STATES

VENEZUELA

AGREEMENT, TREATIES AND CONVENTIONS

INTRODUCTION

Fernando Gascón Inchausti, Astrid Stadler and Magne Strandberg

Whenever a party lacks access to evidence which may support his or her case in a legal dispute and there are reasons to believe that the evidence is in the possession of an opposing party or a third party, these legal questions arise: May the party claim access to evidence from the opposite party or the third party? Have parties a right to access evidence which he or she is not able to access by self-help or has the opposite party a right to keep the evidence within his or her private possession? Is there a right to access evidence only if a set of requirements are met or is there a more or less automatic right to access evidence? Is there a right to access all possibly relevant evidence or only more or less specified groups or categories of evidence? These questions have been relevant for civil proceedings over a very long time in all European countries, and the very problem holds the same basic features across all jurisdictions where proceedings are based on party gathering and party production of evidence. The problem, indeed, may arise both for evidence located in the country where proceedings are pending and for evidence located abroad. **I.001**

The very different attitudes towards the problem at least potentially reflect equally different attitudes towards the "political" ideology of civil procedure law. On the one hand, probably apparent in the Anglo-American tradition, general, broad, and early access to evidence may seem to promote truth seeking and thereby realisation of substantive rights. It may also be regarded as a means for equality: the party having better access to evidence obviously is in possession of a tactical advantage which broad rules on disclosure of evidence seems to extinguish. Finally, broad, general, and early access to evidence may help parties settle at an early stage and to do so based on equally well-informed choices which may enhance the chances of a fair settlement. On the other hand, reluctance towards rights on access to evidence is in line with the need to protect privacy and may be explained by a rather liberalistic procedural ideology where the state should be reluctant to intervene in inter-partes relationships. From such a perspective, a party should not be obliged to provide his enemy with weapons. Furthermore, a reluctant attitude to access to evidence may be justified by a need to avoid high costs, which the Anglo-American experience suggests as a more than potential problem with broad disclosure of evidence. Following from that consequence of broad discovery or disclosure, such rules may lead to new inequalities between the parties – or to be more precise, such rules may let the economically stronger party take **I.002** even greater advantage of his strength and may force the weaker party to close the case simply because of a lack of funding.

I.003 Within this general technical and ideological framework, this book aims to provide a comprehensive and detailed study of the tools available to litigants to overcome the barriers associated with information asymmetry and to access information and evidence held by the opposing party or a third party.

I.004 The scope is focused on access to evidence on a genuinely European level. First, because a significant part of national provisions establishing rules on access to evidence are rooted in EU law. Since a right to access evidence may highly affect the effectiveness of procedural law and the realisation of substantive rights, disclosure of evidence is gaining a higher place on the agenda for the EU. Although the EU has no legislative power to establish general civil procedure law, harmonisation of procedural law for specific branches of substantive law is being expected and achieved.

I.005 Indeed, matters on access to evidence have been directly addressed in five EU Directives: the 2004 Directive on the enforcement of intellectual property rights (Article 8); the 2014 Directive on actions for damages for infringements of the competition law (Articles 5 and 6); the 2020 Directive on representative actions for the protection of the collective interests of consumers (Article 18); the 2024 Directive on corporate sustainability due diligence (Article 29(3)(e)); and the 2024 Directive on liability for defective products (Article 9).

I.006 Since these Directives only apply for a few areas of substantive law, most questions concerning access to evidence are left to national law. Even though the problem of access to evidence is more or less uniform, different procedural traditions seem to fancy very different answers which are remarkably illustrated by the Anglo-American tradition, the Germanic tradition, and the Roman tradition. While the Anglo-American legal family is famous for very generous and broad rules on access to evidence where parties and third parties are obliged to provide a party with access to all relevant and non-privileged evidence, the Germanic and Roman traditions have been far more reluctant and at least as a start have not entailed any rules providing a general right to access evidence. While rules on discovery and disclosure are regarded as cornerstones of procedural law in England and US, traditional German law does not even recognise such rules as procedural – instead, the question of access to evidence has been regarded as a matter of substantive law. The legal situation in Germany has been under some development during the last decades, but neither the procedural nor substantive rules on access to evidence seem to be very generous. The same practical effect is detected in jurisdictions belonging to the Roman tradition, such as France, Italy, or Spain. Even after the Woolf-reform in England in the late 1990s, where less radical rules on disclosure replaced the previous rules on discovery, a remarkable contrast still seems to exist between English law and many of the systems of the continent. This contrast, however, is not necessarily representative for the vast majority of European countries. Quite a few countries, for instance the Netherlands and the Scandinavian countries, seem to have rules on access to evidence which are somewhere between English law and German law. In those countries, parties have a right to access evidence, but only if a number of requirements have been met and the right does not necessarily extend to all relevant and non-privileged evidence.

To what extent are these general statements reflected in legal regulation and, above all, in practice before national courts? In order to dig into that issue, the first chapters of this book are devoted to analyse the situation in representative European jurisdictions: Germany, Austria and Switzerland (by Astrid Stadler); England and Wales (by John Sorabji); France (by Emmanuel Jeuland); Italy (by Elisabetta Silvestri); Spain (by Fernando Gascón); the Netherlands (by Bart Krans and Niek Zondag); and Scandinavia (Sweden, Norway and Denmark, by Magne Strandberg). **I.007**

Although concentrating on a European perspective, the book will deal with some aspects of non-European law which may be relevant for European disputes. Most important is the applicability of US discovery rules for cases which have little to do with American law and which in the end will be handled by the courts in a European country. Especially when a dispute is to be handled in a European country with a very restrictive approach to disclosure rules, parties may ask for access to evidence before US courts and based on US discovery rules if evidence is located in the US or under control of a US company (often an affiliate of the defendant in European proceedings). This is the subject of Nicolò Trocker's analysis. **I.008**

Even though access to evidence has been most intensely debated for litigation before state courts, it may also be necessary in the framework of arbitration – an option which is of high and growing practical importance for commercial disputes. Apart from the powers conferred by the parties and by the regulations on arbitration, there is an additional potential relationship between arbitration and state courts when it comes to access to evidence, since most countries allow the use of state courts for giving access to evidence orders, even though all other aspects of the case are handled by an arbitral tribunal. These issues are addressed in a specific chapter by Michael Stürner and Johannes Landbrecht. **I.009**

The results of all the previous chapters have enabled us, in the last one, to carry out a comparative analysis from which, in turn, it is very clear what the critical points are in this area and the different ways in which national legislators are trying to resolve them, sometimes autonomously, sometimes under the guidance of the European **I.010** legislator. Although there are still important divergences at national level, there is a clear trend towards convergence, especially on the continent, in relation to three basic ideas: access to sources of evidence has a constitutional dimension that allows it to take precedence, subject to criteria of proportionality, over the old concept of *nemo tenetur* and the need to preserve confidential information; indeterminate and open access to any evidence held by the opposing party or a third party is not possible, but requires a reasonable identification of the evidence to be accessed, as well as a justification of its necessity; finally, access to sources of evidence remains a "judge's business", as it is the judges who have to receive requests and grant them, and on whom the legislators rely to find, in each specific case, the right balance between necessary access and procedural abuse.

1

ACCESS TO EVIDENCE IN GERMANY, AUSTRIA AND SWITZERLAND

Astrid Stadler

A. PART I – GERMANY

1. Outset of the German Civil Procedure Code

(a) General rules on evidence

(i) Availability of pre-action access to information?[1]

1.001 The availability of evidence not only regularly determines whether the parties can meet their burden of proof and win the case, it also has knock-on effects. In view

1 It has been rightly pointed out that the term 'information' is complex and not very precise. Wolfgang Hau, *Informationsverantwortung im Zivilprozess*, ZfPW 2022, 154 at 158; the German Civil Procedure Code does not use

of the loser-pays principle that has been largely implemented in German litigation, every plaintiff must be able to assess their chances of success as precisely as possible in advance. Ideally, they will have pre-litigation rights of access to information and disclosure against the potential defendant. The principle of establishing the truth as the basis for a civil judgment would be best served if the parties to the proceedings were required to disclose all available evidence in the proceedings.[2] As an Austrian scholar and judge pointed out: 'A system that is aimed at establishing the material truth must necessarily be characterized by investigative aspects.'[3] This chapter will show that German procedural law is far from this ideal. Contrary to the general international trend towards stronger obligations of the parties to co-operate and provide information,[4] German law remains more or less rooted in the basic approach of the ZPO of the 19th century.

1.002 With a few exceptions, German law does not provide pre-action information rights. If there are no rights to information available in substantive law, it will be left to the plaintiff alone to collect evidence in order to assess his chances of success in court. Pre-litigation information obligations of the parties, as are now common in England and Wales with the pre-action protocols[5] and in some other jurisdictions, are not available in German civil proceedings.

1.003 Even if the claimant has initiated proceedings, they cannot be sure of gaining access to all the relevant evidence. In the interest of an efficient procedure, but also to 'inconvenience' third parties and the opposing party as little as possible, the general requirements for the court to take evidence are rather strict compared for example to US litigation or the Civil Procedure Rules (CPR) of England and Wales. Evidence is only taken on facts that are in dispute between the parties and that are directly relevant to the decision of the case. The strict relevancy standard means that facts must relate to the legal requirements of the plaintiff's claim or the defendant's defense. The party

this term.

2 There is a general consensus that the purpose of civil proceedings is to enforce individual rights under substantive law on the basis of the true facts of the case: Rolf Stürner, *Die Aufklärungspflicht der Parteien des Zivilprozesses*, Tübingen 1976, 43 et seq.; Friedhelm Gaul, AcP 168 (1968), 27 at 49, 53; but a different position is taken, e.g. by Wolfgang Grunsky, *Grundlagen des Verfahrensrechts*, 2d ed. 1974, 4; Christian Heinze, *Liber Amicorum Kostas Beys*, Athen 2003, 515 at 524; Johann Braun, *Wahrheit im Zivilprozess – ein Beitrag zur Prozesszwecklehre*, JZ 2021, 53. Of course, this is not about an absolute concept of truth, because the priniciple of party autonomy and disposition prohibits the court from conducting its own investigations and the parties can also agree on a set of facts to be taken as a basis; Astrid Stadler in: Hans-Joachim Musielak/Wolfgang Voit, *Commentary on the German Civil Procedure Code*, 21st ed. 2024, Sec. 138 mn. 2; for a general discussion see Christian Gomille, *Informationsproblem und Wahrheitspflicht*, Mohr Siebeck, Tübingen 2016.

3 Jürgen Rassi, *Kooperation und Geheimnisschutz bei Beweisschwierigkeiten im Zivilprozess*, Skramek Vienna 2020, 63.

4 The trend is reflected by the ELI/UNIDROIT Model Rules of European Civil Procedure (ECPR), available at: https://www.unidroit.org/english/principles/civilprocedure/eli-unidroit-rules/200925-eli-unidroit-rules-e.pdf.

5 For details see John Sorabji (in this volume), ch. 2.

bearing the burden of proof must not only state the disputed fact as precisely as possible in a motion for evidence,[6] but must also describe the means of evidence precisely.[7] This can be a significant hurdle if, for example, a party does not know the name and address of a witness[8] or can only describe documents in the possession of the opponent in general terms or by categories.

(ii) No fishing expeditions

The taking of evidence is also limited by the so-called ban on fishing expeditions. This admittedly rather vague concept excludes requests for evidence that are too broad and indefinite from the outset and are only aimed at obtaining further evidence. It also excludes requests for evidence that are sufficiently specific, but the specifications have been made 'out of the blue' without any indication of the existence of the facts to be proven.[9] **1.004**

(iii) Substantiation requirements

Three general questions arise from this: firstly, how strict are the requirements for the substantiation of the fact to be proven? Secondly, can any concessions be made in the description of the evidence? And thirdly, the question that will be in the focus of this chapter: provided that a party can specifically identify the facts to be proven and the evidence sought, under what conditions can she demand that the opponent or a third party discloses them in the proceedings (below nn. 1010 et seq.)? **1.005**

---

6 See e.g. BGH, 1.12.1993, VIII ZR 243/92, NJW-RR 1994, 377: 'The necessary content of a motion for evidence is the specified designation of the facts that are to be proven; how specific the respective factual claims must be assessed on the basis of the circumstances of the individual case, in particular the opponent's statement, taking into account the duty of truth and completeness (§ 138 ZPO). A motion to take evidence that lacks sufficient certainty with regard to the facts to be determined is to be rejected.' The general substantiation obligations for parties therefore apply, for more details see Monika Anders in: Monika Anders/Burkhard Gehle, *Commentary on the German Civil Procedure Code*, 82nd ed. 2024, Sec. 138 mn. 21 with further references to case law.

7 The Federal Labour Court (21.3.2024, 2 AZN 785/23, BeckRS 2024, 6283) recently held that the party who files a motion for the examination of a witness need only name the witness and indicate the facts about which the witness is to be examined. The law does not require that the party adducing evidence also comment on the evidence he has for the correctness of the assertion put into the knowledge of the witness.

8 Under certain circumstances, however, the refusal of the opposing party to disclose the name of a witness, for example, can be sanctioned as obstruction of evidence by way of the free evaluation of evidence, BGH, III ZR 239/06, NJW 2008, 982.

In principle, culpable obstruction of evidence may lead to the court drawing adverse inferences or even a reversal of the burden of proof. The prerequisite is fault on the part of the obstructing party, which must relate to the destruction or deprivation of the object of evidence and, also to the elimination of its evidentiary function, i.e. to adversely affecting the opposing party's evidentiary position in a current or future lawsuit, e.g. BGH, III ZR 239/06, NJW 2008, 982 mn. 23; BGH, XI ZR 34/05, NJW 2006, 434 mn. 22.

9 This is established case law, see e.g. BGH, IX ZR 138/84, NJW 1986, 246 at 247; BGH, V ZR 185/85, NJW-RR 1987, 590 at 591, and BGH, IX ZR 195/14, NJW-RR 2015, 829; BGH, VIII ZR 57/19, NJW 2020, 1740 (1741), with further references. It is also the prevailing opinion in legal doctrine, Hanns Prütting in *Munic Commentary on the German Civil Procedure Code*, 6th ed. 2020, Sec. 284 n. 79.

1.006 Although facts must be submitted to the court in as much detail as possible ('strict substantiation standard') this may be eased under limited circumstances. If the plaintiff is unable to assert facts giving rise to a claim in detail because they originate from the sphere of the opponent and he does not have the relevant knowledge and no access, the non-statutory principle of secondary burden of allegation[10] applies. Then, the plaintiff may assert the facts in a more general way and without details. He must, however, not simply pluck his allegations out of thin air, but must plausibly explain where they derive from.

1.007 As a rule, the defendant may simply dispute the factual allegations made by the plaintiff. If, however, the rules of secondary burden of allegation apply, the opponent, who has better access to the facts of the case, must dispute the plaintiff's allegations by giving details. If he fails to do so, the facts presented by the plaintiff are deemed to be undisputed. No evidence will be taken and the plaintiff has met his burden of proof.

1.008 An example from recent case law may illustrate how the mechanism works and how important it can be for the outcome of the litigation. In the lawsuits of the German diesel car owners affected by the cheat software implemented into the diesel cars by *Volkswagen AG*, the plaintiffs had to prove when and what *Volkswagen AG's* board of directors had learned about the installation of the software in order for *Volkswagen AG* to be held liable. Plaintiffs typically cannot know this as it concerns *Volkswagen*'s internal operations. For the plaintiffs, in this case it was sufficient to allege that a fundamental strategic decision had been made by the board of directors of *Volkswagen* to use the cheat software in its diesel cars. This rather general allegation was plausible in view of the fact that all vehicles worldwide with certain engines were affected and that the installation of the software was associated with significant risks for the entire corporation and also with personal liability risks for the decision-makers. It was therefore nearly obvious that this could not happen without the knowledge of the board of directors. *Volkswagen* did not go into details to dispute this allegation. They responded in court that according to their internal investigation there was no evidence that any of its board members had been involved in the development of the software or had known about its development and use. The German Federal Court applied the principle of secondary burden of allegation and did not consider *Volkswagen*'s denial to be sufficiently substantiated. It therefore regarded the plaintiff's allegation regarding the information of the board as undisputed.[11] In view of the clear applicability of this

10 This is settled case law: BGH NJW-RR 2024, 594 mn. 39; NJW-RR 2021, 1669 mn. 27; NJW 2021, 1759 (VIII ZR 316/19); BeckRS 2021, 11170 mn. 30; NJW 2020, 1962; NJW 2018, 2412.

11 BGH NJW-RR 2021, 1029; VI ZR 252/19 NJW 2020, 1962 mn. 39; for a more general discussion of the topic Michael Heese, Sachaufklärung im Dieselsskandal – Probleme und Abhilfen, NJW 2021, 887.

principle, *Volkswagen* was obviously ill-advised in its litigation strategy or resistant to advice.

While the requirement for strict factual substantiation can be eased in some situations, this does not apply to the description of evidence. This will be dealt with later on (n. 1.016). **1.009**

(b) Access to evidence

(i) Nemo tenetur contra se edere

The German Code of Civil Procedure (ZPO) has traditionally taken a cautious approach when it comes to access to evidence in the hands of the opposing party or third parties. This applies in particular to the production of documents and objects for inspection.[12] German procedural law also differentiates between the examination of third-party witnesses and the formal hearing of parties. The latter is considered subsidiary evidence – a principle that will not be discussed in detail in this chapter. Third parties are generally obliged to testify as witnesses, but they can invoke a number of grounds for refusing to testify (Sec. 383–385 German Civil Procedure Code). Parties are not obliged to testify, but they also have no formal privileges. Their statements or non-statements are subject to free evaluation of evidence. **1.010**

German civil procedure imposes no general duties on parties to produce evidence. This is particularly problematic with respect to documents which are a quite reliable sort of evidence and important in many litigations. The legal basis for a court order to produce documents is very restrictive as will be shown below and absent a specific court order, neither party has any obligation to disclose any documents to the party bearing the burden of proof. The reason for this is that as early as in 1958 the German Federal Court of Justice established the principle that 'no party can be expected to provide evidence in order to help the opponent to win its case.' This still has an impact today.[13] **1.011**

(ii) Obligations to produce documents (and tangible things)

In principle, a party to a litigation can only demand that the opposing party produce documents (and objects of inspection) under two conditions. Either the opposing party itself has referred to the documents (Sec. 423 German Civil Procedure Code) or the party bearing the burden of proof is entitled under substantive law to receive the **1.012**

12 For the production of things for inspection by the opponent, the same rules as for the production of documents apply, Sec. 371 para 2 German Civil Procedure Code.

13 See BGH NJW 1958, 1491, at 1492: 'This is because neither party is obliged to provide the other with the material that it already has access to on its own initiative ….' Still today this is the position of German courts, cf. BGH ZZP 104 (1991), 202 (with an annotation by Rolf Stürner); BGH NJW 1997, 128 at 129; NJW 2000, 1108 at 1109; for details see Gerhard Wagner, *Liber Amicorum Dieter Leipold*, Mohr Siebeck, Tübingen 2009, 801 et seq.

documents (Sec. 422–425 German Civil Procedure Code). A clear and strategically thinking defendant will not refer to documents that the claimant may use against him. The first option is, therefore, rarely used if the opponent does not need the document for proving his own case.

1.013 The second option also often comes to nothing. Due to the substantive provisions of the German Civil Code, there are only a few obligations to produce documents that can be invoked in civil proceedings. Even in contract cases it can be difficult to get access to documents. Only Sec. 810 German Civil Code comes into consideration in this respect. However, this provision grants access to documents only to a very limited extent.[14] In addition, the Federal Court of Justice has derived a right to information from good faith and fair dealing (Sec. 242 German Civil Code) in certain constellations – usually cases involving a contractual relationship.[15] This does not even begin to cover all cases. However, in the course of implementing European Directives, additional duties of disclosure, information and submission have been established in certain areas of law (see below nn. 1.018 et seq.). A general duty to give access to evidence as suggested in legal literature by many scholars since the 1970s[16] was never accepted by the Federal Court of Justice.[17]

2. The 2002 reform of evidence rules

(a) *Ex officio* court orders for disclosure

1.014 Although the German Code of Civil Procedure assumes that evidence is only taken at the request of a party, the law has long since recognized the possibility of *ex officio* taking of evidence (Sec. 273 German Civil Procedure Code). This includes all types of evidence except for testimonial evidence. A reform enacted in 2002 formally expanded

---

14 Sec. 810 German Civil Code reads as follows: 'A person who has a legal interest in inspecting a document in the possession of another person may require the holder to permit inspection if the document was drawn up in his interest or if a legal relationship existing between him and another person is recorded in the document or if the document contains negotiations on a legal transaction which took place between him and another person or between one of them and a joint intermediary.'

15 For an analysis of this approach and its influence on Scandinavian law Magne Strandberg, Evidentiary contracts in civil proceedings, in Anna Nylund/Antonio Cabral, *Shaping Civil Litigation using Procedural Agreements*, Den Hague 2024, 41 at 46–48.

16 Rolf Stürner, *Die Aufklärungspflicht der Parteien des Zivilprozesses*, Tübingen 1976; ibid, *Zeitschrift für Zivilprozess* (ZZP) 98 (1985), 237; and ZZP 104 (1991), 208 ff.; also in this sense Egbert Peters, Beweisvereitelung und Mitwirkungspflicht des Beweisgegners, 82 *Zeitschrift für Zivilprozess* (ZZP) (1969), 200 ff.; Astrid Stadler, *Der Schutz des Unternehmensgeheimnisses im deutschen und US-amerikanischen Zivilprozeß und im Rechtshilfeverfahren*, Tübingen 1989, 80 et seq.; Peter Gottwald, *Gutachten zum 61. DJT 1996*, A 15–21 (de lege ferenda); Moritz Nissen, *Das Recht auf Beweis im Zivilprozess*, Tübingen 2019; Christian Katzenmeier, *Aufklärungs-/Mitwirkungspflicht der nicht beweisbelasteten Partei im Zivilprozeß*, JZ 2002, 533 ff.

17 BGH NJW 1990, 3151 and accordingly the prevailing opinion in legal literature; also strongly against such a general duty Johann Braun, *Zivilprozessrecht*, Tübingen 2014, 103–106 who argues that a general duty of disclosure does not serve the purpose of establishing the truth, but is rather abused by the parties in order to wear out the opponent.

the power of courts to order disclosure and production of documents as well as tangible things and access to real property (Sec.142, 144 Civil Procedure Code) – but it did not fundamentally change the system. In addition to the rules described above, a new Sec. 142 was enacted under which the court can order a party or a third party to produce documents in its possession to which any party has made reference. In contrast to Sec. 423 of the German Code of Civil Procedure, it is no longer necessary for the opponent who is in possession of the document(s) to refer to the desired document(s) him- or herself. It is sufficient if one of the parties ('any'), including the party having the burden of proof, refers to the document. Due to this difference in wording the dogmatic relationship between Sec. 142 and Sec. 421–429 German Civil Procedure Code has not been fully clarified.

(b) Pre-trial discovery style disclosure rules?

The new Sec. 142 gave rise to criticism, as it might open the door to US-style pretrial discovery. However, case law very quickly made it clear that although the amendment slightly expanded an existing discretionary power of the court, it cannot be interpreted as imposing a general duty on parties to co-operate or to produce evidence needed by the opponent.[18] Court orders based on Sec. 142 German Civil Procedure Code, in any case, must not be used for fishing expeditions.[19] The legislative memorandum accompanying the Federal Parliament's 2001 reform bill amending Sec. 142 specifically explains that the amendment is not meant to introduce US-style discovery into German law or even to permit discovery-like tools.[20] **1.015**

In practice, the provision of Sec. 142 German Civil Procedure Code has not been given much importance to date.[21] The main reason is that the strict substantiation requirements for the description of the documents to be submitted also apply here. Indeed, **1.016**

18 For case law references cf. Christoph Althammer in: Friedrich Stein/Martin Jonas, *Commentary on the German Civil Procedure Code*, 23rd ed., Sec. 142 n. 21; Dieter Leipold, in: Peter Breitschmid/Ingrid Jent-Sørensen/Hans Schmid/Miguel Sogo (eds), *Liber amicorum Isaak Meier*, Schultheiss, Zurich 2015, 421 at 426; Hanns Prütting, Discovery im deutschen Zivilprozess?, *Anwaltsblatt* 2008, 158.

19 This is clearly stated by leading commentaries: Kathrin Brünningmann in: Monika Anders/Burkhard Gehle, *Commentary on the German Civil Procedure Code*, 82nd ed. 2024, Sec. 142 n. 2, 5; Christoph Althammer in: Friedrich Stein/Martin Jonas, *Commentary on the German Civil Procedure Code*, 23rd ed, Sec. 142 n. 20; Dieter Leipold, in: *Liber amicorum Gerhardt*, 2004, 563 et seq. at 568 et seq.; BeckOK/von Selle, *Online Commentary on German Civil Procedure Law*, Sec. 142 n. 15.1 (suggesting that Sec. 142 should generally not be used to ask for documents from the opponent).

20 See Proceedings of the 14th Bundestag, ('BT-Drs.') 14/6036, 120–121: 'The concern, in particular, is unfounded that the proposed amendments would move German civil litigation any closer to the discovery proceedings as a leading principle of U.S. law.'

21 *See* Astrid Stadler in Hans-Joachim Musielak/Wolfgang Voit, *Commentary on the German Civil Procedure Code*, 21st ed. 2024, Sec. 142 n. 1; Christoph Althammer in: Friedrich Stein/Martin Jonas, *Commentary on the German Civil Procedure Code*, 23rd ed, Sec. 142 n. 6; Ingo Saenger, Grundfragen und aktuelle Probleme des Beweisrechts aus deutscher Sicht, 121 *Zeitschrift für Zivilprozess* (ZZP) (2008), 139 at 152 (with empirical data on the reluctance of courts to use Sec. 142).

to obtain an order against the opponent (and for a third party the requirements apply accordingly) the motion must include both a precise, substantiated description of the documents sought (Sec. 424 no. 1 German Civil Procedure Code) and an explanation why the applicant believes they exist and are in the opponent's possession or control (Sec. 424 no. 4; Sec. 430 ZPO).[22] It is not sufficient to refer to the documents by categories or general description.

(c) Protection of confidential information

1.017 These very strict requirements also ensure that business information is protected, because many documents in the possession of the opponent or a third party do not have to be disclosed to the court and to the party bearing the burden of proof in the first place. Specific procedural safeguards in the event that it becomes necessary to present confidential information will be discussed below nn. 1022 et seq.

3. Transposition of European Directives

1.018 In the last 20 years, the European legislature has significantly interfered with the Member States' rules of evidence and created additional information rights, thus improving access to evidence.

(a) Enforcement of intellectual property rights (Directive 2004/48/EC)

(i) Transposition into German law

1.019 Article 6 para 1 of the Directive stipulates that

> Member States shall ensure that, on application by a party which has presented reasonably available evidence sufficient to support its claims, and has, in substantiating those claims, specified evidence which lies in the control of the opposing party, the competent judicial authorities may order that such evidence be presented by the opposing party, subject to the protection of confidential information. For the purposes of this paragraph, Member States may provide that a reasonable sample of a substantial number of copies of a work or any other protected object be considered by the competent judicial authorities to constitute reasonable evidence.

1.020 Article 7 allows pre-action measures for preserving evidence. According to Article 8 there are more far-reaching possibilities to get access to banking, financial or commercial documents, if there is sufficient probability of an infringement on a commercial scale. Sec. 142 German Civil Procedure Code was considered insufficient to comply with the requirements of the Enforcement Directive because the Directive demands

22 BGH, VII ZR 230/06, NJW-RR 2007, 1393; BGH, XI ZR 277/05, NJW 2007, 2989, 2992; Court of Appeal Stuttgart, January 21, 2016, case no. 2 U 89/15, *BeckRS* 2016, 07931 at no. 85; Court of Appeal Düsseldorf, August 13, 2014, case no. VI-2 U (Kart) 2/13, *BeckRS* 2014, 19052 at no. 24; Kammergericht Berlin, March 30, 2015, case no. 2 U 124/11 EnWG, NJOZ 2015, 1158, at no. 28; cf. Gerhard Wagner, *Urkundenedition durch Prozessparteien – Auskunftspflicht und Weigerungsrechte,* JZ 2007, 707, 713.

an enforceable right of access to information,[23] whereas a refusal under Sec. 142 only allows drawing adverse conclusions (see Sec. 427 German Civil Procedure Code). The legislator implemented the Enforcement Directive with effect from 1 September 2008 and introduced a couple of new provisions in sector specific laws.[24] According to all new provisions, it is a prerequisite for the claim that a violation of rights by the opponent has been demonstrated with sufficient probability. All provisions provide substantive rights for the production of documents or the inspection of objects.[25]

Unfortunately, the legislator did not take the transposition of the Directive as an opportunity to establish a general concept of procedural obligations to co-operate.[26] This would have improved access to information and evidence not only in cases within the scope of the Directive. However, the political will to implement such a concept was lacking. **1.021**

(ii) Protection of trade secrets

Traditional approach

A main criticism raised against the Directive referred to its provision of access to bank, financial and business records in the event of a suspected commercial infringement. The broad access to information and evidence may increase the risk of abuse and fishing expeditions.[27] This can have far-reaching consequences because the transposition does not list specific measures for the protection of trade and business secrets, but leaves it to the discretion of the court. In practice, this meant that the courts continued to apply only the traditional safeguards that do not provide adequate protection. **1.022**

23 For details Astrid Stadler, Was drei wissen, das erfahren hundert – Auskunftspflichten und Geheimnisschutz im Zivilprozess, in: Rolf Stürner/Hiroyuki Matsumoto/ Wolfgang Lüke/Masahisa Deguchi (eds), *Liber Amicorum Dieter Leipold*, Tübingen 2009, 201 at 203.

24 Sec. 140c of the Patent Act, Sec. 24c Utility Model Act, Sec. 19a, 128, 135 Trade Mark Act, Sec. 9 Semiconductor Protection Act, Sec. 101a Copyright Act, Sec. 46a Design Act, Sec. 37c Plant Variety Protection Act. For details see Dennis Amschewitz, *Die Durchsetzungsrichtlinie und ihre Umsetzung im deutschen Recht*, Mohr Siebeck, Tübingen 2008.

25 The legislator followed suggestions made in legal literature: Joachim Bornkamm, Der Schutz vertraulicher Informationen im Gesetz zur Durchsetzung von Rechten des geistigen Eigentums – in camera-Verfahren im Zivilprozess?, in: Hans-Jürgen Ahrens/Joachim Bornkamm/Hans-Peter Kunz-Hallstein (eds), *Liber Amicorum Ullmann*, 2006, 893 at 896; Hans-Jürgen Ahrens, Gesetzgebungsvorschlag zur Beweisermittlung bei Verletzung von Rechten des geistigen Eigentums, *GRUR* 2005, 837; Winfried Tilmann, Beweissicherung nach Art. 7 der Richtlinie zur Durchsetzung der Rechte des geistigen Eigentums, *GRUR* 2005, 737.

26 In favor of procedural obligations Astrid Stadler, Was drei wissen, das erfahren hundert – Auskunftspflichten und Geheimnisschutz im Zivilprozess, in: Rolf Stürner/Hiroyuki Matsumoto/ Wolfgang Lüke/Masahisa Deguchi (eds), *Liber Amicorum Dieter Leipold*, Tübingen 2009, 201 et seq.

27 Maximilian Haedicke, Urkundenvorlagepflichten des vermeintlichen Patentverletzers im Gesetz zur Verbesserung der Durchsetzung von Rechten des geistigen Eigentums, in: Rolf Stürner/Hiroyuki Matsumoto/ Wolfgang Lüke/ Masahisa Deguchi (eds), *Liber Amicorium Dieter Leipold*, Tübingen 2009, 53 at 61.

1.023 In principle, the public can be excluded from hearings,[28] but this does not provide sufficient protection against disclosing documents during the hearing to the opposing party that will in many cases be a competitor of the claimant. If trade secrets had to be described in the statement of claim in order to establish a prima facie case or if they became part of the court files otherwise, no adequate protection was available.[29] Until now, there were no rules restricting the parties' access to the files of their case.

1.024 German courts and the majority of authors in legal doctrine have always rejected 'in camera' proceedings in which the opponent is not present and is not allowed to inspect documents himself.[30] Such a restriction is considered to violate the right to be heard and the right to a fair hearing of the excluded party – which, however, on closer inspection can and should be reconciled with the oppontent's right of access to justice.[31] A party that would have to produce trade secrets in order to win her case will often choose not to pursue her claim from the outset if there is no adequate protection for the trade secrets. A lack of protection mechanisms therefore sometimes prevents access to the court.

1.025 Only in a few cases, including patent law, have the courts granted protection by only allowing a court expert access to confidential information in a first step.[32] The expert can then report, for example, in anonymized form whether the information is really

---

28 Sec. 172 Judicial Act. Moreover Sec. 174 para 3 Judicial Act stipulates that the court may require the persons present in the hearing to maintain confidentiality with regard to facts that come to their knowledge through the proceedings.

29 For details Astrid Stadler, Gerichtliche Verschwiegenheitsanordnungen zum Schutz von Unternehmensgeheimnissen, in: Moritz Brinkmann/Daniel Effer-Uhe/Barbara Völzmann-Stickelbrock/Sabine Wesser/Stephan Weth, *Liber Amicorum Hanns Prütting*, Wolters Kluver, Köln 2018, 559.

30 In favor of 'in camera' proceedings with varying details: Astrid Stadler, *Der Schutz des Unternehmensgeheimnisses im deutschen und US-amerikanischen Zivilprozeß und im Rechtshilfeverfahren,* Mohr Siebeck, Tübingen 1989; ibid, Geheimnisschutz im Zivilprozess aus deutscher Sicht, *Zeitschrift für Zivilprozess* [2010], 261; Edmund James Melzer, *§ 33g GWB: Offenlegung versus Geheimnisschutz,* Berliner Wissenschaftsverlag 2020; Andreas Götz, *Der Schutz von Betriebs- und Geschäftsgeheimnissen im Zivilverfahren*, Mohr Siebeck, Tübingen 2014; Marc Wrede, *Das Geheimverfahren im Zivilprozess*, 2014, 149 et seq.; see also Joachim Bornkamm, Der Schutz vertraulicher Informationen im Gesetz zur Durchsetzung von Rechten des geistigen Eigentums – in camera-Verfahren im Zivilprozess?, in: Hans-Jürgen Ahrens/Joachim Bornkamm/Hans-Peter Kunz-Hallstein (eds), *Liber Amicorum Ullmann*, 2006, 893; the Federal Court of Justice has declined such in camera proceedings, BGH NJW-RR 2007, 106 at 107; so do commentators in leading commentaries: Hanns Prütting, *Munic Commentary on the Civil Procedure Code*, 6th ed. 2020, Sec. 285 mn. 10–16.

31 This is also the position of the Federal Constitutional Court, BVerfGE 115, 205 ff. with concurring opinion of Judge Gaier mn. 144–166. The court held that 'in camera' proceedings do not violate constitutional rights, but require a legal basis in procedural law.

32 This is the so-called 'Düsseldorfer Verfahren' (as it was firstly applied by the Patent Court in Düsseldorf).
Often a mixture of provisional injunctions and preservation of evidence procedure apply, for details see Hermann Deichfuß, Rechtsdurchsetzung unter Wahrung von Vertraulichkeit von Geschäftsgeheimnissen, *GRUR* 2015, 436 with further references; an overview of traditional measures to protect trade secrets is given by Björn Kalbfus in: Henning/Harte-Bavendamm/Ansgar Ohly/Björn Kalbfus (eds), *Gesetz zum Schutz von Geschäftsgeheimnissen*, Munich 2020, Vor §§ 16–19 mn. 22–42.

a trade secret and whether it is relevant to the decision.[33] If necessary, the 'counsel's eyes only' principle applies at that stage of the proceedings. However, if a final decision on the infringement of property rights cannot yet be made without taking the confidential information into account, there has so far been no solution for effectively protecting it.

New in camera proceedings

A recently introduced general provision of the Civil Procedure Code, however, now allows the court *in all proceedings* to classify information as a business secret and to apply a variety of protective measures.[34] Sec. 273a German Civil Procedure Code refers to Sec. 16–20 German Trade Secrets Protection Act (TSPA): **1.026**

> At the request of a party, the court may classify all or part of the information in dispute as confidential if it may constitute a trade secret pursuant to Section 2 (1) of the German Trade Secrets Protection Act; Sections 16 to 20 of the German Trade Secrets Protection Act shall apply accordingly.

The TSPA came into force in 2019 in order to implement the Directive (EU) 2016/943 on the protection of undisclosed know-how and business information. However, the TSPA of 2019 at that time had a very narrow scope of application and was only applicable in proceedings in which the violation of the trade secret itself was the matter of controversy. Due to a special provision in the German Patent Act, it also applied accordingly in patent infringement litigation. **1.027**

Now, from April 2025 on, Sec. 16–19 of the TSPA apply in general to confidential information. The following measures can be taken: **1.028**

(1) The parties, their legal representatives, witnesses, experts, other representatives and any other persons involved in trade secret litigation or having access to documents of such proceedings shall keep confidential information classified as secret and shall not use or disclose such information outside of judicial proceedings (also after the end of proceedings). In the event of a breach of these obligations the court may impose a fine of up to 100.000 Euros or a prison sentence of up to six months;
(2) if third parties inspect files, parts of the file may be blackened;
(3) furthermore, the court may restrict access to confidential documents and information during hearings, taking of evidence, including to the minutes and recordings according to Sec. 19 Trade Secrets Act.

Sec. 19 para 1 sentence 2 TSPA provides that these restrictions 'shall apply only to the extent that, after weighing all the circumstances, the interest in maintaining **1.029**

33 Astrid Stadler, Was drei wissen, das erfahren hundert – Auskunftspflichten und Geheimnisschutz im Zivilprozess, in: Rolf Stürner/Hiroyuki Matsumoto/ Wolfgang Lüke/Masahisa Deguchi (eds), *Liber Amicorum Dieter Leipold*, Tübingen 2009, 201 at 213–214.

34 Sec. 273a German Civil Procedure Code has taken effect from April 1, 2025.

confidentiality outweighs the right of the parties to be heard, also having regard to their right to effective legal protection and a fair trial.' If a party has been excluded from access to information in the proceedings, at least their lawyers and a person whom they trust should be granted access. It lies within the court's discretion to make the necessary orders. So a kind of modified 'in camera' procedure now comes into play.

1.030 The fact that protection is still not optimal is due to the Directive (EU) 2016/943. Contrary to an earlier draft of the Directive[35] that had allowed a 'counsel's eyes only' principle, the European legislature decided to also allow a 'trusted person' to be present during the 'in camera' proceedings at the last minute. As a result, there is now a 'confidentiality club' including persons that are not lawyers and are therefore not subject to the ethical standards of lawyers. The risk of illegal disclosure of information, which will be difficult to prove, therefore continues to exist.

(b) Cartel damages claims

1.031 Directive 2014/104/EU on actions for damages of competition law[36] includes some approaches that are intended to simplify the enforcement of claims for damages, e.g. the right to full compensation, the presumption of damage, the burden of proof on the defendant for the passing-on defense. In addition, German case law allows applying a prima facie evidence.[37] The Directive follows the example of the Enforcement Directive. Articles 5 and 6 establish rules on access to evidence. Article 5 grants 'disclosure of specified items of evidence or relevant categories of evidence circumscribed precisely and as narrowly as possible on the basis of reasonably available facts.' Member States should limit the disclosure to that which is proportionate. According to Article 5 para 4, national courts should have the power to order the disclosure of evidence containing confidential information if it is relevant to the action for damages. In such a situation national courts must have at their disposal effective measures to protect the information.

1.032 Based on the Directive, in 2017 the German legislator implemented new substantive claims for information and for disclosure of evidence in Sec. 33g Antitrust Act.[38] For

---

35 COM(2013)813 final, Article 8 para 2 ('counsel's eyes only' solution). This was not included in the final version of the guideline, partly due to reservations on the German side; Björn Kalbfus in: Henning/Harte-Bavendamm/Ansgar Ohly/Björn Kalbfus (eds), *Gesetz zum Schutz von Geschäftsgeheimnissen*, Munich 2020, Vor §§ 16–19 mn. 9.

36 OJ 5.12.2014, L 349/1.

37 BGH NJOZ 2021, 84; NJOZ 2021, 292 and 848; NJW 2020, 1430, NJW 2019, 661. For a detailed analysis of German cartel damages law and the Directive 2014/104/EU see Franziska Weber, *Der Kartellschaden*, Tübingen 2021.

38 The provision applies in legal disputes in which an action was brought after December 26, 2016, regardless of when the damages claims arose.

reasons of equality of arms, this section applies to both parties.[39] Once again, the German transposition reverts primarily to a substantive legal claim.[40] This allows raising such claims also before a lawsuit has been initiated and thus possibly helps to reach an out-of-court settlement.[41] Sec. 33g para 1 Antitrust Act reads as follows:

> Any person in possession of evidence necessary for the assertion of a claim for damages under Section 33a Antitrust Act shall be obliged to deliver to any person who credibly demonstrates that they have such a claim for damages, provided that the person credibly demonstrating such a claim describes the evidence in as much detail as is possible on the basis of the facts reasonably available.

The disclosure obligations under paragraph 1 (and paragraph 2 for the plaintiff) is limited by proportionality criteria in paragraph 3, such as the scope and costs of the disclosure, the ban on fishing expeditions, the protection of trade secrets, but also the effectiveness of antitrust enforcement. To some extent, the privileges for witnesses also apply. **1.033**

However, the transposition also touches upon procedural law. Sec. 89b Antitrust Act is a rule that applies during court proceedings and it gives the court the power to order production of evidence *ex officio*. The court's authority to issue such an order can, however, only be derived from the legislative documents. The wording of Sec 89b only mentions 'information,' not 'evidence':[42] **1.034**

> (1) Sec. 33g Antitrust Act applies mutatis mutandis to the access to information under Sec. 142 of the Code of Civil Procedure.
>
> (2) Sec. 142 of the Code of Civil Procedure shall apply with the proviso that reasonableness shall be determined in accordance with Sec. 33g Antitrust Act.

The reference to Sec. 142 Civil Procedure Code is somewhat inconsistent, since Sec. 142 Civil Procedure Code leaves it to the discretion of the court to order access to evidence, whereas Sec. 33g Antitrust Act establishes an enforceable right of the party. Sec. 142 Civil Procedure Code has been taken out of its purely procedural context and has been 're-materialized.'[43] We now see a mixture of procedural and substantive law **1.035**

---

39 This possibility is mentioned in Article 13 sentence 2 of the Directive with respect to the defendants burden of proof for the passing-on defense.

40 In favor of a solution in procedural law: Gerhard Klumpe/Thomas Thiede, Regierungsentwurf zur 9. GWB-Novelle: Änderungsbedarf aus der Praxis, Betriebsberater 2016, 3013; Rupprecht Podzsun/Stephan Kreifels, Kommt der Ausforschungsanspruch? – Anmerkung zum geplanten § 33g GWB, GWR 2017, 69.

41 BT-Drs. 18/10207, 62/63. This also goes beyond the requirements of the Directive (permissibly).

42 BT-Drs. 18/10207, 101; Christoph Althammer, Beweismittelherausgabe und Auskunftserteilung nach § 33g GWB und § 89b GWB n.F., in: Moritz Brinkmann/Daniel Effer-Uhe/Barbara Völzmann-Stickelbrock/Sabine Wesser/Stephan Weth, *Liber Amicorum Hanns Prütting*, Wolters Kluwer, Köln 2018, 207 at 209.

43 Christoph Althammer, Beweismittelherausgabe und Auskunftserteilung nach § 33g GWB und § 89b GWB n.F., in: Moritz Brinkmann/Daniel Effer-Uhe/Barbara Völzmann-Stickelbrock/Sabine Wesser/Stephan Weth, *Liber Amicorum Hanns Prütting*, Wolters Kluwer, Köln 2018, 207 at 215/216.

rules for access to evidence and, as a result, it means a step backwards. Although Sec. 142 Civil Procedure Code does not require the existence of any substantive claim for access to information and evidence, in competition litigation courts are now inclined to issue an *ex officio* order for disclosure only if the substantive requirements of Sec. 33g of the Antitrust Act are met.

1.036 Despite this restriction of Sec. 142 that may not have been intended by the legislator, the Directive has lowered the standard for identifying the desired evidence and thus improved the situation of claimants. The description of the documents must only be as precise as possible, i.e. a summary of the content is not required in any case. The party bearing the burden of proof must identify evidence only to the extent that facts are reasonably accessible. This is a considerable advantage over the general provision in Sec. 142 German Civil Procedure Code and its interpretation given by German courts (nn. 1014 et seq.).[44] Furthermore, the Directive clearly states that it suffices to identify the categories of documents and Sec. 33g of the Antitrust Act must be interpreted in conformity with the Directive.[45]

1.037 Article 5 para 4 requires the Member States to provide for the protection of business secrets. This is now being realized by means of the new regulation in § 273a Civil Procedure Code, as already mentioned.

(c) Directive 2020/1828/EU on representative actions in the collective interest of consumers

1.038 The most recent intervention in national evidence law took place by Directive 2020/1828.[46] The Directive improves the enforcement of consumer rights and requires Member States to make a representative redress action available. Qualified entities, such as consumer associations, must be able to apply in court for injunctions and for redress measures against companies in case of infringements of European consumer law listed in the Annex of the Directive (representative actions). The Directive also improves access to evidence for qualified entities. Article 18 requires the Member States to ensure that 'where a qualified entity has provided reasonably available evidence sufficient to support a representative action, and has indicated that additional evidence lies in the control of the defendant or a third party, if requested by that qualified entity, the court or administrative authority is able to order that such evidence be disclosed by the defendant or the third party in accordance with national procedural law, subject to the applicable Union and national rules

---

44 Verena Kern, *Urkundenvorlage bei Kartellschadensklagen*, Tübingen 2020, 165/166.

45 Verena Kern, *Urkundenvorlage bei Kartellschadensklagen*, Tübingen 2020, 149.

46 The appendix of the Directive lists 66 Directives and Regulations to which the Representative Actions Directive applies.

on confidentiality and proportionality.'[47] Unlike earlier Directives, Article 19 para 1 b Directive 2020/2818 explicitly requires sanctions if parties do not comply with court orders under Article 18.

Somewhat surprisingly, the German legislator assumed that all that was required in order to implement Articles 18 and 19 of the Directive into national law was to grant courts the power of imposing a sanction for non-compliance with evidence court orders.[48] Sec. 6 of the Consumer Rights Enforcement Act therefore stipulates that a fine of up to € 250.000 can be imposed on a party for failure to comply with a court order to provide evidence. It is a sector specific rule that applies only for representative actions and is indeed a completely new approach in German civil procedure. Otherwise, lawmakers considered Sec. 142 of the Civil Procedure Code to be already in line with Article 18 of the Directive. However, this is only true if Sec. 142 despite its wording is being interpreted as a mandatory provision. **1.039**

4. Summary

The principle of *nemo tenetur edere contra se* still largely dominates German procedural law. The general duty to disclose evidence and to give access to information proposed by some leading German legal scholars has not been adopted by the courts or the majority of legal scholars. The German legislature has also never taken this step, preferring to implement European Directives on a sector-specific basis and to establish substantive rather than procedural duties of co-operation. As a result, German procedural law differs profoundly from other European legal systems and is not in line with international trends in civil procedure. **1.040**

The German rules on evidence differ significantly from the ELI/UNIDROIT Model Rules of European Civil Procedure. The Model Rules have adopted as an overarching principle the concept of party co-operation (Rule 2) and the approach in evidence law is one that aims at making available all relevant, non-privileged evidence regardless of whether it is in the possession of the opponent or a third party (Rules 25 para 2, 92, 94, 96, 100). The Model Rules not only allow a lower standard for substantiating facts (Rule 53) and evidence (Rule 102[49]), but also establish pre-action rights to information and disclosure in Rules 101 and 106 that are unknown in German law unless required **1.041**

47 In the second sentence, the provision states that this also applies conversely to a motion for disclosure by the defendant if evidence is in the hands of the qualified entity or a third party.

48 Transposition into German law was accomplished primarily by a new procedural act: the Consumer Rights Enforcement Act of 2023.

49 It is sufficient that a party (or prospective party) identifies evidence 'as accurately as possible in the light of the circumstances of the case, the specific sources of evidence to which access is sought, or alternatively identify closely defined categories of evidence by reference to their nature, content or date.'

by EU Directives. It is hardly surprising that the Model Rules contain a purely procedural concept, since the harmonization of substantive legal provisions was not the subject of the ELI/UNIDROIT project.

1.042 The rules on the protection of trade secrets in Rules 103–104 also provide a wide range of measures unknown in German law. German law traditionally required the party bearing the burden of proof to disclose trade and business secrets if they want to win the case and has so far only offered protection from disclosure to the public during hearings and trials.

1.043 The newly enacted Sec. 273a of the German Civil Procedure Code provides a more modern concept. If one is wondering why the German legislator suddenly wants to provide more protection for trade secrets in general, the answer is simple. Sec. 273a of the German Civil Procedure Code is part of a new act 'to strengthen Germany as a location for justice by introducing commercial courts and English as the language of civil proceedings.'[50] This, in turn, is the result of more than 10 years of discussions on how to make German courts attractive for international commercial disputes and to prevent a shift towards arbitration. Other Member States have been trying to compete with English courts for some time by establishing commercial courts, such as the Netherlands Commercial Court (NCC District Court and NCC Court of Appeal) with proceedings in English,[51] and the Belgium Commercial Court in Brussels.[52] It remains to be seen whether the reform that includes English-language proceedings, the possibility of a verbatim protocol and the new protective measures for trade secrets will be sufficient to prevent choice-of-forum clauses or arbitration agreements in the future.

B. PART II – AUSTRIA

1. General principles

1.044 In Austria, the initial situation is very similar to that in Germany. Both Codes of Civil Procedure date from the same period (German Civil Procedure Code: 1 October 1879; Austrian Civil Procedure Code: 1 August 1895). In line with the prevailing opinion at the time, both laws assumed that the parties themselves have the necessary evidence at their disposal. Nevertheless, the Austrian Civil Procedure Code has had mechanisms in place from the outset to help the parties. In Austria, the judge's right to

---

50 Official Journal, Law of October 7, 2024, BGBl. 2024 I, No. 304.

51 https://www.rechtspraak.nl/English/NCC/Pages/default.aspx (last visit October 15, 2024).

52 https://www.eylaw.be/2017/11/30/an-international-english-speaking-commercial-court-in-brussels-the-brussels-international-business-court-bibc/ (last visit October 15, 2024).

ask questions (Sec. 182 Austrian Civil Procedure Code) and the possibility of *ex officio* taking of evidence are intended to help the party that is in need of evidence. However, as in Germany, the latter is rarely used because the court often lacks the necessary information.[53] Moreover, Austrian courts have adopted German case law on the secondary burden of allegation. In Austrian law, the burden of proof may be reversed if the opponent does not dispute facts in detail,[54] and otherwise tend to be rather generous in reversing the burden of proof for facts that are within the control of the opposing party based on the principle of good faith and fair dealing.[55] The concept of the ban on fishing expeditions also exists in Austria, albeit with rather vague contours.[56]

2. Access to documents

The statutory provisions on the production of documents are almost identical in Austria and Germany, at least at first glance. In Austria, a party must present documents in its possession to the opposing party if it has itself referred to these (Sec. 82 Austrian Civil Procedure Code), if it is obliged to present them under substantive civil law or if they are a joint document, such as a contract (Sec. 304 – so-called unconditional production of documents). Unlike German law, however, Austrian procedural law also provides a general obligation to submit documents. According to Sec. 305, the presentation of other documents (not mentioned in Sec. 304) may (only!) be refused: 1. if the content concerns matters of family life; 2. if the opponent would violate a duty of honor by presenting the document; 3. if disclosure of the document would result in the party or third parties being disgraced or would result in the risk of criminal prosecution; 4. if, by producing the document, the party would violate a state-recognized duty of confidentiality from which it has not been validly released or would violate an artistic or business secret; 5. if there are other equally important reasons that justify **1.045**

53 Georg Kodek/Peter Mayer, *Zivilprozessrecht,* 6th ed. Vienna 2024, mn. 856/2. Sec. 183 Austrian Civil Procedure Code is very similar to Sec. 141-144 German Civil Proedure Code.

54 Jürgen Rassi, *Kooperation und Geheimnisschutz bei Beweisschwierigkeiten im Zivilprozess*, Skramek Vienna 2020, 74; OGH (Austrian Federal High Court) RIS-JustizRS0062591; OGH 4 Ob 348/72 = Österreichische Blätter (ÖBl) 1973, 53; OGH 4 Ob 329//74 = Österreichische Blätter (ÖBl) 1975, 57.

55 Jürgen Rassi, *Kooperation und Geheimnisschutz bei Beweisschwierigkeiten im Zivilprozess*, Skramek Vienna 2020, 26 et seq.; ibid, Die Aufklärungs- und Mitwirkungspflicht der nicht beweisbelasteten Partei, 121 *Zeitschrift für Zivilprozess* (ZZP) (2008), 165, 173 et seq. referring to the following decision of the Austrian Federal High Court: 4 Ob 1638/95; 6 Ob 191/04p ecolex 2005, 613 [Wilhelm]; 6 Ob 198/10a; 5 Ob 133/92 wobl 1993, 187 [Strobl]; 2 Ob 275/98z; 1 Ob 254/99f Juristische Blätter 2000, 657 [Jabornegg]; 4 Ob 77/02f ÖBl. 2003, 250 [Dittrich]; 6 Ob 191/04p ecolex 2005, 613 [Wilhelm]; 7 Ob 311/04t ecolex 2006, 960 [Ertl]; 1 Ob 88/05f; 7 Ob 164/06b; 1 Ob 190/06g; 10 Ob 21/08y ecolex 2009 / 257 [Wilhelm]; 9 Ob 91/09m; 8 ObA 71/09p; 6 Ob 198/10a; RIS-Justiz RS0040182 (T4, T5, T9), RS0006261 (T10), RS0037797 (T48). 5 Ob 133/92 wobl1993, 187 [Strobl]; 6 Ob 602/93; 1 Ob 88/05f; 3 Ob 106/06v; 4 Ob 133/14h EvBl 2015 / 90 [Hartlieb]; 8 Ob 53/14y ÖJZ 2014 / 155 [Burtscher]; 8 ObA 9/15d; 6 Ob 20/15f EF-Z 2015 / 151 [Körber-Risak]; RIS-Justiz RS0006261 (T11), RS0040182 (T9).

56 Pavel Bachleda, *Ausforschungsbeweis im Zivilprozess*, Diss. Vienna 2017.

refusal to submit the document.[57] By drawing a reverse conclusion, it follows that all other documents must be presented.

1.046 Like in Germany third parties are subject to the requirement to produce a document only if it is a joint document or if there is an obligation under substantive law. This means that the parties' obligation to co-operate goes well beyond what is required by the German Code of Civil Procedure. Unlike German law, the requirements for the disclosure of documents are identical for *ex officio* court orders and those made at the request of a party.[58]

1.047 Austrian substantive law provides a wide range of disclosure, information, inspection and accounting obligations. As in German law, according to case law these rules are supplemented by duties based on good faith. In both countries, the Federal Courts of Justice assume that information must be provided if the nature of the legal relationship entails that the entitled party is inexcusably unaware of the existence and extent of certain facts, but the other party is able to provide information about them without difficulty and can be expected to do so in accordance with the principles of good faith.[59] For a long time, substantive law was therefore the most important basis for the obligation to provide information in both countries, although it does not apply in many cases.

3. General obligation to co-operate based on procedural law

1.048 In Austria, the general obligation of the parties to give information and access to evidence, which is highly controversial in German procedural law, has a rudimentary legal basis in Sec. 184 para 1 of the Austrian Civil Procedure Code:

> Each party may, for the purpose of clarifying the facts of the case, ask the presiding judge, or with the presiding judge's consent, ask questions to the opposing party present or its representative regarding all circumstances relevant to the subject matter of the dispute or the oral hearing and relevant to the proceedings, and in particular regarding the existence and nature of documents useful for the proceedings, matters of inquiry and matters of personal inspection.

1.049 This right to information was already included in the original version of the Austrian Civil Procedure Code, but it has only been used in court practice since around 2002.[60] The provision must be read together with Sec. 178, which imposes a duty of telling the

---

57 All provisions dealing with the production of documents are also applicable for the inspection of things, Sec. 368–370 Austrian Civil Procedure Code.

58 Jürgen Rassi, Die Aufklärungs- und Mitwirkungspflicht der nicht beweisbelasteten Partei, 121 *Zeitschrift für Zivilprozess* (ZZP) (2008), 165 at 193.

59 Austria: OGH RIS-Justiz RS0035050; Germany: established cases law e.g. BGH BeckRS 2016, 13688 mn. 7; BGHZ 148, 27; BGHZ 95, 274; BGHZ 10, 385 at 387; BGH NJW 1957, 669.

60 For the scope of the right of information cf. Markus Keller/Fabian Liebel/Kevin Labner, Zum Umfang des Fragerechts nach § 1484 ZPO, *BankArchiv* 2023, 733.

truth on the parties. According to the prevailing opinion in legal literature, each party must not only speak truthfully on its own behalf, but must also answer questions and assertions of the opponent correctly.[61] Austrian judges are held to ask questions and to discuss the case with the parties (Sec. 182, 182a Austrian Civil Procedure Code). The court must clarify contradictions, ambiguities and gaps in the parties' submissions. Rolf Stürner, in his justification of the general duty of the parties to provide information and access to evidence in German law, already emphasized the central importance of establishing the truth.[62] The constitutional guarantee of access to justice and the rule of law require a comprehensive investigation of the true facts underlying a particular lawsuit. According to the legislative materials in Austria, the idea of finding the truth is clearly behind the rules for inspection and documentary evidence. As a consequence, Franz Klein, the father of the Austrian Code of Civil Procedure, already called for 'mutual support of the parties to the proceedings.'[63]

Based on Sec. 184, 178 and 182 of the Austrian Civil Procedure Code, an increasing number of authors in Austria today assume that the parties have a very extensive duty to co-operate in giving access to evidence.[64] Their concept was directed against existing case law that preferred to rely on a reversal of the burden of proof in the case of the opponent's 'proximity of evidence.' Such case law was based on considerations of equity and it remains unclear what is a principle and what is an exception.[65] The Austrian Federal Court of Justice has finally also accepted Sec. 184 Austrian Civil Procedure Code as a basis for a general duty to co-operate.[66] A recent decision even seems to suggest that the deciding factor for a party's duty of disclosure is no longer the sphere to which the relevant circumstance can be attributed ('proximity of evidence'), but rather a 'deficiency of information' on the part of the party seeking **1.050**

61 Renate Bienert-Nießl, *Materielle Auskunftspflichten im Zivilprozess – zugleich eine Untersuchung der prozessualen Mitwirkungspflichten der Parteien*, Verlag Österreich 2003, 340; Jürgen Rassi, *Kooperation und Geheimnisschutz bei Beweisschwierigkeiten im Zivilprozess*, Skramek Vienna 2020, 79/80.

62 Rolf Stürner, *Die Aufklärungspflicht der Parteien des Zivilprozesses*, Tübingen 1976, 39 et seq.

63 Franz Klein, *Pro futuro – Betrachtungen über Probleme der Zivilprozessrechtsreform in Österreich*, 1871, 36.

64 Jürgen Rassi, *Kooperation und Geheimnisschutz bei Beweisschwierigkeiten im Zivilprozess*, Skramek Vienna 2020, 70 et seq.; Renate Bienert-Nießl, *Materielle Auskunftspflichten im Zivilprozess – zugleich eine Untersuchung der prozessualen Mitwirkungspflichten der Parteien*, Verlag Österreich 2003; Thomas Klicka, Juristische Blätter (JBl) 1992, 235; Trenker in: Georg Kodek/Paul Oberhammer, ZPO-ON, § 184 (9.10.223) rdb.at; Nicole Konrad, in Jusline.at, Sec. 184 ZPO (15.4.214); contrary to this approach *Schragel*, in: *Fasching / Konecny*, 2nd ed., § 184 ZPO mn. 4.

65 Jürgen Rassi, Die Aufklärungs- und Mitwirkungspflicht der nicht beweisbelasteten Partei, 121 *Zeitschrift für Zivilprozess* (ZZP) (2008), 165, 179 et seq.

66 OGH, 11/5/2005, 9 Ob 12/OSp: 'Rather, it must be assumed that, in principle, there is an obligation to disclose circumstances that are relevant to the proceedings and would otherwise not be accessible to the opponent, and that a breach of this obligation may have adverse consequences for the party concerned (see Klicka, Aufklärungspflichten der Prozessparteien im österreichischen Zivilprozess, JBl 1992, 235; for a more detailed discussion, see Bienert-Nießl, Materiellrechtliche Aufklärungspflichten im Zivilprozess, 339 et seq.)'; see also the following cases of the Federal High Court of Justice: 9 Ob 12/05p; 6 Ob 257/07y; 6 Ob 44/09b; 1 Ob 128/10w ZVR 2011/142 [Kathrein]; 7 Ob 186/10v; 7 Ob 216/10f.

evidence.[67] If a party violates its general duty to co-operate, courts are free to evaluate the refusal,[68] but the alleged facts are not automatically deemed to be admitted.[69] A free evaluation of the refusing party's behavior is also the preferred solution in existing legal provisions: Sec. 307 para 2, 318, 369 Austrian Civil Procedure Code. It provides a flexible way to handle each individual case adequately.

4. Transposition of European Directives

1.051 When implementing the Enforcement Directive, Austria was able to limit itself to the insertion of the substantive rights to information required by the Directive (e.g. Sec. 87b Copyright Act; Sec. 151a Patent Act). Apart from that, the legislator assumed that the existing procedural rules already complied with the Directive. The reason was the following: after the entry into force of the 1995 TRIPS Agreement, which contains a provision on the preservation of evidence by provisional measures similar to that of the Enforcement Directive and which is directly applicable in Austria, Austrian courts had already allowed preliminary injunctions to secure evidence.[70] There was therefore only a limited need for legislative action in Austria.

1.052 With regard to the implementation of the Antitrust Damages Directive, it should be emphasized that Austria, unlike Germany, relies on a purely procedural concept of access to evidence. Accordingly, the implementation of the Directive by Sec. 37j of the Austrian Antitrust Act only regulates the duty to disclose and present evidence in civil litigation.[71] In competition law, it is sufficient if the claim is substantiated at least to the extent that it contains those facts and evidence that are reasonably accessible to the plaintiff and that sufficiently support the plausibility of a claim for damages. Paragraphs 2–3 provide clear rules on access to evidence that is as precisely and accurately as possible described on the basis of reasonably available facts. In order to protect confidentiality, Sec. 37j (7) allows for a temporarily 'in camera' procedure. The party obliged to disclose evidence may request that certain specifically designated evidence

67 OGH, October 18, 2022, 4 Ob 78/22g; Thomas Klicka/Gerd Konezny, Der OGH und das neue Fragerecht nach § 184 ZPO – Eine Analyse der E OGH October 18, 2022, 4 Ob 78/22g, *Österreichische Juristenzeitung (ÖJZ)*, 2024, 105.

68 Jürgen Rassi, Die Aufklärungs- und Mitwirkungspflicht der nicht beweisbelasteten Partei, 121 *Zeitschrift für Zivilprozess* (ZZP) (2008), 165, 198; Thomas Klicka, *Aufklärungspflichten der Prozessparteien im österreichischen Zivilprozess*, Juristische Blätter (JBl) 1992, 233; Walter Rechberger in: Hans Fasching/Andreas Konecny, *Zivilprozessordnung*, vol III, Vor § 266 ZPO mn. 35.

69 This was, however, the idea of Franz Klein, *Pro futuro futuro – Betrachtungen über Probleme der Zivilprozessrechtsreform in Österreich*, 1871, 48.

70 Autrian Federal Court of Justice, (OGH), 4 R 6/99b, MR 1999, 167.

71 Austrian Official Journal, ÖBGBl. I, 2017, 56; Verena Kern, *Urkundenvorlage bei Kartellschadensklagen*, Tübingen 2020, 134.

be disclosed only to the court if there is a duty of confidentiality or a privilege according to the Code of Criminal Procedure. In such a situation the court shall decide, after inspecting the evidence without the participation of the parties ('counsel's eyes only') whether it shall also be disclosed to the party requesting the disclosure.

5. Summary

Compared to the German Civil Procedure Code, the situation in Austria is much more favorable to access to information and evidence. The doctrine of a general duty to co-operate is widely accepted today based on a comprehensive right to ask questions (Sec. 184 Austrian Civil Procedure Code) which enables parties to obtain information on evidence in the hands of the opponent and, subsequently, to submit corresponding requests for evidence. In Austria, the principle of procedural disclosure and co-operation of the parties is also followed when implementing EU Directives whenever the Directive leaves it to the discretion of the Member State. **1.053**

C. PART III – SWITZERLAND

1. Background and general principles of Swiss Federal Civil Procedure Code

The starting point in Switzerland is different from that in Germany and Austria, if only because the Swiss Federal Code of Civil Procedure is one of the youngest in Western Europe. For a long time, legislation for civil proceedings in Switzerland was the exclusive responsibility of the cantons so then there were 26 different codes of civil procedure. The cantonal procedural rules differed considerably in some respects. Depending on their geographical location and history, they were influenced partly by French and partly by German procedural law. Only for the Federal Supreme Court in Lausanne was there a Federal Code of Civil Procedure. It was only in 1999 that the preliminary work began on a harmonized Federal Swiss Code of Civil Procedure. Parliamentary deliberations began in the summer of 2007 and resulted in December 2008 in a definitive version. The new Federal Act came into force on 1 January 2011 and replaced all cantonal procedural codes. **1.054**

The law of evidence is regulated in Article 150 et seq. and explicitly provides, for example, a right to evidence that even includes the use of illegally obtained evidence if the interest in establishing the truth prevails. In this respect, the new Civil Procedure Code has explicitly addressed many issues that have been debated also in German law. Like the German Civil Procedure Code, Article 150, 151 of the Swiss Civil Procedure Code limit the taking of evidence to disputed facts that are directly relevant in law. **1.055**

2. Parties' obligation to co-operate in the taking of evidence

1.056 A noteworthy deviation from German law is the fact that there is a separate section on the parties' obligations to co-operate (Articles 160–167), which begins by stating a general obligation on the parties to co-operate in the taking of evidence by giving testimony and producing documents and objects for inspection.[72] A distinction between parties and third parties is only made to the extent that third parties have further rights to refuse co-operation in Articles 165 and 166 than a litigant (Articles 163 and 164).

1.057 Article 160 para 1 reads as follows:

> Duty to cooperate
> The parties and third parties are obliged to cooperate in the taking of evidence. In particular, they must:
> a. testify truthfully as a party or as a witness;
> b. surrender documents; excepted are documents arising from the dealings of a party or a third party with an attorney who is authorised to represent them professionally, or with a patent attorney within the meaning of Article 2 of the Patent Attorney
> c. to tolerate an inspection of a person or property by experts.

1.058 The only documents exempt from the requirement to be disclosed are legal correspondence. The right to refuse to produce documents does not only apply to the lawyer or patent attorney themselves, but also to parties and third parties, regardless of where the documents are located.[73]

1.059 In legal literature, Article 160 para 1 (c) is interpreted broadly and also includes the taking of evidence by the court itself by way of an inspection.[74] Despite the narrow wording, which seems to only allow an external inspection of things, the expert is also permitted to open and disassemble things, if necessary. In case of a party's unjustified refusal to co-operate, the court may draw adverse conclusions (Article 164), real fines and the enforcement of a court order (Article 167 Swiss Civil Procedure Code) are available against a refusing third party. Apparently, the French principle of the *astreinte*, a fine that can also be imposed on a refusing party, was not adopted.

72 A detailed analysis is made by Niclas Bacher, *Mitwirkungspflichten und Verweigerungsrechte Dritter bei der Beweiserhebung im Zivilprozess,* Diss. Basel 2011.

73 Samuel Baumgartner in: Paul Oberhammer/Tanja Domej/Ulrich Haas, *Schweizerische Zivilprozessordnung*, 3rd ed. 2021, Article 160 mn. 6a.

74 Issak Meier, *Schweizer Zivilprozessrecht – eine kritische Darstellung aus der Sicht von Praxis und Lehre*, Schulthess Zurich 2010, 300; Samuel Baumgartner in: Paul Oberhammer/Tanja Domej/Ulrich Haas, *Schweizerische Zivilprozessordnung*, 3rd ed. 2021, Article 160 mn. 7 refers to Article 181 instead for any inspection by the court. This Article, however, does not provide any obligation of parties or third parties to provide access for inspections.

In addition to the procedural duty to co-operate, Swiss law also recognizes supplementary duties of disclosure, production and accounting under substantive law, which are intended to enable or facilitate the enforcement of rights. **1.060**

3. Protection of confidential information

The Swiss Civil Procedure Code provides only a single, very general rule for the protection of confidential information in the context of the taking of evidence, which leaves it to the court to take the 'necessary measures' (Article 156).[75] In Switzerland, the possible protective measures traditionally extend very far and can restrict the right to a fair hearing and the right of the parties to participate in the taking of evidence (Article 155), their right to inspect files (Article 53 para 2) and also the right to comment on the outcome of the evidence (Article 232 para 1). It is possible to exclude the public and to restrict access to evidence to the lawyers of the parties. This means that one or both parties (in the case of business secrets of a third party) can be excluded from evidence or parts thereof, for example by blackening certain parts of a document or by not admitting them to respective parts of a hearing. The far-reaching measures can be explained, among other things, by the fact that the catalogue of third-party privileges does not provide for any right to withhold trade secrets. In Germany, the situation is much better for third parties in this respect.[76] **1.061**

When selecting a measure in a court order based on Article 156 Swiss Civil Procedure Code, the court must weigh the party's or third party's interest in protection against the affected party's right to be heard and select the mildest measure within the scope of proportionality.[77] **1.062**

However, the protection of trade secrets is not a complete one. If a party has been excluded from the taking of evidence or has had its right to inspect files restricted, the court may only use the evidence in question in its judgment if the party has at least been informed of the essential content and has had the opportunity to comment and to provide counterevidence.[78] This is another attempt to reconcile the protection of secrets with the right to be heard. **1.063**

75 For a detailed discussion see Richard Stäuber, *Der Schutz von Geschäftsgeheimnissen im Zivilprozess*, Diss. Zurich 2011 who advocates for a more concrete list of protective measures.

76 For third-party privileges in Germany see, Sec. 384 no. 3 [witness testimony]; Sec. 142 para 2 [documents], 144 para 2 [inspection of property and tangible things].

77 Samuel Baumgartner in: Paul Oberhammer/Tanja Domej/Ulrich Haas, *Schweizerische Zivilprozessordnung*, 3rd ed. 2021, Article 156 mn. 5.

78 Thomas Sutter-Somm/Franz Hasenböhler/Christoph Leuenberger, *Kommentar zu Schweizer Zivilprozes-sordnung*, 3rd ed. 2016, Article 156 mn. 20; Samuel Baumgartner in: Paul Oberhammer/Tanja Domej/Ulrich Haas, *Schweizerische Zivilprozessordnung*, 3rd ed. 2021, Article 156 mn. 6.

1.064 Another important practical restriction is that the protective measures are limited to the taking of evidence. Each party must present the facts fully and truthfully in their written submissions and cannot hold back trade secrets.[79] In the EU, protection is provided by the Directive 2016/943/EU on the protection of know-how and business secrets, which enables a more comprehensive protection for the entire proceedings and, in particular, provides for general confidentiality obligations and prohibitions on abuse. This covers all information that was disclosed in the pleadings, the contents of the case file, the judgment or otherwise in the proceedings. The Directive is, however, not applicable in Switzerland and there is no indication that the Swiss legislator will comply with the Directive on voluntary basis.

4. Pre-action access to evidence?

1.065 Article 158 Swiss Civil Procedure Code provides that the court shall take evidence at any time if: (a) the law grants a corresponding claim; or (b) the applicant party demonstrates the necessity to preserve evidence or any other legitimate interest. The provision thus not only allows for the preservation of evidence before the start of proceedings. According to the explanatory memorandum,[80] a 'legitimate interest' within the meaning of the provision should also be deemed to exist if a party claims that it wishes to clarify the prospects of evidence and the proceedings. This goes beyond what is possible under German procedural law. Sec. 485 para 2 sentence 2 of the German Civil Procedure Code allows for evidence to be taken by an expert (no other evidence![81]) before proceedings are initiated if it serves to preserve evidence or if a legal interest can be assumed because the determination can serve to avoid a legal dispute. The scope of application is therefore narrower and does not include a party's interest in clarifying the prospects of her case.

1.066 The Swiss Federal Court of Justice's case law, however, interprets Article 158 narrowly and sets strict requirements. It is by no means sufficient for the claimant to assert that they want to clarify the prospects of a particular claim. Rather, they must already credibly establish the facts of the case from which a claim arises against the defendant under substantive law.[82] This has been criticized in legal literature as being too strict and incompatible with the wording. In particular, the Federal Court of Justice thus

79 Samuel Baumgartner in: Paul Oberhammer/Tanja Domej/Ulrich Haas, *Schweizerische Zivilprozessordnung*, 3rd ed. 2021, Article 1221 mn. 26.

80 Botschaft ZPO 7315; Samuel Baumgartner in: Paul Oberhammer/Tanja Domej/Ulrich Haas, *Schweizerische Zivilprozessordnung*, 3rd ed. 2021, Article 158 mn. 8: The pre-action taking of evidence to assess the prospects of success was previously only included in a few cantonal codes of civil procedure.

81 Other evidence can only be collected outside and before a trial if there is a risk of its loss, Sec. 485 para 1 German Civil Procedure Code.

82 BGE 140 III 16 E.2.2.2.; BGE 138 III 76 E. 2.4.2.

establishes requirements that do not otherwise exist in the proceedings for the taking of evidence.[83] Some authors instead propose that only the fact that the amount and validity of a claim are in dispute must be stated and that the taking of evidence is likely to settle the dispute.[84] A lower level of substantiation would help to prevent litigation from the outset, which is also an objective of Article 158. So far, however, the Federal Court has not relaxed its strict requirements. In a sense, the Court has significantly scaled back the legislator's very liberal approach that is now largely in line with the ELI/UNIDROIT Model Rules.

D. PART IV – SUMMARY

Although German, Austrian and Swiss law have common roots to some extent, the parties' procedural duty to co-operate is quite different today. Germany is taking the most cautious approach and is only gradually abolishing the principle of the *nemo tenetur contra se edere* under the pressure of European Directives. Compared to German civil procedure law, particularly Switzerland has a very progressive concept of parties' obligations to co-operate, which is matched by comprehensive protective measures for trade secrets. The Swiss Civil Procedure Code is therefore very similar to the ELI/UNIDROIT Model Rules of European Civil Procedure in many respects. However, compared to the Model Rules, all three legal systems are very cautious when it comes to pre-litigation access to evidence *and* information obligations. **1.067**

83 Samuel Baumgartner in: Paul Oberhammer/Tanja Domej/Ulrich Haas, *Schweizerische Zivilprozessordnung*, 3rd ed. 2021, Article 158 mn. 10; Tanja Domej, Art. 158 ZPO in der Praxis – Ende einer Hoffnung? in: Walter Fellmann/Stephan Weber (eds), *Haftpflichtprozess*, Zurich 2014, 69 at 75 et seq.

84 Samuel Baumgartner in: Paul Oberhammer/Tanja Domej/Ulrich Haas, *Schweizerische Zivilprozessordnung*, 3rd ed. 2021, Article 158 mn. 11; Marc Schweizer, Vorsorgliche Beweisaufnahme nach schweizerischer Zivilprozessordnung un Patentgesetzt, 123 *Zeitschrift für Zivilprozess* (ZZP) (2010), 1; Tanja Domej, Art. 158 ZPO in der Praxis – Ende einer Hoffnung? in: Walter Fellmann/Stephan Weber (eds), *Haftpflichtprozess*, Zurich 2014, 69 at 77.

2

EVIDENCE-GATHERING IN ENGLAND AND WALES

John Sorabji

A. INTRODUCTION

2.001 The English and Welsh civil justice system places responsibility for evidence-gathering primarily in the hands of the parties to litigation. It understands access to evidence as inherently related to the principle of party autonomy or party disposition. For a considerable part of its procedural history, it understood the court's role as simply being facilitative: it was the means by which parties could secure the evidence they sought from the opposing party in litigation. Equally, for a considerable part of its history, this precedence given to party autonomy meant that it was entirely a matter for the parties what evidence they adduced in support of their claims and defences. If a party wished to hold back evidence that would otherwise support their claim, that was a matter for them. Equally it was a matter for them what witnesses, whether lay or expert, they called to support their claims. The court had no power to either require evidence to be adduced nor did it have any power to control the nature and amount of evidence adduced.[1]

1 There was and is, however, a limited power that the court has to call a witness to give evidence on its own initiative. That power is, nevertheless, subject to party consent: *In re Enoch and Zaretsky, Bock & Co's Arbitration* [1901] 1 KB 327 at 332–334; *Fallon v Calvert* [1960] 2 QB 201 at 205.

Since the introduction of the Civil Procedure Rules in 1999 there has, however, been substantial change. The historic position is now much reformed. Party autonomy and control over evidence remains in place. No power, for instance, has been introduced to enable English and Welsh courts to engage in what might be called substantive case management, i.e., to manage the substance of proceedings through the court itself identifying issues, facts and evidence necessary to resolve the parties' dispute and requiring such evidence to be adduced. However, party autonomy is now subject to court control over evidence. Where documentary evidence, including e-documents and data, is concerned two regimes exist: a generally applicable disclosure regime and one that is specifically applied to disputes brought in the Business and Property Courts.[2] Both require evidence-gathering and presentation to be tailored to the nature of the dispute and, hence, consistent with an overarching commitment to procedural proportionality. Before the court will make an order for disclosure, it will thus need to be satisfied that the order sought is consistent with the approach specified in the applicable regime. Where expert evidence is concerned, it too is now subject to the requirements of procedural proportionality, which is enforced through the requirement, amongst other things, that no expert evidence may be adduced without the court's permission. **2.002**

This chapter considers these procedural requirements. It particularly looks at the two regimes that govern documentary disclosure, as well as the power to order pre-action disclosure, and that which applies to expert evidence. It also makes reference to the jurisdiction to obtain information from third parties to proceedings.[3] It should be noted at the outset that access to evidence is subject to a range of limitations provided for through the application of evidentiary privileges. Consideration of those matters are beyond the scope of this chapter.[4] Finally, while the United Kingdom withdrew from the European Union in 2020, both the Intellectual Property Directive[5] and the Damages Directive[6] were implemented prior to that date. Their implementation did not require any steps to be taken to amend or revise the approach taken to evidence-gathering in England and Wales, as provision for ordering a party to disclose evidence on application had been a feature of English civil procedure since the development of the Bill of Discovery prior to 1873 and was set out within the Civil Procedure Rules **2.003**

2 The former under CPR Pt 31. The latter under CPR PD57AD.

3 Evidence gathering concerning physical evidence is not covered. Provision for access to such evidence is provided for by, amongst other things, CPR Pt 25.

4 For a discussion of the variations evidentiary privileges see, A. Zuckerman, *Zuckerman on Civil Procedure – Principles of Practice*, (Sweet & Maxwell, 2021), chaps. 16, 17, 18 and 19.

5 Directive 2004/48/EC of the European Parliament and of the Council of 29 April 2004 on the enforcement of intellectual property rights, article 8.

6 Directive 2014/104/EU of the European Parliament and of the Council of 26 November 2014 on certain rules governing actions for damages under national law for infringements of the competition law provisions of the Member States and the European Union, articles 5 and 6.

(CPR), and specifically their Pt 31. The Representative Actions Directive,[7] however, came into force after the UK's withdrawal. The provision it makes for disclosure of third party litigation funding does not therefore apply to England and Wales. That being said, the power to order disclosure of such information has been acknowledged by the courts in two contexts.[8] First, disclosure of the fact of such funding arrangements can be required where a defendant to proceedings applies for an order for security of costs to be made against a claimant. In such a situation, for the court to consider whether to grant the application effectively because it is being made on the grounds that the claimant is funded by a third party funder and the order for security is to be made against the funder, the fact and identity of the funder must be made available to the court. In such circumstances the court has a power, ancillary to its power to grant an order for security of costs, to order disclosure of the third party funder's identity.[9] More generally, in exercising its jurisdiction to make an adverse costs award against a funded party to litigation, the court can order the disclosure of the funder's identity, the amount of funding they provided and, hence, the general terms of the funding agreement: such disclosure being necessary for the court to determine whether to order the funder to pay costs and, if so, the amount of such costs.[10]

B. THE RATIONALES UNDERPINNING EVIDENCE-GATHERING

2.004 There are several rationales that underpin the English and Welsh approach to evidence-gathering. Andrews, for instance, has suggested what he described as three ignoble purposes, particularly where the documentary disclosure process is concerned. Those were that due to the nature of the process: first, it enabled lawyers to make significant amounts of money, due to the time it took to comply fully with the disclosure obligation and the fact that lawyers, primarily, charge their clients on an hourly basis; secondly, that it enabled defendants to delay the conclusion of cases, i.e., trial and judgement, through disclosing considerable amounts of documents, many of which

7 Directive (EU) 2020/1828 of the European Parliament and of the Council of 25 November 2020 on representative actions for the protection of the collective interests of consumers and repealing Directive 2009/22/EC, articles 10(3) and 18.

8 R. Leinen, *Striking the right balance: disclosure of third-party funding*, Oxford University Commonwealth Law Journal, (2020), 20:1, 115 at 129–131.

9 *Reeves v Sprecher* [2007] EWHC 3226 (Ch); *Wall v Royal Bank of Scotland Plc* [2016] EWHC 2460 (Comm) at [11]–[26], [44]–[45].

10 *Arkin v Borchard Lines Ltd* [2005] EWCA Civ 655, [2005] 1 WLR 3055; *Chapelgate Master Fund Opportunity Ltd v Money* [2020] EWCA Civ 246; [2020] Costs LR 493. Where collective proceedings are taking place in the Competition Appeal Tribunal, disclosure of the fact that the prospective representative party is a third-party funder must be disclosed to the Tribunal as part of the process to consider certifying the proceedings as collective proceedings: see Competition Appeal Tribunal Rules, r.78(3)(b). Where a representative action is on foot in the civil courts, there is no such requirement as only class members may be representative parties.

had no relevance to the proceedings. Thus the process required the receiving party to spend considerable time, at considerable cost, to scrutinise those documents to determine which, if any, were relevant; and, finally, due to the cost and time of the process, it acted as a disincentive to parties to commence proceedings, particularly in cases that were likely to involve considerable documentary disclosure.[11]

While it is well-recognised that documentary disclosure as well as witness evidence and expert evidence have led and can lead to excess litigation cost and the expenditure of significant amounts of time considering evidence by the parties, to characterise evidence-gathering as having ignoble purposes is perhaps a touch cynical.[12] Such matters may well be, and to some degree will inevitably be, consequences of evidence-gathering; they are not, however, when properly construed, its underlying purpose or purposes. There are, however, several well-established purposes that are understood to underpin the various evidence-gathering processes, the primary one of which is that they promote accurate fact-finding, i.e., they promote the ascertainment of truth. That this is the case was outlined by Lord Bingham in Tweed v Parades Commission for Northern Ireland, where he identified this feature as underpinning documentary disclosure. As he put it, **2.005**

> Disclosure of documents in civil litigation has been recognised throughout the common law world as a valuable means of eliciting the truth and thus of enabling courts to base their decisions on a sure foundation of fact.[13]

In this, Lord Bingham was simply echoing a point Bray made in 1885, where he stressed that its role was 'to ascertain facts material to the merits of his case.'[14] This primary purpose is further supported by its ability to prevent surprise at trial,[15] and to place all parties on an equal footing as they all have access to the same evidence both prior to and during the trial process. It thus promotes equality of arms. In that way, as evident from the approach taken to article 6 of the European Convention on **2.006**

11 N. Andrews, *English Civil Procedure*, (OUP, 2003) at 597.

12 Evidence concerning excess litigation cost (and delay) arising from disclosure was given, for instance, to the Atkins Working Party, see R. Atkins et al., *Report and Recommendations of the Commercial Court Long Trials Working Party*, (Judicial Office, 2007) at 26. Evidence was also given to the judiciary of England and Wales by the General Counsel of the FTSE 100 companies in England and Wales concerning excess disclosure and its attendant adverse consequences on cost in 2016–2017, which led to the establishment of the working party that ultimately produced the PD57AD disclosure regime. See, for instance, Dame Elizabeth Gloster, *Proposals for a Disclosure Pilot for the Business and Property Courts in England and Wales*, (Press Announcement, November 2017). Actual empirical studies of the incidence of cost and disclosures impact on it are, however, lacking.

13 *Tweed v Parades Commission for Northern Ireland* [2006] UKHL 53, [2007] 1 AC 650 at [2].

14 E. Bray, *The Principles & Practice of Discovery*, (Reeves & Turner, 1885) at 16.

15 *Davies v Eli Lilly* [1987] 1 WLR 428 at 432.

Human Rights, parties are thus also afforded the ability to participate in proceedings effectively.[16]

2.007 The ability to obtain evidence and thus secure equality of arms and effective participation is particularly important where one party to proceedings is likely to be the only one who has access to relevant evidence.[17] The provision of evidence prior to trial is thus one of the ways in which parties can ascertain the case that is to be put against them to determine how best to test that case, including the evidence, and which evidence, if any, they wish to adduce to challenge that which is to be relied upon by their opponent. Contrary to Andrews' point, particularly where documentary disclosure is concerned, evidence-gathering serves the purpose of reducing litigation cost. By enabling a party to obtain evidence from their opponent via disclosure, they are saved the expense of obtaining it in other ways. Equally, they can avoid having to engage in potentially long and difficult investigative or other processes to obtain relevant evidence. And where evidence is provided to a party it may also promote cost-savings as it can lead to parties narrowing the issues in dispute or to the disclosing party or party who would otherwise have to disclose material, admitting the claim.[18]

2.008 Narrowing issues leads to a wider, and to arguably the second significant rationale that underpins the evidence-gathering process and particularly that of documentary disclosure: settlement's promotion. As Donaldson MR explained it in *Naylor v Preston Area Health Authority*,

> anything which enables the parties to appreciate the true strength and weakness of their positions at the earliest possible moment and at the same time enables them to enter on fully informed and realistic discussions designed to achieve a consensual resolution of the dispute is very much in the public interest.[19]

2.009 The provision of evidence, both supportive and adverse to a parties' case, is one of the key means by which this is achieved. Since the introduction of the CPR in 1999, the promotion of settlement has become all the more important a rationale. The CPR's emphasis on the need for parties to seek to resolve their disputes consensually, and at an early stage in the dispute, as part of its promotion of procedural proportionality (both for the parties and systemically across the whole of the civil justice system) makes it all the more important for parties to mutually disclose information and, not least, to do so before litigation commences.[20]

---

16 O. J. Settem, *Applications for the 'Fair Trial' Norm in ECHR Article 6(1) to Civil Proceedings*, (Springer, 2016) at 337 and following.
17 A. Zuckerman, ibid at 784.
18 E. Bray, ibid at 2.
19 *Naylor v Preston Area Health Authority* [1987] 1 WLR 958 at 967–968.
20 CPR r.1.1(2)(f).

The following key purposes can thus be seen to underpin the English and Welsh approach to evidence-gathering: the promotion of adjudicative accuracy; the promotion of settlement;[21] the promotion of equality of arms and effective participation in proceedings; the reduction in litigation cost and time; and, procedural proportionality. 2.010

C. VOLUNTARY AND COMPULSORY PRE-ACTION DISCLOSURE

The initial means by which the various rationales that underpin evidence-gathering are put into effect is through the process for pre-action disclosure. There are two forms of pre-action documentary disclosure: pre-action disclosure under the Pre-Action Protocols (PAPs) and pre-action disclosure under CPR r. 31.16. There is no pre-action witness disclosure in English and Welsh proceedings. Unlike, for instance, in the United States of America, where parties to litigation can depose witnesses prior to trial, there is no comparable general mechanism in England and Wales.[22] 2.011

1. Pre-action protocol disclosure

Pre-Action disclosure under the PAPs was introduced in 1999, when the CPR was introduced. The PAPs do not, however, form part of the rules of court albeit they form part of the wider architecture of the litigation process.[23] They set out best practice guidelines that parties are exhorted to comply with prior to litigation commencing. Their provisions are thus not mandatory; compliance with their requirements is voluntary albeit non-compliance may result in the imposition of adverse procedural consequences on a non-compliant party if proceedings do commence. The most widely applied adverse consequence is the imposition of adverse cost sanctions. Parties are thereby incentivised to comply with the guidelines even in the absence of a power to mandate compliance.[24] Each of the PAPs apply to a discrete type of cause of action. The Practice Direction – Pre-Action Conduct (PD-PAC) applies generally to those causes of action that are not covered by a specific PAP. The PAPs and the PD-PAC 2.012

---

21 As with English civil procedure's application generally, there are no reliable empirical studies on assumed impact of disclosure on settlement rates. It has, however, been a general assumption for policymakers since at least the 1830s that early disclosure promotes settlement: see, for instance, Lord Brougham LC (1828) cited in H. Wigmore, *Evidence*, (Chadbourn Revision) Vol. 6, 1976 at 498. Evidence that increased pre-action disclosure after the introduction of the PAPs resulted in a reduction in disputes leading to claims being issued decreased, as potential claimants concluded that a claim did not have a reasonable prospect of success if brought based on disclosure by the potential defendant: see T. Goriely, R. Moorhead, P. Abrams, *More Civil Justice? The Impact of the Woolf Reforms on Pre-Action Behaviour*, (The Law Society & the Civil Justice Council, 2002) at 102.

22 Depositions can, however, be obtained in England and Wales where a witness is unlikely to be able to give evidence at trial because, for instance, they are too ill to do so or are likely to be outside the jurisdiction: *Re Bradbrook* (1889) 23 QBD 226; The Evidence (Proceedings in Other Jurisdictions) Act 1975; CPR Pt 34.

23 *Jet 2 Holidays Ltd v Hughes* [2019] EWCA Civ 1858; [2020] WLR 844 at [36]–[43].

24 A. Zuckerman, ibid at 50–54.

each have the same specific aim: to promote pre-action information exchange, including evidence, between parties to a potential dispute. They do so, so that they can better understand each other's position, better determine what steps they should take to resolve their dispute, promote settlement before proceedings commence, and where proceedings do commence to narrow or limit the issues between them, they thus reduce the cost and time of litigation and facilitate its effective, i.e., proportionate, management.[25] Where documentary disclosure is concerned, the Personal Injury PAP emphasises the pro-settlement role of this form of voluntary early information exchange when it states its aim,

> The aim of early disclosure of documents by the defendant is not to encourage 'fishing expeditions' by the claimant but to promote an early exchange of relevant information to help in clarifying or resolving issues in dispute.[26]

2.013 Early information exchange, including that of evidence, is thus – consistently with the various rationales that underpin evidence-gathering in general – intended to being carried out in a way that minimises the cost of litigation and the time taken to resolve disputes. By being targeted on relevant issues, and hence not the basis of a fishing expedition for potential evidence, it is intended to be focused. It is thus not intended to artificially increase the cost of litigation, or party time taken to consider it. Through helping parties to clarify issues or resolve them, it is intended to promote efficient, cost-effective, and proportionate management of litigation if proceedings commence. This is through enabling the parties to narrow or clearly define the issues in dispute and thus target case management on the real issues between them and thereafter, on an equal footing, have them determined on their substantive merits. That, of course, only arises if the primary aim of information of PAPs is not fulfilled, i.e., that early exchange does not result in pre-action settlement of the dispute.

2. Applications for mandatory pre-action disclosure

2.014 While the PAPs have only been in place since 1999, England and Wales has since 1969 had a limited means by which a party to prospective litigation could apply for a compulsory order requiring pre-action documentary disclosure from a putative defendant.[27] Initially it was limited in scope to applications where personal injury proceedings or proceedings arising out of the death of an individual were in contemplation.[28] This

25 CPR Practice Direction Pre-Action Conduct, para. 3; Pre-Action Protocol Personal Injury Claims, para. 2.1.

26 Pre-Action Protocol for Personal Injury Claims, para. 7.1.1.

27 Additionally, the court has a common law jurisdiction to order pre-action disclosure from a non-party, that is where they are involved, innocently, in the commission of a tort: see, *Norwich Pharmacal v Customs and Excise Commissioners* [1974] AC 133.

28 R. Winn, *Report of the Committee on Personal Injuries Litigation* (HMSO, 1969); Administration of Justice Act 1969, s.21(1).

limitation was abandoned in 1999, since which time such disclosure can be applied for in respect of any potential cause of action,[29] irrespective of whether the claim concerns a private law or public dispute.[30] Since 1999 then its ambit has been the same as the ambit for voluntary pre-action disclosure under the PAPs. Unlike the PAPs, its primary rationale was to enable potential claimants to determine if they had a cause of action against the potential defendant. Its primary aim was thus focused on promoting access to justice, in the sense of access to the court. As Zuckerman explains, where evidence is in the hands of one party to a potential personal injury or wrongful death claim, such as a hospital, 'considerable hardship,' in terms of cost and time in trying to obtain the evidence, would likely be incurred by the claimant or the person acting on a deceased claimant's behalf.[31] Providing a means to obtain compulsory pre-action disclosure can thus be seen as an important means to promote cost-effective and timely access to the court, and equality of arms, through enabling the putative claimant to obtain such information. Its secondary aim was, however akin to that of the PAPs, to promote the early exchange of information where parties already knew a claim was viable. As a necessary corollary, this secondary aim gave effect to the rationales that also underpinned the PAPs. Taken together both aims of the mandatory pre-action disclosure process can readily be seen as intended to give effect to the rationales that inform the evidence-gathering process generally.

Due to the potentially wide-ranging nature of an application for pre-action disclosure the CPR places specific requirements on the court's discretion, not least to ensure that it cannot be mis-used to enable a potential claimant to engage in a fishing expedition for evidence of potential litigation, or as the Court of Appeal put it, as a 'roving inquisition'[32] against individuals who may or may not be potential defendants to potential claims. The discretion to grant such an order only arises if: i) the respondent to the application is likely to be a party to subsequent proceedings. In other words it cannot be used as a fishing expedition against any individual. Moreover it cannot, as a consequence be used to harass and put to expense an individual who is unlikely to be party to any subsequent proceedings;[33] ii) the applicant must also be likely to be party to the subsequent proceedings. Again, this is intended to ensure that the application is not brought for anything other than the genuine pursuit of proceedings; iii) the respondent would, if proceedings had already commenced, have had to give disclosure of the **2.015**

29 Senior Courts Act 1981, s.33; County Courts Act 1984, s.52; CPR r.31.16.

30 It is, however, rarely the case that such disclosure would be ordered in respect of putative public law proceedings; see *British Union for the Abolition of Vivisection (BUAV) v Secretary of State for the Home Department* [2014] EWHC 43 (Admin), [3024] AVD 69 at [32]–[34].

31 A. Zuckerman, ibid at 839.

32 *Black v Sumitomo* [2001] EWCA Civ 1819, [2002] 1 WLR 1562 at [92].

33 *Black v Sumitomo* [2001] EWCA Civ 1819, [2002] 1 WLR 1562 at [71]–[73].

documents sought; iv) and, pre-action disclosure is desirable to enable the anticipated proceedings to be disposed of fairly, it would assist in pre-action settlement, or save costs (the discretionary criteria).[34]

2.016 The test for the grant of pre-action disclosure can best be understood as focusing on the court's jurisdiction and, if it has such, whether the discretion to grant the order should be exercised.[35] The initial questions concerning the nature of the parties and their relationship to potential proceedings and then whether it is desirable to grant the application form the jurisdictional tests. Assuming the jurisdictional tests are met, the court then turns to its discretion: would an order promote accurate adjudication, settlement, or cost-savings, i.e., would an order give effect to the rationales that underpin evidence-gathering. Here there is a distinct link with pre-action disclosure under the PAPs, as that is one of the criteria that the court must consider in determining whether to exercise its discretion. In *Black v Sumitomo*, for instance, the Court of Appeal stressed that in considering the discretionary criteria a court should consider,

> the nature of the injury or loss complained of; the clarity and identification of the issues raised by the complaint; the nature of the documents requested; the relevance of any protocol or pre-action inquiries; and the opportunity which the complainant has to make his case without pre-action disclosure.[36]

2.017 In considering these factors, it has also been stressed that apart from cases where the potential defendant is likely to be solely in possession of the evidence sought via the application, it would be exceptional for the court to exercise its discretion to grant pre-action disclosure.[37] In reality then, these types of application are limited to personal injury or death cases where the potential defendant has and is the only one who has access to medical or similar records, and other cases where similar issues arise, e.g., where a local authority or a school is the only body who has access to records concerning safety assessments or employees in, for instance, potential negligence, product liability or employment rights cases. In this way, the courts ensure that this type of application is not misused, and particularly is not used in a speculative manner in the hope that it brings to light a potential claim.[38] To further limit the possibility of misuse, the courts have further held that the discretion cannot be exercised unless the potential subsequent claim has a real prospect of success. The applicant for such an order must not therefore merely demonstrate that they have a potential claim against the respondent, but that the claim is not fanciful, i.e., it is a genuine claim that has a

34 CPR r.31.16.

35 *Bermuda International Securities Ltd v KPMG* [2001] EWCA Civ 269, [2001] Lloyd's Rep PN 392 at [26].

36 *Black v Sumitomo* [2001] EWCA Civ 1819, [2002] 1 WLR 1562 at [88].

37 *Phoenix Natural Gas Ltd v British gas Trading Ltd* [2004] EWHC 451 (Comm) at [2].

38 *Black v Sumitomo* [2001] EWCA Civ 1819, [2002] 1 WLR 1562 at [83].

good prospect of being made out at trial.[39] The applicant must therefore have sufficient evidence,[40] in the absence of the evidence sought via the application for pre-action disclosure, to persuade the court that they have a viable claim. Thus, again, the application cannot be used as a fishing expedition to enable a putative claimant to determine if they have a claim. It is, as a consequence of these restrictive aspects of the criteria courts must consider where such applications are concerned, that such applications have declined since the introduction of voluntary evidence-gathering via the PAPs.[41]

D. DISCLOSURE DURING THE COURSE OF PROCEEDINGS

One of the criteria for the award of pre-action disclosure was that range and nature of documents sought under the order fell within the scope of 'standard disclosure.' That is to say they would have to be capable of being made subject to one form of order for disclosure following the commencement of proceedings. Applications for pre-action disclosure thus point to a specific feature of the English and Welsh approach to disclosure following the commencement of proceedings: that there are differential approaches to it within the CPR. There are, in fact, two different disclosure schemes within the CPR, one of general application and one of specific application to proceedings that take place in the Business and Property Courts of England and Wales, i.e., specialist courts within the High Court (the BPC scheme). Within each of those schemes, further differentiation exists. **2.018**

Before turning to the exact nature of the two schemes, it is important to note that the development of the more recent of the two, the BPC scheme, marks a departure from the English and Welsh general procedural approach. As a general rule, English and Welsh civil procedure is trans-substantive: the same procedural rules generally apply to all civil (including commercial) proceedings irrespective of the substantive cause of action. Specifically and historically a rudimentary form of claim-size trans-substantivity existed. Different rules applied in the county courts, which dealt with lower value, less complex claims, to those that applied in the High Court, which dealt with higher value, more complex claims.[42] This early form of procedural proportionality was replaced when the CPR was introduced in 1999. It provided the same procedure for all civil claims, irrespective of court in which they were pursued. It **2.019**

39 *Carillion Plc v KPMG LLP* [2020] EWHC 1416 (Com) at [66].

40 Evidence could take the form of the information set out in the application for pre-action disclosure where that is supported by a statement of truth or it may take the form of an affidavit in support of the application. See, for instance, *Bermuda International Securities Ltd v KPMG* [2001] EWCA Civ 269, [2001] CP Rep 73.

41 T. Goriely, R. Moorhead and P. Abrams, ibid at xxvi.

42 The County Court Rules applied in the county courts, while the Rules of the Supreme Court applied in the High Court (and Court of Appeal).

did, however, introduce a more sophisticated form of proportionality-based claim-size trans-substantivity. This was achieved, primarily, by introducing procedural case tracks, in which the nature and extent of civil process was matched to each claim by reference to, for instance, its value, complexity, importance to the parties and the public.[43] It was also to be achieved through the introduction of proportionate court-based case management, which is discussed further below.

2.020 Within the CPR's approach a single set of rules, which could be adapted flexibly to different types of case by reference to their nature (value, complexity, etc.), applied to documentary disclosure was introduced. It was set out in CPR Pt 31. With the introduction of the BPC scheme, English and Welsh civil procedure has moved back towards the cruder pre-CPR size-based proportionality approach, with a general disclosure scheme and one that was only applicable to higher, value more complex claims in the Business and Property Courts. It would have, arguably, been more effective and more consistent with the CPR's overarching structure to incorporate the BPC scheme's features within a revised CPR Pt 31 and thus make it available to any claim irrespective of the nature of the claim or which specialist court or otherwise in which the claim was being pursued.

2.021 Where both schemes are concerned, however, there is a key common feature: court control. One of the consistent complaints about documentary disclosure in England and Wales is that it generates excessive litigation cost and delay. This was exemplified in the late 19th century where the then Lord Chancellor's Legal Procedure Committee in 1881 identified 'unnecessary discovery' as 'the greatest source of needless expense' in litigation.[44] The same complaint was echoed over 100 years later in the Interim Woolf Report, which concluded that

> The scale of discovery, at least in the larger cases, is completely out of control. The principle of full, candid disclosure in the interests of justice has been devalued because discovery is pursued without sufficient regard to economy and efficiency in terms of the usefulness of the information which is likely to be obtained from the documents disclosed.[45]

2.022 The reason for this was arguably twofold. In the first instance, there was no effective court control over the disclosure process. Party autonomy was given precedence and parties were generally permitted to obtain orders for disclosure that were wide-ranging in the extreme, such that it was rightly described as 'virtually unlimited.'[46] Those orders paid no attention to either litigation cost or the time taken to obtain and assess

---

43 CPR Pts 26, 27, 28 and 29.

44 S. Rosenbaum, *The Rule-making Authority in the English Supreme Court*, (1917, Hardpress reprint) at 74.

45 H. Woolf, *Access to Justice: Interim Report to the Lord Chancellor on the Civil Justice System in England and Wales* (HMSO) (1995), chap. 3, para. 10.

46 H. Woolf, ibid, chap. 3, paras. 1, 15–17.

the materials subject to the disclosure order. This was not, however, entirely a function of disclosure being subject to effectively unrestrained party autonomy. The second reason why the disclosure process was generally uncontrolled in extent was due to the Court of Appeal's decision in *Compagnie Financiere du Pacifique v Peruvian Guano Company* (1882)[47]. In that case Brett LJ held that

> … it seems to me that every document relates to the matters in question in the action, which not only would be evidence upon any issue, but also, which, it is reasonable to suppose, contains information which may – not which must – either directly or indirectly enable the party requiring the affidavit either to advance his own case or to damage the case of his adversary. I have put the words 'either directly or indirectly,' because, as it seems to me, a document can properly be said to contain information which may enable the party requiring the affidavit either to advance his own case or to damage the case of his adversary, if it is a document which may fairly lead him to a train of inquiry …[48]

The consequence of the test laid down by Brett LJ was that parties would apply for and be granted orders for disclosure of the greatest possible breadth. Parties would be required to disclose not only documents they intended to rely upon, those that tended to support their opponent's case, those that tended to harm their own case (as English and Welsh procedure does not provide make provision for the effective extension of the principle of self-incrimination to documents[49]), and any which could fairly lead to other documents that fell into the previous categories. It was the last category of document, those that led to a train of inquiry, that caused the untrammelled expansion of disclosure and turned the disclosure process into a source of excessive litigation cost and delay. 2.023

This approach was, however, subject to the reforms introduced in 1999, which were referred to earlier, concerning the introduction of procedural case tracks and the introduction of court-controlled procedural case management.[50] With the CPR's introduction at that time, effective party control over the management of proceedings came to an end. One significant feature of this was court control over the disclosure process and the requirement that it, as with procedure generally, was subject to a proportionality requirement. This was to be achieved in two ways, first through the court having to apply a proportionality test to the interpretation of specific procedural rules, including those governing disclosure, and secondly, court control over the disclosure process itself through the application of CPR Pt 31, which made specific provision to enable 2.024

---

47 *Compagnie Financiere du Pacifique v Peruvian Guano Company* (1882) 11 QBD 5.

48 *Compagnie Financiere du Pacifique v Peruvian Guano Company* (1882) 11 QBD 5 at 62–63. For a critique see, A. Zuckerman, ibid at 785–787.

49 Compare, for instance, with the approach set out in the Italian Code of Civil Procedure, articles 183, 187 and 188.

50 CPR r.1 and Pt 3.

the court and parties to match the nature and extent of disclosure to the requirements of each particular case. As Zuckerman rightly noted, the

> aim of the disclosure arrangements under the CPR was to avoid the waste and excesses of the previous system without losing the principal advantages that mutual disclosure of documents is meant to produce.[51]

2.025 This approach is considered further below. The reform aim was not, however, achieved. In both 2007 and 2009 the approach to disclosure continued to cause excess litigation cost and delay. In 2007, the Aikens Review of commercial claims concluded that disclosure continued to generate very significant amounts of disclosure, most of which resulted in irrelevant or useless documents being disclosed at great cost. As significantly, this approach continued to undermine the court's ability to achieve the primary objective of disclosure: the production of documents that concerned the actual merits of the dispute. And hence, it also resulted in the second aim, the promotion of settlement, to be undermined.[52] In 2009, the Jackson Costs Review reached similar conclusions.[53] Despite these two reviews, and attempts in the light of them, to more effectively implement a proportionate approach to disclosure, disproportionate cost and delay remained endemic. That in turn led not to further reforms of the general scheme concerning disclosure contained in CPR Pt 31, which might have been expected, but rather the introduction of the special scheme applicable to business and property claims.

1. The general scheme – CPR Pt 31

2.026 The generally applicable scheme for documentary disclosure is contained in CPR Pt 31. It makes provision for a two-stage process. First, a party who seeks the compulsory disclosure of such evidence from their opponent must apply for an order to that effect. Absent the order there is no compulsory disclosure. If the order is granted, the party subject to it must disclose the nature and existence of documents relevant to the issues in dispute by list, i.e., they must set out in a list those documents that come within the scope of the order. That list should also identify documents it has and which are subject to an evidentiary privilege.[54] They should also state if they believe that it would be disproportionate for them to be required to permit the party in whose favour the order was made to inspect the document. Inspection is the second part of the disclosure process. Except where a document the existence of which has been disclosed by

51 A. Zuckerman, ibid at 786.

52 R. Aikens, *Report and Recommendations of the Commercial Court Long Trials Working Party*, (Judicial Office, 2007) at 58.

53 R. Jackson, *Review of Civil Litigation Costs: Final Report*, (HMSO, 2010) at 364–368.

54 CPR r.31.3.

list can properly be withheld from the party in whose favour the order has been made, that party has a right to inspect the listed documents.

The nature and extent to which a party must disclose by list and permit inspection of documents as part of the disclosure process is case-specific. In claims that are of low value and hence are allocated to the small claims track, disclosure is limited by reference to procedural proportionality. As a consequence, disclosure is strictly limited to those documents that a party intends to rely upon.[55] Where claims are allocated to the fast track (claims between the value of £10,000 and £25,000), the parties are generally required to try to agree the scope of disclosure, with courts as part of their oversight ensuring that what is agreed is proportionate.[56] Judicial oversight can and does result in disclosure being limited to less than 'standard disclosure.' Standard disclosure is, generally, the most common form of disclosure order made for claims allocated to the intermediate and multi-tracks, although it is not the presumptive form of order. On those tracks, the court is required to ensure that the order matches the needs of the particular case, which militates against the maintenance of a default or presumptive form of order.[57] Standard disclosure requires disclosure of documents on which a party relies, those which adversely affect their case, adversely affect their opponent's case, those that support their opponent's case and those required to be disclosure by specific provision within a Practice Direction. It thus is intended to avoid disclosure of 'train of inquiry' documents, and thereby provide a more focused form of disclosure than was the case prior to the CPR's introduction.[58] The court, and hence also the parties, must however consider whether another form of disclosure should be made in order to promote procedural proportionality and ensure costs and the time taken in litigation are minimised.[59] **2.027**

Depending on the nature and circumstances of an individual case, to give effect to these matters, such other forms of disclosure order range from the court ordering that there be no disclosure, to disclosure on an issue by issue basis, to disclosure of documents on which a party relies combined with the specific disclosure of individually identified documents, to any other order the court concludes is appropriate.[60] Specific disclosure can also be ordered separately from the orders made under standard disclosure, i.e., parties can apply for this form of disclosure to obtain disclosure of particular documents that have not otherwise been disclosed. More broadly, this form **2.028**

55 CPR r.27.2. It is thus excluded from the CPR PR 31 regime, see CPR r.31.1(2).

56 CPR PD 28 para. 3.6(1)(d).

57 CPR r.31.5. Prior to April 2024, standard disclosure was a presumptive form of order, see Civil Procedure (Amendment) Rules 2024 (SI 2024/106)).

58 CPR r.31.6.

59 CPR r.31.7.

60 CPR r.31.7(a)–(f).

of disclosure can, in those cases where it is justified, be relied upon to secure 'train of inquiry' disclosure. Thus the CPR maintains a commitment to providing a mechanism that can increase the cost and time of the disclosure process where that is necessary to promote adjudicative accuracy and also settlement.[61]

2.029 CPR Pt 31 is focused on disclosure from parties (as is the special scheme under PD57AD). Both are supplemented by the means by which an individual who is in possession of a document can be compelled to attend trial to produce the document.[62] As with the general approach to disclosure, this measure, which is effected via a witness summons, is designed to ensure that a witness can only be compelled to attend to produce specified documents. It cannot therefore be used to secure train of inquiry documents or as Gross J put it in *South Tyneside MBC v Wickes Building Supplies Ltd*,[63] secure attendance to enable the party in whose favour the order is made to secure disclosure generally or to secure disclosure of a 'fishing or speculative nature.'[64] Such an order must only be granted where it facilitate 'the fair disposal of the matter or … save costs.'[65] Again, we see the aims of securing adjudicative accuracy or settlement (fair disposal) and of ensuring that the process does not unnecessarily increase litigation cost, and attendant delay given effect through the limits placed on the witness summons process.

2. The special scheme – CPR PD 57AD

2.030 The special scheme, which is implemented via CPR PD 57AD, arose as a consequence of continuing complaints that the approach to disclosure under CPR Pt 31 failed to ensure that the cost and time involved in disclosure was proportionate. This engendered the introduction of a pilot scheme, applicable in the Business and Property Courts, which introduced a new scheme that had new and distinctive features. Those features were incorporated into CPR PD 57AD when the pilot scheme was made permanent within the CPR.

2.031 The first distinctive feature of the special scheme is that it is expressly intended to be applied to secure procedural proportionality. It thus supplements the general proportionality requirement under CPR r.1 with a specific focus on the need for parties to co-operate with each other and the court to ensure that disclosure is conducted to minimise cost and time, and thus secure proportionality. As the High Court explained, the special scheme was to ensure that disclosure operated 'along different lines [from

61 CPR r.31.12.

62 An individual can, equally, be compelled to attend trial to give oral evidence: see CPR r.34.2.

63 *South Tyneside MBC v Wickes Building Supplies Ltd* [2004] EWHC 2428 (Comm).

64 *South Tyneside MBC v Wickes Building Supplies Ltd* [2004] EWHC 2428 (Comm) at [23].

65 *South Tyneside MBC v Wickes Building Supplies Ltd* [2004] EWHC 2428 (Comm) at [23].

Pt 31] driven by reasonableness and proportionality.'[66] It was to create a new culture of disclosure, which was to be a proportionate one. It further stressed that the courts would expect the parties to co-operate in this respect: party co-operation was to be at the heart of the new approach.[67]

Secondly, it did away with standard disclosure and specific disclosure. In their place it made provision for 'Initial Disclosure' and 'Extended Disclosure.' The former is the requirement that in all claims subject to the scheme parties must disclose by list (the first stage of the disclosure process) the details of key documents. This list must be provided with the parties' statements of case, i.e., no disclosure order is required. Key documents are those on which a party intends to rely and those that are necessary to enable the other parties to understand the claim or defences to it.[68] Extended disclosure, which is subject to close court management, enables parties to seek further documents, albeit any such disclosure process must be 'reasonable and proportionate having regard to the overriding objective.'[69] In this way specific force is given to the first distinctive feature of the scheme. **2.032**

Within extended disclosure four specific options are available: Model A Extended Disclosure, which provides for no or no further disclosure than provided for by Initial Disclosure; Model B Extended Disclosure, which is comparable to Initial Disclosure; Model C Extended Disclosure, which directs the party subject to it to search for and disclose specific documents or specific classes of document; Model D Extended Disclosure, which in essence is the same as standard disclosure under CPR Pt 31; and Model E Extended Disclosure, which is equivalent to standard disclosure and specific disclosure under Pt 31.[70] In this way a more nuanced and tailored approach to disclosure is available. The final distinctive feature is that is the introduction of the Disclosure Review Document and an explicit provision that enables parties to seek the advice of the court on the approach to be taken to disclosure. The former is intended to guide the parties and the court through the disclosure process; i.e., to focus the parties' minds on the proportionate approach to disclosure and to facilitate their co-operation over the disclosure process. The latter is intended to facilitate more effective court oversight of the process, and enable parties to proactively seek the court's advice on the proportionate approach to take to disclosure.[71] **2.033**

---

66 *UTB LLC v Sheffield United Ltd* [2019] EWHC 914 (Ch); [2019] 3 All ER 698 at [75].
67 *UTB LLC v Sheffield United Ltd* [2019] EWHC 914 (Ch); [2019] 3 All ER 698 at [4], [53]–[54], [58].
68 CPR PD 57AD, para. 5.
69 CPR PD 57AD, para. 6.4
70 CPR PD 57AD para. 8.
71 CPR PD paras. 10 and 11.

2.034 This approach, which appears to be working well to achieve its objectives, has now been in place formally since 2022. It is difficult to see why its approach and the benefits that flow from it could not be applied more broadly. It was introduced to resolve problems of cost and delay in primarily commercial disputes. Non-commercial disputes can be of equally high value, complexity and be potentially document-heavy. It is difficult to see why its approach should not be available to them. Nor is it immediately clear why it could not be beneficially applied as a replacement for CPR Pt 31 generally. It incorporates the provisions of that scheme in its Models D and E for Extended Disclosure. It incorporates the facility to order no disclosure further than Initial Disclosure, which could readily be adapted to the approach to disclosure on the small claims track and fast track. If applied more broadly and consistently with the general approach to procedural trans-substantivity, it might provide the basis for English and Welsh civil procedure to finally cure the long-standing problems associated with the disclosure process, rendering it a means to promote adjudicative accuracy and settlement without the additional detrimental consequences of the promotion of excessive cost and delay. At the present, however, there appears to be no intention to generalise its application.

E. WITNESS EVIDENCE

2.035 Turning away from documentary evidence, the CPR provides the means by which parties can secure lay witness evidence. Historically, such evidence was given orally at trial, with each party hearing for the first time what their opponent's witnesses would say. There was, and remains, no general facility for the taking of witness evidence prior to trial in England and Wales. This posed, at least, two potential problems. First, it could generate surprise at trial for both parties. A party's witness may not give the evidence it had anticipated. Equally, for the opposing party, they would hear the nature of their opponent's witness evidence for the first time. In both cases, this could hamper the parties' ability to present and test evidence. It could also increase the cost and time of hearings, as parties would need more time to consider how to examine and cross-examine witnesses than they might otherwise have needed if they had had advance notice of the witness's evidence. Secondly, this approach failed to adequately promote settlement endeavours. Advance notice of lay witness evidence, as with advance provision of documentary evidence, can properly assist the parties to consider the merits of their dispute and help prompt settlement or, at the least, narrowing of the issues between them.

2.036 In 1978, a form of advance notice of witness evidence was introduced via the introduction of written witness statements. The original intention behind this development, which was incorrectly referred to in 1991 as adding witness evidence to the discovery (disclosure) process,[72] was to enable parties to litigation to provide each other with 'epitomes of evidence of fact,' i.e., short precis of the evidence a witness was to give at trial.[73] In 1986 this innovation was formalised.[74] Since that time witness statements supported by a statement of truth,[75] which are prepared by each party and then exchanged by parties shortly in advance of trial, stand as each witness's evidence at trial, i.e., oral witness evidence is generally limited now to cross-examination and re-examination.[76] Their introduction was intended to further the rationales that underpin evidence-gathering in general. As the Court of Appeal noted in *Mercer v Chief Constable of the Lancashire* in 1991, their introduction was intended to reduce the cost and time of litigation, and particularly trials, while promoting settlement.[77]

As with documentary evidence, two schemes now govern witness statements, a general one and one specifically applicable to the Business and Property Courts. Again, as with documentary disclosure, there is little principled justification for this dual-track approach.[78] The rationale for the introduction of the latter scheme was to promote a more cost-effective and efficient use of witness statements and, particularly to do so, by ensuing that they focus on witness evidence. A general problem with witness statements is that there is a tendency for them to be drafted by a party's lawyer and thus they are not set out in the words of the witness; that they contain opinion evidence where that can only properly be given by an expert witness; they go beyond the evidence that the witness can properly give; contain extracts from documents or, impermissibly, give evidence as to the law. The need to eliminate these problems and to have properly focused witness statements that are confined to the witness's actual evidence set out in their own words and not mediated through lawyerly revisions or redrafting is not just a matter that is important for the type of commercial claim that is heard in the Business and Property Courts, it is applicable to all types of proceeding. **2.037**

---

72 *Mercer v Chief Constable of Lancashire* [1991] 1 WLR 367.

73 *Philadelphia Manufacturers Mutual Insurance Co Ltd* (3 July 1978, unreported). See J. Sorabji, *A Model Civil Procedure Code for England and Wales*, (Oxford, 2024) at 335 for a discussion.

74 They are now provided for in CPR Pt 32.

75 The requirement to sign a statement of truth is intended, amongst other things, to reduce the prospect that dishonest claims or defences will be set out: *Clarke v Marlborough Fine Art (London) Ltd (Amendments)* [2002] 1 WLR 1731. Were a false statement of truth to be made the party or witness making it would expose themselves to proceedings for contempt of court, which could result in a fine and/or imprisonment. It would not lead to perjury proceedings as that only applies to false statements made under oath at trial: Perjury Act 1911, s.1. Contempt of court proceedings concerning false witness statements thus mirror the approach to perjury proceedings were oral evidence is concerned.

76 A witness may also add to their witness statement when giving evidence at trial where, for instance, new matters have arisen since they prepared their witness statement or there is a need to amplify matters set out in their statement: CPR r.32.5(3). It is often the case that parties and witnesses will prepare multiple versions of their witness statements prior to finalising them for service on the other party and filing with the court in advance of trial.

77 *Mercer v Chief Constable of Lancashire* [1991] 1 WLR 367 at 373.

78 J. Sorabji, ibid at 336. CPR Pt 32 and CPR PD 57AC.

2.038 Where a witness is unable to give evidence at trial, two mechanisms exist to facilitate it being given. First, a party may seek to depose the witness in advance of trial. In this way, a party takes the witness's evidence on oath and the written statement of evidence (the deposition) stands as their evidence at trial. This method can only be used where a witness is unable to attend trial because, for instance they would be too ill to attend trial, or they are outside the jurisdiction.[79] Secondly, where a witness is uncooperative with the party who would otherwise call them to give evidence at trial and the witness has refused to give evidence, a party may rely on a 'witness summary.'[80] This is, as the name suggests, a short summary of the evidence that the witness would have been expected to give at trial. As, however, it is both less developed than a witness statement and, again unlike a witness statement, neither accompanied by a statement of truth, which is the written version of the oath a witness gives at trial, nor renders the witness subject to cross-examination at trial due to their non-attendance, such summaries are of limited evidential value. This is particularly the case given the latter point, as the value of witness evidence comes with the fact that evidence given by witness statement can be tested at trial. Testing at trial is the means by which evidence is capable of playing a credible and reliable role in the discharge of the court's adjudicative function through more effectively promoting findings of right fact. That being said, where both depositions and witness summaries are concerned, their provision prior to trial can nevertheless play a role in promoting settlement through alerting the opposing parties to relevant potential evidence.

F. CONCLUSION

2.039 The general approach to evidence-gathering in England and Wales can properly be seen to place the primary responsibility for it in the hands of the parties: its scope and ambit is initially determined by them. However, that is not the end of the story. Evidence-gathering in all respects is subject to court supervision and approval: party autonomy is limited by the courts and particularly by the requirement that courts manage proceedings to ensure that they are conducted proportionately. This is the case whether documentary disclosure is in issue or whether witness evidence is in issue.

79 They do not therefore operate in the same manner as depositions in the United States of America. On the use of depositions in England and Wales, as a means to obtain evidence for trial of a witness who would otherwise be unable to give evidence at trial, see S. Cockerill, *The Law and Practice of Compelled Evidence in Civil Proceedings*, (Oxford, 2011).

80 CPR r. 32.9; *Otuo v Watch Tower Bible & Tract Society of Britain* [2019] EWHC 346 (QB).

Such court oversight is intended to particularly ensure that an effective balance is struck between the need to minimise the cost and time associated with the evidence-gathering process, and the presentation and testing of evidence at trial, with the need to secure the primary rationales that underpin that process: the aims of promoting adjudicative accuracy and settlement.

3

ACCESS TO EVIDENCE IN FRANCE

Emmanuel Jeuland

A. INTRODUCTION: THE FRENCH APPROACH TO EVIDENCE LAW

3.001 The French system of proof in civil procedure directly dates back to the Middle Ages. It has its own style, which favours written evidence. Additionally, the Court of Cassation's role and the French conception of evidence do not make way for deeper interest in evidence. The first thing to understand about the French system of proof is that it is not directly linked to the judge. Evidence rules are enshrined in the Civil Code, not in the Code of Civil Procedure. Evidence law ignores the judge. The second thing to understand is that the system of civil procedure disregards evidence.

3.002 The famous shift, which occurred during the Middle Ages in all Continental Europe, between so-called irrational proofs and rational proofs, took specific forms in France.[1]

1 E. Vergès, G. Vial, O. Leclerc, *Droit de la preuve*, 2° éd., PUF, 2022, "histoire du droit de la preuve", no. 55 s.; v. aussi R. Jacob, *La grâce des juges*, O. Jacob, 2014.

The system of proof which used to favour ordeal, oath and duel was transformed, in order to favour testimony and written documents (documentary evidence). Taking an oath is still possible in French civil proceedings and may be used in practice when the case is almost lost, as a last resort. Some expert reports may be seen as a kind of ordeal. For example, handwriting analysis is not considered as totally scientific but may be accepted. The etymology of the word "expertise" – "expert report" – is trial or ordeal. **3.003**

The shift between irrational proof and rational proof did not occur to unearth a higher number of true statements but because it fitted in the new kind of procedure. Ecclesiastical Courts involved ecclesiastical judges, who were not superior to religious parties. Judges were part of the hierarchical Church and there was a need to standardise the type of proof. It was held that judges should not have too much leeway. So, a scale of proof was invented, which included plain proof, semi proof and even quarter of proof. The level of proof spoke for itself. Judges were not entitled to personal appreciation. **3.004**

The French specificity lies on the importance placed on written documents in civil law. The reason why is still not completely clear in legal history. It might be the consequence of the split in France between written and oral law, between the South – where Roman law had always been applied – and the North – where oral customs were predominant. In order to centralise France, it was necessary, on the one hand, to prohibit duels and, on the other hand, to balance oral proof or testimony and written documents. Whatever the reason, a new legal profession developed around the 15th and 16th centuries in the South of France: notaries. Before the intervention of notaries, proof through witnesses prevailed over written proof. After the coming into existence of the new legal profession, it became clear that the action of the notary provided sufficient certainty; consequently, written documents were favoured and superseded oral proof. **3.005**

Today, a contract, the amount of which exceeds €1500, must still be evidenced in writing.[2] A party is not entitled to prove it through testimony or on the basis of a presumption. The probative force of this evidence is considered to be full if it is made through an authentic document or deed, signed in front of a notary. To demonstrate the contrary will be extremely difficult and lengthy. The cogency of the evidence is actually very high. A notary who would be charged with forged document may be sent to jail for ten years.[3] The system rests on the notary's reliance and organisation. Private deeds signed by parties may be admitted but might easily be challenged in court. In **3.006**

2 Article 1359 Civil Code and Decree no. 2016–1278 Article 1.
3 Article 441–4 Criminal code.

such a situation, French judges have no leeway at all. If a fact cannot be proven by a written statement, it simply does not exist.

3.007 Broadly speaking, in France, evidence law works without judges. The decision was made deliberately since judges were considered by the revolutionaries (who were often lawyers) to be simple mouths of the law. The importance of written documents has to be connected to the predominance of written statutes over customs. This method of evidence in civil procedure is a formalised legality, undertaken in order to avoid discretionary and arbitrary decisions.

3.008 Digital proof has been easily accepted as part of the system of legal proof. The principle of equivalence between written proof and digital proof has been set out in Article 1366 of the Civil Code.

3.009 Proof by confession is also considered in civil procedure as full. If a party asks his opponent to take an oath in relation to a fact, the proof is considered full as well. In all these situations, the judge has nothing to say.

3.010 If a party cannot provide written documents, a prima facie written document is admissible, for example a letter or nowadays an email. But such prima facie written document is not a perfect proof. It opens the door to other complementary proofs such as testimonies and presumptions, which means here indications.

3.011 Only in this situation will the judge have some leeway to appreciate the proof. So, the idea of standard of proof might here gain some acceptance but that will be a low one.[4]

3.012 For contracts below €1500 or when establishing facts, the system of free proof prevails (Article 1358 CC). Actually, litigations where facts have to be proven are frequent. It is the reason why the 2016 statute reversed the principle: free proof is now the principle, while legal proof has become the exception. It is nevertheless only a matter of presentation.

3.013 The centrality of written evidence in French law may be explained by the bureaucratic, Paris-centred and paper-centred French government. New technologies have not eliminated this aspect of French law, but have transformed it considerably. Today the electronic document has become a central piece of evidence in French law.

3.014 Rules on the manner in which evidence can be presented (expertise, inquiry, etc.) were spread across the Civil Code (means of evidence) and the Code of Civil Procedure (CCP) after the French Revolution in order to avoid making evidence a judicial matter.

---

4 E. Jeuland, "The Standard of Proof in France", in *The Standard of Proof in Europe*, L. Tichy (ed.), Mohr Siebeck, 2019.

The principal means of evidence do not need to be judged: for example, a written contract is evidence of an agreement between the parties.

When French judges have to assess evidence in civil procedure, they need to be convinced. It could be hence said that the standard of proof is conceived according to a subjective approach (the judge has to be fully convinced) rather than an objective one, as in Common law (where a standard of proof of 51% may be enough). However, judges must provide the grounds for their judgments and cannot avail themselves of dubious reasons.[5] They cannot say for example: "It seems that it happened in such a way". Judges cannot stand by the likeliness of the facts only.[6] Facts and documents have to be certain to apply judicial syllogism, which is still formally favoured in the French system. **3.015**

The Court of Cassation does not control the evidence assessment made by lower Courts. The Court insists on the lower Courts' sovereign power of assessment while prohibiting dubious reasons. There has almost never been a Court of Cassation landmark case on a question of evidence, except recently on the duty of loyalty when taking evidence, which may be seen as the starting point of an evolution. Although trial judges do face problems of evidence every day, the subject remains in the background. Evidence law does not really exist. Until a few years ago, no books at all were even dedicated to evidence law. It is obviously not an autonomous field taught at law schools, but mainly taught as part of civil procedure lectures. However, things are changing and there is now an emerging interest in evidence law. **3.016**

Traditionally, the civil judge from the Frankish period was neutral and passive (still according to the 1806 Code): he could not participate in the taking of evidence. Then in the 20th century certain reforms made in 1937 and 1965 authorised judges to be more "interventionist", but these reforms were limited. Case management ("la mise en état") did not work very well because the judges did not have enough power. The new CCP of 1976 broadened the powers of the judges in this respect. This reform was influenced by Alsatian procedural law, which was of German origin,[7] and by German procedure directly by Henri Motulsky.[8] **3.017**

5 F. Ferrand, *Rép. p. civ. Dalloz 2016, V° Preuve, no. 569.art.*

6 See e.g. Cass., Civ. 2e, 18 June 2002, no. 01-03.429; the Court of Cassation considers that dubious reasons (e.g. it seems that there was a contract) is the equivalent of an absence of reason.

7 It should be noted that the Alsace region was part of Germany from 1870 until World War I, and its civil procedure was of German origin. When the region became part of France after World War I, it maintained its civil procedural rules until the reform of 1976, which unified French civil procedure and was, in part, influenced by Alsatian case management.

8 This great scholar who influenced the new Code of Civil Procedure of 1976 was educated in Germany, where he practiced law.

3.018 Since this reform, the judge and the parties must cooperate to find a solution for their dispute. The scope of cooperation is different depending on whether facts or the law are concerned. The Latin adage *Da mihi factum, dabo tibi jus* ("Give me the facts, I will give you the law") is more or less applicable in France, but it is much more subtle than it seems.

3.019 Normally, a party must present the facts to the judge. If the opposing party contests certain facts, the party presenting the facts has to prove them. The burden of proof lies on the party who introduces the facts to justify a claim (Article 6 CCP and Article 1353 Civil Code). In the event of a counterclaim, the burden shifts to the defendant, who must establish his claim. Each party must try to prove his case; if he fails, the judge may order a particular type of proof (the hearing of witnesses, experts, etc.). However, Article 146 of the Code of Civil Procedure prohibits the court from making up for the failure of the party who has the burden of proof. Moreover, on the basis of Articles 11, paragraph 2 and 141 of the Code of Civil Procedure, any request to produce or obtain evidence may be opposed on the grounds of a "legitimate impediment". The judge may give these orders at the request of a party or *ex officio*. In the latter case, the proceedings are inquisitorial rather than adversarial. But the judge cannot base his decision on facts which are not on the record, whether these facts are presented by a party or the result of his orders for proof taking (Article 7 CCP). For example, the judge cannot use personal knowledge of the case.

3.020 The judge may use any fact that is on the record even though no party relied on the fact as a basis for an argument. For example, in one case, a French judge used a minor provision in an insurance contract that no party had relied on or seen, as the basis for his decision. Since the contract was part of the record, the judge was entitled to do so.[9] In this chapter, we will examine the French domestic rules on access to evidence, the rules of access to evidence coming from EU Law and the European and international rules of access to evidence for cross-border cases.

B. DOMESTIC RULES ON ACCESS TO EVIDENCE

3.021 In domestic French procedural law, rules on access to evidence relate to transmission of evidence, investigative measures and the new legal concept of right to evidence.

9 Cass. 2° civ., 22 October 2015, no. 14-13994.

1. Presentation of evidence

The claimant may prove his/her arguments using documents either in paper or electronically. The veracity of these documents is very difficult to fight. The proceedings to contest the truth of a document are quite long and difficult, so usually parties are discouraged to bring a special action to contest a document (forgery proceedings). It is possible but it is rarely used especially as far as a "public" document is concerned (e.g. a notarised deed). The party who refers to a document in her/his complaint has to provide the document to the other party for examination (the rule is intended to secure that the document is not "invented");[10] otherwise, a judge's injunction may impose this under threat of a monetary penalty which increases daily ("astreinte"). If the document is in the hands of someone other than the party who would like to use it in court, this party may ask the judge to order the holder of the document (who may be the other party) to transmit it under threat of a similar monetary penalty.[11] Proceedings to obtain a document are the functional equivalent of Common law discovery or disclosure; the difference is that the document has to be specified or at least identifiable (i.e. easy to find among other documents; for example, the sale contract between such and such of the year 2024: there is no date or number but the holder of the document may find it easily). The holder may refuse to present the document for legitimate reasons such as a professional privilege (if the holder is a lawyer who represents parties at court), but trade secrecy is not enough to justify a refusal.[12] 3.022

Where evidence can be obtained free of charge or the case relates to a contract valued at under €1500, or where evidence is being presented on factual matters (such as liability cases), the documents may be very diverse: even witness testimony can take the form of a written declaration. It is rare in civil proceedings that the witness appears in court. For example, in divorce proceedings, the parties will generally present the written testimony of parents and friends. 3.023

The electronic document is admitted under certain conditions and the judgment itself can be provided digitally. The judge assesses the evidence and must check that it is relevant and conclusive. 3.024

2. Court-ordered evidence

If the claimant tries to prove what s/he is arguing but does not succeed, s/he may ask the judge to order on evidence ("mesures d'instruction"). The measures available to 3.025

10 Article132 to 135 CCp.
11 Article 138 CCp.
12 Article 141 CCp.

the court are manifold: the judge may decide to inspect premises like a scene of an accident or any other real property or hear the parties and their testimony. In civil law, oral testimony is very rarely offered in court and there is no cross-examination: witness accounts are generally provided in written, signed documents. Lastly, the judge may order a technician to advise, provide a report, or offer an expert opinion. Normally, an expert opinion is subsidiary means of evidence because the claimant has to prove her/his claim through documentary evidence and if s/he is unsuccessful, the judge may order an expert opinion only if it is not possible to use another means of proof that is quicker and cheaper. Expert opinions are ordered in about 5% of the civil cases as a whole, which means that there is always an expert opinion ordered in tort cases (relating, for example, to medical, property, or environmental issues). The main difference between French law and Common law is that under French law, the judge may choose one expert who is paid by both parties (the losing party may have to pay the full cost at the end of the proceeding except if the court decides otherwise for equitable reasons).[13] The expert is not a witness in French law; s/he is an auxiliary person of the judge. Usually there are lists of experts from which a judge may choose. In the majority of French cases, experts are chosen from official lists of experts accredited by tribunals, appeal courts, and the Court of Cassation under the statute of 29 June 1971. How an expert comes to be registered on the list is not always clear and this is one of the principal disadvantages of expert lists. Nevertheless, the technical level of experts seems to be correct. Experts are trained in procedural law and must comply with the right for the parties to be heard. An "expertise" under French law is often considered a small trial within the trial. The "expertise" meetings (outside the court where the accident or other event took place) are very important and decisions may be made during these meetings. A study conducted in the commercial tribunal of Paris several years ago demonstrated that expert reports led to a settlement in many cases and where this was not the case, the report was followed by the judge in 9 out of 10 cases.[14] "Expertise" is therefore pivotal in French civil proceedings. Testimony, on the other hand, is not very important, and written documents remain very central.

3.026 It is important to note that a summary court-order ("référé probatoire") may be obtained regarding matters of evidence. This is similar to pre-trial discovery proceedings, which occur before a decision is taken on the merits. Under Article 145 CCP: "[i]If there is a legitimate reason to preserve or to establish, before any commencement of a legal process on the merits, the evidence of the facts upon which the resolution of the dispute depends, legally permissible preparatory inquiries may be ordered at the request of any interested party, by way of a petition or by way of a summary procedure".

---

13 Article 695 CCP.

14 Not published, study made by master students of the University Paris 1 Pantheon-Sorbonne.

The purpose is to enable a party to preserve or establish evidence that it can rely on in any future proceedings.[15] This technique is particularly useful when an item of evidence is threatened with loss or decay.[16] However, this is not its only justification; it can also be used to assess the conditions of existence or even the relevance of a potential action, but there is a great risk that this could lead to the judge hearing the application for interim measures being transformed into a legal consultancy (since this proceeding allows to know if a future case on the merits has a real chance to win). It is true that the dividing line is sometimes difficult to draw. The Court of Cassation must then keep Article 145 within its narrow limit. Article 145 of the Code of Civil Procedure is of great practical importance. It derogates from the rules applicable to ordinary measures of inquiry, in particular Articles 146, 150 and 152 CCP, just as it derogates from the rules applicable to ordinary summary proceedings and applications. An investigative measure *in futurum* may only be ordered if the conditions required by Article 145 relating to time (a), subject matter (b), and the measure ordered (c) are fulfilled. **3.027**

(a) Time of application

The claim must be lodged before any lawsuit on the merits has been initiated, which is understood to mean "before referral to the competent court" and which is assessed on the date on which a copy of the writ of summons is delivered to the registry. The court having jurisdiction on the merits may be a state court or an arbitral tribunal. It is sufficient that such a trial is possible. The plaintiff does not therefore have to establish the merits of the action for which the measure is sought.[17] **3.028**

(b) Conditions relating to the purpose of the application

This involves "preserving or establishing evidence of facts on which the outcome of a dispute may depend", which must be based on a legitimate reason that is sufficient to justify the request and which is assessed in the light of a reasonably foreseeable subsequent dispute. This is a question of fact that has given rise to a wide range of case law.[18] Article 145 does not require the person bearing the measure to be the potential **3.029**

15 The procedure provided for in this Article is not limited to the *preservation of* evidence; it may also aim to *establish* it.

16 The point is to enable a party to avoid the complaint of failure to provide evidence which might otherwise be made against him in the event of subsequent proceedings: see Article 146, see also Paris, 31 July 2019: *D.* 2019, 2394, note Strickler, based on a real risk of evidence being lost.

17 Cass. 2° civ. 4 November 2021, no. 21-14023, *Gaz. Pal.* 18 January 2022, p. 52 obs. Mayer; *RPR* 2021, no. 10, p. 8 obs. Laher, but the boundary is not always clear between checking the legitimate reason and not checking the possible merits: Cass. Com, 18 January 2023, no. 22-19539 and Cass. 2° civ., 19 January 2023, no. 21-21265, *JCP G* 2023, 239, note M. Cormier.

18 The right of access to health data constitutes a legitimate reason: Cass. 2° civ., 30 September 2021, no. 19-25045, *JCP G* 2021, 1229, note G. Deharo.

defendant in the future litigation on the merits of the potential dispute. A third party may be ordered to produce a document if there is no legitimate impediment to do so.

(c) Conditions relating to the measure ordered

3.030 It must be a legally admissible investigative measure,[19] which means that it must be necessary for the exercise of the applicant's right to evidence and proportionate to the conflicting interests at stake, while being confined to a certain perimeter.[20] Thus, the *right to privacy* cannot as such prevent the taking of evidence *in futurum* unless the necessity and proportionality of the measure are reviewed. Similarly, business secrecy is not "in itself"[21] an obstacle to an investigative measure *in futurum*, but the court must review the proportionality of the measure by balancing the applicants' right to establish the expected evidence against the preservation of the *business secrets* of the parties seeking its rejection.[22] In addition, when the court is seized of an application under Article 145 of the Code of Civil Procedure, it may order *ex officio* the temporary sequestration of the documents requested in order to protect business secrets.[23] If these conditions are met and the court to which the matter is referred has jurisdiction,[24] there is nothing to prevent the court from taking a decision, which will

---

19 Broadly interpreted to include an *inspection* (Cass. 1re civ., 3 November 2016), a *visit to the premises* (Cass. 3e civ., 24 April 2003: *Bull. civ.* 2003, III, no. 85), or the *production of documents* (Cass. 2e civ., 23 September 2004: *Bull. civ.* 2004, II, no. 428; *JCP* G 2005, I, 125, no. 9, obs. Serinet; even internationally: Cass. 1re civ. 27 January 2021, no. 19-16917, *JCP G* 2021, 591 no. 10 obs. Jeuland; *Gaz. Pal.* 27 January 2021, 66 obs. Egéa. – Versailles, 11 March 2008 (also allowing *named persons to be heard)*, including *documents held by third parties* (Cass. 2e civ. 26 May 2011, no. 10-20.048: *Procédures* 2011, no. 256, obs. Perrot; *D.* 2012, pan. 2896, obs. Bretzner without being able to constitute a *general* investigative measure: Cass. 2e civ. 7 January 1999: *Bull. civ.* 1999, II, no. 3; on the refusal to order *in futurum*, an internet service provider, to communicate information allowing the identification of alleged infringers when the IP addresses used to support the request had been collected and processed in violation of the rules of European Regulation No. 2016/679 of 27 April 2019 (known as "RGPD") and the Act of 6 January 1978: TGI Paris, ord., 2 August 2019, No. 19/53997: *Dalloz actualité*, 17 September 2019, obs. Maximin.

20 Cass. soc. 22 September 2021, no. 19-26144, *JCP G* 2021, 1054 obs. Dedessus-Le Moustier and 1341, no. 5 obs. Mayer; *JCP S* 2021, 1279, note Blanquart; *Gaz. Pal.* 18 January 2022, p. 50 obs. Mayer; *D.* 2022, p. 437 obs. Aynès and p. 438 obs. Bretzner; *RTDciv.* 2022, p. 857 obs. Barbier; there has been an evolution in the case law which, until 2020, did not precisely limit the scope of the documents at the risk of creating a "French-style *discovery*" without the safeguard of a solicitor-client privilege (since French lawyers do not benefit from solicitor-client privilege like American in-house counsel, see F. G'sell, "Qu'est-ce que le *legal privilege*?" *JCP G* 2021, 337).

21 Cass. 2e civ. 7 January 1999: *Bull. civ.* 1999, II, no. 4; *Procédures* 1999, no. 60, obs. Perrot.

22 V. Cass. 1re civ. 22 June 2017, no. 15-27.845: *Dalloz actualité*, 7 July 2017, obs. Kebir and *D.* 2017, 2444, obs. Auguet; *RTD civ.* 2017, 661, obs. Barbier.

23 C. com., Article R. 153-1, red. dec. no. 2018-1126, 11 December 2018. Business secrecy may be protected at the stage of communication or production of documents in the form of an interim injunction to prevent infringement of business secrecy: Article L. 153-1, compl. of the Commercial Code, Article R. 152-2 et seq. V. M.-P. Mourre-Schreiber, *Levée du secret des affaires et rétractation de l'ordonnance encadrant insuffisamment une mesure d'instruction in futurum: RPR* 2020/4, p. 23, à propos de Lyon, 10 mars 2020, no. 19/04792; le référé à fin de mainlevée du séquestre des documents recueillis interrompte la prescription: Cass. 2° civ., 14 janv. 2021, no. 19-20316, *JCP G* 2021, 289, note J-J. Taisne.

24 The petitioner has the option of choosing between the president of the court in whose jurisdiction the measure is to be carried out and the president of the court likely to have jurisdiction on the merits: A clause conferring territorial jurisdiction is unenforceable against a party who applies to the motions judge for an investigative measure to be carried

take the form of an interim order or an *ex parte* order, depending on whether "the law permits or necessity dictates that (the) measure be ordered without knowledge".[25] By ordering the interim relief, the judge has exhausted his powers. Her/His decision may be appealed.[26] It should be noted that Article 2239 of the Civil Code, enacted by the Act of 17 June 2008, specifies that the limitation period for the action on the merits is suspended if the court grants the request for an investigative measure *in futurum*.

3. Right to evidence and loyalty principle[27]

The right to be heard in evidence matters is encompassed in the principle of equality of arms as established in the ECtHR case *Montavanelli v France*.[28] The principle is rarely referred to alone, but rather in conjunction with the right to be heard in French case law. But there are other human rights applicable to evidence matters. **3.031**

The idea of "fundamentalisation" of evidence law refers to the development of human rights and human rights reasoning in the field of evidence; it is not a mere deduction, but rather a balance of interests according to the principle of proportionality. More precisely, there is a right to evidence. This right is not totally clear. It concerns not only the party's right to have evidence taking ordered on request, but also to something more complex: the right to use a piece of evidence which may not have been obtained in good faith or the idea of obtaining, from the legislature and the judge, a court-order on evidence. The nature of the right to evidence is not clearly presented as a human right, but the human rights reasoning is applied although there is no treaty provision on this particular question and it is not so clear in the ECtHR case law. **3.032**

The right to evidence appears for the first time in a 2012 case law of the Court of Cassation. The right to evidence mirrors the loyalty principle in the taking of evidence. **3.033**

The parties must exercise good faith when obtaining evidence. The principle of loyalty prohibits e.g. the use of tricks and telephone recordings without the speaker's **3.034**

---

out *in futurum*: Cass. com., 13 September 2017, no. 16-12.196: *Procédures* 2017, 258, obs. Strickler; *Dalloz actualité*, 20 September 2017, obs. Dargent; *D.* 2018, 700, obs. Fricero; *Gaz. Pal.* 31 October 2017, 58, obs. Hoffschir; *D.* 2019, 164, obs. Bretzner.

25 Article 17 Urgent measures under Article 145 may only be ordered by petition when the circumstances require that they are not taken in adversarial proceedings: Cass. 2e civ. 26 June 2014, no. 13-18.895: *Gaz. Pal.* 7–9 September 2014, 32, note Raschel.

26 Article 490 CCP.

27 E. Jeuland, "The 'Right to Proof' and the 'Loyalty Principle': A French Perspective", in *Evidence in Contemporary Civil Procedure*, C.H. van Rhee and Alan Uzelac (ed.), Intersentia, 2015, pp. 79 ff and "Le changement de rôle des témoins et des conseils dans quelques pays de droit civil et en particulier en France," in *Common Law Civil Law and the Future of Categories*, J. Walker and O.G. Chase (ed.), LexisNexis, 2009, pp. 193–204.

28 *Montavanelli v France* (18 March 1997), ECtHR, no. 21497/93.

knowledge,[29] surveillance by video or other means[30] (e.g. of a spouse in order to obtain a divorce or of an employee in order to obtain dismissal for cause).[31] The principle of loyalty is specific to evidence and does not apply to procedure in general, except in arbitration. The general principle of loyalty may be too broad and difficult to distinguish from the legality principle or the good faith principle. The principle of loyalty may even be misplaced as far as evidence is concerned, since nowadays everybody knows that a telephone call may be recorded.

3.035 The principle of loyalty in evidence taking has exceptions. For example, an employee may produce a piece of evidence obtained without authorisation on his company's computers. Today, there is a so-called right to evidence.[32] In the case decided on 5 April 2012 by the Court of Cassation, the French Court of Appeal had rejected a private letter as inadmissible since it was obtained in violation of the privacy principle, against the will of its author. The Court of Cassation reversed the decision of the Court of Appeal to set aside the letter "without checking whether the letter was necessary for the exercise of the right to evidence and proportionate to the … conflicting interests". In other words, the Court of Cassation reversed the judgment because the Court of Appeal should have checked whether this piece of evidence was necessary for the claimant to exercise his right to evidence and was proportionate to the rights of the different parties. In this case, the right to evidence is not a right to obtain a court order; it is the right to use a piece of evidence, such as a document.

3.036 Moreover, the principle of loyalty does not prohibit evidence by email, Short Message Service (SMS)[33] or USB key (it is a matter of free evaluation of proof). In one case, a USB stick was presented in evidence by an employer. There was no privacy issue, so the USB key could be used as a trial document. The same rule was found to apply to an SMS when the person who wrote the SMS knew that it could be read and preserved for litigation. An employer can even use a personal file found on an employee's work computer against the employee since the computer is used in a professional context.

29 Cass. 2nd civ., 7 October 2004: *JCP* 2005, II, 10025 Léger; *D.* 2005, 122, Bonfils referring to Article 6 ECHR – Cass. com., 3 June 2008: *Bull. civ.* 2008, IV, no. 112; *D.* 2008, 2476, Boursier-Mauderly; Cass. ass. plén., 7 janv. 2011, no. 09-14.316 et no. 09-14.667: *JCP* 2011, 43, Malaurie-Vignal.

30 Cass. soc., 26 November 2002: *JCP* 2003, I, 156, no. 5, Cesaro; *D.* 2003, 1858, note Bruguière; then Cass. 1st civ., 31 October 2012, no. 11-17.476: *JCP* 2012, 1229, Abravanel-Jolly; *D.* 2013, 227, Dupont; *RTD civ.* 2012, 117, no. 9, Fages.

31 Cass. soc., 18 March 2008: *D.* 2008, 993; *Rev. huissiers* 2008, 218, Fricero; *Procédures* 2008, no. 137, then: Cass. soc. 4 July 2012, no. 11-30.266: *Procédures* 2012, no. 286, Bugada.

32 Cass. 1st civ., 5 April 2012, no. 11-14177: *D.* 2012, 1596, Lardeux; *D.* 2013, pan. 274. Fricéro; *RTD civ.* 2012, 506, Hauser, free translation of "*sans rechercher si la production litigieuse n'était pas indispensable à l'exercice de son droit à la preuve, et proportionnée aux intérêts antinomiques en présence*".

33 See about emails Cass. 1st civ., 18 May 2005: *Gaz. Pal.* 16–18 October 2005, 19, Massip and Cass. 1re civ., 17 June 2009, no. 07-21.796: *D.* 2009, 1758, obs. Egea in divorce matters if there is no fraud or violence, then Cass. soc., 12 February 2013, no. 11-28.649, *Procédures* 2013, no. 152 obs. Bugada (USB key).

Conversely, an employee can use secret files of his employer in a trial against the employer if this means of evidence is necessary to prove the claim.[34] In October 2012, evidence obtained by a detective hired to follow someone was found admissible and not contrary to the principles of loyalty or privacy, since the detective took pictures in a public area.[35]

In a case from 2007, an SMS was used by an employee to prove harassment by an employer.[36] Harassment and discrimination claims raise important issues in relation to the right to evidence in a wider sense. The European Directive of 27 November 2000 establishing a general framework for equal treatment in employment and occupation has been implemented in France. Under this Directive evidence is used to protect a fundamental right. The employee's burden of proof is alleviated because of the asymmetry of access to information as compared to the employer (Article 10 of the Directive). The employer may only establish that his decision was objective (i.e. without discrimination). To respect the right to evidence, the Directive considers that the employee only has to present facts which establish a presumption of discrimination or harassment. In 2002, the French Constitutional Council reviewed the implementation of the Directive in France. The implementing statute stated that the victim had to present the facts establishing discrimination and that it was up to the defendant to prove there was no discrimination. The Constitutional Council considered that in order to avoid creating an imbalance in the relationship between employers and employees, the victims had to establish the facts raising a presumption of discrimination or harassment. The statute had to be modified: instead of "facts which supposedly establish discrimination", the statute now provides that the employee has to present facts which establish a presumption of discrimination (Article L1132-3-3 Labor Code). This solution complies with the right to defence. **3.037**

Moreover, the Court of Cassation (Soc. 24 September 2008)[37] decided that it would review the qualification of harassment and discrimination to verify how judges decided on the merits after hearing evidence of an employer's behaviour. Whether it was a matter of qualification or a matter of evidence was unclear. In 2011, the Court of Cassation specified that judges should decide on the merits of a case after an appreciation of all of the elements taken together rather than after an assessment of separate elements. Then in 2013 (Soc. 29 January 2013) the Court of Cassation specified that a medical certificate was not enough to establish a presumption of discrimination or **3.038**

34 If strictly necessary to the employee: Cass. soc., 30 juin 2004: *Bull. civ.* 2004, V, no. 187; *JCP* 2005, I, 122, no. 16, Pétele-Teyssié.

35 Cass. 1st civ., 31 October 2012, no. 11-17476, JCP 2012, 1229 Abravanel-Jolly; D. 2013, 227 Dupont.

36 Cass. Soc., 23 May 2007, Bull. 2007, no. 85.

37 No. 06-45.747.

harassment.[38] The right to evidence allows the admission of a large set of information even obtained without loyalty but, in a way, the right to evidence is also recognised in favour of the employee who cannot establish the discrimination or harassment. The employee may request an order from the judge in order to alleviate his burden of proof.

3.039 The principle of loyalty is different from the legality principle of evidence (a principle according to which only legally obtained evidence is admissible), but is more or less a moral principle. It may be without limitations and may, therefore, be dangerous. It is limited by the right to evidence and even regarding specific means of evidence, such as expert evidence.

3.040 In civil proceedings, the defendant must establish the facts s/he alleges in support of his/her defence. The judge may supplement the evidence provided by the parties. This solution is sometimes presented as an aspect of the right to evidence[39] which was enshrined by the ECtHR[40] before being enshrined by the Court of Cassation:[41] each party has a right to have the production of evidence ordered by the judge, when he is not in a position to do so himself. This is not a human right, as it is not found in any international text. The concept of the "right to evidence" stems from a judgment of the European Court of Human Rights[42] which the Court of Cassation has applied. In fact, this Strasbourg Court ruling is the only one to invoke the right to evidence, without linking it to Article 6 of the European Convention on Human Rights on the right to a fair trial. The decision refers to the Dombo Beheer ruling,[43] which concerns equality of arms but does not establish a fundamental right to evidence. Between these two rulings, we moved from equality of arms to the right to evidence. However, the concept of "right to evidence" was not used again in subsequent rulings by the Strasbourg Court. It is only mentioned in the pleadings submitted in the litigations. If we refer to the English-language versions of the judgments, the "right to evidence" does not appear either. The Court of Cassation uses the concept of "droit à la preuve" but its citations refer mainly to the Articles on the protection of privacy. The leading case is that of the First Civil Chamber of the Court of Cassation on the confidentiality of correspondence.[44] In this case, in the context of a controversy related to an inheritance, a letter was presented to the Court without the consent of the writer of the

38 No. 11-22174.

39 A. Burgeaud, *Le droit à la preuve*, LGDJ, Paris, 2010.

40 *LL v France* (10 October 2006), ECtHR, no. 7508/02, *RTD civ.* 2007, 95, obs. Hauser.

41 Cass. 1e civ. 5 April 2012, no. 1-14177: *D.* 2012, 1596, Lardeux; *D.* 2013, pan. 274. Fricero; *RTD civ.* 2012, 506, Hauser, "without investigating whether the disputed production was not indispensable to the exercise of its right to evidence, and proportionate to the conflicting interests at stake". Cass. 1re civ. 4 June 2014, *JCP* G 2014, no. 986, note E. Raschel (the notary's professional secrecy takes precedence over the right to evidence).

42 ECHR, 10 October 2006, no. 7508/02, L.L. v/France

43 ECHR, 27 October 1993, no. 14448/88, Dombo Beheer v Netherlands.

44 Cass. civ. 1ere, 5 April 2012, no. 11-14.177.

missive. According to the First Civil Chamber, it was necessary to determine whether "the production of the letter was indispensable to the exercise of his right to evidence and proportionate to the conflicting interests at stake". The right to evidence can only justify the production of material that infringes privacy if such production was necessary for the exercise of a right and proportionate to the aim pursued.[45] The right to evidence may be limited by a notary's professional secrecy[46] but not by a banking secrecy.[47] Other chambers of the Court of Cassation have since adopted this reasoning. In the Facebook case,[48] a photograph displayed on the private account of a Petit Bateau employee was reported to the employer by one of the dismissed employee's colleagues (the picture was proof that the dismissed employee revealed to competitors the date and content of the future collection of children's clothes Petit Bateau). The two employees were "friends" on Facebook. The ruling held that the invasion of privacy is not disproportionate in this specific case. The ruling contrasts a freedom, the right to privacy, with the right to evidence, a more technical principle. The Court of Cassation intends to apply a review of proportionality *in abstracto*. The Second Civil Chamber has drawn up a report on the principle of proportionality. It recommends a review *in abstracto* in order to avoid violating the principle of equality. In case of an *in concreto* review, it considers that there would be subtle nuances of fact and outcomes that would be too different. The Labour Court involved in the Facebook case takes a position on the borderline between *in concreto* and *in abstracto* review. In the Facebook case, several *in concreto* elements were taken into account.[49] Nevertheless, certain factual elements were not addressed. For example, did the employer suffer as a result of the fact that the dismissed employee unveiled the Petit Bateau collection? Did competitors react to the publication of the photograph on the employee's Facebook account? The Labour Division of the Court of Cassation uses only two criteria: the indispensable nature of the exercise of the right to evidence and a balance of interests that remains somewhat abstract and does not go to the end of the reasoning. In the case law of the ECJ on the principle of proportionality, there are more criteria: the first two are common to the social chamber of the Court of Cassation (indispensability and balance of interests), and the ECJ adds "the appropriateness of the means in the light of the aim pursued".[50] Courts of appeal must also carry out more thorough proportionality checks. Logic would dictate that this control should fall to them (since this control is conducted in fact and not in law and since the Court of Cassation controls only in law).

45 Cass. 1re civ. 25 February 2016, *D.* 2016, 884, note J.-C. Saint-Pau.
46 Cass. 1re civ. 4 June 2014, no. 12-21244, *RTD civ.* 2014, 658, obs. Barbier.
47 CJEU, 16 July 2015, aff. C-580/13, *Coty Germany GmbH*, *D.* 2015, 2168, note C. Kleiner and *D.* 2016, 96, note G. Lardeux.
48 Cass. soc., 30 September 2020, no. 19-12.058
49 Cass. Soc. 30 September 2020, *D.* 2020, 2383, note C. Golhen.
50 CJEU, "Johnston v Chief Constable of the Royal Ulster Constabulary", 1986, Case 222/84, §38.

3.041 One might wonder whether the right to evidence does not require the judge to take investigative measures. This development in case law also raises more theoretical questions. O. Leclerc dates the right to evidence back to the 18th century.[51] Behind the right to evidence lies a search for rationally established truth. The difficulty in establishing harassment is that we are looking for truths that are more internal and more elusive. The Labour Court could have considered the nature of the employee's relationship with her Facebook "friends" (competitors or clients?). Were they technical or commercial relationships? Professional? Commercial? In the AFP ruling, the Court of Cassation[52] accepted that an employer could use an employee's IP address to prove that he had committed a fault in breach of CNIL rules.[53] In the Renault Trucks ruling of 16 December 2020,[54] it was accepted that Article 145 CPC could be used by an employee to request the production of documents from his employer relating to discrimination. The right to evidence thus becomes a condition for obtaining an investigative measure *in futurum*.[55] The rise of the concept of the right to evidence can also be seen as a rebalancing of the procedure in favour of the parties and a new recognition of the traditional principle that the trial is controlled by the parties.[56]

3.042 Recently, the Court of Cassation decided to reverse its caselaw in favour of the right to evidence:[57] an employer complained that the judgment declared inadmissible the evidence he had obtained by means of clandestine recordings and consequently set aside its exhibits without real and serious cause. Furthermore, the Court had ordered that the employer must pay the employee various sums by way of damages for dismissal without real and serious cause, compensation, and related paid leave. The Court decided:

> Having regard to Article 6(1) of the European Convention for the Protection of Human Rights and Fundamental Freedoms and Article 9 of the Code of Civil Procedure: 5. Following the principles laid down by the European Court of Human Rights (see in particular ECHR, judgment of 10 October 2006, L.L. v. France, no. 7508/02), the Cour de Cassation has established, in civil matters, a right to evidence which makes it possible to declare admissible unlawful evidence where that evidence is essential to the success of the claim of the person relying on it and where the infringement of the conflicting rights in question is strictly proportionate to the aim pursued (Com., 15 May 2007, Appeal no. 06-10.606, Bull. IV 2007, no. 130; 1st Civil Division, 5 April 2012, Appeal no. 11-14.177, Bull. I 2012, no. 85; Soc. 9 November 2016, appeal no. 15-10.203, Bull. V 2016, no. 209; Soc., 30 September 2020, no. 19-12.058, published; Soc., 25 November 2020, no. 17-19.523,

---

51 O. Leclerc, "Le droit à la preuve à l'assaut de la vie privée du salariée", Dr. Ouvr. déc. 2020, p. 1.

52 Cass. Soc., 25 November 2020, no. 17-19.523, Published; see also Cass. soc. 10 November 2021, no. 20-12263, *D.* 2021, 117, note G. Loiseau.

53 *JCP G* 2021, 159, note Bossu.

54 Cass. soc., 16 December 2020, no. 19-17.637.

55 See also Cass. 2° civ. 25 March 2021, no. 20-14309 and no. 19-20156, *JCP G* 2021, 708, note X. Vuitton.

56 I owe this idea to X. Lagarde.

57 Cass. Ass. Plen., 22 December 2023, no. 20-20.648 and no. 21-11.330 B+R.

> published; Soc. 8 March 2023, no. 21-17.802, 21-20.798 and 20-21.848, published). 6. On the basis of the aforementioned texts and the principle of loyalty in the administration of evidence, the Cour de cassation nevertheless holds that the production of evidence gathered without the person's knowledge or obtained through a manoeuvre or stratagem is inadmissible (Ass. plén. 7 January 2011, no. 09-14.316 and 09-14.667, Bull. 2011, Ass. plén. no. 1; 2nd Civ, 9 January 2014, no. 12-23.387 and 12-17.875, Com. 10 November 2021, no. 20-14.669 and 20-14.670, Soc. 18 March 2008, no. 06-40.852, Bull. 2008, V, no. 65; Soc. 4 July 2012, no. 11-30.266, Bull. 2012, V, no. 208). 7. This solution is based on the consideration that justice must be done fairly on the basis of evidence gathered and produced in a manner that does not undermine its dignity and credibility. 8. The application of this case law may, however, result in a party being deprived of any means of proving her/his rights. 9. The European Court of Human Rights does not as a matter of principle hold that evidence considered to be unfair is inadmissible. It considers that, where the right to evidence as guaranteed by Article 6(1) of the European Convention for the Protection of Human Rights and Fundamental Freedoms conflicts with other rights and freedoms, in particular the right to respect for private life, it is for the court to weigh up the various rights and interests involved. It adds that "equality of arms implies the obligation to afford each party in disputes between private interests a reasonable opportunity of presenting his case under conditions which do not place him at a distinct disadvantage compared with his opponent". It emphasises that this provision imposes on the court the obligation to carry out an effective examination of the parties' pleas, arguments and offers of proof, unless it wishes to assess their relevance to the decision to be handed down (N.N. and T.A. v. Belgium, 13 May 2008, ECtHR, req. no. 65087/01).

As a result, the Court of Cassation decided: **3.043**

> 12. It should therefore now be considered that, in civil proceedings, unlawfulness or unloyalty in obtaining or producing evidence does not necessarily mean that it should be excluded from the proceedings. The court must, when asked to do so, assess whether such evidence prejudices the loyalty of the proceedings as a whole, by balancing the right to evidence against the conflicting rights in issue, the right to evidence being able to justify the production of material prejudicial to other rights provided that such production is essential to the exercise of that right and that the prejudice is strictly proportionate to the aim pursued.

This decision has been widely discussed and criticised,[58] in particular because it favours the employer and risks creating permanent suspicion regarding the recording of an interview. **3.044**

C. FRENCH DISCOVERY EMERGING FROM EUROPEAN LAW

Types of discovery procedures exist in France in certain specific areas where European law has been influential: intellectual property and private enforcement of competition law. **3.045**

---

58 Cass., ass. plén., 22 déc. 2023, no. 20-20.648 et no. 21-11.330. Dalloz actualité, 9 janv. 2024, obs. N. Hoffschir; *D.* 2024. 291, note G. Lardeux; ibid. 275, obs. R. Boffa et M. Mekki; ibid. 296, note T. Pasquier; ibid. 570, obs. J.-D. Bretzner et A. Aynès; ibid. 613, obs. N. Fricero; JA 2024, no. 697, p. 39, étude F. Mananga; AJ fam. 2024. 8, obs. F. Eudier; AJ pénal 2024. 40, chron.; AJCT 2024. 315, obs. A. Balossi; Dr. soc. 2024. 293, obs. C. Radé; Légipresse 2024. 11 et les obs.; ibid. 62, obs. G. Loiseau; RCJPP 2024. 20, obs. M.-P. Mourre-Schreiber; RTD civ. 2024. 186, obs. J. Klein; JCP 2024. 119, rapp. D. Ponsot et H. Fulchiron; ibid. 120, note G. Vial; JCP E 2024. 1042, note C. Golhen; JCP S 2024. 1028, note S. Brissy; Procédures 2024. 37, note A. Bugada.

1. Discovery in intellectual property litigation

3.046 Article 8 of the Directive 2004/48/EC of the European Parliament and of the Council of 29 April 2004 on the enforcement of intellectual property rights provides a right of information. This Directive has been implemented in French law by the statute no. 2007-1544 of 29 October 2007 to combat counterfeiting.[59] The right to information, incorporated by the 2007 reform, is autonomous from the seizure-infringement, and may be invoked in addition to the latter or independently (Article L. 615-5-2 Intellectual Property Code (IPC)). If so requested, the court hearing a civil action for infringement

> may order, if necessary under penalty, in order to determine the origin and distribution networks of the allegedly infringing products or processes that infringe the plaintiff's rights, the production of any documents or information held by the defendant or by any person who has been found in possession of allegedly infringement or implementing allegedly infringing processes or who provides services used in allegedly infringing activities or has been reported as being involved in the production, manufacture or distribution of such products, the implementation of such processes or the provision of such services.

3.047 This right to information enables the owner of the infringed patent to obtain information on the conditions under which the infringer distributes its goods, and to know the consistency and extent of the infringement in order to better assess the extent of the infringement and bring an action. This measure allows the information obtained in the context of seizure-counterfeiting to be supplemented. This proceeding is reminiscent of the pretrial discovery procedure used in the United States.

3.048 In order to protect business secrecy, the production of documents or information may only be ordered if there is no legitimate impediment. It is up to the judge to assess these impediments. The documents or information that may be disclosed are listed exhaustively by the legislator.[60] Firstly, it includes the names and addresses of producers, manufacturers, distributors, suppliers, and other previous holders of the goods or services, as well as wholesalers and retailers. It also includes the quantities produced, marketed, delivered, received or ordered, as well as the price obtained for the goods or services in question. This first set of information relates to the production-distribution network of the counterfeit. The second set of information concerns the determination of the extent of the infringement to enable the victim to assess his or her claim for compensation. Article 8(3)(e) of Directive 2004/48/EC precludes a national provision which authorises, in an unlimited and unconditional manner, a banking institution to rely on banking secrecy in order to refuse to provide information relating to the name

---

59 See Répertoire de droit commercial / Brevet d'invention Com. – Nicolas BINCTIN – Mise à jour de juillet 2024, no. 301 ss.

60 Article L. 615-5-2 Intellectual Property Code.

and address of the holder of an account. The case managing judge can give access to this information.[61] The court hearing the merits of an action for infringement may order the defendant to produce information and items, of a commercial or accounting nature, likely to enable the patent owner, who has otherwise provided proof of the alleged infringement, to determine the origin and extent of the infringement and to perfect its claims.[62]

2. Discovery in private enforcement of competition law

The Directive 2014/104/EU of the European Parliament and of the Council of 26 November 2014 on certain rules governing actions for damages under national law for infringements of the competition law provisions of the Member States and the European Union provides a kind of discovery proceedings (Articles 5 and 6).[63] **3.049**

These rules require national courts to balance conflicting interests in the form of a triple test of relevance, necessity, and proportionality in order to give an injunction to the party or third party who detains a document to produce it. The requirement that the evidence be "relevant" derives from Article 5(1) and is understood to mean the relevance of the factual elements sought in the documents collected. The test of necessity derives from Article 5(2) and requires the requesting party to limit as narrowly as possible the "evidence" or "relevant categories of evidence ... on the basis of factual data reasonably available in the reasoned justification". This requirement may find its *ratio legis* in the desire not to encourage fishing expeditions and not to make up for the failure of the parties. Article 5(3) states that the test or proportionality constitutes the basis on which the court may balance the right to evidence of the party seeking access to certain documents against any interests that may be opposed to it. The same provision goes on to list some of these interests: the cost of the investigative measure for the party or third party being investigated, the protection of legitimate interests that they may oppose (business secrecy), and the preservation of the effectiveness of *public enforcement*. **3.050**

These rules have been quite literally transposed.[64] The Court of Cassation has censured the lower Courts for lack of a legal basis under Article L. 483-1 of the French **3.051**

61 Cass. Com. 13 déc. 2011, no. 10-28.088, D. 2012. 90; CCE 2012. Comm. 14, obs. C. Caron.

62 Com. 8 October 2013, no. 12-23.349, Bull. civ. IV, no. 149; JCP E 2013. Actu. 782.

63 Fasc. 317: PRIVATE ACTION IN RESPECT OF ANTI-COMPETITION INFRINGEMENT – Evidence: judicial administration of evidence and admissible methods of proof, Rafael AMARO15/05/2024JurisClasseur Concurrence – Consommation, Fasc. 317.

64 Statute-order no. 2017-303 of 9 March 2017 relating to actions for damages as a result of anti-competitive practices and Decree no. 2017-305 of 9 March 2017 and Circ. 23 March 2017 transposing the Directive 2014/104/EU 26 November 2014 AJDA 2017, 548, M.-C. De Montecler; RLC/60 2017, no. 3165, M. Cousin and M. Dumarcay, "La

Commercial Code when they fail to carry out the balancing required by the law.[65] The requirement of necessity is also set out in Article L. 483-4 of the French Commercial Code for documents in the files of competition authorities: "The judge may not order the Autorité de la Concurrence, the Minister for Economic Affairs, any competition authority of another Member State or the European Commission to produce a document in its file when one of the parties or a third party is reasonably able to provide the document". The Paris Court of Appeal has already had occasion to carry out an Article 5(1) test in one of the truck cartel cases.[66] It was asked to order the production of the following five categories of documents: extracts from the confidential version of the cartel decision containing the full text of certain footnotes which, it is understood from the grounds of the judgment, transcribe information "in support of the finding of an infringement of the competition rules"; extracts from the index to the Commission's decision listing all the file numbers; all references to certain footnotes with the exception of leniency statements; the average selling prices achieved on sales of Daimler heavy goods vehicles in France and in the European Union between 1995 and 2010 for each of the seven models purchased by the plaintiffs; the margins achieved by Daimler on these same models. At the end of its review, the Court agreed to order the production of only one category of documents, that relating to sales prices (the fourth), on the grounds that it was useful in assessing the loss. It refuses to order the production of the other categories of documents for three reasons. The first reason is: the documents are of no use to the claimant in assessing his loss; the second reason is: producing the document is a disproportionate measure; and the third reason is: the document is blacklisted under Article L. 483-5 of the French Commercial Code, which transposes Article 6(6)(a) of the Damages Directive and prohibits the disclosure of statements made by beneficiaries of a leniency programme.

3.052 Business secrets are covered by the new provisions of Title V of Book I of the French Commercial Code, which transpose the Directive 2016/943/EU.[67]

3.053 The European Court of Justice clarified that the concept of "relevant" evidence within the meaning of Article 5(1) could cover so-called ex novo evidence, i.e. evidence that involves aggregating, classifying and formatting in order to create a document that does not exist as it stands in the documentation of the litigant or third party.[68]

---

transposition de la directive 'dommages' en droit français: vers une nouvelle architecture des contentieux du droit des pratiques anticoncurrentielles?", RLC/62, 3204 (2017).

65 see Cass. com, 8 July 2020, no. 19-25.065.

66 CA Paris, division 1, ch. 8, 25 October 2019, no. 19/05356, Sté Renault Trucks: *Concurrences* no. 1-2020, note by R. Amaro, p. 226.

67 Article L153-1, L153-2, R153-1 to R 153-9.

68 ECJ, 10 November 2022, Case C-163/21, Paccar and DAF, pt 69.

The Court adds, however, that the national court must ensure that the investigative measure relating to such evidence is proportionate (paragraph 64).

3. Directive on representative actions in the collective interest of consumers

3.054 The Directive (EU) 2020/1828 of the European Parliament and of the Council of 25 November 2020 on representative actions for the protection of the collective interests of consumers and repealing Directive 2009/22/EC has been recently transposed in French law[69] not only for consumers but for all potential victims. Article 18 of the Directive contains a right to access to evidence, but only insofar as "in accordance with national procedural law". Article 10(3) requires disclosure of third-party funding of representative action. The French statute does not provide a specific right to evidence but only a disclosure of third-party funding (Article 16.D.):

> The persons mentioned in 1, 2 and 3 of C of the present I may receive funding from third parties, provided that such funding has neither the purpose nor the effect of influencing the introduction or conduct of group actions likely to harm the interests of the persons represented. Such third-party funding is published under conditions determined by decree.

D. EUROPEAN AND INTERNATIONAL RULES ON ACCESS TO EVIDENCE IN CROSS-BORDER CASES

3.055 As far as the type of evidence (written or oral) is concerned, the relevant law is the law applicable to the merits of the case; it is not the *lex fori*. Conversely the *lex fori* applies to evidence proceedings. Under Article 145 CCP and to know whether or not the claimant has a legitimate cause, French law has to be applied. For example, in a contract case between a German company and a French company, German law was applicable to the contract according to a choice-of-law clause therein. The German company terminated the contract rather brutally and the French enterprise needed to obtain a statement regarding this breach. The French company asked a French judge to rule on the matter on the basis of Article 145 CCP; however, the French judge said that the French enterprise had no legitimate cause since such a contract could be terminated subject to German law. But the Court of Cassation considers that French law may be applied to determine whether there was a legitimate reason to get an order under Article 145. Therefore, a summary judgment was granted in this case.[70] I will distinguish the access to evidence in international litigation in front of an ordinary court (1.) and the international litigation in front of an International Chamber (2.).

69 LOI no. 2025-391 du 30 avril 2025 portant diverses dispositions d'adaptation au droit de l'Union européenne en matière économique, financière, environnementale, énergétique, de transport, de santé et de circulation des personnes, Dalloz actualité 14 May 2025 K. Castanier.

70 Cass. 1st civ., 4 July 2007, *Bull. Civ.* I, no. 255; *Procédures* 2007, no. 215, Perrot; *Rev. crit. DIP* 2007, 840, Muir Watt.

1. Access to evidence in international disputes before an ordinary court

3.056 As far as international litigation is concerned there are three sets of rules for the taking of evidence: the EU regulation, the Hague Convention of 1970, and the traditional rules on international letters rogatory when neither the EU regulation nor the Hague Convention apply. The traditional rule is as follows: the competent judge in a case sends a letters rogatory to the Ministry of Justice, which sends the request to the Ministry of Foreign Affairs, which, in turn, requests the respective counterpart in the foreign country to perform the rogatory commission. Then, the request follows its course abroad. These diplomatic proceedings may be long and the request may be refused where national economic interests are threatened.

3.057 Under the Hague Convention of 1970, the diplomatic channel may disappear. A request can be sent directly by the French Ministry of Justice to the foreign Central Authority, which may be the foreign Ministry of Justice or a court in the Contracting State. When this Hague Convention was negotiated, the French government made a reservation regarding Article 23 on United States' pre-trial discovery, which does (did?) not exist in French law. By the statute of 19 January 1987, France agreed to accept requests in the context of pre-trial discovery if documents subject to discovery were clearly specified and closely connected to the case. A previous statute of 16 July 1980 prevented a French party from offering any financial information in response to requests made outside the scope of the Hague Convention. That statute is known as a blocking statute. Article 1 of the statute of 26 July 1968, modified by the statute of 16 July 1980, provides as follows:

> French nationals, French residents and other entities present in France are prohibited from communicating economic, commercial, industrial, financial or technical information to foreign public officials if such communication is harmful to France. It applies "anywhere", including extraterritorially and to all communications, whether in writing, orally, or by any other means. The communications that are prohibited are those capable or likely of harming or prejudicing the sovereignty, security or essential economic interests of France or public order.

3.058 Article 1-*bis* prohibits "any person in France from requesting, investigating or communicating the same kind of documents or information to be used in foreign judicial or administrative proceedings". Unlike the prohibition provided for by Article 1, the scope of the prohibition of Article 1-*bis* is not defined by the nature of the documents, but by their intended use (as potential evidence in connection with foreign judicial or administrative proceedings, whether pending or prospective). The provisions of Article 1 and Article 1-*bis* are subject to treaties and international agreements such as the Hague Convention of 1970. Any violation of the provisions of Article 1 and Article 1-*bis* is punishable either by imprisonment (maximum six months) or fine (maximum 18000 Euros) or both. The 1980 blocking statute was intended to block the extraterritorial application of foreign procedural rules on the French territory and to force foreign authorities to comply with the strict requirements and procedures provided by the Hague Convention. The 1970 Hague Convention is, thus, not exclusive in the United States (U.S. Supreme Court, *Aerospatiale* case, 1988[71]). For example: a party to a U.S. civil litigation can obtain pre-trial discovery according to the U.S. domestic rules of procedure, by asking a French subsidiary in the United States to provide all of the information about a case. The sanction, if the French subsidiary is not in compliance and fails to provide the documents, even if said documents are coming from France, is contempt of court.

A French lawyer was criminally convicted for the first time in the 2007 *Executive life* case, but the amount of the fine was quite low (10000 Euros).[72] This explains why a U.S. judge decided in another case to impose an injunction on a French person for offering evidence without respecting the blocking statute.[73] In this case, documents were given to the U.S. Court by the French government in a U.S. criminal case under a Mutual Legal Assistance Treaty between France and the United States. The companies that were victim of a competition infringement brought a class action lawsuit in a U.S. Civil Court and asked to benefit from these documents. The French party objected, indicating that this information would not have been available if the Hague Convention had been applied. The U.S. civil judge balanced the interests of the victims against those of the defendant, taking into account the low risk of sanctions in France. The judge decided that the documents obtained in the criminal proceedings could be used in the civil class action. As such, this blocking statute has no real effect as long as the case is brought in the U.S. Nevertheless, a French agency specialised in the protection of freedoms as they relate to database storage and use of personal information, try to prevent the transmission of personal information such as personal banking information through a general recommendation.[74] Conversely, in a South African case, a U.S. judge did not require a person to offer evidence because the amount of the potential fine under a South African blocking statute was significantly higher than in France. It should be noted that the Hague Convention is not considered to be the exclusive way of obtaining evidence under French law. Thus, an expert appointed by a French judge may have to conduct research for evidence abroad.[75] 3.059

71 482 U.S. 522 (1987).

72 Cass. crim, 12 December 2007, no. 07-83228, *Christopher X.*

73 Air Cargo Shipping Services Antitrust Litigation, case no. 1:06-md-1775-JG (VVP) (EDNy mar. 29 March 2010).

74 Deliberation CNIL, 23 July 2009 no. 2009-474.

75 Court of Appeal Paris 23 September 2003, RG no. 2002/18509, which has been accepted by ECJ, 6 September 2012, C-170/11 *Lippens*; ECJ, 21 February 2013, C-332/11, *ProRail BV.* Case C-199/92 P, *Hüls* v *Commission* [1999] ECR I-4287, paragraphs 149 and 150. Does that also apply for third states? In Switzerland, for example, the research of the expert would be considered a violation of national sovereignty and he could be sent to prison.

3.060 On the other hand, the EU Regulation (Regulation (EU) 2020/1783 of 25 November 2020 replacing Regulation (EC) No 1206/2001 of 28 May 2001) on cooperation between the courts of the Member States in the taking of evidence in civil or commercial matters is exclusive.[76] A testimony may not be obtained by a provisional measure in application of Article 35 of the Brussels I recast.[77] A Member State Court may ask a judge of another Member State to hear a witness or ask for the production of documents or other objects.

3.061 It should be noted that *discovery* could be requested in the United States in the context of proceedings commenced in France against a U.S. defendant under section 1782 of the U.S. Code of Federal Claims.[78] A court order obtained in France by a party on the basis of Article 145 CCP may relate to computer documents stored on a computer concerning relations between French lawyers and U.S. lawyers without application of the foreign law on the merits and without taking account of the professional secrecy of U.S. lawyers (who enjoy the same *privilege* as lawyers).[79] One may wonder whether the French procedure has not introduced a form of *discovery* that does not provide all the procedural guarantees. However, the Court of Cassation is careful to ensure that the conditions of Article 145 are met, even at the international level, in particular that the purpose of the measure is to preserve evidence,[80] that there is a legitimate interest under French law (and not under the foreign law applicable to the merits of the case, so that the measure is proportionate to the aim to be achieved), and that there is standing to bring an action under the law of the grouping.[81]

2. Access to evidence in international disputes before an International Chamber

3.062 The International Chamber of the Paris Commercial Court and the International Chamber of the Paris Court of Appeal compose the new International Commercial Courts of Paris (ICCP in English, CCIP in French).[82] This Court is quasi-autonomous and self-regulated with a hybrid and specific procedure.

---

76 ECJ, 28 April 2005, St Paul Dairy, *Rev. crit. DIP* 2005, 742, Pataut.

77 ECJ, 6 September 2012, C-170/11 *Lippens*, Procédures 2012, no. 352, Nourissat.

78 A. Kirry and R. Chapon, "Un outil probatoire méconnu: l'utilisation de la procédure de *discovery* devant les tribunaux français", *Gaz. Pal.* 10 December 2013, no. 344, p. 17.

79 Cass. 1re civ. 3 November 2016, no. 15-20495, *D. avocats* 2016, 31, note G. Royer; *D.* 2017, 1019, obs. H. G-T; *JCP* 2017, 105, note E. Jeuland; *adde* F. G'sell, "Qu'est-ce que le *legal privilege* ?" *JCP G* 2021, 337.

80 Cass. 1re civ, 27 January 2021, no. 19-16917, *JCP G* 2021, 315, note G. Cuniberti (in relation to the application of Article 35 of the Brussels 1 bis regulation on provisional and protective measures) making an adjustment to previous decisions Cass. 1re civ, 14 March 2018, no. 16-27913, *JCP G* 2018, 702, note F. Mailhé.

81 Cass. 1re civ, 9 March 2022, no. 20-22244, *JCP G* 2022, 552, note O. Boskovic and chron. 661, no. 9 obs. Larribère (concerning an association acting in defence of the environment).

82 E. Jeuland, "The International Chambers of Paris: A Gaul Village", in *International Business Courts: A European and Global Perspective*, X. Kramer and J. Sorabji (dir.), Eleven International Publishing, 2019, chap. 4, p. 65; F. Ancel, "La chambre commerciale internationale de la cour d'appel de Paris", *D.* 2018, 1904; J.-S. Bazile, "Chambres

The International Chamber is hence to be found at the first-instance level of the Paris Commercial Court (thereinafter referred to as the CCIP-TC, which used to exist until 1993 but was re-established in 2011 and 2017) and the International Chamber at the second instance level of the Paris Court of Appeal (thereinafter referred to as the CCIP-CA since March 2018).[83] Both Courts accept documents and hold hearings in English and adapt the French justice system to international cases. Nevertheless, these Chambers comply, at least formally, with French procedure rules. **3.063**

The French case management judge of the international chamber is not only in charge of the case schedule but also of the evidentiary part (but this judge does not decide the case). This judge may have consequently greater power than his counterpart in Common law countries (who issues nevertheless a scheduling order and may hold a pretrial conference to prevent wasteful discovery). In particular, the French judge may act as an examining judge even though s/he does not usually use much of such examining powers for time reasons. The creation of the CCIP-CA (Rules of International Chamber of the Paris Court of appeal) might be a good opportunity for French case management judges to act as investigative judges in ordering expert opinions to be obtained and other technical experts to be heard. The focus is, however, on testimonies and not on the evidence orders reserved to judges, such as asking for expert opinions or other technical advices and statements. What is clearly favoured is witness testimony. The CCIP-CA and ITCP Protocol (Commercial Court) preambles state that there is a focus on testimonial evidence. Many rules of the Protocols also concern witnesses and hearings. French Commercial Courts (and French Civil Courts generally speaking) virtually never hear witnesses, so the issue of the language in which they may address the Court normally does not arise (in ordinary sections). The attractiveness of foreign courts (e.g. London courts) is certainly due to the possibility of hearing witnesses and disclosing documents. **3.064**

It has been argued that Article 145 of the French CCP allows a kind of pretrial disclosure[84] However, as for the procedure on the merits the documents have to be precisely specified to get a disclosure order from the judge. This rule deters fishing expeditions of American-like discovery, but this is not convenient in the event of big commercial cases. It is the reason why the Protocol brings some flexibility in this matter. Rule 5.1.1 **3.065**

---

commerciales internationales. Deux ans après leur création: bilan et perspectives dans un contexte remanié," *JCP G* 2020, 769.

83 Protocole relatif à la procédure devant la Chambre Internationale de la Cour d'appel de Paris, CCIP-CA, available at: www.avocatparis.org/system/files/editos/protocoles_signes_creation_juridiction_commerciale_internationale_1.pdf and www.lja.fr/wp-content/uploads/2018/02/ProtocolesCIC and www.shearman.com/-/media/Files/Perspectives/2018/04/Protocol_relating_to_the_procedure_before_the_International_Chamber_of_the_Paris_Court_of_Appeal.pdf?la=en&hash=8539B15BCD02C6140DF2FDE5212C1B364FBCC1F4.

84 See B.2.

of the CCIP-CA Protocol actually provides that: "Requests for mandatory production of documents held by a party or by a third party are examined by the judge in charge of the procedure ('conseiller de la mise en état'), pursuant to the rules set forth in Articles 11 and 138 to 142 of the French Code of Civil Procedure". This rule seems to be in line with the normal procedure so that only specified documents may be considered by the judge when making an evidence order. However, Rule 5.1.2 CCIP-CA Protocol (Article 4.1.3 CCIP-TC Protocol) provides that "Parties may seek the production of precisely identified categories of documents". This rule opens the door to a French disclosure of documents since it refers to identified categories of documents and not to identified documents. For example, instead of requesting a business contract number Y of a precise date, a party may request an order from the judge imposing the other party or a third party to disclose a series of contracts concluded between the parties during such or such period of time. It is quite similar to the procedure of disclosure implemented in France for the private enforcement of competition infringement.[85] The advantage of the Common law's flexible rules of disclosure or discovery is to offer better access to relevant pieces of evidence that the claimant does/may not precisely know. The disadvantage is the cost incurred, which can be huge and disproportionate. This is why the American discovery system is only plainly available for the biggest cases (see Article 26 and seq. Federal rules). So, the compromise entails a reasonable cost of disclosing documents.

3.066 The rules concerning witnesses also illustrate another kind of compromise. Usually, in France, written evidence is favoured in civil matters, whereas written documents are not necessary in commercial matters.[86] Some facts, however, cannot be proved by written documents. The French tradition is to be cautious with witnesses. According to a famous French adage, written evidence outweighs oral evidence ("lettres passent témoins"). The practice of written testimony has the advantage of being costless but the drawback of not being reliable even though it has to be written and signed by the hand of the witness (however the court is not in the position to ask further questions directly to the witness). The Protocols provide that the written statement may be drafted by way of computer, which creates some new flexibility (Article 4.3.2 CCIP-TC Protocol and 5.3.2 CCIP-CA Protocol). In addition, witnesses may be interrogated before the Court, which is possible in normal procedure but quite rare. The Protocols add the possibility, which in France only exists in criminal procedure, to cross-examine witnesses and parties. Rule 5.4.4 provides that "The judge carries out the examination of witnesses; by asking those questions he considers useful on all facts for which evidence is admitted by law. Witnesses may thereafter be invited by the judge to respond to

85 See C.2.
86 Article L110-3 Commercial Code.

the questions that the parties wish to ask". It means that cross-examination is possible under the supervision of the Court. This should lead to an unknown practice in France, which is the preparation of witnesses. This is still an issue since the preparation of witnesses by the parties' lawyers may be considered as a criminal offence called "subornation de témoin" (witness tampering), which is an attempt to influence and to corrupt a witness. It is possible to cross-examine a party under the supervision of the Court under Article 5.2.1: "Each party may thereafter be invited by the judge to respond to the questions that the other parties wish to ask". It should be added that under French law parties do not have a complete obligation to reveal all relevant facts to the Court, such as in Common law with the sanction provided by the principle of contempt of court. Quite the contrary, French rules usually try to prevent parties from self-incrimination. This difference of rules and culture reveals a huge gap between Common law procedure and French International Chambers procedure.

As a whole, the special procedure set by the Paris International Chambers is original and autonomous. Some specific improvements will probably be necessary in the future (e.g. witness preparation, amicus curiae such as an expert in foreign law, etc.). **3.067**

In conclusion, these new flexible rules, whether on access to evidence in International Chambers, or in applying Article 145 CCP, or in specific fields such as intellectual property litigation and private enforcement of competition rules may, one day, lead to the wider acceptance in France of the effect of a U.S. discovery order in spite of the blocking statute of 1980.[87] It is also important to stress that French in-house lawyers do not benefit from privileges so that they cannot refuse, like American lawyers, to comply with a discovery order. Many French in-house lawyers would like to benefit from such a privilege, but it is not likely to happen because these lawyers are not independent from their companies and EU law opposes this extension of privilege.[88] **3.068**

87 See D.1.
88 ECJ, 10 September 2009, Case C-97/08 P, Akzo Nobel NV and Others.

4

ACCESS TO EVIDENCE IN ITALY

Elisabetta Silvestri

A. INTRODUCTION

4.001 If someone ventured to peruse the rich Italian literature on the topic of evidence in civil procedure, he would discover that the issue of access to information and evidence is rarely mentioned. Of course, it is clear that the reality of legal disputes often brings about the need for a party to acquire information and evidence that are in the control of the opponent or a third party, but, in principle, the range of the legal tools available to allow the party to obtain that very information and evidence is quite limited. Therefore, the Italian approach, like the approach of other legal systems rooted in the Roman tradition, can be illustrated synthetically by stating that 'a general obligation of a party to deliver necessary information and evidence in the interest of an opponent does not exist or that a party is not bound to make available to a counterparty all material useful for his success'.[1]

1 Marco Gradi, 'The Right of Access to Information and Evidence and the Duty of Truthful Disclosure of Parties in Comparative Perspective', in Loïc Cadiet, Burkhard Hess, Marta Requejo Isidro (eds), *Procedural Science at the Crossroads of Different Generations* (Nomos 2015) 93. It may be of interest to mention that even comprehensive studies on the obligations (whether legal or ethical) of the parties in the conduct of civil proceedings do not address the issue of how to secure access to evidence or information in the control of the opponent or non-parties. This, despite the fact that a supposedly existing duty of cooperation with a view to fostering the fair resolution of the dispute is described as an underlying influence permeating the whole adjudication: see, for instance, the essays collected in

If this statement holds true, then it is clear that in order to ascertain the facts of a case the court can only rely on the evidence each party is able to offer in support of his allegations, according to the burden of proof and the rules (often derived from substantive law) that modify such burden. This is so unless courts are entrusted with the power to order (upon request of either the claimant or the defendant, or even *ex officio*) the taking of evidence deemed relevant, to fill the gap – so to speak – left by the parties in their efforts to substantiate their narratives of the facts in dispute through evidence.[2] But the power of the courts, if they have any, is meaningless if their orders are not strengthened by a body of effective sanctions that can be imposed on the defaulting party, or somehow enforceable. This is an aspect of a wider issue regarding the effectiveness of the courts' orders concerning the taking of evidence, an issue extensively explored by the academic literature in the framework of the debate revolving around the powers entrusted with the courts for what is nowadays called 'the management of evidence'.[3] **4.002**

In short, since under Italian law a party to a case has no legal obligation to disclose information that is likely to adversely affect his case or can support the opponent's case, the only available avenue open to each party to collect relevant information held by the opponent or by third parties is to rely on the court's initiative, in the form of either an order for the inspection of places, persons or things or an order for the exhibition of documents or other items, hoping that the sanctions threatened for non-compliance work. Another procedural device, one which sounds quite outdated and is of limited practical relevance, is the so-called formal examination of a party (*interrogatorio formale*) upon request of the opponent. Its purpose is to induce the party under examination to acknowledge the truth of facts that are adverse to the party himself, and favourable to his opponent: it is a particular form of what the Italian law defines as a confession, a relic of a long-gone concept of evidence.[4] **4.003**

In light of all this, one may state that the right to evidence, which is a paramount component of the due process principle enshrined in article 111, section 1 of the Italian **4.004**

Quaderni dell'Associazione italiana fra gli studiosi del processo civile, *Etica del processo e doveri delle parti (Atti del XXIX Convegno Nazionale, Genova, 20–21 settembre 2013)* (Bononia University Press 2015).

2 On the balance between the obligations of the parties to support their 'truth' of the facts they allege in order to validate their claims and the inquisitorial powers that the court can exercise, on the assumption that such powers are 'accessory and supplementary' (my translation), see extensively Michele Taruffo, *La semplice verità. Il giudice e la costruzione dei fatti* (Editori Laterza 2009) 174.

3 On the issue mentioned, see specifically Angelo Dondi, *Effettività dei provvedimenti istruttori del giudice civile* (CEDAM 1985). The passage of time since the publication of this study has not detracted from the depth of the analysis conducted by the author, confirming the impression that nothing is new under the sun, in spite of the many winds of reform affecting Italian civil procedure.

4 See Elisabetta Silvestri, 'The Antique Shop of Italian Civil Procedure: Oath and Confession as Evidence', in CH van Rhee and A Uzelac (eds), *Truth and Efficiency in Civil Litigation. Fundamental Aspects of Fact-finding and Evidence-taking in a Comparative Context* (Intersentia 2012) 47.

Constitution,[5] does not seem to include a wide-ranging right of access to information and evidence, such as the one that is familiar to the legal systems relying on discovery (the well-known 'asset' of the U.S. pre-trial phase of adjudication) or disclosure (the English, more limited equivalent of American discovery) as legal tools specifically aimed at eliciting information to be used as evidence from the opponent party or a non-party.

4.005 It is worth emphasising, though, that as a consequence of recent, extensive reforms of Italian civil procedure,[6] the amendments to several articles of the Code of Civil Procedure, including the articles devoted to inspection and exhibition, are seen by a number of scholars as an important step toward a positive enhancement of the parties' duty to loyal cooperation in the management of the case:[7] a duty that has never been taken seriously enough, in spite of the fact that article 88, section 1 of the Code provides that 'loyalty and probity' must govern the behaviour of the parties (and their lawyers as well) in their conduct during the proceeding. The reform is too recent to state with certainty that the parties' duty to loyal cooperation in the establishment of the facts in dispute now exists as a positive obligation even in the absence of a specific rule on the subject. Similarly, it is still doubtful whether the amended rules will have a significant and beneficial effect on the right of access to information and evidence.

B. INSPECTION AND EXHIBITION (ACCORDING TO THE CODE OF CIVIL PROCEDURE)

4.006 According to article 118 of the Italian Code of Civil Procedure, the court can order *ex officio* the parties or non-parties to allow an inspection of their persons or tangible items that are in their possession, insofar as the inspection is 'indispensable' in gaining knowledge of the facts in dispute. Further limits surround the availability of an order for inspection: the order cannot cause any 'serious harm' to its intended recipient, nor can its intended recipient be forced to disclose privileged information, in particular information pertaining to professional or State secrets.

---

5 'Jurisdiction shall be administered through due process regulated by law.'

6 See Legislative decree no 149 of 10 October 2022 (*Attuazione della legge 26 novembre 2021, n. 206, recante delega al Governo per l'efficienza del processo civile e per la revisione della disciplina degli strumenti di risoluzione alternativa delle controversie e misure urgenti di razionalizzazione dei procedimenti in materia di diritti delle persone e delle famiglie nonché in materia di esecuzione forzata*), commonly referred to as *Riforma Cartabia*, from the name of the Minister of Justice then in office.

7 See, in particular, Marco Gradi, 'Doveri delle parti dei terzi (artt. 96, 118, 121, 210, 213 c.p.c.)', in Roberta Tiscini (a cura di), *La riforma Cartabia del processo civile. Commento al d. lgs. 10 ottobre 2022, n. 149* (Pacini Giuridica 2023). The author offers a copious bibliography on the subject matter in support of (as well as against) his main theory, which postulates that the parties are not only under the obligation of loyal cooperation, but are also expected to abide by a 'duty to truth' with respect to the facts in dispute and the evidence substantiating those very facts.

It is clear that courts enjoy discretionary powers in evaluating whether the inspection appears to be 'indispensable' or the harm to which the party (or the non-party) would be exposed as a consequence of the court's order qualifies as 'serious'. The published case law is virtually nonexistent and, in any event, only the specific circumstances of the case at stake could shed light on the reasons given in support of the granting of an order for inspection. **4.007**

Probably the only interesting aspects of the rule governing orders for inspection are the sanctions applicable to the party failing to comply with the order. A recent amendment to article 118 of the Code of Civil Procedure provides for a fine, ranging from €500 to €3,000, that the court can impose on the defaulting party;[8] the fine is paid into the public purse. Furthermore, adverse inferences can be drawn from the party's refusal to allow the inspection. Leaving aside the questionable effectiveness of fines, the power of the court to draw negative inferences from the behaviour of the uncooperative party is a sort of blunt weapon, since the prevailing interpretation of the evidentiary value of these inferences rules out the possibility that they are sufficient, by themselves, to prove the facts in dispute, in particular when such facts are adverse to the party who fails to comply with the court's order. By the same token, it can be emphasised that the threat of the adverse inferences that can be drawn by the court from the party's refusal to comply with an order for inspection does not seem serious enough to prompt a change of heart in the party.[9] **4.008**

As far as the exhibition is concerned,[10] article 210 of the Code of Civil Procedure provides that either party can apply for an order directing his opponent or a non-party to exhibit documents or other items in their possession insofar as the documents or other items are deemed by the court to be the sources of evidence that are necessary (or better yet, indispensable) to secure in order to prove the facts in dispute. Simply put, the exhibition can be ordered only if the applicant cannot resort to any other legitimate ways to get hold of the document or the items at issue: this holds true, in particular, for a variety of official documents to which special statutes grant interested parties specific rights of access. According to the established case law, the exhibition is a 'residual' means of gathering evidence, which can be resorted to only when the facts in dispute cannot be proven in any other ways. It cannot be ordered to remedy the fault of a party who failed to discharge his burden of proof; and, in any event, whether **4.009**

8 For the non-party, the fine ranges from €150 to €1,500.

9 See Diego Volpino, 'L'ispezione', in Michele Taruffo (a cura di), *La prova nel processo civile* (Giuffrè Editore 2012).

10 See extensively Fabio Rota, 'Commento all'art. 210', in Federico Carpi – Michele Taruffo (a cura di), *Commentario breve al codice di procedura civile* (10th edn, Wolters Kluwer – Cedam 2023).

or not to issue an order for exhibition is a discretionary choice of the court left to its 'prudent appreciation'.[11]

4.010 Like the inspection, the exhibition cannot be ordered if it causes any 'serious harm' to its intended recipient or forces him to disclose privileged information, such as that covered by professional or State secrets. The applicant is required to identify specifically the document or the item to be exhibited, offering also evidence of the fact that the former or the latter are in the possession of the opponent or the non-party.

4.011 The party neglecting to comply with the order for exhibition is subject to the same sanctions provided for failure to discharge an order for inspection. Mention has already been made of the disputable evidentiary value of the adverse inferences the court can draw from the conduct of the non-cooperative party.[12] As to the fine, it is worth emphasising that it is conceived as a lump sum: this means that if the party (or the non-party) pays the fine, there is no way to gain access to the document or the item that was required to be exhibited. The situation would be different if the fine had been designed as a pecuniary penalty accruing each day of non-compliance, but even the latest reform of Italian civil procedure does not seem to have remedied this untenable situation: since the court's order cannot be enforced directly and the fine, by itself, is far from compelling compliance, the possibility for the party who requested an order for exhibition to get hold of the document he needs for evidentiary purposes is left to the good will of the person (his opponent or a non-party) in control of that very document.

4.012 A final word on the non-party who is the recipient of an order for exhibition: according to article 211 of the Code of Civil Procedure, the court, when it issues the order, 'must balance in the best way possible the interest of justice against the respect due to the third party's rights' (my translation). The non-party can be heard and he can also intervene in the procedure for the sole purpose of challenging the order.

C. LEGISLATION GOVERNING EXHIBITION IN SPECIAL AREAS OF SUBSTANTIVE LAW

4.013 The general principles on exhibition laid down by the Code of Civil Procedure are overridden, at least to a certain extent, by several provisions having to do with specific subject matters.

---

11 Several judgements issued by the Italian Court of Cassation state this principle: see, for instance, Cass. Civ., Sez. III, 20 August 2024; Cass. Civ., Sez. I, 11 June 2024, no 16233; Cass. Civ., Sez. II, 27 December 2023.

12 Curiously enough, the rules governing collective proceedings provide that if the court orders the defendant to exhibit relevant evidence in his control and the order is not complied with, the facts that the evidence refers to can be considered proven: see Code of Civil Procedure, art 840-*quinquies*, s 13.

Pursuant to the Civil Code and the rules devoted to company law,[13] the exhibition of all of the accounting ledgers of a company can be ordered by the court only if the dispute concerns the winding up of the company itself or other limited circumstances. Furthermore, the court can order, even *ex officio*, the exhibition of the accounting ledgers and other accounting records that are relevant for the case at hand. It is unclear what consequences are brought about by failure to comply with the court's order: since the Code is silent on this point, it seems reasonable to conclude that article 210 of the Code of Civil Procedure is applicable, therefore exposing the defaulting party to the fine provided by this rule and to the possibility for the court to draw adverse inferences against the uncooperative party. **4.014**

In the field of intellectual property litigation, when a party has offered reliable elements to support the merits of his claim and has identified documents, elements or information in the control of the opposing party, the court can be petitioned to order the exhibition of these items or to address a request for information from the opposing party. The same party can be ordered by the court 'to provide the elements suitable to identifying the subjects involved in the production and distribution of goods or services constituting infringement of industrial property rights'.[14] Furthermore, in the case of an infringement committed on a commercial scale, the court, on application by a party, can order the exhibition of banking, financial or commercial documents in the control of the opposing party. The court's orders must ensure the protection of confidential information, giving the recipient of the order the possibility to have his say on the issue. From the behaviour of the party or his unjustified refusal to comply with the order the court – as usual – can draw adverse inferences. **4.015**

The academic literature refers to the orders just mentioned as orders for 'discovery',[15] as if the Italian legislators had bravely decided to enrich the evidence-taking phase of intellectual property rights litigation with a tool unknown to the national legal system. It has been emphasised, though, that the rules governing the alleged 'discovery' of evidence in reality follow the pattern of the exhibition as well as the interrogation of a party (when the party is requested to provide information) according to the precepts of the Code of Civil Procedure.[16] No subpoenas can be issued by the court to foster **4.016**

---

13 Civil Code, art 2711.

14 Reference here is made to the Industrial Property Code, established by Legislative decree no 30 of 10 February 2005, and specifically to art 121. An English translation of the Code can be found at <https://www.wipo.int/wipolex/en/legislation/details/22344> accessed 6 January 2025.

15 See, for instance, Leonardo Benvenuto, 'Il sistema della *discovery* e del diritto di "informazione" nel codice della proprietà industriale' (2007) Rivista di diritto industriale 118.

16 In particular, see Gina Gioia, 'La tutela giurisdizionale della proprietà industriale (artt. 117-146 d.lgs. 10 febbraio 2005, n. 30 "Codice della proprietà industriale, a norma dell'art. 15 della legge 12 dicembre 2002, n. 273", in G.U. n. 52 del 4 marzo 2005, s.o. n. 28)' (2006) Le Nuove Leggi Civili Commentate 3.

compliance with its orders, and it is questionable whether the new fine provided for non-fulfilment of a 'regular' order for exhibition[17] can be applicable to a sector-specific type of litigation.

1. Disclosure of evidence in actions for damages for infringement of competition law

4.017 EU Directive no. 104 of 2014 was implemented (well beyond the deadline set by the Directive) by a statutory instrument[18] that is not much more than a repetition of the Italian version of the EU rules, which shows the lack of any real attempt at coordinating the new provisions with the preexisting ones. This is particularly noticeable if one looks at the rules concerning the disclosure of evidence,[19] which mark a gap between the exhibition of evidence in the actions for damages for infringement of competition law and the exhibition of documents and other items according to the Code of Civil Procedure. In other words, the implementation of the Directive could have offered a good opportunity to review the whole subject of access to information and evidence, reconfiguring the regulation of exhibition and its strict limits by adopting a more modern and structured approach. Unfortunately, not only was such an opportunity missed, but also the reform passed in 2022 did not bring about any real novelties related to the evidence-taking phase, overlooking the suggestions coming from sector-specific rules, such as the ones on the disclosure of evidence in actions for damages in the field of antitrust law.

4.018 According to article 3, section 1 of Legislative decree no. 3 of 2017, the disclosure can be ordered upon request of a party who must identify the facts to be proven and the evidence that is 'reasonably' supposed to be in the control of the opponent or a non-party. These elements (facts and evidence) must be sufficient to support the 'plausibility' of the party's claim. Here, too, the fact that the Italian legislators did not care at all to expand on the meaning of the expression *plausibilità della domanda* has brought about a variety of interpretations, all … plausible. A reasonable approach seems to indicate that, in light of the allegations made by the claimant, the evidence whose disclosure is sought makes the claim prima facie well-founded, so that the disclosure can be denied only insofar as the claim appears to be blatantly groundless.[20] From this

---

17 ibid, para 2.

18 Legislative decree no 3 of 19 January 2017 (*Attuazione della direttiva 2014/104/UE del Parlamento e del Consiglio, del 26 novembre 2014, relativa a determinate norme che regolano le azioni per il risarcimento del danno ai sensi del diritto nazionale per violazioni delle disposizioni del diritto della concorrenza degli Stati membri e dell'Unione Europea*).

19 ibid, art 3 (*Ordine di esibizione*).

20 See, in particular, Giuseppe Finocchiaro, 'La disciplina dell'esibizione delle prove nei giudizi risarcitori per violazione delle norme *antitrust* in attuazione della dir. 2014/104/UE' (2018) Le nuove leggi civili commentate 415; Paolo Comoglio, 'Note a una prima lettura del d.lgs. n. 3 del 2017. Novità processuali e parziali inadeguatezze in tema di

point of view, it is emphasised that the disclosure provided by article 3 goes beyond the strict limit of the 'regular' exhibition, even though the heading of the article reads 'order of exhibition:' again, the lack of coordination of the sector-specific rules with the general provisions of the Code of Civil Procedure is crystal clear.

Other aspects of the disclosure of evidence in the actions for damages for antitrust infringement do not seem to deserve special analysis, since they repeat what is provided for in the Italian version of Directive 2014/104. With no intention to minimise their importance, this author thinks that their study is better left to those who can claim expertise in the field of antitrust law. It is worth mentioning, though, the consequences of unjustified failure to comply with an order for disclosure: besides huge administrative penalties imposed on the non-cooperative party (or non-party), the court, taking into account any other pieces of evidence, can deem the facts that the evidence for which the disclosure sought was supposed to demonstrate as being proven. This is again something quite different from what the Code of Civil Procedure provides for in case of failure to comply with an order for exhibition, an event that the court may sanction (so to speak) by drawing adverse inferences to the detriment of the defaulting party. **4.019**

D. REQUEST FOR INFORMATION

Here and there in the Code of Civil Procedure, as well as in the Civil Code and a panoply of special statutes, reference is made to the 'information' that the court can acquire, either upon party's request or *ex officio*, with a view to collecting data of various kinds leading to a more accurate decision of the issues in dispute.[21] It would be of little worth to list the relevant rules, while it is worthwhile to emphasise that the 'information', often accompanied by adjectives such as 'summary' or 'necessary', does not fall into a single coherent category, but, to the contrary, can be defined as a bunch of sources of knowledge that are equally diverse as the rules, whether substantive or procedural, mentioning them. **4.020**

Scholars discuss extensively the probative value of the information,[22] but the different schools of thought seem to agree on the fact that the power to acquire information **4.021**

danno *antitrust*' (2017) Rivista trimestrale di diritto e procedura civile 991; Andrea Giussani, 'Direttiva e principi del processo civile italiano' (2015) AIDA-Annali italiani del diritto d'autore, della cultura e dello spettacolo 251.

21 See Luca Passanante, 'Le informazioni', in Michele Taruffo (a cura di), *La prova nel processo civile* (Giuffè Editore 2012) 957.

22 According to Michele Taruffo, *La prova dei fatti giuridici* (Giuffre Editore 1992) 463, since the information is acquired by the court directly from third parties or by means of third parties, it is in practice akin to witness statements. Other scholars qualify the information as a peculiar type of evidence, called 'atypical evidence', that is not included in the normative catalogue of the evidence considered admissible by the law, but that is quite often relied upon by the courts:

offers the court the possibility to search elements of knowledge beyond the scope of the strict rules governing the taking of evidence. If this holds true, though, it is of paramount importance that the court, most of all when acting *ex officio*, abide by the due process principle, allowing the parties to have their say on the information collected.

1. Request for information addressed to public agencies

4.022 Mention has already been made of the fact that an order for exhibition (in particular, when the object to be exhibited is a document) can be issued only insofar as the applicant is unable to get hold of the document in any other legitimate way. The problem concerns most of all documents retained by public bodies and agencies. Even though Italy, like many other countries, has statutes aimed at granting citizens a right to freedom of information and the ensuing possibility to gain access to a variety of public documents and records, there are still a few 'grey areas' in which access to the relevant information is not publicly available, even though such information is not protected from disclosure by any specific statutes, concerning, for instance, national security or foreign policy.

4.023 According to article 213 of the Code of Civil Procedure, the court before which the proceeding is pending may, in its discretion, act *ex officio* and request a public agency to provide written information related to documents that are 'necessary' to acquire, meaning that these documents are likely to provide valuable information to be used as evidence in the case at hand.

4.024 The latest reform of Italian civil procedure has added to article 213 a new section, assigning to the public agency a deadline of sixty days in which either to comply with the request or to explain the reasons justifying the refusal to comply. The new rule is silent on the consequences ensuing from the expiration of the deadline and, as a matter of fact, the lack of any sanctions for failure to discharge the court's request seems to make the rule of limited usefulness, if even that. It has been suggested that the agency clerk who is supposedly in charge of providing the court with the documents requested and who fails to do so could be charged with a felony known as 'Dereliction of duty' (in Italian, *Omissione di atti d'ufficio*) as contemplated by article 328 of the Criminal Code:[23] an interesting suggestion that seems at odds with the Kafkaesque structure of Italian public agencies, which is likely to make it extremely difficult to identify the real culprit.

---

see, for instance, Gian France Ricci, *Le prove atipiche* (Giuffrè Editore 1999) 285; Bruno Capponi, 'Le "informazioni" del giudice civile (appunti per una ricerca)' (1990) Rivista trimestrale di diritto e procedura civile 929.

23 Gradi (n 7) 58.

E. EVIDENCE PRESERVATION PROCEDURE

The Italian Code of Civil Procedure allows the collection of certain types of evidence (other than documents) before the commencement of a judicial procedure when it is assumed that later on, and therefore when adjudication is pending, the evidence will be difficult, if not impossible, to take.[24] **4.025**

Procedurally speaking, the evidence preservation procedure is designed as an interim measure. This can be inferred from the fact that in the architecture of the Code the evidence preservation procedure finds its location within the rules governing interim measures. In spite of that, the general discipline of the procedure leading to the granting of interim measures (which is known as *procedimento cautelare uniforme*[25]) does not apply to the evidence preservation procedure: in particular, such procedure is not controlled by the rule according to which an interim measure lapses whenever the proceeding on the merits is not initiated within a specific deadline. **4.026**

Through the evidence preservation procedure it is possible to collect a witness statement, to inspect places or persons, and to secure the written report of an expert. **4.027**

As far as the witness statement is concerned, the rationale supporting the procedure is the reasonable concern that a prospective witness may become unavailable in the future due, for instance, to old age or a serious illness. Therefore, it is necessary to acquire from the witness a sort of affidavit to be used in the proceeding that a potential party to a lawsuit could institute. In order for a pre-filing order allowing the examination of the witness to be granted by the court, the potential litigant must state the compelling reasons justifying his application and the facts on which the witness is expected to testify with reference to the prospective claim or defense that could be supported by the evidence offered by that very witness. **4.028**

A pre-filing inspection order can be petitioned whenever there is an urgent need to ascertain the state of places or the condition of certain items, since the status quo is likely to be modified by the passage of time and therefore by the inevitable delay of a prospective adjudication. The inspection of persons (the applicant included) can be ordered only with the consent of the interested subject. **4.029**

The evidence preservation procedure aimed at collecting the written report of an expert implies that if the application is granted, the court will appoint an expert. The **4.030**

24 In Italian, the evidence preservation procedure is known as *istruzione preventiva*: see in general Giulio Nicola Nardo, *Contributo allo studio della istruzione preventiva* (Edizioni Scientifiche Italiane 2005); Chiara Besso, *La prova prima del processo* (Giappichelli Editore 2004).

25 The general rules on interim measures are articles 669 *bis* – 669 *quaterdecies* of the Code of Civil Procedure. For a general overview, see Antonio Carratta (a cura di), *I procedimenti cautelari* (Zanichelli Editore 2013).

expert's task is not limited to giving his opinion on the matter which is the object of his investigation. In fact, the expert may also extend his report to an evaluation of the causes of personal injury or the amount of damages for harm caused to property, if the potential litigant has an interest in establishing these circumstances.

4.031 It is worth mentioning that there is a particular type of pre-filing order for appointing an expert when the prospective lawsuit concerns the financial losses caused by contract non-compliance or torts.[26] Based on his written report, the expert is expected to engage in an attempt at prompting the potential parties to reach a settlement. If a settlement is reached, the court will make it enforceable; otherwise, each party can request that the expert's written report be made available as evidence in the forthcoming adjudication. At present, this specific type of pre-filing order is widely resorted to in civil cases, keeping in mind that, according to the Code, an application can be lodged even when there are no compelling reasons justifying the use of an evidence preservation procedure. Interestingly, one of the fields recording the most recurring use of the pre-filing order at issue is medical malpractice: medical malpractice lawsuits cannot be instituted unless the parties have previously attempted to reach a settlement either through an out-of-court mediation or on the basis of the written report of the expert appointed by the court via a pre-filing order.[27]

F. UNCHARTERED TERRITORY: ASSISTED NEGOTIATION AND THE EXTRAJUDICIAL TAKING OF EVIDENCE

4.032 In 2014, the Italian legislators passed a statutory instrument aimed at reducing the caseload of the courts by resorting to an ADR procedure known as 'assisted negotiation', namely a negotiation conducted by the parties' lawyers with a view to reaching an amicable resolution of the dispute before the commencement of the judicial procedure.[28] The assisted negotiation is set in motion when the parties, assisted by their lawyers, sign a written agreement by which they commit themselves to cooperate loyally and in good faith with a view to resolving their dispute amicably. In order to increase the chances of success of the new ADR tool, the legislators made assisted negotiation mandatory in a variety of cases, exactly as they had done previously with mediation: both mediation and assisted negotiation are compulsory steps to be taken

26 Vincenzo Ansanelli, 'La consulenza tecnica preventiva ai fini della composizione della lite', in Michele Taruffo (a cura di), *La prova nel processo civile* (Giuffrè Editore 2012) 1070.

27 Laura Giraldi, 'Questioni processuali e pratiche ricorrenti in tema di accertamento tecnico preventivo in materia di responsabilità sanitaria' (13 May 2024) Judicium <https://www.judicium.it> accessed 6 January 2025.

28 Elisabetta Silvestri, 'La negoziazione assistita', in Elisabetta Silvestri (a cura di), *Forme alternative di risoluzione delle controversie e strumenti di giustizia riparativa* (Giappichelli Editore 2020). Assisted negotiation is governed by Statutory instrument no 132 of 12 September 2014.

in almost all civil and commercial cases on the assumption that people are not very inclined to choose either voluntarily.

The reform passed in 2022 extended the scope of application of assisted negotiation and authorised the lawyers for the parties to resort to particular forms of extrajudicial taking of evidence.[29] The rationale supporting this innovation is that the more information each party (or better yet, his lawyer) can gather from a third party or the opponent about the facts in dispute, the higher the chances are that the controversy can be resolved by a settlement. **4.033**

Leaving aside the details of the procedure, the lawyer for each party can 'invite' a third party 'to make statements regarding facts that are specifically singled out and relevant with respect to the dispute' (my translation). The third party is unhappily called the 'informant' (*informatore*). In practice, he is heard as a witness. The replies given by the informant to the questions asked by the lawyer are recorded in a transcript, which provides irrefutable evidence of the information collected (namely, the questions asked by the lawyer and the replies given by the third party) or, more precisely, of what the lawyers for the parties certify took place before them. Therefore, the transcript becomes a new type of 'legal proof',[30] whose probative weight is not objectionable if, thanks to the information collected, the assisted negotiation results in a settlement. If no settlement is reached and a litigation ensues, the transcript can be used as documentary evidence that the court can freely evaluate according to its 'prudent appreciation', in consonance with the rule laid down by article 116, section 1 of the Code of Civil Procedure. Furthermore, the court can deem it appropriate to hear again the informant as a witness. Should the informant not show up or refuse to reply to the questions, and provided that the assisted negotiation has failed, the party interested in the information can ask the court to take the steps necessary to obtain from the informant a sort of affidavit, according to the rules governing a particular procedure aimed at securing specific items of evidence by interim measures before the inception of the judicial proceeding. **4.034**

Moreover, each party can be 'invited' by the opponent's lawyer to make written statements 'regarding facts that are specifically singled out and relevant with respect to the dispute' (my translation), facts that are adverse to the party himself and favourable to the party who is interested in obtaining the statement. If a settlement is reached, the **4.035**

29 See Statutory instrument no 132 of 12 September 2014, arts 4-*bis* and 4-*ter*, extensively analysed by Luigi Rosario Luongo, 'L'istruttoria stragiudiziale nel procedimento di negoziazione assistita' (20 February 2024) Judicium <https://www.judicium.it> accessed 2 November 2024.

30 On the concept of legal proofs, whose predetermined probative value overrides the general rule of the free evaluation of evidence, see Michele Taruffo, 'Evidence', in Mauro Cappelletti (ed), *Civil Procedure, Chapter 7, International Encyclopedia of Comparative Law* (Mohr Sieback/Martinus Nijhoff Publishers 2010) paras 54, 89–90.

probative value of the statement seems to be the same as the transcript of the replies given by the informant, but, if the negotiation fails, the statement can be used in the judicial proceeding as an out-of-court confession: this means that the statement provides conclusive evidence as to the facts stated by the party, so that the court is bound to regard the same facts as indisputably true. If the party refuses to provide the required statement, the court can sanction his behaviour by increasing the costs of the proceeding, namely applying the rules provided for abusive litigation.

4.036 If the legislators designing the extrajudicial taking of evidence intended to add a touch of modernity to assisted negotiation with a view to promoting its appeal, the results are far from satisfactory. The new rules are badly conceived, to the point that as yet they have never been applied even though, as mentioned previously, assisted negotiation is a mandatory ADR technique in a wide variety of cases.

4.037 It is unclear whether the sources of inspiration for the new rules were the deposition and interrogatories of American pre-trial discovery or the English pre-action protocols. In any event, the extrajudicial taking of evidence 'Italian style' seems to be a complex procedure that is incompatible with the objective to foster settlements within the framework of assisted negotiation.[31] Furthermore, it is hard to believe that Italian lawyers are ready (and inclined) to get involved in an activity (the preparation of a new example of 'legal proof') that is typically reserved to public officers entrusted with the power to draw up the so-called 'authentic deeds'.[32]

4.038 While waiting for the 'epiphany' of practical applications of the reform, one school of thought subscribes to a future extension of the extrajudicial taking of evidence beyond the limits of assisted negotiation[33] – a drift toward a privatisation of the evidence-taking procedure that this author does not look forward to.

---

31 See, in particular, Angelo Dondi and Vincenzo Ansanelli, 'Istruzione stragiudiziale e *discovery* nei recenti "Interventi per l'efficienza del processo civile". Qualche rapida impressione' (2019) Rivista trimestrale di diritto e procedura civile 757.

32 For this remark, see Beatrice Ficcarelli, 'L'istruzione stragiudiziale nella negoziazione assistita da avvocati' (2023) Rivista trimestrale di diritto e procedura civile 520.

33 Giuliano Scarselli, 'L'istruzione stragiudiziale affidata agli avvocati: una buona idea al momento tutta da disciplinare' (4 November 2024) Judicium <https://www.judicium.it> accessed 6 November 2024.

5

ACCESS TO EVIDENCE IN SPAIN

Fernando Gascón Inchausti

A. SOME RELEVANT FEATURES OF SPANISH CIVIL PROCEDURE, WITH AN IMPACT ON ACCESS TO EVIDENCE

Spanish civil procedure is mainly regulated in the Code of Civil Procedure (*Ley de Enjuiciamiento Civil*, LEC hereinafter), passed in 2000 and in force since January 2001. The approval of the LEC led to a radical change in the Spanish civil justice system, with significant consequences also in the field of evidence. Until then civil proceedings in Spain – defined in a Code from 1882 that, in turn, was a light remake of an 1855 previous one – was slow, unnecessarily complicated and written with a much-reduced presence of the judge. Not unsurprisingly, the system led to unsatisfactory outcomes, inacceptable from a modern perspective: the main claim lawyers made at that time was that judges had not been able to 'understand' the dispute, due to the reduced contact of the court with the subject-matter of the case. **5.001**

5.002 The main aim of civil procedure, as enacted in 2000, is precisely to ensure the quality of first instance judgments, trying to place the judge in the best possible position to make the best possible decision on the case: the course of proceedings, as well as the duties of parties and judges, have been arranged to serve this purpose. Some general overriding principles explain the architecture of the system and are necessary to understand it properly – also when it comes to the rules on evidence.[1]

1. A lawyer's procedure

5.003 Spanish procedure is, in general terms, a procedure meant to be used and driven by lawyers, not by lay people. Legal representation is mandatory if the value of the case exceeds 2000 euros.[2] In practice, however, it is frequent to have lawyers in cases where the amount at stake is lower. Historical tradition and the high rate of lawyers could be an explanation.[3] The procedural protagonism of lawyers allows the system to be demanding with the parties, also in evidentiary matters: many of the rules that will be discussed below, hard and rigid in appearance, become explicable when it is assumed that their real addressee is a lawyer, i.e., a person with legal knowledge and expert in the management of judicial proceedings.

2. The Spanish way to understand the principle of party disposition and judicial impartiality

5.004 Spanish civil procedure rests in a very intense manner on the principle of party disposition,[4] which is understood in a rather strict and rigid way, sometimes hard to explain to a foreign observer. This rigidity is especially visible regarding two issues.

5.005 a) On the one hand, the claimant bears the burden to identify not only the factual, but also the legal grounds sustaining the claim; as a consequence, the court is not allowed to change nor to amend them.[5] The *iura novit curia* principle, hence, has a narrow scope of application: the court may consider different legal provisions as those alleged by the

---

1 See A. De la Oliva Santos, 'Sobre la Ley 1/2000, de 7 de enero, de Enjuiciamiento Civil: criterios inspiradores e innovaciones principales', *Tribunales de Justicia*, 2000–2, pp. 127–141; A. de la Oliva Santos, *El papel del juez en el proceso civil* (Civitas, Madrid, 2012); J. Montero Aroca, *Los principios políticos de la nueva Ley de enjuiciamiento civil. Los poderes del juez y la oralidad* (Tirant lo Blanch, Valencia, 2001).

2 Article 31 LEC.

3 The number of practising lawyers in 2023 was over 153,000, for a population of around 49 million; this means more than 300 lawyers for every 100,000 persons, whereas there are only 12.1 judges per inhabitant or 27.3 lawyers per judge. This information has been retrieved from an official publication of the Spanish General Council of the Judiciary (Consejo General del Poder Judicial) appearing yearly, titled *La Justicia Dato a Dato – The Spanish Judiciary in figures*, published both in Spanish and in English. See https://www.poderjudicial.es/cgpj/es/Temas/Estadistica-Judicial/Estadistica-por-temas/Actividad-de-los-organos-judiciales/Juzgados-y-Tribunales/Justicia-Dato-a-Dato/ (accessed 30 November 2024). I have used the data that appear in the 2023 report.

4 Article 216 LEC.

5 Article 218.1 II LEC, Section VI of the preamble.

claimant, but the legal grounds (i.e., the legal perspective) cannot be altered.[6] As a consequence, for instance, a claimfor damages for damages founded on contract could not be granted by the court on the basis of tort. The real extent of this provision is still controversial in case law, since sometimes there is a very subtle border between different possible legal grounds (e.g., *culpa in eligendo* v. *culpa in vigilando* when attributing responsibility arising from the conduct of a third party or an employee). The same burden applies to the defendants' defences: except for the voidness or nullity of the contract,[7] especially in the case of unfair contract terms in consumer contracts, they cannot be appreciated *ex officio* by the court if they have not been timely alleged by the defendant.

b) On the other hand, when it comes to evidence, it is an exclusive prerogative of the parties to produce pieces of evidence and to propose the taking of evidence.[8] As a general rule the court is not empowered to order *sua sponte* the taking of evidence not previously proposed by a party; this possibility is only permitted in some family law procedures, where the interests of children are at stake, and in procedures on the capacity of natural persons[9] or in some procedures on patent law.[10] Outside those very limited fields, no *ex officio* taking of evidence is possible.[11] This legal decision might appear strange to other legal systems, especially when it comes to expertise – see, for instance, the situation in France or in Germany. The Spanish approach to this issue is based on a very strict notion of judicial impartiality: the judge would be favouring the position of one of the parties by doing so and he/she would also be compensating the lack of diligence of the lawyer in complying with the burden to propose evidence. An active role of the judge – always under the perspective of this strict notion of impartiality – could only be justified if one, or even both, parties are not legally represented; but this is a very rare situation under Spanish law, where, as mentioned above, legal representation is mandatory in cases above 2000 euros. 5.006

What the court may do, nevertheless, is suggesting what evidence not previously proposed by a party it sees to be relevant and useful. Pursuant to Article 429.1 LEC, during the preliminary hearing, if the court considers that the evidence put forward by the parties could turn out to be insufficient to clarify the facts at stake, it shall inform them, indicating the fact or facts which in its opinion could be affected by insufficient evidence. Upon making this statement, the court may also point out the evidence which it may deem appropriate, taking into consideration the evidentiary elements 5.007

---

6 On this issue, see A. De la Oliva Santos, *Objeto del proceso y cosa juzgada en el proceso civil* (Civitas, Madrid, 2005); I. Tapia Fernández, *Objeto del proceso. Alegaciones. Sentencia. Cosa juzgada* (La Ley, Madrid, 2000); G. Ormazabal Sánchez, *Iura novit curia* (Marcial Pons, Madrid-Barcelona, 2007).

7 See, for instance, judgment of the Civil Chamber of the Supreme Court No. 314/2016 of 12 May 2016.

8 Article 282 LEC.

9 Article 752 LEC.

10 Article 120.7 of the Spanish Patent Act.

11 The judgment of the Court of Appeal of Málaga (4th Division) No. 540/2013 of 23 October 2013, for instance, reverses the first instance judgment on the basis that it had been rendered assessing evidence taken by the court on its own motion (since the party that had initially proposed it had later withdrawn it).

whose existence is already reflected in the files of the procedure. If a party accepts that suggestion, the court will then order the taking of that evidence. This possibility raised some academic discussion at the time of the enactment of the LEC;[12] in practice, however, it is not very much used, since judges are not obliged to make recourse to it.[13]

5.008 In any event, the limited role of the judge in identifying and proposing evidence places a greater burden on the parties; and this, in turn, forces the system to make sufficient tools available to the parties to lift that burden. A system that places the burden on the parties to identify and bring evidence to the proceedings, but does not allow them access to it when it is not initially within their sphere of control, would not be fair.

3. Preclusion and procedural rigidity

5.009 A strong rule of preclusion is also one of the defining features of Spanish civil procedure, also leading to a very rigid development of the procedure.[14] The Code establishes a fixed track for each kind of procedure, as well as the timing and the deadlines for each of the pieces or elements of every procedure: the space left to wide case-management is therefore very small, and parties are not allowed to negotiate a development of proceedings that would deviate from what is legally established. Judicial mentality and judicial training help keeping this *status quo*: judges are not expected to be creative; and many lawyers are also used to this way of proceeding.[15] There is no real contestation of this in practice.

5.010 Preclusion, as already mentioned, is also very strong: the parties have the heavy burden to include all possible causes of action – i.e., contentions of fact and of law – in their first written pleadings; any contention which would have been possible at that time is precluded and will no longer be permitted at a subsequent stage of proceedings (not even at the appeal phase).[16] The same applies to the production of pre-existing evidence and to the proposal for the taking of personal evidence, also under strict preclusion rules. Obviously, fresh or freshly discovered facts, as well as fresh or freshly discovered evidence can be successfully included into the proceedings.[17] The purpose

---

12 See J.F. Etxeberria Guridi, *Las facultades judiciales en materia probatoria en la LEC* (Tirant lo Blanch, Valencia, 2003).

13 See, for instance, the judgments of the Superior Court of Justice of Catalonia (Civil and Criminal Chamber) No. 79/2012 of 17 December 2012; of the Court of Appeal of Barcelona (19th Division) No. 446/2011 of 17 October 2011; or of the Court of Appeal of Murcia (1st Division) No. 442/2009 of 6 October 2009.

14 See E. Vallines García, *La preclusión en el proceso civil* (Civitas, Madrid, 2004).

15 See G. Schumann Barragán, 'La gestión y la flexibilidad del procedimiento: ¿un proceso civil convergente con Europa?' in F. Gascón Inchausti, P. Peiteado Mariscal (eds.), *Estándares europeos y proceso civil* (Atelier, Barcelona, 2022) pp. 117–153.

16 Article 400 LEC.

17 Article 286 LEC.

of this rigid preclusion is twofold. On the one hand, it serves the goal of having all factual, legal and evidentiary elements of the dispute presented before the court of first instance at the very beginning, which should foster an early disposition of the dispute, since each one knows in advance all the 'weapons' in the hands of the opponent. On the other hand, it prevents the parties from keeping contentions and evidence from the proceedings, nor reserving them, as a sort of surprise, for advanced moments of the proceedings or for a superior court in the appeal phase and to force them to present their position in a clear and extensive manner.

These preclusion rules add further pressure on the parties to lift the burden of accessing relevant information and the evidence that can support it. Not only do they need access tools that are effective; they also need those tools to allow them access at an appropriate procedural time, that is, at a procedural time when the evidence eventually obtained can be used effectively. Here, it is desirable to have access to information and sources of evidence even before the claim is filed, so that what is alleged in the claim is consistent with the information and evidence available. Obtaining information and evidence when the process is already advanced may force the parties to modify their claims, something for which a rigid procedural model such as the Spanish one is not well prepared. **5.011**

4. Structure of first instance proceedings

The structure of declaratory proceedings in the first instance is rather simple. The parties will first submit their written statements of claim and of defence, where they will have to assert all legal and factual grounds to sustain their claims and defences. They have the burden to produce with their statements all relevant pre-existing pieces of evidence: documents, files, electronically stored information and written expertise prepared by experts appointed by each one.[18] The parties are then summoned to a preliminary hearing (*audiencia previa al juicio*), to try to reach a settlement, to solve procedural problems, to delineate the scope of the proceedings and to propose evidence and decide on the evidence to be taken. A very active involvement and management from the judge is expected at this stage. Finally, a trial (*juicio*) will ordinarily be celebrated a month after the closing of the preliminary hearing, where evidence will be taken and parties will submit final conclusions on the case. In exceptional cases, evidence that could not be taken during the trial will be taken separately, before judgment is given (*diligencias finales*). **5.012**

The development of proceedings expresses a classical combination between written and oral activities. The pleadings will always have to be presented in writing. From **5.013**

18 Article 265 LEC.

that point on, the procedure becomes oral and concentrated to ensure immediacy and direct contact of the judge with the evidence. The principle of immediacy is granted the highest qualification as a procedural safeguard: it is compulsory for the judge to be present at the hearings and only the judge who attended the hearing will be entitled to give judgment; the infringement of the rules on immediacy will lead to the nullity – totally or partially – of the proceedings.[19]

5.014 If the value of the case does not exceed 15,000 euros, as well as for some specific matters,[20] the procedural track is simplified (*juicio verbal*): the deadline to present the written answer to the claim is reduced to 10 days and the preliminary hearing is replaced by a written exchange of pleadings on procedural issues and on the proposal of evidence. Admitted evidence will be taken at a hearing (*vista*), which will not necessarily take place.

5. A comprehensive regulation of evidence

5.015 The overriding aim to enhance the quality of first instance decisions can only be reached if the judge gets the best possible knowledge of the relevant facts. A poor regulation of evidence, or shortcomings in practice, may lead to judgments based on an incorrect assessment of the facts; and this will certainly frustrate the legitimate expectations of litigants, entitled to assume that the system grants the parties and the judge proper tools to cope with the factual issues of every proceeding. The right to evidence is considered an essential part of the right to effective judicial protection, enshrined in Article 24 of the Spanish Constitution, in terms equivalent to Article 6.1 ECHR or Article 47 CFREU.[21] Access to evidence, which is instrumental to the right to evidence, therefore has equivalent constitutional dimension and deserves equivalent constitutional protection.

5.016 The Spanish LEC deals with civil evidence in a comprehensive and systematic way:[22] the core of the regulation is to be found in Articles 281 to 386 LEC; other provisions, scattered along the LEC, also deal with evidentiary matters (e.g., the rule on the burden of proof, included with those addressing the internal requirements of judicial decisions; or the rules on the taking of evidence in the second instance). The rules are common and general, i.e., they are not associated with specific types of procedure or

---

19 Article 137 LEC.

20 Article 250 LEC.

21 See, among others, the following Judgments of the Spanish Constitutional Court: STC 107/2019, of 30 September; STC 91/2021, of 22 April; STC 121/2021, of 2 June; STC 45/2022, of 23 March; STC 47/2022, of 24 March; STC 46/2022, of 30 March; STC 119/2022, of 20 September.

22 See also F. López Simó, F. Alba Cladera, *Disposiciones generales sobre la prueba en el proceso civil. Estudio breve de los artículos 281 a 298 y concordantes de la Ley de Enjuiciamiento Civil* (La Ley, Madrid, 2019).

with specific courts. Indeed, they apply in a subsidiary manner also to administrative and labour proceedings. It is also necessary to have in mind that in Spain there is no jury in civil matters: the rules on evidence have been designed for professional judges – and for lawyers.

There is not a general provision addressing the *evaluation of evidence*; the LEC deals with this issue separately for each specific type of evidence. The criterion that prevails is free evaluation of the evidence by the judge, subject to an important requirement of motivation. There are, however, certain types of evidence whose evaluation is not free: public deeds and non-contested private documents,[23] and the examination of a counterparty, in case she would admit personal facts prejudicial to her claims.[24] This special evidentiary value of documents makes access to them essential for anyone who does not have them in their possession. **5.017**

The notion of *standard of proof* is not commonly used by the law or by case law:[25] the rule is that a contested issue of fact is proven when the court is convinced of its truth, assuming that 'full' conviction is only an ideal, but also that the degree of conviction reached should be as close to full conviction as possible. The standard is therefore high and more demanding than what would be required by a 'balance of probabilities' (i.e., the judge considering more probable the existence of a fact than its non-existence). This makes it particularly relevant to have evidence of 'quality', even though it is often in the possession of the opposing party. **5.018**

Article 217 LEC establishes the rules on the *burden of proof*. In case of doubt on a relevant fact, the court must decide to the detriment of the party having the burden to prove a doubtful issue of fact (burden of proof in its material sense). The plaintiff, therefore, bears the burden of proving the facts sustaining the claim, whereas the defendant is responsible for proving the facts that support the defences (burden of proof in a formal sense). Some specific criteria alleviate a strict application of these rules, namely those of evidential proximity and facility, which can be used by the judge to distribute the burden of proof by attributing to each of the parties the burden to prove facts which, in principle, are 'closer' to them and, therefore, 'easier' to prove. Alleviations and reversals of the burden of the proof are established also in certain matters, like consumer protection, product liability, unfair competition, illegal **5.019**

23 Articles 319 and 326 LEC.

24 Article 316 LEC.

25 See, on this, E. Vallines García, 'Evaluation of evidence by the Spanish civil courts' in K. Makridou, G. Diamantopoulos (eds.), *Evidence in Spanish and Greek Procedural Law* (Sakkoulas, Athens-Thessaloniki, 2018) pp. 106–108 (available online at https://iaplaw.org/images/PDF/Greek-and-foreign_Vol.-4.pdf).

advertising or gender discrimination.[26] These rules on burden of proof also have an impact on access to evidence: it is not uncommon that alleviations and reversals are foreseen for the benefit of the party suffering from an information asymmetry, i.e. the party who may have difficulties in proving certain facts to their advantage, especially if that party is perceived or treated by the law as vulnerable. In such cases, the rule on burden of proof may reduce the need to resort to tools of access to sources of evidence – or it may place the burden of resorting to such tools on the party who has to overcome the consequences of the special rule.

5.020 Finally, Spanish law has opted for a strict exclusionary rule regarding *illegally obtained evidence*, i.e., evidence obtained infringing, directly or indirectly, a fundamental right.[27] A typical example would occur if the plaintiff seeks to provide as a basis for a claim some images recorded inside the domicile of the defendant without their consent; or produces a letter or an electronic message addressed by a non-party to the defendant that the claimant had detained or hacked (evidence obtained, then, infringing the defendant's fundamental right of privacy). The legal reaction against illegally obtained evidence is clear and direct: such evidence will have no evidentiary value and must be excluded from the proceedings. This strict exclusionary rule is associated with the will of the lawmaker to grant a reinforced protection to fundamental rights: there will be no room for any balance of interests at stake, not even with the fundamental right to evidence. There is at this point a relevant divergence between the Spanish legal system and the more flexible approach that prevails in other legal systems and namely in the case law of the European Court of Human Rights[28] and of the Court of Justice of the European Union.[29] This, again, has its consequences with regard to access to sources of evidence: the difficulty of 'legally' accessing a source of evidence cannot be considered as an exceptional circumstance that could justify the acceptance, in a specific case, of illegal evidence. And this, in turn, increases the pressure on the system, which has to offer access tools that take into account that there is no possible alternative.

---

26 G. Ormazabal Sánchez, 'Facilitaciones probatorias y acceso a las fuentes de prueba en el proceso civil' in J.M. Asencio Mellado (dir.), *Derecho probatorio y otros estudios procesales* (Ediciones Jurídicas Castillo de Luna, Madrid, 2020) pp. 1481–1495, G. Ormazabal Sánchez, *Discriminación y carga de la prueba en el proceso civil* (Marcial Pons, Madrid-Barcelona, 2011).

27 Article 11.1 of the Organic Act on the Judiciary. On this, See F. Gascón Inchausti, 'La prueba ilícita en el proceso civil, entre la exclusión y la ponderación' in J.M. Asencio Mellado (dir.), *Derecho probatorio y otros estudios procesales* (Ediciones Jurídicas Castillo de Luna, Madrid, 2020) pp. 783–800.

28 See ECtHR 10 October 2006, *L.L. v. France*, appl. no 7508/02; ECtHR 13 May 2008, *N.N.and T.A. v. Belgium*, appl. no 65097/01.

29 See the above mentioned ECJ ruling in the *Peter Puškár* case (C-73/16, judgment of 27 September 2017, ECLI:EU:C:2017:725).

6. Identification, production and proposal of evidence in first instance proceedings

The legal regulation on evidence draws a very important distinction between 'pre-existing evidence' and 'personal evidence'. The notion of 'pre-existing evidence' describes documents and equivalent pieces of evidence, like expert reports, pen drives, CDs or other supports of electronically stored information. In a certain way, their existence is autonomous from the procedure, i.e., they need to be introduced in it. On the other hand, it is usual to refer as 'personal evidence' those types of evidence that are created in the procedure itself: this is the case of the examination of parties, witnesses and expert witnesses, as well as judicial inspections, since they can only exist as such in the framework of an ongoing procedure, with the common intervention of the court and the parties. Against this background, the parties have different burdens regarding the identification and the production of the evidence in their possession. **5.021**

Pre-existing evidence has to be identified and produced by each party with their written statements of claim and defence.[30] This means that claim and defence will have to be accompanied by (i) all relevant documents that each party intends to use as evidence in support of their claim, (ii) any means to record sounds and images, (iii) any electronically stored information and (iv) the reports drafted by party-appointed experts.[31] This burden refers only to the evidence that each party intends to use in support of their own position. There is no duty to identify all the evidence available in relation to the dispute, including that which might benefit the other party. Lack of compliance with this requirement entails preclusion: the evidence will not be admissible at any later stage of the procedure.[32] In addition, production of evidence with the statements of claim and defence does not necessarily mean that this evidence will be admitted and evaluated by the court: each party has to propose formally the admission at the preliminary hearing. The preclusion rule only covers, obviously, documents and other pre-existing evidence which were already in the possession of the party or, at least, which were known to the party. Article 270 LEC establishes different means of flexibility, allowing the parties to produce documents at a later stage in the following situations: (i) documents created after the moment the party filed the claim or the defence, provided that it had not been possible for them to draft them prior to those moments; (ii) documents dated prior to the moment the party filed the claim or the defence, if the party submitting them later justifies not having been aware of their existence before; (iii) documents that the party was not able to obtain for reasons not attributable to her, **5.022**

30 Article 265 LEC.

31 In the current context of e-Justice and 'zero paper' policy, the production of pre-existing evidence will have to be performed electronically, so documents in paper will have to be scanned.

32 Articles 269 and 272 LEC.

provided that the party had mentioned them in her statement of claim or defence and had announced that she would submit them as soon as she could have access to them.

5.023 As for expert evidence, the ways to make the preclusion rule more flexible are in line with those just described for documents. Under Spanish law, two different approaches to expert evidence co-exist: expertise provided by party-appointed experts[33] and expertise provided by court-appointed experts.[34] Each party is free to choose if she will appoint any suitable expert or if she prefers the court to appoint one from a list in the possession of the court. Party-appointed experts offer the advantages of 'free market': the party chooses the expert and, of course, the report will only be produced if it is favourable; the risk, obviously, is that those experts may appear biased to the court, thus diminishing the probative weight of their reports. If a party has decided to use expertise provided by an expert appointed by her, then she will have to produce the report together with her written statement of claim or defence. The case may appear, however, that the party claims that she has had not sufficient time to produce the report: e.g., the report is complicated to elaborate and expiration of time limits is threatening; the situation is easier to imagine in the case of the defendant, who is always granted a fixed deadline to submit their written statement of defence, which may be insufficient to prepare an accurate expert report. In such case, the party may announce in her written statement that an expert report will follow, provided that it is submitted to the counterparty at least five days in advance to the date of the preliminary hearing.[35]

5.024 If the party prefers to have the report drafted by an expert appointed by the court, then she will have to ask for it in her written statement of claim or defence;[36] once the deadline to submit the statement of defence has expired the court will identify the expertise required timely by the parties and will appoint as many experts as necessary, who will be required to present their reports within a deadline established by the court.[37] Preclusion operates also with regard to the timely request to the court to appoint an expert.

5.025 In both cases, for party-appointed and court-appointed experts, the need to have recourse to expert evidence may appear at a later moment, i.e., after the party has submitted her claim or defence; this may happen namely when such need of a report arises in view of the contentions of fact stated by the defendant in his/her statement of defence or by any of the parties at the preliminary hearing. In that case, the parties are

---

33 Article 337 LEC.
34 Article 339 LEC.
35 Again, Article 337 LEC.
36 Again, Article 339 LEC.
37 Article 346 LEC.

granted an opportunity to announce party-appointed expert reports or to require the appointment of an expert by the court.[38]

To sum up with 'pre-existing' evidence: (i) documents, audio and video records, electronically stored information and reports drafted by party-appointed experts will be ordinarily produced with the claim or with the defence; (ii) they will have to be expressly proposed as evidence at the preliminary hearing; (iii) the appointment by the court of experts has to be sought in the claim or in the defence; (iv) exoneration from preclusion is admissible when new facts or new evidence appear or are known to the party at a later moment. **5.026**

This duty to provide pre-existing evidence at an early stage has a clear consequence: it is important to be able to access it before the claim is filed, something that must be taken into account in the regulation of the measures of access to sources of evidence. In particular, it is important to gain access to the material elements on the basis of which, if necessary, the expert report is to be drawn up, which, in turn, has to be submitted with the claim. **5.027**

The rules are different when it comes to 'personal' evidence, i.e., examination of parties, of witnesses and of expert witnesses, and judicial inspection, since there is here no pre-existing element to produce and to introduce into the records. Identification of these types of evidence is not necessary at the first stages of the procedure: witnesses do not need to be mentioned in the written statements of claim and defence; the parties do not need either to announce in their first contentions their intention to examine the counterparty or any witness or expert witness, nor to perform judicial inspection. Identification and proposal are left to the preliminary hearing: at this stage each party has to propose formally all relevant evidence she wants to use[39] and provide the whereabouts of the witnesses she intends to examine.[40] **5.028**

Expert evidence presents here a singular situation of duplicity. As a general rule, expert reports are presented in writing – like documents – and in most cases this may be sufficient for the court to assess them: they are treated, hence, as pre-existing evidence. However, namely when each party has appointed her own experts, they may have an interest in the expert being examined – and cross-examined – before the court, in order to increase the probative value of their reports or to diminish the value of the counterparty's one: the rules on personal evidence, therefore, would apply. The court can also on its own motion summon any expert who is the author of any of the **5.029**

38 Article 427 LEC.
39 Article 429.1 LEC.
40 Article 284 LEC.

produced reports to appear during the trial or the main hearing, when it considers it necessary to a better understanding and evaluation of the written report. It is a very limited *ex officio* power, which is considered instrumental to the court's duty to perform a reasonable understanding of evidence as a logical basis for a reasonable evaluation.

5.030 These rules on personal evidence also have consequences regarding access to sources of evidence: even if witness evidence is proposed later, it may be necessary to know at an early stage whether there are witnesses to any relevant facts. If information regarding the identity of such persons is in the possession of the opposing party or third parties, access measures become, again, of utmost importance.

B. PROCEDURAL MECHANISMS ENABLING ACCESS TO INFORMATION AND TO EVIDENCE

5.031 These general rules allocating the burden of proof to the parties and imposing on them strict and preclusive time frames to identify and produce pre-existing pieces of evidence from the outset are based on the assumption that they have had previous access to the sources of evidence, i.e., to the documents (in a wide sense), objects, persons (e.g.,witnesses) and information which will formally be used later as evidence. In other words, the parties are expected to know who the witnesses are they may want to examine; or to have access to the documents or files they may want to produce for evidentiary purposes.

5.032 Consequently, a more or less general regulation could be expected which, in development of the fundamental right to evidence, would establish mechanisms of access to information and sources of evidence in the possession of the opposing party, the potential opposing party or third parties. Unfortunately, when the LEC was drafted the belief still prevailed in the Spanish legal and procedural mentality that a subject could not be compelled to collaborate with the opposing party by providing them with those means of evidence that could be detrimental to the party's position.[41]

5.033 Therefore, the regulation adopted in 2000 was based on a simple rule: it is the parties' burden to procure themselves access to the relevant information and to the sources of evidence, since it belongs to the most elementary procedural strategy to found the

41 The non-cooperative party, at most, risked the consequences of the judge, in the judgment, applying the rules on the burden of proof taking into account the standard of proof, i.e., taking into account which of the parties has the easier burden of proof to prove a fact or to rebut a possible presumption.

claims or defences only on facts that the parties can reasonably expect to establish as true.

In line with this general rule, the LEC did not regulate general mechanisms through which parties can get access to the sources of evidence.[42] The lawmaker at this point assumed that each party will have to make use of any possible means available to them, provided that they are legal – otherwise, the strict exclusionary rule will apply. 5.034

However, two tools were foreseen which, although incomplete and not very well articulated, allowed, in some cases and under certain conditions, access to evidence that was not initially under the litigant's control: the so-called 'preliminary measures' and the 'requests for the production of documents', which I will deal with shortly. 5.035

Outside the LEC – even before its approval – the mentality was partially different regarding patent law, where 'fact-finding measures' (*diligencias de comprobación de hechos*) which granted access to internal information of a potential defendant, had been incorporated into Spanish law as early as 1986 due to the influence of supranational legislation. 5.036

After the enactment of the LEC, it has been the influence of European law that has led to a certain evolution. The transposition of the 2004 IP Rights Directive in 2006[43] expanded the catalogue of preliminary measures and requests for production of documents and contributed, albeit perhaps to a limited extent, to changing the mentality. The turning point came a decade later with the transposition of the 2014 Directive on competition damages claims. The transposition of the 2020 Directive on representative actions and of the recent 2024 Directive on due diligence will certainly put the focus back on this issue. 5.037

1. Preliminary measures (*diligencias preliminares*)

Under the generic name of 'preliminary measures' (*diligencias preliminaries*), Articles 256 to 263 LEC[44] establish a system that can be used by prospective claimants in 5.038

---

42 See G. Ormazabal Sánchez, 'La investigación en el proceso civil. Hacia una nueva ordenación de los mecanismos de averiguación de hechos y de obtención de fuentes de prueba', *Revista de la Asociación de Profesores de Derecho Procesal de las Universidades Españolas*, núm. 1, 2020.

43 Directive 2004/48/EC of the European Parliament and of the Council of 29 April 2004 on the enforcement of intellectual property rights (OJ L 157, 30.4.2004). It was incorporated into Spanish law through Law 19/2006, of 5 June, which extends the means of protection of intellectual and industrial property rights and establishes procedural rules to facilitate the application of various Community regulations.

44 See J. Banacloche Palao, *Las diligencias preliminares* (Civitas, Madrid, 2003); R. Castrillo Santamaría, *La preparación del proceso civil: las diligencias preliminares* (J.M. Bosch, Barcelona, 2018).

order to prepare their claims, gathering with the assistance of the court some information and, sometimes, some sources of evidence which could be necessary to prepare a future claim. This information can relate to two main types of questions:

- Who has standing to be sued, i.e., against whom the claim must be directed.
- Certain basic facts, the knowledge and identification of which are necessary for the claim to succeed.

5.039 The LEC uses here a *numerus clausus* system, i.e., the prospective claimant is only entitled to apply for a number of possible measures, specifically addressed by Article 256 that can in turn help gathering certain pieces of information. Specifically, these are the following:

5.040 a) Statement of the party against whom the claim may be lodged on a fact concerning his/her capacity, representation or standing that might be relevant for the litigation, and/or exhibition of the documents proving such capacity, representation or standing. This measure can be used to find out, for example, whether one person is the successor or legal representative of another, or whether there are several persons involved in the legal relationship in dispute.

5.041 b) Exhibition of the thing in the possession of the prospective defendant to which the litigation will be referred. Particularly when a claim for possession of a movable thing is brought, the passive standing corresponds to the person who possesses the thing; a claim against a different person would be unsuccessful. This measure makes it possible to ascertain that the person believed to be in the possession of the thing really has it, as well as to verify its state of conservation (e.g., for the purpose of claiming compensation for any damage or deterioration caused to it).

5.042 c) An individual considering himself/herself to be an heir, a co-heir or a legatee may request the exhibition of the deed of last will of the testator.

5.043 d) A partner or co-owner may request for the documents and accounts of the partnership or community to be produced. Thus, for example, if a partner wants to claim the payment of dividends in court, he will need to know the company's profit and loss account.

5.044 e) A person who considers themself injured by an event that could be covered by civil liability insurance may request the exhibition of the insurance contract by whoever has it in his possession. Indeed, under Spanish law, if there is an insurance contract, the claim may be directed directly against the insurance company, rather than against the insured, or against both jointly.[45]

5.045 f) A prospective claimant may request access to their medical records that are in the custody of a health centre or professional.

5.046 g) A consumer association seeking to bring proceedings for the defence of the collective interests of consumers may apply to the court for the purpose of identifying the members of the group of affected persons where they are not determined but can be easily ascertained. This type of request has, on some occasions, been confronted with the allegation

45 Article 76 of Act 50/1980 on insurance contract.

by the requested party that the provision of this information may violate the rules on the protection of personal data.[46]

h) As implementation of Directive 2004/48 on the protection of IP rights, a prospective claimant may request access to information and documents related to a possible infringement, including, e.g., identification of producers, manufacturers, distributors, suppliers, providers of goods and services; amounts produced, manufactured, delivered, received or ordered; exhibition of bank, financial, commercial or customs documents; identification by internet services providers of a user who is apparently infringing IP rights.[47] **5.047**

Although the list may appear to be long, the fact is that it comprises only very specific situations and receives in practice a restrictive interpretation.[48] Thus, for example, it is common to try to use the second measure – i.e., the exhibition of the thing to which the litigation is referred – to obtain evidentiary documents in the possession of the opposing party, but this has been almost unanimously rejected, as the document is not the 'thing' to which the litigation will refer.[49] It is not, therefore, an ordinary means to have access to information and evidence that may be necessary for a proper definition of the procedural strategy of the parties. **5.048**

In addition to its limited scope, its procedural regime also fails to ensure maximum effectiveness of these preliminary measures. **5.049**

When requesting a preliminary measure, it is necessary to identify, as far as possible, the matter that will constitute the scope of the proceedings to be prepared, so that the court can assess the appropriateness of the request. Even if the applicant is not yet in a position to fully identify the claim – that is why they ask for a preliminary measure – it is reasonable to require them to make an effort to specify the potential core of their hypothetical claim. **5.050**

---

46 See Judgment of the Constitutional Court 96/2012, of 7 May 2012 (ECLI:ES:TC:2012:96). A consumer association, which intended to bring collective proceedings against a bank for misselling of financial products, requested from the bank the lists of customers who had contracted these products. The bank resisted on the grounds that the measure was disproportionate and compromised its customers' right to data protection. The lower court's decision to grant the measure eventually reached the Constitutional Court, which annulled it on the grounds that no proportionality test had been carried out that could justify the sacrifice of the right to data protection of customers for the sake of the effective judicial protection of the beneficiaries of the collective action.

47 See J. Massaguer Fuentes, *Acciones y procesos de infracción de derechos de propiedad industrial* (Aranzadi, Madrid, 2020) pp. 218–231; M. Cantos Pardo, *El proceso civil para la cesación de la infracción de patentes* (Tirant lo Blanch, Valencia, 2023) pp. 252–267; J. López Sánchez, 'Las nuevas diligencias preliminares en materia de propiedad intelectual y propiedad industrial: el denominado "derecho de información" y la exhibición de documentos comerciales', *Diario La Ley*, núm. 6429, 2006; A. Armengot Vilaplana, 'Las nuevas diligencias preliminares y las normas sobre prueba en materia de propiedad intelectual e industrial', *Diario La Ley*, núm. 6819, 2007.

48 Decision of the Spanish Supreme Court of 11 November 2002 (ECLI:ES:TS:2002:3037A).

49 See, among many others, the decisions of the Provincial Courts of Barcelona (19 January 2010), Madrid (23 July 2010) or Seville (30 September 2010).

5.051 Upon receipt of the application, the court shall decide whether or not to grant it, without hearing the party against whom it has been made. If the request is granted, the interested parties will be summoned for its implementation.

5.052 Compliance with a preliminary measure may have a cost for the person who has to take part in it. According to Article 256.3 LEC, such costs shall be borne by the applicant. Therefore, the court will require the applicant to provide security for the costs of the measure and for any additional damages that may be caused to the requested persons if the applicant does not bring proceedings within a period of one month after implementation – even if the applicant, in view of the results of the preliminary measure, comes to the conclusion that the claim is not viable. The law does not allow the applicant to obtain reimbursement of these costs, even if he or she eventually brings a claim and wins the case.

5.053 The requested party may either voluntarily comply with the measure or oppose it. The grounds for opposition are not specified in the law. In practice they are usually of two types, factual and legal. It is often argued that the order cannot be complied with because the requested information or documentation is not available. But it is also common for the refusal to be justified on the grounds of the confidential nature of the information or documentation requested.

5.054 When the requested party does oppose, an adversarial procedure will take place, after which the court will have to decide whether to uphold the measure or to lift it. If the court upholds the measure (or if there was no opposition), the measure will be enforced at the place and at the time specified by the court: documents or things will be exhibited; or a statement will be taken from the prospective defendant on facts concerning their capacity, representation or standing; a remote implementation is possible for the exhibition of documents and equivalents.

5.055 There is also a special rule on the usability of the information obtained by means of the measures provided for the protection of intellectual and industrial property rights: it may not be used for any purpose other than to seek judicial protection of the rights that gave rise to the request, and it may not be disclosed or communicated to third parties.

5.056 In the event of a refusal to comply, the consequences vary depending on the content of the measure that has been ordered:

5.057 a) If a statement has been requested on facts relating to the capacity, representation or standing of the summoned person, the questions that the applicant intends to put to them may be deemed to have been answered in the affirmative and the relevant facts will be deemed to be admitted for the purposes of the subsequent proceedings. The sanction may provide a clear procedural advantage, but it is not automatic and in practice it is difficult to implement: it is not easy to hold a person liable for damage simply because they have not agreed to produce a document that would prove their passive standing in the framework of preliminary measures, especially if during the subsequent proceedings the defendant provides evidence to the contrary or if the plaintiff is not in a position to provide any additional evidence.

b) If the production of documents has been requested and the court considers that there is sufficient indication that they can be found in a particular place, it shall order the entry and search of that place so that, if they are found, they can be made available to the applicant.[50] **5.058**

c) The same shall be done if it is a question of the production of a thing and the place where it is to be found is known or well suspected; the applicant may, in addition, request, as a protective measure, its custody in order to ensure its preservation during the course of the proceedings. **5.059**

d) If the production of accounting documents has been requested, the accounts and data submitted by the applicant may be deemed to be true for the purposes of the subsequent proceedings. **5.060**

5.061 As can be seen, the level of enforceability is inevitably low, as it is strongly conditioned by the circumstances of the specific case. The law provides certain means to achieve the maximum possible effectiveness, such as entry and search. But if they do not work, the position of the litigant interested in obtaining the information and evidence is not a comfortable one: going into the proceedings without evidence is risky, even with the expectation of an adverse inference, the real impact of which cannot be known until the proceedings are completed.

2. Requests for the production of documents held by the opposing party or a third party (*deber de exhibición documental*)

5.062 The second general tool foreseen to try to mitigate the asymmetry of information in civil proceedings is the duty to produce documents imposed on the parties and third parties in Articles 328 to 332 LEC (*deber de exhibición documental*).[51]

5.063 The general rule is stated very broadly: each party may request the other parties and third parties to produce those documents that relate to the subject matter of the proceedings or to the effectiveness of the means of evidence; and they, of course, have the duty to comply with this request. This formulation would suggest that we are dealing

---

50 The search will be performed by officers of the court, with the assistance of the police, where necessary.

51 See S. Pereira Puigvert, *La exhibición de documentos y soportes informáticos en el proceso civil* (Aranzadi, Cizur Menor, 2013). See also Judgment of the Provincial Court of Palencia (Section 1) núm. 186/2024 [ECLI: ES:APP:2024:295]; Provincial Court of Badajoz (Section 3) 268/2024 [ECLI: ES:APBA:2024:1343]; and Provincial Court of Madrid (Section 25) 333/2024 [ECLI: ES:APM:2024:12322].

with a duty equivalent to that which justifies American discovery or English disclosure. The reality, however, is somewhat more disappointing. Let us see why:

5.064 a) The request must be accompanied by a simple copy of the document to be produced, if such a copy exists and is available; if not, the content of the document must be indicated in the most exact terms possible. This is a requirement designed precisely to avoid the implementation of the American discovery rules and also to prevent very open or generic requests from being made: documents whose existence is known may be requested, but not fishing expeditions. However, a copy of the document will not always be available and, above all, it will not always be easy to identify the document in question, especially when the opposing party denies the very existence of the document requested. In practice it is common to try to make broad discovery requests, e.g., by asking for copies of e-mails between certain dates. But such requests are not always considered to reach a sufficient level of precision.

5.065 b) The LEC does not indicate the appropriate procedural moment to request the production of documents. As Article 328 speaks of 'parties', the interpretation has been consolidated that the proceedings must already be underway and that it is not, therefore, a request that can be made prior to their commencement. This limits effectiveness, as it does not serve to properly prepare the proceedings, but only to obtain a document that corroborates or proves information that is considered to be certain and on which the procedural strategy has been built. In practice, however, the information deduced from the documents obtained in this way may be different from what the litigant had guessed or thought they knew. And this forces the party to modify their claim at a later stage, something that is not at all easy in a rigid and preclusive procedural model such as the Spanish one. In any case, it would be reasonable to understand that this request for production must be made before the time at which the possibility of producing the document in question would lapse, if it were in the possession of the interested party. In practice, however, this type of request is made directly at the pre-trial hearing (*audiencia previa al juicio*); at that moment, once the request has been made, the court may endorse it, so that what was initially a request between the parties becomes a court order for production.

5.066 c) The law only allows for an exhibition of the document, i.e., for the interested party to see and examine it, but not its delivery to the applicant. If the requested party complies with the request but is unwilling to part with the document, the court clerk will make a copy.[52] This rule is designed for physical documents. Its adaptation to electronic documents should lead to allowing their viewing, but not their downloading.

5.067 d) The production of documents may entail costs for the requested party, but the law is silent on this point – perhaps because the law is thinking of the production of a small number of easily traceable documents. Although these measures are granted in the framework of a pending procedure, their cost does not seem to be reimbursable to the litigant who finally wins, as they are not included in the list of items eligible for reimbursement (Article 241 LEC).

5.068 e) The law makes no provision for the possibility for the requested party to oppose production or, consequently, the possible valid reasons for such opposition. In practice, refusal is often justified on the grounds that the requested document does not exist or that, in any

52 Article 332 LEC.

case, the requested party does not have it in its possession. It is then up to the court to assess the credibility of these assertions. In other cases, the confidentiality of the document is invoked. Here again, Spanish civil procedural law does not contain a list of cases in which a document – or the information contained in it – is to be considered confidential. Some substantive rules recognise this: this is the case, e.g., with documents reflecting the professional relationship between lawyer and client,[53] with medical records[54] or with trade secrets. But unless the law gives the privilege an absolute value, it is up to the court to weigh up in a specific case whether the right to evidence of the party requesting the disclosure or the rights underpinning confidentiality should prevail. In the event that it agrees to the disclosure of a confidential document, the court is entitled to agree on ancillary measures to ensure the preservation of confidentiality. The catalogue of measures, however, is not unique, but depends on the context and is particularly developed for trade secrets due to the transposition of the 2016 Directive.[55]

f) If the requested party unreasonably refuses production, the court, taking into account the other evidence, may attribute evidentiary value to the simple copy submitted when applying for production and also to the version given by the applicant of the content of the document. This rule, however, does not apply automatically and is only clearly useful when the litigant at least possesses a simple copy; when he/she does not have such a copy, it is not easy to imagine which version of the content of the document would be the one to attribute evidentiary value to, especially when the requested party categorically denies the existence of the document or that the document is in his/her possession. Therefore, this consequence will only be operative when the court comes to the conclusion that the document exists and that the party requested to produce it does not want to do so, despite being in possession of it.[56] Beyond such an adverse inference, it is not clear in the law what the court can do in the event that its request is not complied with; an analogy with what is laid down for preliminary measures could sustain the possibility for the court to order entry and search – in principle, by officers of the court, with the assistance of the police, if this turns out to be necessary. The system is therefore at odds with any similarity with the feared US-style fishing expeditions. **5.069**

g) Where documents are in the possession of third parties, the duty to cooperate is lesser. In principle, third parties will only be requested to produce documents in their possession if the court considers that knowledge of them is 'of fundamental importance' to give judgment – a higher standard than that required for agreeing the production of documents between parties, for which it is sufficient that the document 'relates to the subject matter of the proceedings or to the effectiveness of the evidence'. **5.070**

---

53 Article 16 of Organic Act 5/2024 on the right of defence.

54 Article 16 of Act 41/2002, of 14 November regulating patient autonomy and the rights and obligations regarding clinical information and documentation.

55 On this see F. Gascón Inchausti, 'Las medidas para la protección de los secretos empresariales en el proceso civil: el problema de su efectividad', *Revista de la Asociación de Profesores de Derecho Procesal de las Universidades Españolas*, Nº 10, 2024, pp. 9–57 (available online at https://apdpue.es/wp-content/uploads/2025/01/Revista-APDPUE-10.pdf). For a broader study of confidentiality in civil proceedings, see G. Schumann Barragán, *Información confidencial y proceso civil. Las inmunidades procesales en materia probatoria* (Atelier, Barcelona, 2025).

56 The non-application of adverse inference may justify the filing of an appeal against the judgment. However, the Supreme Court has recently pointed out that, to this end, it is necessary for the party to insist on its request for production at later stages of the proceedings (Judgment of 6 March 2024, ECLI:ES:TS:2024:1385).

5.071 Where appropriate, the court will order the personal appearance of the third party who has the documents in his or her possession and, after hearing him or her, will decide whether or not they should be asked to produce them.[57] The problem is that the refusal of the third party to produce the documents does not have the same consequences as the refusal of the opposing party. A possible entry and search of the third party's premises could be justified on the basis of the general duty to cooperate with the administration of justice, enshrined in Article 118 of the Spanish Constitution. However, taking the version of the document provided by the party requesting the disclosure as true may be somewhat excessive, at least in principle, because the conduct of a third party should not harm a litigant; however, in many cases there are links between the requested third party and the party that would be harmed by the disclosure (e.g., they are companies belonging to the same corporate group).

5.072 In the special case where the third party is a public body, it may not refuse to issue the certifications requested by the courts, nor object to the production of any documents held in its premises and archives (exception: in the case of state secrets and highly confidential information). This obligation extends to entities and companies that perform public services.[58]

5.073 It should be noted, on the other hand, that the implementation in Spain of the 2004 Directive on IP rights was not only carried out by extending the catalogue of preliminary measures (as seen above), but also by using this tool: Article 328.3 LEC makes it clear that, in proceedings for infringement of an industrial property right or an intellectual property right, committed on a commercial scale, the request for production may include banking, financial, commercial or customs documents produced in a certain period of time and which are presumed to be in the possession of the defendant. In such cases, the request must be accompanied by prima facie evidence, such as the production of specimens, goods or products in which the infringement has materialised.

3. Evidence preservation measures

5.074 Articles 297 and 298 LEC regulate the mechanisms for the securing or the preservation of evidence, 'to avoid that, due to human conduct or natural events, which may destroy or alter material objects or states of things, it is impossible, when the time comes, to take relevant evidence or even pointless to propose it' (Article 297.1 LEC). At the time the LEC was passed (2000), the legislator was probably thinking of physical objects to be subject to judicial inspection or to be taken as a basis for

57 Article 330.1 LEC.
58 Article 332 LEC.

the preparation of an expert opinion. But measures can also be used to prevent the destruction of documents and, in particular, for the preservation of information in electronic form.

These measures can be requested both before and during the course of the proceedings, subject to verification that the evidence to be secured or preserved is relevant and useful, at least at the time when it is proposed to secure it. In cases of urgency or where there are indications of bad faith, they may be granted without hearing the person who must bear the burden of securing the evidence. **5.075**

Although the law regulates them autonomously, it is clear that these measures can be connected with prior measures of access to sources of evidence: in some cases, they can be requested and agreed in a complementary manner – as was seen above, in fact, with regard to the preliminary measure consisting of the exhibition of a movable thing; in other cases, an access measure can be the necessary instrument to make the securing of evidence possible. **5.076**

4. Two additional (but 'minor') tools

Preliminary measures and requests for the production of documents are the basic mechanisms for access to sources of evidence at present, except for what will be seen below for certain special sectors. Alongside them, and also on a general level, the LEC has two additional provisions rules which, in theory, may also be used to force one of the parties to collaborate in the opposing party's access to evidence. **5.077**

Regarding expert evidence, the provisions of Article 336.5 LEC must be taken into account, granting access to information in order to prepare the expert report. At the request of a party, the court or tribunal may order that the defendant be permitted to examine, through a lawyer or expert, the things and places whose condition and circumstances are relevant to their defence or to the preparation of the expert reports that they intend to submit. Likewise, in the case of claims for personal injury, the court or tribunal may order the plaintiff to allow an examination by a medical practitioner in order to prepare an expert's report. **5.078**

Something similar happens in relation to the application for some provisional measures, in the terms of Article 732.2 LEC. Where interim relief is sought in support to claims seeking the prohibition or cessation of unlawful activities, it may also be proposed to the court that, as a matter of urgency and without notice of the application to the other party, it require such reports or order such investigations as the applicant is unable to provide or carry out and which are necessary to decide on the application. **5.079**

5.080 The absence of case law on these matters is a clear indication, however, that they have little practical impact – or, less likely, that their application does not give rise to difficulties.

5. Specific measures in patent litigation: fact-finding measures (*diligencias de comprobación de hechos*)

5.081 Patent litigation is handled in accordance with the general rules of the LEC, although since 1986 patent law has established a series of procedural specialities which, in practice, have contributed to the creation of a special kind of litigation in this area. Among the procedural specialities of the current Patent Act[59] there is a special mechanism for accessing information held by others, the so-called 'fact-finding measures' (*diligencias de comprobación de hechos*).[60] By means of these measures, the patent holder requests the court to check whether facts that may constitute an infringement of the exclusive right granted by the patent are taking place. The measures consist of the entry of the judge, accompanied by one or more experts, without prior notice, into places and premises to verify whether the infringement of the patent is taking place: e.g., by examining machines, devices, products, processes, installations or by interviewing persons found there. Other special laws refer to these rules for the investigation of infringement of trademarks,[61] unfair competition,[62] trade secrets,[63] industrial designs[64] and plant variety rights.[65]

5.082 The judge will only grant these measures if it is previously shown to him that the infringement is presumable and there are no alternatives to prove it. In return, the applicant must provide security for any damages that may be caused by the measure; furthermore, in order to avoid undue disclosure of confidential information, the applicant does not participate in the execution of the measures. Only if the judge considers that the alleged infringement is indeed taking place will he provide the applicant with a detailed description of the elements presumably used to commit the infringement – which the applicant may only use to bring his legal action and may not disclose or use for any other purpose. The applicant must also file the claim within 30 working days,

59 Act 24/2015, of 24 July.

60 Articles 123 to 126 of the Patent Act. See J. Massaguer Fuentes, *Acciones y procesos de infracción de derechos de propiedad industrial* (Aranzadi, Madrid, 2020) pp. 231–240, M. Cantos Pardo, *El proceso civil para la cesación de la infracción de patentes* (Tirant lo Blanch, Valencia, 2023) pp. 267–281.

61 Additional Disposition 1 of Act 17/2001, of 7 December, on Trademarks (*Ley de Marcas*).

62 Article 36 of Act 3/1991, of 10 January, on Unfair Competition (*Ley de Competencia Desleal*).

63 Article 17 of Act 1/2019, of 20 February, on Trade Secrets (*Ley de Secretos Empresariales*).

64 Additional Disposition 1 of Act 20/2003, of 7 July, on Legal Protection of Industrial Designs (*Ley de Protección Jurídica del Diseño Industrial*).

65 Final Disposition 2 of Act Ley 3/2000, of 7 January, on Plant Variety Rights (*Ley de régimen jurídico de la protección de las obtenciones vegetales*).

failing which the measures become ineffective and may not be used in any other legal action.

These last legal provisions show that, in practice, although the name is misleading, the purpose of the 'fact-finding' is evidential, and not only informative: it is clear that it serves for the applicant to analyse the viability of their case; but, above all, it identifies objects, places and persons that qualify as sources of evidence and which, without doubt, will be the scope of evidentiary activity in the proceedings to be initiated. These measures are offered to future plaintiffs in addition to the preliminary measures, not as an alternative; and they also coexist with requests for the production of documents, which, as seen before, are also applicable in patent and trademark litigation.[66] **5.083**

6. Specific measures in the field of competition law: measures of access to sources of evidence (*medidas de acceso a fuentes de prueba*)

The implementation of the 2014 Directive, as noted above, has meant – albeit to a lesser extent than desirable – a turning point in the way access to sources of evidence is dealt with in Spanish civil procedural law.[67] To do so, the legislator could have followed the same scheme that was used in 2006 to implement the equivalent rules of the 2004 Directive on IP rights enforcement, fitting the provisions of Articles 5 to 8 of the 2014 Directive within the system of preliminary measures and production of documents of the LEC. However, it was noted at the time that this would not have been a good solution, precisely because of the shortcomings of both instruments, which have already been made clear. On the one hand, because of the procedural moment to implement the mechanisms of access to sources of evidence, which are not temporarily limited in the Directive, but which would be limited if the channels of preliminary measures and production of documents were to be used. Moreover, because the pre-existing mechanisms would not ensure the prior hearing of the addressee before the evidence is ordered to be made available to the opponent, which is also required by the Directive. Finally, because these channels seem to be primarily designed for the claimant, although the Directive makes no distinction and also mentions the defendant as a beneficiary of the measures necessary to improve access to sources of evidence (in particular as regards the passing-on defence). In addition to the above technical reasons, a further, purely policy-related reason was added: it is discriminatory that the mechanisms of access to sources of evidence foreseen in the Directive, which clearly improve the right to effective judicial protection, are provided for only in respect of **5.084**

66 See the Decisions of the Provincial Court of Valencia (Section 9) 40/24 [ECLI: ES:APV:2024:173A]; Provincial Court of Barcelona (Section 15) 118/2023 [ECLI: ES:APB:2023:10771A] and 74/2023 [ECLI: ES:APB:2023:5118A].

67 On this, P. Hitchings, *La influencia del Derecho europeo en los procesos de daños por infracción del Derecho de la competencia* (Tirant lo Blanch, Valencia, 2024).

very specific areas of the legal system, which are characterised by the fact that they have been subject to substantive harmonisation by the European legislator, and yet cannot be used in a generalised manner by any litigant who, in order to properly prepare the judicial defence of a right, needs access to information or sources of evidence held by their opponent or by a third party who is unwilling to provide it to him.

5.085 For this reason, in 2015, a transposition law proposal was drafted that sought to take advantage of the implementation of the Directive to carry out a general reform of the evidentiary system of the LEC. Specifically, it was proposed to introduce a new general tool, the 'measures of access to sources of evidence' (*medidas de acceso a fuentes de prueba*), which could be granted by the court before or at any stage of the proceedings at the request of any party and after hearing the opposing party. This new tool would replace preliminary measures and requests for the production of documents, which would be repealed. It would be used not only for antitrust damages or IP rights claims, but in general for any kind of litigation.

5.086 This proposal, however, was strongly resisted, as it was understood by some sectors that an 'American-style' discovery system was being introduced and that it would distort the national procedural culture too much. For this reason, it was finally 'mutilated' in the Decree-Law 9/2017, through which the transposition was made operative: the LEC was reformed, but the reform did not make the proposed general change, and instead limited itself to the minimum necessary to comply with the requirements of the Directive, restricting its scope of application to actions for damages for infringement of competition law. Specifically, a new section was introduced in the LEC, within the chapter devoted to the general provisions on evidence, under the heading 'On access to sources of evidence in proceedings for damages claims for infringement of competition law', comprising 11 Articles, from 283 bis a) to 283 bis k) LEC.[68] Despite the failure of the proposed reform, it generated an academic and legal debate that has not been closed. There are more and more voices regretting the limited nature of the mechanism introduced in 2017 and proposing its generalisation.

5.087 The regulation rests on the classic distinction between sources of evidence and means of evidence:[69] the purpose of the measures is to allow access to sources of evidence,

68 See F. Gascón Inchausti, 'El acceso a las fuentes de prueba en los procesos civiles por daños derivados de infracciones de las normas sobre defensa de la competencia', *La Ley Mercantil*, No. 38, 2017; F. Gascón Inchausti, 'Aspectos procesales de las acciones de daños derivados de infracciones de las normas sobre defensa de la competencia: apuntes a la luz de la directiva 2014/104 y de la propuesta de ley de transposición', *Cuadernos de Derecho Transnacional*, vol. 9, núm. 1, 2017, pp. 122–152; P. Hitchings, *La influencia del Derecho europeo en los procesos de daños por infracción del Derecho de la competencia* (Tirant lo Blanch, Valencia, 2024) pp. 533–608: E. Pastor Martínez, *La compensación del daño antitrust* (Tirant Lo Blanch, Valencia, 2024).

69 See J. Montero Aroca, *La prueba en el proceso civil* (Civitas, Madrid, 2002, 3rd ed) pp. 108–110.

i.e., to persons or objects which, where appropriate, may be used in the proceedings to convince the judge of disputed facts through appropriate means of evidence. Thus, they allow access to documents, reports, electronic files, places or persons with the potential to prove in the proceedings the factual assertions on which the claims of the parties are based. If the request for access to sources of evidence is successful, it will be the responsibility of the requesting party to propose, in due time and form, the means of evidence that it considers appropriate to transfer to the judge the persuasive force that can be deduced from the source of evidence.

As to the content of the measures, the system is open and allows access to any sources **5.088** of evidence in support of any possible claim or defence: it is open to both the future claimant and the defendant. The law allows the court to order the disclosure of 'specific pieces of evidence' (i.e., concrete and identified elements), but also of 'relevant categories of evidence', as limited and narrow as possible (e.g., list of e-mails received and sent between certain subjects in a given period of time). In any case, a list of possible data and information that may be requested is offered, which, strictly by way of example, are specified in Article 283 bis a) 1 LEC as follows: 1) the identity and addresses of the alleged infringers; 2) the conduct and practices that would have constituted the alleged infringement; 3) the identification and volume of the goods and services affected; 4) the identity and addresses of the direct and indirect purchasers of the goods and services affected; 5) the prices applied successively to the goods and services affected, from the first transmission to the making available to consumers or end users; and 6) the identity of the group of affected parties. This catalogue expresses a clear reality: these general rules envisage potential defendants (rather than third parties) as the addressees of the measures and, therefore, their use makes sense, above all, when the exercise of independent damages actions, of the stand-alone type, is considered.

The system, moreover, is based on the validity of a general rule in favour of access to **5.089** or production of evidence in the possession of the opposing party or third parties, so that the interest of companies in avoiding actions for damages will not constitute an interest that can be adduced to justify a refusal to comply with them.

The measures, however, shall be adopted subject to very strict conditions, in order to **5.090** prevent them from being used as a basis for prospective and indiscriminate investigations. To this end, the applicant will have to provide with the request a prima facie evidence of his case. The request must also be specific and not generic. In addition, the principle of proportionality (necessity, subsidiarity, instrumentality, least onerousness and speciality) will be applied to assess whether or not to grant the request.

5.091 Measures of access to sources of evidence shall be dealt with in an ad hoc oral and adversarial procedure,[70] in parallel with or prior to the main proceedings in which the claim for damages for infringement of competition law is being heard. The applicant will be required to provide security for the costs of the measures and, where appropriate, for any damages that they may cause. Measures of access to sources of evidence may be requested prior to the claim, in the claim, or during the pendency of the proceedings. If they are requested before the claim, they will be subject to a regime of strict instrumentality which obliges the filing of the claim within a maximum period of twenty days from its practice.[71] Failure to file the application within this time limit will have potentially serious consequences for the applicant: a) the court will order them to pay the costs and declare that they are liable for the damage they have caused to the person with regard to whom the measures were taken; b) the court, at the request of the affected party, may order the necessary measures to revoke the acts of performance that have been carried out, including, in particular, the return of all types of documents, minutes, testimonies and objects. It may also, at the request of the aggrieved party, declare that the data and information obtained by the applicant may not be used by the latter in any other proceedings where there is evidence of abuse on his part.

5.092 If the court grants the request for measures, voluntary compliance can be expected. If this is not the case, the court will use whatever means are necessary for the execution of the measure, including the entry and search of closed premises and homes, and the seizure of documents and objects found there.[72] Additionally, Article 283 bis h) LEC regulates the consequences attached to conduct that goes beyond mere refusal and constitutes obstruction: destroying or concealing sources of evidence, or making effective access to them impossible in any other way. In such a case, and apart from possible criminal liability for disobedience, the applicant may request the court to impose one or more of the following consequences: a) to declare as admitted facts to which the sources of evidence allegedly referred; b) to consider the defendant or future defendant as having tacitly accepted the claims made or to be made; c) to dismiss in whole or in part the defences or counterclaims that the person affected by the measure could raise in the main proceedings; d) to impose on the addressee of the measures a coercive fine ranging from 600 to 60,000 euros per day of delay in complying with the measure; e) to order the addressee to pay the costs of the motion for access to sources of evidence and the costs of the main proceedings, whatever the outcome of the latter.

70 Article 283 bis f) LEC.
71 Article 283 bis e) 2 LEC.
72 Article 283 bis g) LEC.

The issue of confidentiality. The confidential nature of the documents or information to which access is sought is not an absolute bar to the granting of a measure of access to sources of evidence.[73] If deemed proportionate in view of the circumstances of the specific case, the disclosure of confidential information or documents shall be agreed and accompanied by appropriate additional measures to protect confidentiality:[74] 1) Dissociating sensitive passages in documents or on other media; 2) Conducting hearings in camera or restricting access to hearings, 3) Limiting the persons allowed to examine the evidence; 4) Commissioning experts to prepare summaries of the information in a non-confidential aggregated form or in any other non-confidential form; 5) Drafting a non-confidential version of a court decision in which passages containing confidential information have been deleted; 6) Limiting access to certain sources of evidence to the parties' legal representatives and counsel and to experts subject to confidentiality obligations. The protection of confidentiality is reinforced by very tough provisions in case of breach of confidentiality obligations.[75] In addition to possible criminal liability for disobedience, the court may, at the request of the injured party, impose one of the following sanctions: a) The total or partial dismissal of the claim or defences brought or raised in the main proceedings, if they are still pending; b) Declare the infringer civilly liable for the damages caused and order him to pay them; c) Order the infringer to pay the costs of the proceedings for access to sources of evidence and the costs of the main proceedings, whatever the outcome of the latter; d) If the breach is not serious, a fine of between 6,000 and 1,000,000 euros. **5.093**

In the case of evidence contained in the file of a national competition authority, Articles 283 bis (i) and 283 bis (j) LEC transpose into domestic law the provisions of the Directive, which grant absolute protection to some elements of the file – leniency statements and settlement submissions – and which, for others, only allow deferred access once the proceedings before the competition authority have been completed – information that was prepared by a natural or legal person specifically for a competition authority proceeding; information that competition authorities have prepared and that has been sent to the parties in the course of their proceedings; and settlement submissions that have been withdrawn. **5.094**

---

73 P. Peiteado Mariscal, 'El derecho a un proceso con todas las garantías y la protección de información confidencial en el proceso civil. Modelos europeos y convergencias' in F. Gascón Inchausti, P. Peiteado Mariscal (dirs.), *Estándares Europeos y Proceso Civil* (Barcelona, Atelier, 2022).

74 Article 283 bis b) 1 *i.f.* LEC, following the suggestions in recital 18 of the Directive.

75 Article 283 bis k) LEC. See also the Decision of Commercial Court 3 of Valencia 717/19 [ECLI:ES:JMV:2020:391A].

7. Cross-border settings

5.095 Under Spanish law, there are no special rules on access to sources of evidence in cross-border contexts. This does not mean that it is neither possible nor necessary: the most easily imaginable situation will arise in the framework of a request for the production of documents, where the addressee is a third party located outside Spain; if the addressee of the request is one of the parties to the proceedings, the fact that the documents are located abroad should not be significant, unless the court considers that direct access to them cannot be replaced by alternative consequences, such as drawing adverse inferences. In order to obtain access, in these cases, it will be necessary to resort to the applicable international cooperation instruments: the European Regulation on the taking of evidence, the 1970 Hague Convention and, ultimately, Law 29/2015 on international legal cooperation in civil matters. These will be the same instruments to be used by those who need the cooperation of Spanish judges to ensure access to sources of evidence located in Spain in support of proceedings pending abroad.

5.096 Specifically, Article 31 c) of Law 29/2015 envisages the cases in which (i) a Spanish court needs to request the cooperation of a foreign court to access documents or other information supports located abroad – which can be granted in execution of a request for the production of documents – or (ii) a foreign court requests the cooperation of Spanish judges to access documents or information supports located in Spain. In order to activate the request in the first case (i) or to comply with the request in the second (ii), it is necessary that the documents or other information supports to be produced are reasonably identified; furthermore, those facts or circumstances must be specified, which makes it possible to maintain that the documents requested are in the control or custody of the person from whom they are requested; and the right not to produce documents according to the legislation of the requesting State must be specified, if applicable, in case (ii).

C. FINAL REMARKS

5.097 The picture described is fragmentary and unsatisfactory. For certain specific matters, and thanks to the influence of supranational and European harmonisation, there are reasonable tools for accessing evidence held by the other party or third parties, subject to proportionality criteria and which have not, in these sectors, produced consequences comparable to those of a US-style discovery.

5.098 But, in general, the two instruments available to litigants do not adequately meet the expectations of those who need to assert their rights but are exposed to situations of informational asymmetry and evidentiary insufficiency. Preliminary measures fall short in their material scope of application. Documentary production requirements in practice are often effective, i.e., litigants usually produce documents when requested to do so by a judge. But their procedural design is inefficient, as they can only be activated when the proceedings are already advanced and their scope has been defined by the parties, which renders the information obtained in this way useless or forces the reorganisation of the claims and expert reports already provided, which is not easy in a very inflexible procedural environment.

5.099 The Spanish 'official' procedural culture is still allergic to a paradigm shift and to accepting a more cooperative approach to the management of access to information and evidence. And this is paradoxical to a large extent, because the Spanish procedural culture has assimilated with great force the constitutional dimension of civil procedure and the relevance of the right to evidence as an essential element of the right to effective judicial protection enshrined in Article 24 of the Spanish Constitution. It is not difficult to see that refusal to provide the other party with information or sources of evidence could therefore amount into a limitation on the right to an effective judicial remedy.[76] It is to be hoped that, sooner or later, the lawmaker will eventually generate sufficient consensus to bring about a change that will lead to a generalisation of effective mechanisms of access to sources of evidence that, for the time being, are only reserved for singular areas.

76 This view has been endorsed, from an Article 47 CFREU point of view, by the ECJ in the *Peter Puškár* case (C-73/16, judgment of 27 September 2017, ECLI:EU:C:2017:725).

6

ACCESS TO EVIDENCE IN THE NETHERLANDS[1]

Bart Krans and Niek Zondag

A. INTRODUCTION: A TOPICAL SUBJECT

6.001 How is access to evidence regulated in Dutch law? Needless to explain, that question is, on the one hand, of great importance for legal practice and, on the other, involves

1 This contribution was finalised on 1 March 2025.

several interesting scientific facets. Moreover, the question is unquestionably topical for Dutch civil procedure law. This is because Dutch civil evidence law has changed as of 2025. As of that year the 'Wet vereenvoudiging en modernisering bewijsrecht' (the Act on simplification and modernisation of law of evidence) has come into force.[2] That Act aims to simplify and clarify the possibilities for parties to obtain information about a dispute before and during civil proceedings. In addition, that Act aims to give the judge and parties more clarity on the latitude the judge has during the hearing to discuss information with the parties in order to prevent certain facts from being underexposed or misinterpreted in the eyes of the parties.[3]

In this chapter, we discuss access to evidence under Dutch civil law. We first discuss some principles of Dutch law of evidence in general (Section B). In Part II, we look more specifically at access to information (sections C–G). Then, in Part III, we discuss three European Directives and their role in Dutch civil procedure law: the Directive on enforcement of intellectual property rights (section H), the Competition Law Directive (section I) and the Directive on Representative Actions (section J). By no means do we discuss those Directives and their significance for Dutch law in their entirety, but for each of those three Directives we only discuss the main facets around access to evidence in relation to those Directives. The discussion of the Directives will show that the consequences of their implementation differ as a result of the previously applicable rules in Dutch procedural law. **6.002**

B. PART I – CIVIL LAW OF EVIDENCE IN GENERAL

1. Obligation to furnish facts and burden of proof

Before discussing access to evidence in Dutch civil procedural law, we turn to the principles of civil law of evidence in general. To this end, we first turn our attention to the necessity of establishing facts in civil proceedings (section (a)), the parties' duty of truth (section (b)) and the system of apportioning the duty and burden of proof (section (c)). **6.003**

(a) Furnishing facts

The main rule of Dutch civil law of evidence also directly entails important information duties for the parties. Indeed, the basic principle of Dutch civil law of evidence is that the court may only base its decision on facts or rights that have come to its attention in the proceedings or that have been alleged and established according to **6.004**

2 Dutch Bulletin of Acts, Orders and Decrees 2024, 62 and Dutch Bulletin of Acts, Orders and Decrees 2024, 72.

3 See Justice and Security Ministry news release: https://www.rijksoverheid.nl/actueel/nieuws/2024/03/22/vereenvoudiging-en-verduidelijking-van-bewijsrecht-in-civiele-procedures-per-1-januari-2025.

the Code of Civil Procedure (CCP).[4] Those facts or rights that have been furnished by one party and which have not been sufficiently disputed by the other, the court must consider as established.[5] Facts and circumstances of common knowledge need not be furnished by the parties.[6]

6.005 The plaintiff must furnish sufficient facts to support his claim. Exactly what the plaintiff must allege depends on what burden of proof falls on him. For the claim to be allowed, the plaintiff must furnish all the factual elements that follow directly from the legal requirements of the statutory provision invoked.[7] The relevant contentions must be sufficiently specified. The defendant must then – in order to prevent the claim from being upheld – contest the assertions made with reasons. Whether an assertion has been sufficiently substantiated will depend partly on the extent to which the plaintiff has substantiated its assertion. The more elaborately a plaintiff has substantiated his assertions, the more reasoned a defendant must contest. In other words, the more substantiated the claims is, the more is expected from the plaintiff regarding the substantiation of his claim either at this stage or later in the proceedings.

6.006 This starting point on furnishing facts entails a duty of information for the parties. After all, if the claimant fails to provide sufficient information to make his claim plausible, the court will not get around to dealing with the substance of the claim. And if a defendant does not contest with sufficient reasons, certain facts will be considered as established.

(b) The duty of truth

6.007 It is for the parties to set out the factual content and scope of the case. According to Article 21 CCP, the parties must furnish those facts fully and truthfully. This is commonly called the duty of truth.[8] This duty of truth entails the obligation of the parties to fully and truthfully disclose all facts and circumstances relevant to the decision, both to each other and to the court. This includes the grounds that lead to acceptance or rejection, the arguments that support these grounds and the documents that support these arguments.[9]

---

4 Article 149 (1) first sentence CCP.

5 Article 149 (1) second sentence CCP.

6 Article 149 (2) CCP.

7 See on the burden of proof below section B.1 (c).

8 Article 21 CCP.

9 AIM van Mierlo & FM Bart (compilers), *Parlementaire Geschiedenis. Herziening van het burgerlijk procesrecht voor burgerlijke zaken, in het bijzonder de wijze van procederen in eerste aanleg* (Wolters Kluwer 2002), p. 146; This refers to the Dutch legislative history of the revision of the Code of Civil Procedure in 2002; see also about this topic CJA Seinen, 'De waarheidsplicht en de geraden gevolgtrekking anno 2020: een zoektocht naar proportionaliteit' (2020) TCR, p. 33.

The main purpose of this duty is to prevent parties from knowingly lying.[10] Viewed in this way, this provision aims to ensure that no facts relevant to the decision are withheld or obscured so that the court's decision is as true as possible. **6.008**

This duty of truth may mean that, in circumstances, a party may have a duty of disclosure in relation to facts that are unfavourable to its own legal position but may contribute to the other party's right and which it knew or ought to have known that the other party did not know or ought reasonably to have known those facts.[11] Denying facts that one knows or ought to know to be true may constitute a violation of the duty of truth.[12] **6.009**

On the other hand, the obligation again does not go as far as requiring a party to reveal its weak positions. It has also been noted that this duty of truth does not prevent parties from selecting what they consider relevant facts and presenting them from their own perspective.[13] **6.010**

This does not mean, however, that the plaintiff can suffice with stating facts that are in its favour only. As an extension of the duty of truth, according to the Article 111(3) CCP, which sets out the requirements for the statement of claim, the plaintiff is required to state in its claim the defences raised by the defendant and the grounds for them. Obviously, the plaintiff cannot mention defences of the defendant of which he is unaware. This is the case, for example, if the defendant has not responded to correspondence. It is usually assumed that it is prudent for the plaintiff to then mention in his statement of claims that the defendant simply has not responded. Violation of the obligation to state defences does not lead to nullity of the summons. In principle, a plaintiff will then be able to rectify this omission at a later stage of the proceedings. Only in special circumstances can the court refuse new facts or evidence if at an earlier stage a relevant duty to disclose or provide evidence was neglected.[14] **6.011**

---

10 AIM van Mierlo & FM Bart (compilers), *Parlementaire Geschiedenis. Herziening van het burgerlijk procesrecht voor burgerlijke zaken, in het bijzonder de wijze van procederen in eerste aanleg* (Wolters Kluwer 2002), pp. 146–147.

11 AIM van Mierlo, 'Commentaar op art. 21 Rv', in FJP Lock, AIM van Mierlo and CJJC van Nispen (eds), *Tekst en Commentaar Burgerlijke rechtsvordering* (Wolters Kluwer 2024), para 2; see Supreme Court 4 October 1996, NJ 1998/45 (Goosen/Goosen) in the context of a claim based on fraud.

12 See Court of Appeal Arnhem 27 July 2004, ECLI:NL:GHARN:2004:AR4652, para 4.4, Court of Appeal Den Bosch 7 June 2016, ECLI:NL:GHSHE:2016:2302, para 3.7.2, court of Appeal Den Bosch 7 March 2017, ECLI:NL:GHSHE:2017:890, para 6.13–6.15; Court of Appeal Amsterdam (Enterprise Chamber) 21 May 2019, ECLI:NL:GHAMS:2019:1720, para 3.4.

13 AIM van Mierlo, 'Commentaar op art. 21 Rv', in FJP Lock, AIM van Mierlo and CJJC van Nispen (eds), *Tekst en Commentaar Burgerlijke rechtsvordering* (Wolters Kluwer 2024), para 2.

14 AIM van Mierlo & FM Bart (compilers), *Parlementaire Geschiedenis. Herziening van het burgerlijk procesrecht voor burgerlijke zaken, in het bijzonder de wijze van procederen in eerste aanleg* (Wolters Kluwer 2002), p. 280.

6.012 The general duty of truth is not an 'absolute' duty. The exact scope of the duty of truth isn't clear either. However, it is beyond dispute that parties may never (i) state facts that they know are not or cannot be correct, (ii) deny facts that they know are correct, and (iii) withhold facts that could mislead the judge (and the other party). The latter also includes the case where a party only tells part of the story and submits only the relevant documents.[15] Apart from these more obvious cases, a court must assess on a case-by-case basis whether a party has withheld information that it knew was relevant to the assessment of the dispute and whether or not this behaviour constitutes a breach of the duty of truth that must be sanctioned. A clear example of violating the duty of truth is when a party substantiates a claim with fake messages.[16]

6.013 If the court concludes that a litigant has not fully and truthfully presented all relevant facts, it may on statutory basis draw the inference it deems appropriate.[17] Those inferences may include, for example, declaring a party's claim inadmissible, rejecting a claim in its entirety or ordering the party that violates the duty of truth to pay the costs of the proceedings. As we stated above, the court will assess on a case-by-case basis whether or not a party violated the duty of truth. Therefore, the type of sanction depends on the seriousness of the violation.[18] The principle of the duty of truth has attracted more scholarly attention in recent years.[19]

(c) Distribution of the burden of proof

6.014 Strongly linked to the aforementioned duty to furnish facts is the important question of the distribution of the burden of proof: which party has to prove certain facts where necessary? In other words, which party bears the risk that relevant facts are not established?[20] In this regard, the party invoking legal consequences of facts or rights bears the burden of proving those facts or rights.[21] This important rule in Dutch civil procedure law entails that substantive law is decisive for the distribution of the burden of proof. This is in line with the idea that procedural law should enable parties to

---

15 Advisory opinion advocate-general De Bock, 15 January 2021, ECLI:NL:PHR:2021:38, sub 3.11.

16 District court Limburg (Maastricht), 2 February 2019, ECLI:NL:RBLIM:2019:1129, sub. 4.7.

17 The statutory basis consists of the legal framework for the duty of truth (Article 21 CCP). The legislator added the following provision: 'Where parties fail to comply with this obligation, the court may draw the inference 'as it deems appropriate'.

18 CJA Seinen, 'De waarheidsplicht en de geraden gevolgtrekking anno 2020: een zoektocht naar proportionaliteit' (2020) TCR 2.

19 See, inter alia R de Bock, *Tussen waarheid en onzekerheid: over het vaststellen van feiten in de civiele procedure*, dissertatie UvT 2011 (Kluwer 2011) (translated: Between truth and uncertainty: on establishing facts in civil proceedings; with a summary in English) and CJA Seinen, 'De waarheidsplicht en de geraden gevolgtrekking anno 2020: een zoektocht naar proportionaliteit' (2020) TCR 2 and CJA Seinen, 'Dutch Law', in CJA Seinen and others (eds), *Fact Finding in Civil Proceedings* (Boom Juridisch 2024), sub 5.

20 Article 150 CCP.

21 Rights in this context mean subjective rights (such as property rights).

realise substantive civil rights and duties.[22] In addition, this way it is foreseeable for litigants which party bears the burden of proving certain facts.

The law formulates two exceptions to this main rule. Firstly, a different distribution of the burden of proof may result from any special statutory rule. Secondly, a different distribution of the burden of proof may result from the requirements of reasonableness and fairness. An example of a rule of special distribution of burden of proof based on a statutory rule can be found in the doctrine of employers' liability. If the employee suffers damage while performing his duties, the employer must furnish facts and prove that he fulfilled his duty of care by creating a safe working environment.[23] The court may deviate from the main rule of burden of proof if it deems it reasonable and fair. In general, it can be required that there is a structural imbalance in proceedings that frustrates legal protection for the party bearing the risk of proof under the main rule of burden of proof.[24] A different burden of proof is thus applied if the legal protection of a party requires so. In addition, a different burden of proof may be applied to encourage the party with the aggravated evidentiary position to behave in accordance with a rule of substantive law. This is referred to as the 'legal policy' reasons for a different burden of proof.[25] **6.015**

In addition to these two exceptions there are several other ways in which the burden of proof can be relieved for one of the parties. The so-called strengthened obligation to state reasons is one of them.[26] **6.016**

C. PART II – ACCESS TO INFORMATION

1. Judicial power to request information

In this section, we address access to information in Dutch law of evidence. In section 2, we will go into the so-called strengthened obligation to state reasons. That topic is closely related to the division of the burden of proof and the obligation to present evidence as discussed in the previous sections, but we deal with it here (in section 2) **6.017**

---

22 G de Groot, 'Commentaar op art. 843a Rv', in P Vlas, TFE Tjong Tjin Tai and AIM van Mierlo (eds), *Groene Serie Burgerlijke rechtsvordering* (Wolters Kluwer 2024), para 2.1 and WDH Asser, *Mr. C. Assers Handleiding tot de beoefening van het Nederlands Burgerlijk Recht. Procesrecht. 3. Bewijs* (Wolters Kluwer 2023), nrs 279–285.

23 Article 7:658 Civil Code.

24 WDH Asser, *Mr. C. Assers Handleiding tot de beoefening van het Nederlands Burgerlijk Recht. Procesrecht. 3. Bewijs* (Wolters Kluwer 2023), nr. 294.

25 WDH Asser, *Mr. C. Assers Handleiding tot de beoefening van het Nederlands Burgerlijk Recht. Procesrecht. 3. Bewijs* (Wolters Kluwer 2023), nr. 294 and I Giesen, *Bewijs en aansprakelijkheid: Een rechtsvergelijkend onderzoek naar de bewijslast, de bewijsvoeringslast, het bewijsrisico en de bewijsrisico-omkering in het aansprakelijkheidsrecht* (Boom Juridische Uitgevers 2001), chapter XII.

26 See para 4.

because it is also a mechanism explicitly aimed at providing information by one of the parties to the other party. We also look at prima facie evidence (section 3) and the Dutch disclosure regime (section 4). To conclude this section on access to evidence, we look at the possibilities of seizure from the other party (section 5). This topic has developed expressly in the Netherlands under the influence of European regulations. We start with the judicial power to request information at any stage of the proceedings.

6.018 The judge has the authority, in all cases and at any stage of the proceedings, to order the parties to clarify certain contentions or to produce certain documents relating to the case.[27] The judge may reinforce this order with a penalty payment.[28] The parties may refuse if there are compelling reasons for doing so. Substantial reasons may include personal or corporate confidential information. The judge will assess whether this refusal is justified. To do so, it will generally have to take cognisance of the relevant documents or information. The judge will therefore require the refusing party to cooperate. If the judge concludes that the refusal is justified, the obligation to produce the documents will cease to exist. It is also possible for the judge to decide that only inspection of the documents by him is justified. He may then, with the other party's consent, rule partly based on the relevant documents, explanations or information without the other party being able to inspect them.[29] Should the court rule that no compelling reasons exist, it may draw the conclusion it deems appropriate from the non-disclosure. What the latter means exactly is not specified, but it is obvious that it does no good to the case of the party who did not comply with the request. It has been surveyed in the literature that the judge usually chooses from nine different sanctions.[30] As written above, these sanctions vary according to the seriousness of the breach. At one end of the 'spectrum' is the sanction that the court just states that the duty of truth has been violated. This is the least punitive sanction. At the other end of the spectrum is the sanction that the court does not assess the claim. The court will then declare the claim inadmissible or will directly grant or reject the claim in its entirety. Also, the court can opt for one of the following sanctions: qualify the statements of parties in a certain way, change the burden of proof or order a party to pay the costs of the proceedings. One last example is that, when estimating profits to be

---

27 Article 22 CCP.

28 AIM van Mierlo & FM Bart (compilers), *Parlementaire Geschiedenis. Herziening van het burgerlijk procesrecht voor burgerlijke zaken, in het bijzonder de wijze van procederen in eerste aanleg* (Wolters Kluwer 2002), p. 154.

29 Usually a party shall consent due to the statutory obligation that parties are obliged towards each other to avoid unreasonable delay of the proceedings.

30 CJA Seinen, 'De waarheidsplicht en de geraden gevolgtrekking anno 2020: een zoektocht naar proportionaliteit' (2020) TCR 1, p. 38.

remitted, the court will leave any uncertainties to be borne by the party that failed to preserve and produce documents regarding the profit.[31]

Furthermore, it is important to stress that the court's power to order parties to produce documents is a discretionary power. Therefore, this power does not give the parties an independent right of action against each other for exhibits.[32] However, a party that wishes to inspect a particular document of its opposing party can request the court to exercise its discretion. However, as this is thus a discretionary power of the court, it is not obliged to proceed to a comprehensive assessment of such a request.[33] Regarding the amount and kind of documents the court will require, the guiding principle is that the court will request the information he finds absolutely necessary to assess the claim. **6.019**

Finally, we see in case law that the judge uses his power to request information in a varied number of cases. For example, by ordering a claim vehicle which launches a class action to produce the litigation funding agreement,[34] requesting information to assess whether the liquidation of an estate has been completed[35] and ordering an employer to produce all information relating to any overtime worked by the employee.[36] **6.020**

Since the renewal of the civil law of evidence as of 2025, the Code of Civil Procedure contains a special rule for cases where a party wishes to submit certain confidential information to support its contention, under the condition that only the judge will take cognisance of the confidential information.[37] According to the parliamentary history, the judge will have to be reluctant when a party requests to withhold certain information from the opposing party. Derogations from the duty of truth and the fundamental principle of adversarial proceedings should be limited to exceptional cases.[38] An appeal by a party to secrecy may result in the judge hearing the case and ruling on the appeal to secrecy having knowledge of information that may affect his judgment, but on which he may not base his ruling. Therefore, the Code of Civil Procedure contains a rule that the case should then be transferred to another chamber of the court.[39] **6.021**

31 Supreme Court 14 November 2014, ECLI:NL:HR:2014:3241, *NJ* 2015/193, with case note DWF Verkade, para 4.2.4.

32 See Court of Appeal Arnhem-Leeuwarden 29 July 2014, ECLI:NL:GHARL:2014:6079, para 4.4.

33 See inter alia Court of Appeal Arnhem-Leeuwarden 20 September 2022, ECLI:NL:GHARL:2022:8111, para 3.7.

34 District Court Amsterdam 17 July 2024, ECLI:NL:RBAMS:2024:4264, para 5.13.6.

35 Supreme Court 19 May 2017, ECLI:NL:HR:2017:939, para 4.3.4.

36 Supreme Court 10 February 2023, ECLI:NL:HR:2023:193, para 4.11.

37 Article 22, para 7 CCP.

38 HB Krans and JLN Reynders (compilers), *Parlementaire Geschiedenis Wet vereenvoudiging en modernisering bewijsrecht* (Wolters Kluwer 2024), pp. 122–123; This refers to the Dutch legislative history of the revision of the Code of Civil Procedure in 2024.

39 Article 22, para 4–7 CCP.

The other chamber does not get to know the information that a party does not want to bring into the proceedings.[40]

6.022 Another way to ensure confidentiality and comply at the same time with the aforementioned principles is to let the documents be inspected by an authorised representative who is a lawyer or doctor or has obtained special permission from the court to do so.[41] This method can be applied if 'full disclosure' of the documents would disproportionately harm the physical or mental health of a party or the privacy of others.

2. The strengthened obligation to state reasons[42]

(a) Started in the area of medical liability

6.023 The principles of assertion and proof were discussed above. The strengthened obligation to state reasons is related to this.[43] We discuss the issue here because it specifically concerns a party's duty to provide certain information to the other party in certain cases. If that party fails to do so, several legal consequences are possible. Therefore, the strengthened obligation to state reasons is an effective instrument for parties to gain access to relevant information that is in the domain of the other party. Although the legislator does not always put it like that, this instrument is one of the reasons that Directives do not always need to be implemented.

6.024 The now familiar doctrine of the strengthened obligation to state reasons was initially applied in the field of medical liability, among others. In principle, a patient who sues a doctor for damages must prove that the doctor failed to fulfil an obligation owed to him. This can be difficult because the doctor usually has more medical knowledge and can better assess the facts from a medical perspective. In the context of legal proceedings, this can lead to a procedural imbalance. The Timmer/Deutman (1987) judgment is often characterised as the starting point of the strengthened obligation to state reasons.[44] If a doctor is sued for compensation for damage as a result of an operation he performed and he disputes that he committed an 'art error',[45] the burden of proof does not rest on the patient but on the doctor, the Supreme Court was told in cassation. The Supreme Court did not accept this argument, even in case it was established that

40 HB Krans and JLN Reynders (compilers), *Parlementaire Geschiedenis Wet vereenvoudiging en modernisering bewijsrecht* (Wolters Kluwer 2024), p. 121.

41 Article 22a CCP.

42 This para 4 on the strengthened duty to state reasons is a translated version of HB Krans, 'De verzwaarde motiveringsplicht in het privaatrecht', in M Sombroek-van Doorn and others (eds), *Cuim Suis* (Boom Juridisch 2021), pp. 53–61.

43 Although the strengthened obligation to state reasons is related to Articles 149 and 150 CCP, there are no explicit rules of procedural law on which the rule is based but only case law.

44 Supreme Court 20 November 1987, *NJ* 1988/500 (Timmer/Deutman), with case note W.L. Haardt.

45 As it was described in our former Rector Magnificus Stolker's thesis.

the injury could have been caused by an art error.[46] However, the Supreme Court did accommodate the patient in question by considering that the doctor could be required to provide sufficient factual information to justify his contestation of the patient's assertions in order to provide the patient with leads for possible proof of his claim.[47]

Timmer/Deutman is not the only judgment on medical liability in which the strengthened obligation to state reasons has come up. In 2007, the Supreme Court ruled on a gynaecologist's professional liability claim. The Supreme Court applied the strengthened obligation to state reasons and added something to it, thus giving some substance to the obligation: the information must be specific in the sense that that information enables plaintiffs to assess on which point they would have to focus their possible evidence. That specification is no one-hit wonder.[48] Less than two months later, the Supreme Court repeated this approach in another medical case.[49] Providing data to enable the other to assess the point on which it should focus its possible evidence was apparently the required interpretation of the standard in these cases.[50] **6.025**

(b) Other forms of professional liability

The expertise of the professional called upon and the fact that he has a certain file in possession are important reasons for assuming this strengthened obligation to state reasons. If this strengthened obligation to state reasons did not exist, as Asser notes, the burden of proof could become illusory. The consequence could be that the legal protection that substantive law is intended to offer to this party would be unduly compromised.[51] This ratio also makes it clear that this strengthened obligation to state reasons need not be limited to medical liability. In other professional liability cases, too, the defendant may very well be the expert in the field in which he is accused of a breach of standards. **6.026**

An aggrieved party wishing to claim against a civil-law notary in connection with the latter's actions will have to assert and, if necessary, prove that the civil-law notary did not exercise the care that can be expected of a reasonably competent and reasonably **6.027**

46 Sub 3.4, first and second sentence.

47 Sub 3.4, third sentence; Once the defendant has provided information, the plaintiff is given the opportunity to prove its claim with those documents.

48 Supreme Court 20 April 2007, *RvdW* 2007/423, para 3.4.4.

49 Supreme Court 15 June 2007, *NJ* 2007/335, para 3.3.2.

50 The strengthened duty to state reasons may be at issue once a claim is filed. Even before a claim is formally filed, a plaintiff may rely on the fact that a defendant must provide additional reasons why it did not fail; see HB Krans and JLN Reynders (compilers), *Parlementaire Geschiedenis Wet vereenvoudiging en modernisering bewijsrecht* (Wolters Kluwer 2024), p. 114.

51 WDH Asser, *Mr. C. Assers Handleiding tot de beoefening van het Nederlands Burgerlijk Recht. Procesrecht. 3. Bewijs* (Wolters Kluwer 2023), nr. 307.

acting professional.[52] However, the Supreme Court has deemed the doctrine of the strengthened obligation to state reasons applicable to this form of liability as well. A civil-law notary who is being sued may be required to provide sufficient factual information to substantiate his challenge to the relevant assertions in order to provide the party suing him with evidence.[53] More specifically: under circumstances, a notary may be required, when executing a deed, not only to communicate the substantive content, but also to point out the consequences arising from that content.[54] Making notes of what he discussed in the context of this duty to inform and keeping those notes may be important in the context of fulfilling the strengthened obligation to state reasons. If the civil-law notary does not make or keep these notes, this may result in him not being able to comply with his strengthened obligation to state reasons. And that is at the notary's risk.[55]

6.028 Besides the medical professional and the civil-law notary, the strengthened obligation to state reasons is applied towards other professional service providers. In the NNEK/Mourik judgment, for example, the Supreme Court ruled on the strengthened obligation to state reasons following the liability of an asset manager.[56]

6.029 The strengthened obligation to state reasons is by no means found only in Supreme Court judgments. Given the substance of the matter, it is of course not surprising that District and Appellate Courts apply the strengthened obligation to state reasons in certain professional liability cases. For example, in June 2020, the Gelderland District Court ruled on the potential liability of an insurance intermediary. The court considered that the intermediary could be required to provide sufficient factual information to justify the contestation of the claim in order to provide the person who held him liable with starting points for possible evidence.[57] The court added a consideration that is familiar from the aforementioned judgment on the liability of a notary: to the extent that the insurance intermediary does not keep and preserve notes of what he discussed with the person in question in the context of his duty to provide information, this may result in him not being able to comply with the obligation to provide reasons, which is then at his risk. In 2018, the Den Bosch Court of Appeal also ruled on the liability of an insurance intermediary. The plaintiff bears the burden of furnishing and proving facts and circumstances that can support the claim that the person held liable has failed to fulfil their duty of care. This is in line with the premise of Article 150 CCP.

52 Article 7:401 CC.

53 Supreme Court 10 January 1997, *NJ* 1999/286, with case note WM Kleijn and Supreme Court 19 February 2016, *NJ* 2016/295, with case note S Perrick.

54 See inter alia Supreme Court 20 januari 1989, *NJ* 1989/766.

55 Supreme Court 19 February 2016, *NJ* 2016/295, with case note S Perrick.

56 Supreme Court 15 December 2006, *NJ* 2007/203, with case note MR Mok (NNEK/Mourik), para 3.4.

57 District Court Gelderland 3 June 2020, ECLI:NL:RBGELD:2020:3084, para 4.7.

The court of appeal also ruled that the person held liable can be required to provide subsequent factual information to substantiate their contestation of the alleged shortcoming in order to provide the plaintiff with evidence.[58] On the basis of what had occurred in that case, the court subsequently found that the person held liable had not fulfilled that strengthened obligation to state reasons.[59] And there are more examples where the strengthened obligation to state reasons is applied in factual proceedings.[60]

The scope of this strengthened obligation to state reasons seems to have been broadened a step further in the case Van Dijk/Lenningh.[61] It concerns a possible advantage on the side of a debtor due to the failure to pay as a result of creditor default. If the debtor enjoys a certain advantage due to the failure to pay as a result of the creditor's fault, for example by receiving interest on the amount of the money owed for as long as he has been unable to repay the amount to the creditor, under circumstances it may follow from the requirements of reasonableness and fairness that he owes this advantage to the creditor in whole or in part.[62] Although the burden of proof regarding the existence and extent of the benefit rests on the creditor, the debtor will have to provide information to enable the creditor to meet its burden of proof. The relevant information can be provided by furnishing facts and circumstances from which it follows that he does not enjoy any benefit from the failure to pay.[63] The Supreme Court does not just mention the obligation to provide information, but indicates what the relevant party (in this case, the debtor) must adduce: facts and circumstances from which it follows that the debtor does not enjoy any advantage due to the failure to pay. This judgment specifies the strengthened obligation to state reasons in some detail. This is presumably less special than it looks because the court is free to specify what the fulfilment of the strengthened obligation to state reasons should entail. We recall here the notary case in which the duty to make and keep notes was mentioned. **6.030**

The strengthened obligation is also known in cases where a party states that a contract had been entered into under the influence of an error. In principle, an erring party must prove the causal link between the error and the conclusion of the contract. In certain cases, this burden of proof may not be too high.[64] The erring party may try to make the existence of causal connection plausible by, for example, pointing to certain **6.031**

58 Court of Appeal Den Bosch, 4 September 2018, ECLI:NL:GHSHE:2018:3707, para 3.4.4.
59 Court of Appeal Den Bosch, 4 September 2018, ECLI:NL:GHSHE:2018:3707, para 3.4.7.
60 To mention one more here, the Oost Brabant District Court Oost Brabant ruled on a strengthened obligation to state reasons in partial dispute proceedings and found that that duty had not been met (District Court Oost-Brabant 17 December 2019, ECLI:NL:RBOR:2019:7732, para 4.3 en 4.4).
61 Supreme Court 30 September 2016, ECLI:NL:HR:2016:2227, *NJ* 2017/72 (*Van Dijk/Lenningh*).
62 Supreme Court 30 September 2016, ECLI:NL:HR:2016:2227, *NJ* 2017/72 (*Van Dijk/Lenningh*), para 5.3.4.
63 Supreme Court 30 September 2016, *NJ* 2017/72 (Van Dijk/Lenningh), with case note TFE Tjong Tjin Tai, para 5.3.4.
64 Boonekamp and WL Valk (eds), *Stelplicht & Bewijslast* (Wolters Kluwer 2017), Article 6:228 CC.

facts and circumstances from which something can be deduced about his will or to the general relevance of a certain factor or the special features of a contract.[65] At the same time, depending on the circumstances of the case, strengthened requirements may be imposed on the other party's reasoning for challenging the causal link.[66]

6.032 In the area of liability for governmental decisions, the application of the strengthened obligation to state reasons is possible as well. In the case of governmental liability for wrong decisions, the burden of proof and the obligation to prove the *conditio sine qua non* relationship rests with the injured party. In the special circumstances of the case, the court may find reason to rule that the public authority has a strengthened obligation to state reasons.[67]

6.033 As stated, case law in fact-finding instances offers more examples of cases in which a strengthened obligation to state reasons has been assumed. In a case before the Arnhem-Leeuwarden Court of Appeal, the question was which of the parties had to provide evidence of a number of rented homes and the rent due for a number of e-boilers. The court held that it was up to the appellants, as the most ready party and in order to substantiate their dispute, to provide the other party with sufficient factual information in order to be able to substantiate and, if necessary, prove their position (regarding the rent due).[68]

(c) Legal consequence of violation

6.034 What does failure to comply with the strengthened obligation to state reasons lead to? While the doctrine has gained a firm footing since at least Timmer/Deutman, the sanction for failure to comply with the obligation was still somewhat up in the air. In the aforementioned NNEK/Mourik judgment from 2006, the Supreme Court addressed the consequences of failure to comply with the strengthened obligation to state reasons for the first time. Various routes can be envisaged in this context. First, it is possible to apply a reversal of the burden of proof with regard to the violation of the duty of care. Secondly, the court may find that the violation of the duty of care is established because it has not been sufficiently disputed. Finally, the court can consider the violation of the duty of care to be provisionally proven unless there is evidence to the contrary.

---

65 Jac. Hijma, 'commentaar op art. 6:228 BW', in RJQ Klomp and HN Schelhaas (eds), *Groene Serie Verbintenissenrecht* (Wolters Kluwer 2022), paras 4.6.1, 4.5.4 and 4.5.6.

66 Supreme Court 4 September 2009, ECLI:NL:HR:2009:BH7854, NJ 2009/398 (De Alternatieve), para 3.4.2, final sentence and advisory opinion Attorney General Wissink, 8 maart 2019, ECLI:NL:PHR:2019:331, sub 6.6.

67 Thus considered by the Supreme Court on 25 September 2020, ECLI:NL:HR:2020:1510, para 3.4.

68 Court of Appeal Arnhem-Leeuwarden 16 September 2014, ECLI:NL:GHARL:2014:7178.

However, there is no standard route the court must follow. As follows from NNEK/Mourik, in principle, it is left to the policy of the judge on the facts to decide which sanction he considers appropriate in the given circumstances if a party who has an increased burden of proof does not comply with it. According to the Supreme Court, it is preferable that the judge does not reverse the burden of proof, but either accepts the arguments of the party who has the burden of proof as established due to insufficient contradiction[69] or considers these arguments provisionally proven, subject to counter-evidence by the party who has the strengthened obligation to state reasons.[70] **6.035**

In a judgment of 25 September 2020, the Supreme Court ruled on the causal link in governmental decisions liability.[71] In that judgment, these three possible routes are discussed again. In NNEK/Mourik, the Supreme Court not only mentions those three routes, but also indicates that one of those three routes (reversal) is less preferable than the other two. That explanation is lacking in the most recent judgment. This could mean that the choice between these three routes is now more 'open' than previously seemed to be the case. It could also be that by not mentioning this interpretation again, nothing was intended. It is and remains up to the judge in the fact-finding instance to determine the legal consequence of a breach of the strengthened obligation to state reasons.[72] **6.036**

(d) Questions about three aspects

The strengthened obligation to state reasons in private law has now gained a firm foothold, that much is clear. However, that does not mean that there is complete clarity on the subject. On the contrary: various questions may arise. For example, the question is in which cases exactly a strengthened obligation to state reasons can be required. Can it apply to all cases and forms of professional liability? And if so, are there conditions attached to it? And where can the doctrine be applied outside the area of professional liability? It is not obvious that the aforementioned cases are truly the only cases. The exact content of the duty is a second aspect about which questions may arise. What does providing starting points for possible evidence actually mean? The question is easier asked than answered. 'Providing sufficient factual information to substantiate his dispute of the patient's statements in order to provide these starting points for possible evidence' is, or at least suggests, an open standard. That is probably exactly what **6.037**

69 On the basis of Article 149 section 1 CCP.

70 Supreme Court 15 December 2006, *NJ* 2007/203, with case note MR Mok (NNEK/Mourik), para 3.4.

71 Supreme Court 25 September 2020, ECLI:NL:HR:2020:1510, para 3.4.

72 Incidentally, it is noteworthy that in this judgment of 25 September 2020, unlike in previous judgments, the Supreme Court does not use the term 'aggravated duty to propose' but the words 'aggravated duty to state reasons' (para 3.4).

the Supreme Court intends. It is not possible to indicate with one stroke of the pen for all cases in which the strengthened obligation to state reasons is applied what the duty exactly means for the party on whom the duty rests.[73]

6.038 A simple denial or bald assertion by the person held liable will in any case not suffice. The doctor held liable for damages cannot sit back and wait until the patient has reached a dead end with his evidence. He will have to provide as much insight as possible into the course of events and his files will have to look decent.[74] The person held liable will in fact have to 'come forward' and, to summarise (too) briefly, explain why he acted as he did. On the basis of that explanation, the party on whose behalf the increased duty to provide reasons is assumed must be able to determine whether to proceed with the claim and how he can then substantiate it in fact and prove it where necessary. It may perhaps be helpful to keep the aforementioned rationale of the mechanism in mind: it is the person held liable who has the relevant expertise and/or the file. Perhaps the application of the obligation leads to mutual differences between the various forms of professional liability. If so, is that related to differences between the various professions and the requirements that can be imposed on contractors? If not, what could explain any differences? And can those possible differences also be justified?

6.039 A third aspect of the strengthened obligation to state reasons that may raise questions concerns the legal consequences of violating it. Various questions arise. On what basis does the court of fact choose between the three sanctions mentioned by the Supreme Court for non-compliance with the strengthened obligation to state reasons? Of course, these are the facts of the case, but is it possible to gain more control over the question of when which facts point in which direction? Is one of the three possible legal consequences still less obvious than the others? And could a certain 'increased' obligation to provide reasons be imposed on the (court of fact) judges in connection with the legal consequence?

6.040 This broad scope of application makes the strengthened obligation to state reasons a fully-fledged instrument that provides parties with access to evidence that lies within the domain of their counterparty.

---

73 In Supreme Court 18 February 1994, *NJ* 1994/368, also on medical liability, the Supreme Court also applied this criterion (para 3.3).

74 CJJM Stolker, *Aansprakelijkheid van de arts, in het bijzonder voor mislukte sterilisaties* (Kluwer 1988), pp. 81 and 82.

3. Preliminary provision of evidence

(a) Until 2025

Before proceedings were initiated, the court could, at the request of an interested party, order a 'provisional witness hearing',[75] a 'provisional expert report' or a 'provisional site inspection and inspection'.[76] The interested party often wished to estimate in advance whether it will succeed in providing evidence for the positions it adopts during the proceedings. If the chance of success is small, they will refrain from instituting main proceedings. Furthermore, provisional evidence could promote settlement opportunities in a case. Thirdly, provisional evidence was useful if there was a de facto risk of losing opportunities to provide evidence during the main proceedings.[77] For example, in the case of the hearing of a very elderly or seriously ill witness. **6.041**

If a party had sufficient interest in its request for provisional evidence, the court would in principle grant this request.[78] A request for a provisional witness hearing or provisional expert report could be rejected on three grounds. Firstly, if the request was contrary to proper procedural order. Secondly, if the authority to submit the request was abused, for example because the applicant could not reasonably be allowed to exercise that authority due to the disproportionate nature of the interests involved. Finally, the request could be rejected if the court found that there was another serious objection. **6.042**

(b) As of 2025

With the entry into force of the Act on the simplification and modernisation of the law of evidence, the various options for obtaining information and evidence via the court prior to proceedings are combined.[79] Parties can combine various provisional evidence activities. The legislator aims to promote efficiency in the collection of information and to simplify the request for judicial intervention.[80] At the same time, it offers the court the opportunity to control which form of information collection and provision of evidence is most appropriate and suitable at the stage at which the request or requests are decided.[81] The literature concludes that this change is partly due to the aim of having parties provide evidence as early and as completely as possible.[82] **6.043**

---

75 (Former) Article 186–193 CCP.

76 (Former) Article 202–207 CCP.

77 HJ Snijders and others, *Nederlands burgerlijk procesrecht* 2022 (Wolters Kluwer 2022), nr. 232.

78 See on sufficient interest within the meaning of Article 3:303 of the Civil Code inter alia Supreme Court 11 March 2022, ECLI:NL:HR:2022:347 (*SMMT/Warner*).

79 Article 196 CCP.

80 HB Krans and JLN Reynders (compilers), *Parlementaire Geschiedenis Wet vereenvoudiging en modernisering bewijsrecht* (Wolters Kluwer 2024), p. 2.

81 HB Krans and JLN Reynders (compilers), *Parlementaire Geschiedenis Wet vereenvoudiging en modernisering bewijsrecht* (Wolters Kluwer 2024), p. 12.

82 FJP Lock, 'De Wet vereenvoudiging en modernisering bewijsrecht: wat er (niet) gaat veranderen' (2024) TCR 3, p. 68.

6.044 The starting point under the law as of 2025 continues to be that the court will grant the request for preliminary provision of evidence unless it is of the opinion that a. the information requested is not sufficiently specified or specific; b. there is insufficient interest in the provisional evidence activities; c. the request for provisional evidence activities is contrary to the proper order of the proceedings; d. there is abuse of authority; or e. there are other important reasons which oppose the provisional taking of evidence.[83]

4. The 'duty to disclose'

(a) Until 2025

6.045 Dutch civil procedural law did not contain a general obligation for parties to produce documents. Parties were not obliged to provide each other or the court with information and documents. Whether a right of inspection existed always depended on the context and the actual circumstances. Article 843a of the Dutch Code of Civil Procedure offered parties a basis to claim inspection of certain written documents that the other party had in its possession. The claim was eligible for award if three cumulative conditions were met. The claimant must (i) have a 'legitimate interest' in inspection, copy or extract of (ii) 'certain documents' (iii) concerning a legal relationship in which he or his legal predecessors are a party. The defendant did not have to comply with the claim for production if there were important reasons for doing so or if proper administration of justice was guaranteed even without the requested information (paragraph 4). In addition, persons with a right to refuse to testify were also not obliged to submit the written documents. Finally, a duty to disclose might arise before the beginning of a civil procedure as it could arise during a procedure.

6.046 The various conditions for awarding the claim for disclosure have resulted in an abundance of case law and literature in the Netherlands.[84] We will try to briefly discuss the conditions.

6.047 The first requirement, which concerns the legitimate interest, was not defined in general terms by the legislator or the Supreme Court. The requirement was mainly intended to prevent fishing expeditions. The mere interest of a party in certain documents was therefore insufficient.[85] Sometimes the law provided for a special claim to documents.[86] For example, an employee had the right to inspect documents if his

83 Article 196 CCP.

84 See J Ekelmans, *De exhibitieplicht* (Wolters Kluwer 2010) and JR Sijmonsma, *Het inzagerecht* (Wolters Kluwer 2010).

85 AIM van Mierlo and FM Bart (eds), *Parlementaire geschiedenis. Herziening van het burgerlijk procesrecht voor burgerlijke zaken, in het bijzonder de wijze van procederen in eerste aanleg* (Kluwer 2002), p. 553.

86 J Ekelmans, *De exhibitieplicht* (Wolters Kluwer 2010), para 6.2.2.

salary depended on any data from the employer's administration.[87] The legitimate heir had the right to inspect documents to determine his claim[88] and an agent had the right to inspect documents if it appeared from them what the amount of his commission was.[89] If a claim to documents did not arise from a statutory provision, there was little certainty surrounding the question of how the concept of 'legitimate interest' should be interpreted. Decisive was whether a party needed the specific document in order to be able to meet their burden of proof. In addition, there was a connection between the requirement of a legitimate interest and the second requirement of 'certain documents'. If a claim for inspection was too broad and did not concern certain documents, the claimant might be less likely to have a legitimate interest in it.[90] In other words, the documents must be so specifically defined that it was clear what is being claimed and it must be possible to assess whether the person claiming them also had a legitimate interest in doing so.[91]

As regards the requirement of sufficient specificity, it followed from the Theodoor Gilissen Bankiers judgment that the issue was whether the claim for inspection covers a subject that is sufficiently precisely defined.[92] According to the Expert Group on the Modernisation of Civil Evidence Law, it was then not necessary for the documents to be described individually.[93] **6.048**

Finally, there had to be a legal relationship in which the claimant or his predecessors were a party. Legal relationship refers to any legal relationship, not only an agreement, but also an obligation under the law (tort, undue payment or unjust enrichment). The legal predecessor of the party could also invoke the obligation to provide evidence in this Article, as he might also have an interest in inspection or a copy.[94] **6.049**

(b) As of 2025

With the entry into force of the Act on simplification and modernisation of the law of evidence on 1 January 2025, Article 843a of the Dutch Code of Civil Procedure was **6.050**

87 Article 7:619 section 1 CC.

88 Article 4:78 CC.

89 Article 7:433 section 2 CC.

90 TRB de Greve, 'Commentaar op art. 843a Rv', in P Vlas, TFE Tjong Tjin Tai and AIM van Mierlo (eds), *Groene Serie Burgerlijke rechtsvordering* (Wolters Kluwer 2024), para 4.1.

91 LA Bosch, 'Commentaar op art. 843a Rv', in FJP Lock, AIM van Mierlo and CJJC van Nispen (eds), *Tekst en Commentaar Burgerlijke rechtsvordering* (Wolters Kluwer 2024), para 4.

92 A Hammerstein, RH de Bock and WDH Asser, *Modernisering burgerlijk bewijsrecht* (Boom Juridische uitgevers 2017), nr. 83.

93 A Hammerstein, RH de Bock and WDH Asser, *Modernisering burgerlijk bewijsrecht* (Boom Juridische uitgevers 2017), nr. 83 and advisory opinion advocate-general Wesseling-van Gent, ECLI:NL:PHRT:2020:10, sub 2.29).

94 LA Bosch, 'Commentaar op art. 843a Rv', in FJP Lock, AIM van Mierlo and CJJC van Nispen (eds), *Tekst en Commentaar Burgerlijke rechtsvordering* (Wolters Kluwer 2024), para 5.

repealed.[95] The right of inspection is now laid down in Articles 194, 195 and 195a of the adapted Code of Civil Procedure. This has changed several aspects. Firstly, Article 194 of the renewed Code of Civil Procedure regulates the right of inspection without the need for judicial intervention. The purpose of this Article is to provide parties with a clear arrangement on the basis of which they can, at least in non-complex cases, assess for themselves without judicial intervention when they are entitled to certain information and when they must comply with a request for information.[96] The conditions under which a party must be granted inspection are now the following. There must be a legal relationship between the parties, it must concern certain data and the requesting party must have a sufficient interest in the inspection. The party that has the data does not have to grant access if it has a right to refuse to testify or if there are important reasons that oppose access (paragraph 2).

6.051 The requirement 'party to a legal relationship' must be interpreted broadly. The existence of a legal relationship does not have to be established yet. After all, whether a legal relationship exists can be the focus of the procedure. The party that requests access does not first have to sufficiently demonstrate that it has a right to claim.[97] Another new feature is that the term 'documents' is replaced by the term 'data'. This does not entail any material changes, but the law now states more clearly that not only written documents fall under the right of access, but all forms of information, like video- and audiotapes.

6.052 The ground for refusal in the previous Article 843a paragraph 4 of the Code of Civil Procedure that no right of access exists if it can reasonably be assumed that proper administration of justice is also guaranteed without the provision of the requested data, has been dropped. In this way, the right of access must become a cheap, simple, fast and reliable alternative to, for example, a witness hearing or an expert report.[98]

6.053 If a party refuses to cooperate, the applicant is free to take preliminary evidence. He can then submit a request to the court on the basis of Article 196 et seq. of the new Code of Civil Procedure, for example, to hear witnesses or experts. Also, the court can order the refusing party to cooperate and disclose the relevant information.

---

95 In this contribution, we do not address the situation in which a party tries to gain access to information to which it is not actually entitled by hearing witnesses.

96 HB Krans and JLN Reynders (compilers), *Parlementaire Geschiedenis Wet vereenvoudiging en modernisering bewijsrecht* (Wolters Kluwer 2024), p. 168.

97 Explanatory notes 'Wet vereenvoudiging en modernisering bewijsrecht' (translation: Act simplification and modernisation of the law of evidence), p. 47.

98 Explanatory notes 'Wet vereenvoudiging en modernisering bewijsrecht' (Act simplification and modernisation of the law of evidence), p. 13.

Articles 195 and 195a of the new Code of Civil Procedure serve as a basis for requesting the court during ongoing proceedings to order the other party or a third party to provide access. The same requirements apply to the award as under Article 194 of the new Code of Civil Procedure: party to a legal relationship, specific data and sufficient interest in accessing the specific data. The importance of Article 194 CCP is that it provides legal grounds for pre-trial access to information. **6.054**

Finally, if a party permanently refuses to cooperate, the court can make use of the same sanctions as discussed in the context of the duty of truth (section B.1.(b)) and the judicial power to request information (section C.1). **6.055**

5. Seizure of evidence

(a) Until 2025

If a party feared that relevant evidence would disappear, it could, in addition to requesting a provisional seizure of evidence, have that evidence seized. This possibility has existed in IP law for some time (see section D.1), but for non-IP cases this procedure was recognised in the important Molenbeek/Vergeer judgment.[99] The Supreme Court ruled that seizure could take place under conditions that apply to the right of inspection (see section C.4 (a)) and could only relate to documents as referred to in Article 843a of the Code of Civil Procedure.[100] In this respect, permission to seize evidence only entitled the seized documents to be kept, not to be issued, inspected or copied. Furthermore, strict requirements were imposed on the burden of proof of the person requesting permission to seize evidence, whereby the applicant must clearly state the importance and necessity of the requested seizure of evidence. **6.056**

(b) As of 2025

The amendment to the law means that the Molenbeek/Vergeer judgment is codified as of 1 January 2025.[101] When assessing the request to seize evidence, the conditions that apply to the right of access without a procedure must be tested (see sections C.3 (a) and C.4 (a)). In addition, it is tested whether one of the grounds for refusal that apply to the right of access via the court prior to the procedure does not apply (see section C.3 (a)). The seizure of evidence is imposed by a bailiff's report.[102] **6.057**

99 Supreme Court 13 September 2013, ECLI:NL:HR:2013:BZ9958.

100 The function is to safeguard against the obstruction of evidence; see for the run-up to this scheme hereafter para 8.3.

101 Article 205 en 206 CCP; HB Krans and JLN Reynders (compilers), *Parlementaire Geschiedenis Wet vereenvoudiging en modernisering bewijsrecht* (Wolters Kluwer 2024), p. 17.

102 Article 206 CCP.

D. PART III – THREE DIRECTIVES AND THEIR ROLE IN DUTCH LAW ON EVIDENCE

1. The Enforcement Directive

(a) Obtaining and securing evidence under the IP Enforcement Directive

6.058 We now turn to the implementation of three European Directives in Dutch law. We start with the Directive on the Enforcement of Intellectual Property Rights (hereinafter: the Enforcement Directive). In IP infringement proceedings, the plaintiff depends on others for information facilities. If there is IP infringement over the Internet, think of facilitating illegal downloads of movies, the plaintiff is dependent on Internet service providers regarding information regarding the infringer's data. For example, in cases involving the sale of counterfeit products, the plaintiff will want access to the places where those products are stored.

6.059 On the basis of the Enforcement Directive, Member States are obliged to make it so that parties can, under conditions, have access to evidence located in the control of their counterparty.[103] Access can be granted if a party has substantiated its claims with the reasonably available evidence and the evidence to further substantiate its claims is in the power of its counterpart.[104]

6.060 Furthermore, the IP Enforcement Directive obliges Member States to create, inter alia, the power for courts to order, upon the justified and reasonable request of the claimant, the infringer and/or other persons to provide certain information.[105] This information relates to the origin and distribution channels of the goods or services infringing an intellectual property right. This includes data on the front and back men, on the numbers produced, purchased and sold of the infringing goods as well as the prices charged. Furthermore, Article 8 of the Enforcement Directive introduces the possibility to demand information on origin and distribution channels of goods from third parties not (yet) involved in the proceedings.

6.061 Finally, we note that the Enforcement Directive offers possibilities to take measures to protect evidence.[106] Consideration should be given, for example, to the seizure of disputed goods and the materials and tools used in their production or distribution and the relevant documents.

---

103 Article 6 Enforcement Directive.
104 Article 6 section 1 Enforcement Directive.
105 Article 8 Enforcement Directive.
106 Article 7 Enforcement Directive.

(b) Information obligation of the infringer and third parties

Prior to the Enforcement Directive, Dutch law already offered ample possibilities in several separate IP laws to obtain information from the infringer regarding the origin of the infringing goods. However, Dutch law did not yet have a legal basis to obtain information on the distribution channels of infringing goods. To provide for this substantive right to information, several IP laws were amended.[107] **6.062**

It follows from the law, firstly, that the court will order the infringer to provide information at the request of the right holder.[108] A third party will be obliged to provide information upon court order if the following three conditions are met. First, as in the proceedings against the infringer, the applicant must be the right holder of an IP right. In addition, this right must be infringed on a commercial scale with certain goods. Finally, the third party addressed must fall into one of the following categories: (i) it owns or uses the goods, (ii) it provides services used in the infringement on a commercial scale, and (iii) it has been designated by one of the third parties referred to in (a) and (b) as being involved in the production, manufacture or distribution of those goods or in the provision of those services.[109] **6.063**

If a party is entitled to information, he may obtain such information by filing a claim with the court to order a witness examination on all that the third party knows about the origin and distribution channels of the infringing goods or services.[110] The witness examination can either take place at the hearing or be recorded in writing. It appears from the Explanatory Memorandum that this witness examination is a preliminary witness examination as we discussed in section C.3 (a).[111] This raises the question of the added value of the right to testify specifically for IP proceedings, as this is subject to considerably more stringent requirements than the granting of a 'regular' preliminary examination of witnesses.[112] Indeed, for the regular preliminary examination of witnesses, such a request is in principle granted.[113] **6.064**

---

107 Explanatory notes to the Act implementation of the Enforcement Directive, p. 12; see inter alia Article 28 section 9 Copyright Act and Article 70 section 11 Seeds and Planting Materials Act 2005 and CJJC van Nispen, 'Commentaar op art. 1019f Rv', in FJP Lock, AIM van Mierlo and CJJC van Nispen (eds), *Tekst en Commentaar Burgerlijke rechtsvordering* (Wolters Kluwer 2024), para 3.

108 Inter alia Article 2.22 section 4 Benelux Convention on Intellectual Property; CJJC van Nispen, 'Commentaar op art. 1019f Rv', in FJP Lock, AIM van Mierlo and CJJC van Nispen (eds), *Tekst en Commentaar Burgerlijke rechtsvordering* (Wolters Kluwer 2024), para 3.

109 TFE Tjong Tjin Tai, 'Commentaar op art. 1019f Rv', in P Vlas, TFE Tjong Tjin Tai and AIM van Mierlo (eds), *Groene Serie Burgerlijke rechtsvordering* (Wolters Kluwer 2024), para 3

110 Article 1019f CCP.

111 Explanatory notes to the Act implementation of the Enforcement Directive, p. 24.

112 WJG Maas, C Shannon and C de Boer, *De handhavingsrichtlijn: handhaving van IE-rechten in Nederland* (Boom Juridische Uitgevers 2013), pp. 112–113.

113 WDH Asser, *Mr. C. Assers Handleiding tot de beoefening van het Nederlands Burgerlijk Recht. Procesrecht. 3. Bewijs* (Wolters Kluwer 2023), nr. 242.

6.065 However, the added value of the specific right to witness examination must be sought in the right to written evidence.[114] In addition, once the requirements of Article 1019f CCP are met, it is certain that there is a right to obtain the information referred to in this provision.[115] Finally, Article 1019f CCP makes it clear that the defendant is obliged to prepare summaries if necessary.[116]

6.066 Although the witness hearing for IP cases offers advantages over the ordinary preliminary witness hearing, such a request is not often granted. Thus, the claim often runs aground on the requirement of establishing infringement of an IP right.[117] In general, it can also be concluded that, in practice, Article 1019f CCP does not play a significant role in the Netherlands.[118]

(c) The attachment of evidence in (non-)IP cases

6.067 In the context of IP law, we would like to touch briefly on how the possibility of the seizure of evidence is regulated in Dutch law. This seems useful to us as the Enforcement Directive has had a clear influence on the acceptance of the possibility of evidence attachment in non-IP cases.

6.068 Following the Enforcement Directive, Dutch law has three possible provisional measures to secure evidence in IP cases: precautionary seizure of evidence, detailed description and sampling.[119] In addition, the minister gives examples of other possible measures such as preliminary witness examination, preliminary expert report and hanging a camera in a factory hall.[120] Article 1019b CCP can be invoked if the applicant has made it plausible that his IP right has been infringed or is in danger of being infringed. This requirement differs from Article 7(1) Enforcement Directive. Indeed, there it is not required that the infringement is sufficiently plausible, but the applicant is expected to produce reasonably available evidence in support of the claim.

---

114 TFE Tjong Tjin Tai, 'Commentaar op art. 1019f Rv', in P Vlas, TFE Tjong Tjin Tai and AIM van Mierlo (eds), *Groene Serie Burgerlijke rechtsvordering* (Wolters Kluwer 2024), para 3.

115 TFE Tjong Tjin Tai, 'Commentaar op art. 1019f Rv', in P Vlas, TFE Tjong Tjin Tai and AIM van Mierlo (eds), *Groene Serie Burgerlijke rechtsvordering* (Wolters Kluwer 2024), para 3.

116 TFE Tjong Tjin Tai, 'Commentaar op art. 1019f Rv', in P Vlas, TFE Tjong Tjin Tai and AIM van Mierlo (eds), *Groene Serie Burgerlijke rechtsvordering* (Wolters Kluwer 2024), para 3.

117 District Court Arnhem 10 January 2008, ECLI:NL:RBARN:2008:BC2898 (no IP infringement); District Court Rotterdam 9 December 2010, ECLI:NL:RBROT:2010:BO9561 (uncertain whether claimant is right holder and no large-scale infringement) and District Court Haarlem 22 October 2010, ECLI:NL:RBHAA:2010:BP0127 (no IP-infringement).

118 HB Krans, *Nederlands burgerlijk procesrecht en materieel EU (*Kluwer 2010) and HB Krans, 'Europees recht en Nederlands bewijsrecht', in AS Hartkamp and others (eds), *De invloed van het Europese recht op het Nederlandse privaatrecht* (Kluwer 2014).

119 Article 1019b CCP.

120 Explanatory notes to the Act implementation of the Enforcement Directive, p. 20; see also Supreme Court 13 September 2013, *NJ* 2014/455, para 3.7.1 and TFE Tjong Tjin Tai, 'Commentaar op art. 1019b Rv', in P Vlas, TFE Tjong Tjin Tai and AIM van Mierlo (eds), *Groene Serie Burgerlijke rechtsvordering* (Wolters Kluwer 2024), para 2.

The Supreme Court bridges the difference between the two provisions by first considering that the applicant must furnish (if possible, supported by evidence) facts and circumstances from which a reasonable suspicion of an (imminent) infringement can be derived.[121] Next, the Supreme Court sets the bar lower for requests under Article 1019b CCP by considering that the required plausibility of the infringement may be present earlier than when it comes to a request or claim to be allowed to inspect or obtain a copy or extract of that evidence (Article 1019a CCP).[122]

In conclusion here, we do not want to leave unexposed the fact that the inclusion of a statutory provision has played an important role in the use of evidence seizure in non-IP cases. After the introduction of the possibility of evidence seizure was advocated in the literature in the 1990s, evidence seizure was increasingly applied in practice and the possibility was legally recognised for IP cases.[123] In 2013, in the Molenbeek judgment, the Supreme Court recognised the seizure of evidence as a protective measure for non-IP cases as well.[124] The Supreme Court stated first of all that the right of inspection of Articles 730 and 843a CCP provides a sufficient basis for the seizure of evidence in non-IP cases.[125] One of the arguments for accepting the general seizure of evidence lies in the fact that, since the implementation of the Enforcement Directive, it has been possible to seize evidence in IP cases. If no attachment of evidence was possible in other cases, a curious discrepancy would arise.[126] **6.069**

The Supreme Court stated first of all that the right of inspection of Articles 730 and 843a CCP provides a sufficient basis for the seizure of evidence in non-IP cases. One of the arguments for accepting the general seizure of evidence lies in the fact that since the implementation of the Enforcement Directive, it has been possible to seize evidence in IP cases. If no attachment of evidence was possible in other cases, a curious discrepancy would arise. The Supreme Court does not cite Article 1019c CCP as such as a basis for adopting a general attachment of evidence, but does consider that the statutory provisions on the attachment of evidence in IP cases apply accordingly to the **6.070**

121 Supreme Court 13 November 2015, ECLI:NL:HR:2015:3304 (*AIB/Novisem*), *NJ* 2016/491, with case note Ch. Gielen, para 4.1.5.

122 Supreme Court 13 November 2015, ECLI:NL:HR:2015:3304 (*AIB/Novisem*), *NJ* 2016/491, with case note Ch. Gielen, para 4.1.6.

123 WDH Asser, *Mr. C. Assers Handleiding tot de beoefening van het Nederlands Burgerlijk Recht. Procesrecht. 3. Bewijs* (Wolters Kluwer 2023), nr. 201 and JBM Vranken, *Mr. Asser's handleiding tot de beoefening van het Nederlands burgerlijk recht. Algemeen deel* (Kluwer 1995), nr. 24; WA Hoyng, 'Vier procesrechtelijke wensen', in BWM Nieskens Isphording and others (eds), *In het nu, wat worden zal* (Kluwer 1991), pp. 105–118; JM Barendrecht and WAPJ van den Reek, 'Exhibitieplicht en bewijsbeslag', (1994) WPNR 6155, pp. 739–745.

124 Supreme Court 13 September 2013, ECLI:NL:HR:2013:BZ9958, *NJ* 2014/455, with case note HB Krans (Molenbeek/Begeer c.s.).

125 Supreme Court 13 September 2013, ECLI:NL:HR:2013:BZ9958, *NJ* 2014/455, with case note HB Krans (Molenbeek/Begeer c.s.), para 3.6.1.

126 Case note HB Krans ad Supreme Court 13 September 2013, ECLI:NL:HR:2013:BZ9958, *NJ* 2014/455, nr. 10.

general attachment of evidence to the extent necessary.[127] Finally, the attachment can only take place under the conditions arising from Article 843a CCP which imply that attachment can only relate to 'documents' within the meaning of that provision (see section D.1 (c)). The attachment may, if necessary, also relate to the objects in which, or the data carriers on which these documents are located.[128]

(d) Case law on the IP Enforcement Directive

(i) The public interest in enforcing IP rights

6.071 Illustrative of granting a claim for submission of information is the decision of the District Court of The Hague in the case between Bacardi and Top Logistics.[129] Top Logistics provides, among other things, logistics services, including the storage of various goods. In this capacity, Top Logistics was storing a batch of counterfeit GREY GOOSE products. After Bacardi had established that these were in fact counterfeit products, it filed a claim pursuant to Article 2.22 (4) and (5) of the BTIP and Article 1019f of the Dutch Code of Civil Procedure to order Top Logistics to provide Bacardi with a correct and complete statement of the origin and distribution channels of the counterfeit GREY GOOSE products stored in its warehouse. The court ruled that Top Logistics, as a third party, was required to make a statement of, among other things, exit documents, packing lists, invoices, escrow documents, correspondence, photographs and the entire customer files.[130] Top Logistics further argues that further disclosure cannot be considered justified and reasonable. In doing so, it invoked a duty of confidentiality towards its clients. The court in first instance does not agree and considers (translated):[131]

> A contractual duty of confidentiality on the part of Top Logistics towards its principals (if it existed at all) could not automatically lead to the abrogation of the right to information laid down in Article 2.22(5) BVIE (…). The Enforcement Directive aims to provide effective measures to enforce intellectual property rights. Therefore, a contractually agreed confidentiality obligation cannot simply interfere with the statutory declaration obligation. That could only be different if that obligation thereby no longer meets the required proportionality and subsidiarity.

---

127 Supreme Court 13 September 2013, ECLI:NL:HR:2013:BZ9958, *NJ* 2014/455, with case note HB Krans (Molenbeek/Begeer c.s.), para 3.6.1; seel also para 3.7.2 en 3.7.3.

128 WDH Asser, *Mr. C. Assers Handleiding tot de beoefening van het Nederlands Burgerlijk Recht. Procesrecht. 3. Bewijs* (Wolters Kluwer 2023), nr. 203.

129 District Court The Hague 29 March 2023, ECLI:NL:RBDHA:2023:4857.

130 District Court 29 March 2023, ECLI:NL:RBDHA:2023:4857, para 4.8–4.10.

131 District Court 29 March 2023, ECLI:NL:RBDHA:2023:4857, para 4.11. The text in Dutch: 'Een contractuele geheimhoudingsverplichting van Top Logistics jegens haar opdrachtgevers kan (als die al zou bestaan) niet zonder meer leiden tot opheffing van het in artikel 2.22 section 5 BVIE neergelegde recht op informatie (…). Met de Handhavingsrichtlijn wordt beoogd doeltreffende maatregelen te bieden tot handhaving van intellectuele eigendomsrechten. Een contractueel overeengekomen geheimhoudingsverplichting kan dan ook niet zomaar in de weg staan aan de wettelijke opgaveverplichting. Dat zou alleen anders kunnen zijn als die verplichting daarmee niet meer voldoet aan de vereiste proportionaliteit en subsidiariteit'.

Finally, the court does not follow Top Logistics in its argument that it takes too much time and money to collect and organise all the requested documents. The court recognises that it takes Top Logistics manpower to provide the requested statement to Bacardi. However, this argument is being outweighed by the public interest in preventing counterfeit products with unknown content from being put into circulation outweighs.[132] Nevertheless, Bacardi must reimburse Top Logistics' reasonable and proportionate costs.[133] **6.072**

(ii) Submission of information by a third platform party

A second example of a case where a third party, in this case a platform, is required to provide information to the plaintiff is the BREIN/Google case.[134] The case concerns the following.[135] Google offers e-books through the so-called Google Play Books. At Google Play Books, the content is sold as originating from third parties by Google. In doing so, Google offers the so-called 'Books Partner Center'.[136] This gives third parties a platform to distribute 'originating from them' e-books through Google Play Books and charge money for it. BREIN Foundation notes that a certain publisher 'Flâmanca Hollanda' offers a large number of Dutch-language e-books for sale at too low a price via Google Play Boeken. For example, e-books by various well-known authors were offered on this account at a price of €2.21, instead of the usual €13–15. BREIN claims information about the Publisher Account from Google, such as subscriber information, the IP address of the computer used to create the Publisher Account, the date and time the Google Account was created and various other relevant IP addresses. It bases this claim primarily on Article 28(9) Copyright act (Ca). **6.073**

An important defence raised by Google is that BREIN is not entitled to information from Google as a third party because BREIN has not yet initiated proceedings against the infringer. Google bases its defence on the first sentence of Article 8(1) Enforcement Directive which states that a request for information is made during legal proceedings for infringement of an intellectual property right. Google therefore argues that as long as BREIN has not initiated proceedings against the infringer, it is not obliged to provide information. The court does not follow Google's argument as Article 28 (9) Ca does not state that an information order can only be claimed in proceedings in which the infringer is a party.[137] In addition, it follows from the par- **6.074**

132 District Court Den Haag 29 March 2023, ECLI:NL:RBDHA:2023:4857, para 4.13.

133 District Court Den Haag 29 March 2023, ECLI:NL:RBDHA:2023:4857, para 4.14.

134 District Court Den Haag 5 October 2015, ECLI:NL:RBDHA:2015:11408, *IER* 2016/12, with case note FWE Eijsvogels (Brein/Google).

135 See District Court Den Haag 5 October 2015, ECLI:NL:RBDHA:2015:11408, para 2.1–2.13.

136 In the Netherlands, a new account cannot be created for this purpose since May 2015.

137 District Court Den Haag 5 October 2015, ECLI:NL:RBDHA:2015:11408, r.o 4.7.

liamentary history that in such claims, the plaintiff is expected to make his interest sufficiently plausible, namely the termination or prevention of an infringement.[138]

6.075 The court further considered that Google qualifies as a third party providing services used in infringement on a commercial scale. For the application of Article 28(9) Ca, it is irrelevant that it is a neutral provider of an online platform that does not itself infringe.[139] In doing so, the Court refers to the Coty/Sparkasse judgment[140] and points out that Article 28(9) Ca is an implementation of Article 8 Enforcement Directive.[141]

6.076 Furthermore, the court concluded that BREIN has a real interest in obtaining the identifying data as its objective is the enforcement of its members' copyrights. In addition, Flâmanca Hollanda will be able to continue the infringing activities via Google Play if it is not sued for this and the damage the rights holders suffer will continue. Finally, BREIN cannot find out the details of the holder of the Flâmanca Hollanda account in a less intrusive way. Google is the only point of reference to find out the holder and take legal action against it.[142] The court still weighs these arguments and interests against the interests of Flâmanca Hollanda and Google, but concludes that they do not outweigh the interests of BREIN.[143] Google is therefore obliged to make the requested information about Flâmanca Hollanda's account available to BREIN pursuant to Article 28 (9) Ca.[144]

6.077 In summary, the importance of this ruling lies in the fact that it is now clear that a third party is obliged to provide information if the infringement is sufficiently plausible and the applicant needs the information in order to initiate proceedings against the infringer. In order to allow the third party to be heard, the infringement will first have to be established. After all, this is not a matter of hearing witnesses for the purpose of taking evidence in the pending proceedings themselves, but of obtaining information about the further infringement chain in order to possibly address the other links as well. Therefore, the claim to hear third parties as witnesses cannot be assessed until the court has ruled that there is infringement and assesses the additional measures claimed.

---

138 Parliamentary Documents *II*, 2005/06, 30 392, nr. 6, pp. 2–3.

139 District Court Den Haag 5 October 2015, ECLI:NL:RBDHA:2015:11408, para 4.8.

140 Case C-580/13 *Coty/Sparkasse* [2015].

141 District Court Den Haag 5 October 2015, ECLI:NL:RBDHA:2015:11408, para 4.8.

142 District Court Den Haag 5 October 2015, ECLI:NL:RBDHA:2015:11408, para 4.10.

143 District Court Den Haag 5 October 2015, ECLI:NL:RBDHA:2015:11408, para 4.11.

144 District Court Den Haag 5 October 2015, ECLI:NL:RBDHA:2015:11408, para 4.15

2. The Cartel Damage Directive

(a) Access to evidence under the Cartel Damage Directive

The plaintiff in cartel damages actions has a strong interest in having access to information about the conduct of cartel participants. After all, to make his claim plausible, he needs information about the agreements that were made and what influence those agreements had on the pricing of products. **6.078**

The evidence provisions of the Cartel Damage Directive aim to counter information asymmetry in competition disputes.[145] This is necessary, according to the European legislator, because the evidence plaintiffs need to support their claim for damages is usually in the possession of the opposing party or third parties. To ensure equal means in proceedings, both claimants and defendants should have the possibility to access relevant evidence. The Cartel Damage Directive aims to meet this need.[146] Article 5 of the Cartel Damage Directive regulates the right of access to information held by the opposing party or a third party. Access to information is granted after balancing the legitimate interests of the parties involved. In doing so, the court must expressly take into account (i) the specificity of the claim in light of the information already available, (ii) the scope and cost of the release of information and (iii) the confidential nature of the information. **6.079**

In addition, parties will not be granted access to certain information while the competition authority's investigation procedure is ongoing.[147] Finally, a request for access to information is always rejected if the subject matter of the claim consists of leniency statements and settlement submissions.[148] **6.080**

(b) The Dutch disclosure in cartel damages proceedings

Dutch law, as mentioned above, has a possibility to request access to evidence held by the opposing party or a third party (Article 843a DCCP; see above paragraph 2.7). The Dutch legislator indicates that this regulation offers a wider access to evidence than Article 5 Cartel Damage Directive in all but one respect.[149] Due to this broad scope of application, Article 5 Cartel Damage Directive does not need further implementation. In contrast to the Cartel Damage Directive, however, a request for inspection may be refused if it can reasonably be assumed that the proper administration of justice is guaranteed even without the provision of inspection, copy or extract of the documents. According to the Cartel Damage Directive, only substantial reasons may **6.081**

145 Cartel Damages Directive, preambule nr. 15.
146 See Article 5 en 6 Cartel Damages Directive.
147 Article 6 section 5 Cartel Damages Directive.
148 Article 6 section 6 Cartel Damages Directive.
149 Explanatory notes to the Act implementation of the Cartel Damages Directive, pp. 23–24.

prevent the granting of a request for inspection. In order to bring the Dutch right of inspection into line with the Directive, it is now laid down by law that, in the case of inspection claims in the context of information relating to a competition infringement, only weighty reasons can be the exceptional ground on the basis of which a request for inspection is refused.[150]

6.082 Furthermore, in order to implement the Cartel Damage Directive, a statutory regulation has been introduced regulating the right of inspection in relation to leniency statements.[151] A leniency statement falls under the so-called 'black list documents' and is never provided to the applicant. There is also a provision containing a time-limited exception to the right of access:[152] pending proceedings before a competition authority, no inspection, copy or extract of documents containing information prepared by a natural or legal person specifically for the proceedings of a competition authority, information prepared by a competition authority in the course of its proceedings and sent to the parties and settlement submissions that have been withdrawn shall be provided.[153]

6.083 It is further stipulated by law that a competition authority need only provide inspection, copy or extract of documents if another party is not reasonably able to do so.[154] Inspection of documents of the competition authority is thus a last resort.[155] Finally, it follows from Article 850 CCP, based on Article 6(4)(c) Cartel Damage Directive, that when deciding on the provision of inspection, copies or extracts of documents originating only from a file of a competition authority concerning a claim for damages for an infringement of competition law, the court shall always consider whether the effectiveness of the public enforcement of competition law should be safeguarded.

(c) Leading Dutch case law on access to information during antitrust damages proceedings

(i) Request for information at an early stage of the proceedings

6.084 There are several decisions in competition law by Dutch courts that revolve around whether a party should be given access to information held by its counterparty. The first relevant ruling is that of the Amsterdam District Court of 25 March 2015.[156] The case revolves around collective actions brought by Equilib and SCC (hereinafter: the claim vehicles) against a number of airlines. According to the claim foci, the airlines have in the past entered into prohibited agreements on the prices of their air

150 Article 845 CCP.
151 Article 846 CCP.
152 Article 847 CCP in implementation of Article 6 para 5 Cartel Damages Directive.
153 Explanatory notes to the Act implementation of the Cartel Damages Directive, pp. 23–24.
154 Article 849 CCP.
155 Explanatory notes to the Act implementation of the Cartel Damages Directive, pp. 23–24.
156 District Court Amsterdam 25 March 2015, ECLI:NL:RBAMS:2015:1778.

cargo services. Customers of air cargo services claim to have suffered damages as a result. In the proceedings, both parties apply to the court for access to information held by the other. For example, Equilib requests to be given access to picket lines, European Commission decisions and e-mails and conversation records. The airlines request production of notes of lading and agreements with freight forwarders. Based on this information, the parties intend to further debate issues such as applicable law, prescription and assignment.[157]

6.085 The court puts first that the various requests for inspection are assessed under Article 843a CCP. Furthermore, section 4 of Article 843a CCP implies that inspection need not be granted if this is not necessary for the proper administration of justice. The interests of the parties must therefore be weighed up. For the interpretation of this balancing of interests, the court follows the Directive, which has not yet been implemented. Accordingly, the court expressly takes into account (i) the extent to which the claim or defence justifying the request for access to evidence is supported by available facts and available evidence, (ii) the scope and cost of access, in particular for third parties involved, in order to avoid having to search for non-specific information that is unlikely to be relevant to the parties to the proceedings and (iii) whether or not the evidence to which access is requested contains confidential information, in particular about third parties, and what arrangements apply to protect such confidential information.[158] For the court, the ultimate decisive factor is that the access request is made at an early stage of the proceedings and that the collection of the requested information will take a very long time and involve very high costs.[159] According to the court, months or years could be needed to organise, inventory, copy, study and comment on the millions of pages of documents submitted back and forth.[160] Both parties' discovery requests are therefore rejected.[161]

(ii) The relevance of the type of information requested

6.086 In other proceedings, too, the court considered the status of the proceedings to be a decisive factor and rejected the request for access due to the 'premature' nature of the request.[162] In the context of a follow-on procedure concerning a truck cartel, a request for access was submitted by claims foundation CDC. The request for access was aimed at the Commission's 'Statement of Objections'. The reason for the request was that CDC wanted detailed information on the infringement in order to substantiate its

157 District Court Amsterdam 25 March 2015, ECLI:NL:RBAMS:2015:1778, para 4.25.
158 District Court Amsterdam 25 March 2015, ECLI:NL:RBAMS:2015:1778, para 4.11.
159 District Court Amsterdam 25 March 2015, ECLI:NL:RBAMS:2015:1778, para 4.12.
160 District Court Amsterdam 25 maart 2015, ECLI:NL:RBAMS:2015:1778, para 4.25.
161 District Court Amsterdam 25 maart 2015, ECLI:NL:RBAMS:2015:1778, para 4.12, 4.20 and 4.29.
162 District Court Amsterdam 22 September 2021, ECLI:NL:RBAMS:2021:5297.

factual and economic analysis of causal link and damage to determine the scope of its data and evidence collection and to prepare the assessment of the claims for damages submitted by it. According to CDC, the 'Statement of Objections' was essential in order to be able to take note of the details of the various cartel practices, such as the specific content, scope, moments and duration of the anti-competitive agreements and information exchanges that constitute the infringement. This information would enable CDC to create an economic model of the hypothetical market without the cartel practices. The court agrees with CDC that information must be provided to eliminate the information asymmetry. However, the 'Statement of Objections' is not a suitable document because it concerns a unilateral statement of the Commission on which the parties could not comment.[163] In addition, the request for access is premature because efficient litigation requires that a debate is first held on the question on which information an economic analysis should be based.[164]

(iii) Request for information at a later stage of the procedure

6.087 The rulings discussed above were made at an early stage of the proceedings. At the later stage, once the substance of the case is before the court and the court assesses the damages claim, it follows the 'ordinary rules' of the allocation of the burden of proposition and proof. This division means that plaintiffs must make their claims sufficiently plausible and thus prove, sometimes on a per assignor basis, that damages have been suffered. This causes a narrowing of the debate, and the defendants still have no interest in a broad request for access to the plaintiff's documents. Illustrative of this is an Amsterdam court ruling in the aforementioned air cargo cartel case.[165] The court discusses the requirements for substantiation of the claim. The court takes Articles 149 and 150 of the Dutch Code of Civil Procedure as a starting point, which implies that at the start of the proceedings (i.e. already at the time of the summons), all factual elements that are required by law for the claim to be allowed must be submitted. Those factual elements must be substantiated; generalities will not suffice.[166] In doing so, the court emphasised that Dutch law provides no basis for requiring plaintiffs to bring certain documents into the proceedings.[167] If the airline companies find that plaintiffs have insufficiently substantiated their claims, they may – after having taken cognisance of the information in the database – make this known stating reasons. With regard to the substantive requirements of the duty to state reasons, the court considered in a later ruling that plaintiffs must adequately substantiate their claims from the outset. Plaintiffs failed to request sufficiently specific substantiating data

163 District Court Amsterdam 22 September 2021, ECLI:NL:RBAMS:2021:5297, para 3.4.
164 District Court Amsterdam 22 September 2021, ECLI:NL:RBAMS:2021:5297, para 3.5.
165 District Court Amsterdam 11 September 2019, ECLI:NL:RBAMS:2019:9965.
166 District Court Amsterdam 11 September 2019, ECLI:NL:RBAMS:2019:9965, para 4.2.
167 District Court Amsterdam 11 September 2019, ECLI:NL:RBAMS:2019:9965, para 4.9.

and documents from the underlying parties at the beginning of the proceedings. This resulted in the claim foundations being unable to adequately substantiate their claims at the later stage of the proceedings. The court concludes that these requirements of the duty to substantiate are in line with applicable Dutch (procedural) law and thus, in the court's opinion, the principles of equivalence and effectiveness referred to in the Cartel Damage Directive do not come into play.

(iv) Prevention of 'fishing expeditions'

The last judgment we would like to discuss concerns a judgment of the Court of Appeal of The Hague dated 16 April 2024. The question before us is whether the so-called markdown policy of health insurers with regard to medicines violates the cartel ban as set out in the Treaty on the Functioning of the European Union. As plaintiff, Eureco-Pharma takes the position that it cannot be required to substantiate a claim to the extent that the data required for substantiation are in the domain of its counterparty and it does not have access to them. She therefore submitted a request under Article 843a CCP to inspect the documents in the Zilveren Kruis' possession. The court of appeal considered that Dutch law does not have a general duty of disclosure. Article 843a CCP is an exception to this, but for reliance on this provision certain conditions must be met, in particular to prevent so-called 'fishing expeditions'.[168] This condition has not been met because there is no concrete indication whatsoever that there may have been an agreement or concerted practice prohibited by Article 101 TFEU or Article 6 MW. In that state of affairs, an order to surrender the requested documents under Article 843a CCP would result in a 'fishing expedition'.[169] **6.088**

(d) Are inspection requests judged too timidly?

The view has been expressed in the literature that the Dutch courts assess requests for inspection with a restraint that is inconsistent with the Cartel Damage Directive.[170] It is argued that the courts' considerations for rejecting information requests as premature are not valid and do not constitute reasonable grounds for rejection. In addition, Tuinenga argues that concerns about the confidentiality and volume of information are unjustified. Finally, the interest of injured parties in having access to information at an early stage of the proceedings should outweigh the complications identified by Dutch courts when dealing with such requests. **6.089**

We disagree with the criticism. The effective and efficient conduct of the proceedings may well justify the (provisional) rejection of extensive requests for inspection at an early stage of the proceedings. After all, the rules of the duty to propose and the **6.090**

168 Amsterdam District Court 22 September 2021, ECLI:NL:RBAMS:2021:5297, para 6.31.
169 Amsterdam District Court 22 September 2021, ECLI:NL:RBAMS:2021:5297, at para 6.33.
170 S Tuinenga, 'Exhibitievorderingen in kartelschadezaken: een (te) rigide Nederlandse praktijk?', (2023) MP 2.

burden of proof imply that the debate will become increasingly narrow during the proceedings, so that the defendants in particular will only later gain insight into exactly what information they need to defend themselves. Plaintiffs would do well, at an early stage of the proceedings, to narrow down their access request as much as possible and to focus on concrete documents that are in the defendant's possession.

3. Directive on Representative Actions (DRA)

6.091 Finally, information plays a key role in class actions. Consider, for example, proceedings involving alleged privacy breaches, where the plaintiff benefits from information about a company's internal policies on how to handle personal data. For such cases, the current rules on access to information will suffice as legal basis. According to the minister, there is therefore no need to transpose Article 18 of the Directive on Representative Actions (DRA).[171] We recall that relevant general rules of Dutch civil procedural law include in this context are the duty to disclose information (section C.4) and the strengthened obligation to state reasons (section C.1). Also, the Dutch legal system already provides legal basis for the sanctions as written down in Article 19 DRA. That Article states that there must be sanctions for non-compliance with an order to stop infringement or an obligation to provide information about a ruling or to disclose evidence. The sanctions must be 'effective, proportionate and dissuasive' and fines should be possible as well. The court has the overall power to issue a prohibitory injunction which can be subject to a periodic penalty payment.[172] Regarding the disclosure of information and corresponding sanctions we refer to sections B.1.(b) and C.1. There we described the broad power of the court to sanction the refusal of disclosing relevant information.

6.092 The DRA also aims to provide for legal basis for the courts being able to check whether or not the (external) funding of a proceeding is in compliance with the conditions which are stated in Article 10 section 1 and 2 of the DRA.[173] The minister did not think it was necessary for this to be transposed. Dutch courts have the authority to request documents regarding agreements between the claim vehicle and the litigation funder.[174] Access to those documents by anyone other than the judge is not necessary according to the minister. After all, that could lead to misuse of the information, for example, by the addressed party adjusting its litigation strategy.[175]

---

171 The implementation of this Directive took place in the Netherlands mainly by amending the so-called WAMCA (Act on settlement of mass damage in collective actions).

172 The statutory basis is Article 3:296 CC.

173 Article 3 section 2 DRA.

174 Article 22 CCP.

175 AJ Meijerink, 'Procesfinancieringseisen in de Richtlijn representatieve vorderingen en de WAMCA', (2021) MvV 11, p. 378; see also Explanatory notes to the Settlement of mass damages in collective action Act 2020 (nr. 36034,

The image that emerges from case law is that the existing Articles provide a sufficient basis for understanding the funding sources of claim foundations.[176] An example is the case of claim vehicle NUON-claim against Vattenfall in which the court orders NUON-claim to file the funding agreement.[177] That way the court can – exclusively – assess the agreements made with the funder and see whether or not the claim vehicle complies with the standards that follow from the Settlement of Mass Damages in Collective Action Act. **6.093**

Another useful example is the recent ruling of the district court of Amsterdam in a case concerning a class action against Renault for selling cars with manipulated software regarding the emissions of diesel.[178] The plaintiffs argued they needed information from Renault about the precise functioning of the software. The court agreed and ruled that a strengthened obligation to state reasons applies to the contestation of the claim by Renault. Therefore, Renault was held to provide information about the emission control system installed in each of the vehicles involved, and specifically the software used in it.[179] **6.094**

In conclusion, we can affirm that the general rules of Dutch civil procedural law provide sufficient legal basis for litigants to gain access to relevant information in class actions. **6.095**

4. Final remarks

Access to evidence is an important part of civil evidence law. If parties do not have appropriate access to evidence, it may prevent the realisation of important substantive rights. At the same time, an abundance of access to evidence can lead to unnecessary and unjustified litigation prompts. **6.096**

SOURCES

S Adam and J de Ceuster, 'Informatieverwerving voor schadelijders in mededingingszaken: een kritisch overzicht van de state of play', (2020) SEW 10.

LA Bosch, 'Commentaar op art. 843a Rv', in FJP Lock, AIM van Mierlo and CJJC van Nispen (eds), *Tekst en Commentaar Burgerlijke rechtsvordering* (Wolters Kluwer 2024).

BJ Drijber, 'Privaatrechtelijke handhaving van het mededingingsrecht: nieuwe rechtspraak en nieuwe wetgeving', (2016) Ondernemingsrecht 124.

session year 2021/2022), p. 13; to our knowledge, there is no Dutch case law on whether this limited access to information is considered a violation of the right to be heard

176 Amsterdam District Court 20 November 2019, ECLI:NL:RBAMS:2019:8741, para 8.7.

177 Amsterdam District Court 25 October 2023, ECLI:NL:RBAMS:2023:6683, para 2.10–2.19.

178 Amsterdam District Court 13 November 2024, ECLI:NL:RBAMS:2024:6874.

179 Amsterdam District Court 13 November 2024, ECLI:NL:RBAMS:2024:6874, para 3.13–3.15.

J Ekelmans, *De exhibitieplicht* (Kluwer 2010).
JW Fanoy and T Raats, 'Bewijsvergaring in kartelschadezaken', (2015) *TMP* 3.
TRB de Greve, 'Commentaar op art. 843a Rv', in P Vlas, TFE Tjong Tjin Tai and AIM van Mierlo (eds), *Groene Serie Burgerlijke rechtsvordering* (Wolters Kluwer 2024).
A Hammerstein, RH de Bock and WDH Asser, *Modernisering burgerlijk bewijsrecht* (Boom Juridische uitgevers 2017).
HB Krans, 'Europees recht en Nederlands bewijsrecht', in AS Hartkamp and others (eds) *De invloed van het Europese recht op het Nederlandse privaatrecht* (Kluwer 2014).
HB Krans, 'De verzwaarde motiveringsplicht in het privaatrecht', in M Sombroek-van Doorn and others (eds), *Cuim Suis* (Boom Juridisch 2021).
HB Krans, *Nederlands burgerlijk procesrecht en materieel EU* (Kluwer 2010).
HB Krans and JLN Reynders (eds), *Parlementaire Geschiedenis Wet vereenvoudiging en modernisering bewijsrecht* (Wolters Kluwer 2024).
M Kuijper and F Leeflang, 'De richtlijn betreffende schadevorderingen wegens inbreuken op het mededingingsrecht – gevolgen voor de praktijk', *TMP* 2015/3.
WJG Maas, C Shannon and C de Boer, *De handhavingsrichtlijn: handhaving van IE-rechten in Nederland* (Boom Juridische Uitgevers 2013).
R Meijer and EJ Zippro, '"Elk nadeel heb z'n voordeel": bewijslastproblematiek rondom het passing-on verweer in kartelschadezaken', (2016) M&M 6.2.
AIM van Mierlo and FM Bart (eds), *Parlementaire geschiedenis, herziening van het burgerlijk procesrecht voor burgerlijke zaken, in het bijzonder de wijze van procederen in eerste aanleg* (Kluwer 2002).
JG Reus, 'Persoonsgegevens verkrijgen van een tussenpersoon: omgaan met een privacyverweer', (2017) IER 4.
GR Rutgers and HB Krans, *Bewijs (Pitlo, Het Nederlands burgerlijk recht)* (Kluwer 2014).
CJA Seinen, 'De waarheidsplicht en de geraden gevolgtrekking anno 2020: een zoektocht naar proportionaliteit', (2020) TCR 2.
CJA Seinen, 'Dutch Law', in CJA Seinen and others (eds), *Fact Finding in Civil Proceedings* (Boom Juridisch 2024).
JR Sijmonsma, *Het inzagerecht* (Wolters Kluwer 2017).
TFE Tjong Tjin Tai, 'Commentaar op art. 1019f Rv', in P Vlas, TFE Tjong Tjin Tai and AIM van Mierlo (eds), *Groene Serie Burgerlijke rechtsvordering* (Wolters Kluwer 2024).
TFE Tjong Tjin Tai, *GS Burgerlijke Rechtsvordering*, Article 1019f Rv.
S Tuinenga, 'Exhibitievorderingen in kartelschadezaken: een (te) rigide Nederlandse praktijk?', (2023) MP 2.
EJ Zippro, 'Het voorontwerp van de implementatiewet richtlijn privaatrechtelijke handhaving mededingingsrecht', (2015) MvV 12.1.
SS Zoeteman, 'De implementatie van de richtlijn privaatrechtelijke handhaving mededingingsrecht', (2017) AA 0440.

7

ACCESS TO EVIDENCE IN SCANDINAVIA

Magne Strandberg

A. INTRODUCTION

Scandinavian civil procedure law is characterized by basic principles of party autonomy. In accordance with *forhandlingsprinsippet*,[1] a translation of the German Verhandlungsmaxime, the main responsibilities for pleading of facts and production of evidence are left to the parties.[2] In general, it is for each party to decide which evidence he or she will present, and a party has a right to present any relevant evidence **7.001**

1 Bernhard Gomard and Michael Kistrup, *Civilprocessen* (8th edn, Karnov 2020) 500–511 and 516–517; Bengt Lindell, *Civilprocessen* (5th edn, Iustus 2021) 135–145; Jens Edvin A Skoghøy, *Tvisteløsning* (4th edn, Universitetsforlaget 2022) 571–574.

2 The Norwegian Code of Civil Procedure of 17 June 2005 no 90 (*Tvisteloven*) section 11-2; the Danish Code of Procedure of 22 Sept 2017 no 1101 (*Retsplejeloven*) section 344; the Swedish Code of Procedure of 18 July 1942 (*Rättegångsbalken*) section 35:6. Unofficial translations into the English language: https://lovdata.no/dokument/NLE/lov/2005-06-17-90; https://www.karnovgroup.dk/loesninger/karnov-law; https://www.regeringen.se/contentassets/5503f73d320b4de5bb521dd7ee07500a/the-swedish-code-of-judicial-procedure/.

unless an evidential privilege applies.[3] Whenever a party offers evidence to court, that evidence must be made accessible to the court and the opposing parties.[4] However, a challenge in a party-driven evidentiary system arises when one party's control over crucial evidence gives them an unwarranted advantage. Should a party freely decide over the evidence in his or her possession, or should the opposing parties have a right to access it to ensure a fair opportunity to present it to the court? A similar issue arises when important evidence is under the exclusive possession of a third party. In Scandinavian law, these questions are handled by balancing the respect of party-autonomy against the need for adjustment of strategic powers between the parties and the need for effective mechanisms for truth-finding.

7.002 Before the 20th century, parties had minimal rights to access evidence that had not been offered by another party. Access was obliged when explicitly supported by substantive law, but such obligations were more or less unheard of within procedural law.[5] A party could encourage other parties to disclose evidence, but there was no obligation for the other party to comply. If a party denied having such evidence or argued that the evidence was irrelevant, the only procedural remedy was to demand that the party swear an oath.[6] The first significant step towards establishing genuine procedural rules on access to evidence came with the early 20th-century legal codes. The Norwegian Code of 1915, the Danish Code of 1915, and the Swedish Code of 1948 entailed rules on *edisjonsplikt* that obliged parties to disclose certain evidence.[7] However, the rules only applied when a party specifically identified and requested particular documents or tangible evidence in the possession of another party or a third party. Due to that strict criterion and other legal, technological, and economic factors, rules on access to evidence were rarely applied throughout most of the 20th century.

7.003 From the 1990s onward, access to evidence rules became far more important. A legal development was initiated by the Supreme Courts, in particular by allowing less specified requests for evidence.[8] Legislators also played a role in this transformation. In Norway, for instance, the reform culminating in the 2005 Code of Civil Procedure provided a modernized set of criteria in line with the development initiated by the

---

3 F ex The Norwegian Code of Civil Procedure section 21-3 (1).

4 Gomard and Kistrup (n 1) 609–610; Lars Lindecrone Petersen and Håkun Djurhuus, 'Bevisoptagelse og bevissikring' in Redigeret af Pernille Backhausen, Håkun Djurhuss and Christian Lundblad (eds), *Proceduren* (4th edn, DJØF 2019) 293.

5 Maria Astrup Hjort, *Tilgang til bevis i sivile saker* (Universitetsforlaget 2016) 41.

6 Astrup Hjort, *Tilgang til bevis i sivile saker* (n 5) 40–41.

7 The Norwegian Code of Civil Procedure of 13 Aug 1915 no 6 (*Tvistemålsloven*) sections 250 and 251; The Danish Code of Procedure section 300 (1); The Swedish Code of Procedure sections 38:2 and 38:3.

8 Peter Westberg, *Civilrättskipning I* (3rd edn, Norstedts Juridik 2021) 307.

Supreme Court.[9] The legislator also developed other legal mechanisms to facilitate access to evidence, especially for the period prior to commencement.[10]

In Scandinavian law, access to evidence (*bevistilgang*) is typically treated as a distinct topic separated from presentation or taking of evidence (*bevisføring*).[11] These are viewed as separate issues, resolved through separate court orders. Rules governing the presentation of evidence define which evidence the court can and shall base its judgment on. In general, the evidence must be presented during the main hearing, following an evidentiary offer made during the preparatory stage.[12] The court decides whether evidence should be presented based on general legal criteria, and may disallow evidence on grounds such as lack of relevance or evidential privilege. The court may also encourage a party to produce evidence,[13] and, under exceptional circumstances, take evidence on its own motion.[14] While presentation of evidence is a legal relationship between a party and the court, access to evidence largely involves the relationship between the parties.[15] In contrast to presentation of evidence, access issues can often be resolved by mutual agreement between the parties without court involvement. However, gaining access to evidence does not equate to its presentation in court; rather, the objective of access rules is to enable parties to offer evidence during proceedings. In certain situations, access to evidence and presentation of evidence merge into a single process. This can occur if a request for access to evidence is made at a rather late stage, if the evidence is provided on the court's initiative, or if evidence is taken by visual inspection. **7.004**

In this chapter, I will describe the rules on access to evidence in Denmark, Sweden, and Norway. The analysis will be in the form of a joint presentation where the legal frameworks of the three countries share common elements, and individual presentations for each country where significant differences arise. A joint presentation is preferred where the countries' law is based on common elements, even though the details may differ. While some details and peculiarities in a country's law may be overlooked **7.005**

9 NOU 2001: 32 *Rett på sak* 460–464.

10 See n 7.058 et seq.

11 Hjort, *Tilgang til bevis i sivile saker* (n 5) 20–21; the Norwegian Supreme Court's decision HR-2020-2469 para 41.

12 The Swedish Code of Procedure sections 35:8, 42:2 (1) and 42:8 (1); The Danish Code of Procedure section 340 (1) and (2); The Norwegian Code of Civil Procedure sections 9-2 (2), 9-3 (3) and 9-15. On the main hearing model of Scandinavian civil procedures: Laura Ervo, 'Swedish-Finnish Preparatory Proceedings: Filtering and Process Techniques', Anna Nylund, 'Preparatory Proceedings in Norway: Efficiency by Flexibility and Case Management', and Jakob Juul-Sandberg, 'Reform and Development of Preparatory Proceedings in the Danish Civil Justice System' in Laura Ervo and Anna Nylund (eds), *Current Trends in Preparatory Proceedings. A Comparative Study if Nordic and Former Communist Countries* (Springer 2016).

13 The Danish Code of Procedure section 339; The Norwegian Code of Civil Procedure section 11-5 (4) and (5).

14 The Norwegian Code of Civil Procedure section 21-3 (2) last sentence; the Swedish Code of Procedure 35:6.

15 Astrup Hjort, *Tilgang til bevis i sivile saker* (n 5) 127; the Norwegian Supreme Court's decision HR-2020-2469 para 47.

in this approach, the benefit of emphasizing the defining characteristics of the shared model outweighs this limitation.

7.006 However, the countries diverge significantly on some issues, such as access to evidence prior to the commencement of proceedings. In these areas, a common model does not exist and the differences between the countries are more significant than their similarities. I will start by discussing whether the countries have developed general principles of cooperation or similar frameworks for fair litigation (Section B). This will be followed by a discussion of the rules on *edisjonsplikt* (Section C), the rules applicable before the commencement of proceedings (Section D), and special rules for intellectual property cases (Section E) and competition cases (Section F). Finally, I will conclude with some overarching observations in Section G.

7.007 Following the framework set up in the book's introduction, the focus will be limited to civil and commercial cases. Since the procedural codes of Denmark, Sweden, and Norway apply to these types of cases, I will not stress the differences in scope of application of these codes apart from mentioning that they apply also to other cases. For instance, the Norwegian and Danish codes apply also to administrative cases while that is subject for specialised legislation in Sweden.

7.008 I will constrain my analysis to procedural rules, meaning rules applying after commencement of a civil proceeding or in the context of preparing for or considering the initiation of such a lawsuit. Substantive law forms an important element of the legal landscape in which the procedural rules operate. In Scandinavia, many documents are accessible in accordance with generous freedom of information acts.[16] Claiming for access to information under these administrative rules may be easier than relying on procedural rules. On the other hand, procedural rules often provide broader access to evidence, as the exceptions to access under administrative law are more extensive.

7.009 Access to evidence may also be grounded in private law. For instance, a party who owns a document or another piece of evidence in possession of the opposing or a third party may claim access based on ownership rights. Contract law can also serve as an alternative basis for access, allowing parties to agree on broader disclosure rights.[17] However, such contractual agreements cannot override procedural obligations or narrow the rights established by procedural codes. It is unlikely that parties could replace

16 See the Danish *Lov om offentlighed i forvaltningen* (Offentlighedsloven) of 19 Dec 1985 no 572; the Norwegian Freedom of Information Act of 19 May 2006 no 16 (*offentleglova*); the Swedish *Offentlighets- och sekretesslag* of 20 May 2009 no 400.

17 Lindecrone Petersen and Djurhuus (n 4) 287; Westberg, *Civilrättskipning I* (n 8) 300; Magne Strandberg, 'Evidentiary Contracts in Civil Proceedings' in Anna Nylund and Antonio Cabral (eds), *Shaping Civil Litigation Using Procedural Agreements* (Eleven 2024) 46–48.

the access to evidence framework provided in the procedural codes with contract-based criteria.[18] While a contract may enhance a party's right to access evidence, it cannot diminish or replace the rights guaranteed under procedural law.

B. GENERAL DUTY ON COOPERATION OR SELF-INITIATED ACCESS TO EVIDENCE?

While the Scandinavian rules on the concept of *edisjonsplikt* become relevant upon request, there is an ongoing debate about whether a party might also have an obligation to proactively disclose evidence, even in the absence of such a request. A duty of self-initiated disclosure might seem consistent with the key purposes of access to evidence rules, promoting fairness, transparency, and search for truth. On the other hand, such a duty could conflict with fundamental principles of party autonomy, and the balancing of these considerations seems to be a bit different from one Scandinavian country to another. **7.010**

In Norway, a general duty of self-initiated disclosure was introduced as part of the 2005 reform. This duty applies both before and after commencement of proceedings. Before commencement, the obligation is tied to the exchange of notice of claims and responses, as stated in the Code of Civil Procedure (CCP) section 5-3: **7.011**

> A person who gives notice of claim or who contests a notified claim is also obligated to provide information about important documents or other evidence of which he/she is aware and of which he/she cannot expect the opposite party to be aware. This applies irrespective of whether such evidence supports his/her position or the position of the opposite party.

After commencement, the duty is further reinforced in the CCP section 21-4 (2). The preparatory works describe this duty as stemming from general principles of fair litigation and cooperative behavior.[19] However, these rules merely oblige a party to inform the opposing party about the existence of important evidence; they do not oblige a party to give access to that information. These obligations cannot be enforced by a court order. Instead, non-compliance may lead to indirect consequences, such as cost-shifting, shifts in the burden of proof, or adjustments to the standard of **7.012**

---

18 In Sweden, this is due to a general approach saying that a procedural contract is binding only when supported by a statutory provision, see e.g. Peter Westberg, *Konflikt och Kontrakt* (Jure 2020) 649; The Norwegian Code of Civil Procedure section 21-5 suggests that the rules on access to evidence can only be limited by provisions in the Code of Civil Procedure, see Strandberg, 'Evidentiary Contracts in Civil Proceedings' (n 17) 51.

19 NOU 2001: 32 *Rett på sak* 716 and 946.

evidence.[20] Additionally, the purposes underlying these obligations may influence the interpretation of the rules on *edisjonsplikt*.[21]

7.013 In Denmark, there is no statutory provision imposing a self-initiated duty to disclose evidence. However, elements of such a duty are applied in court practice. The concept is closely tied to the non-statutory rule of *oplysningsplikt*, which involves an obligation to inform the court and the opposing party about relevant facts and evidence.[22] Non-compliance with this obligation may imply that the rules on the burden of proof do not apply, which in practice means that the fact alleged by the non-compliant party will be deemed unproven.[23] Additionally, non-compliance can impact cost-shifting, placing greater financial liability on the non-cooperative party.[24]

7.014 In Sweden, a duty of loyal cooperation can neither be based on the code nor a non-statutory rule.[25] However, certain elements of such a rule are found. For instance, if a party fails to produce evidence they are reasonably expected to provide, this may influence the allocation of the burden of proof or the standard of evidence.[26] In particular, such an effect may take place if a party demolishes or damages evidence.

C. *EDISJONSPLIKT*

1. Introduction

7.015 As outlined in my introduction, rules on *edisjonsplikt* have quite a long history in Scandinavia. These rules are still the most important procedural tools for access to evidence in Scandinavia. Upon request from a party,[27] rules on *edisjonsplikt* may oblige another party or a third party to disclose evidence. Typically, the process begins with a party encouraging the opposing party to disclose specific evidence.[28] If the opposing party complies or the parties reach an agreement on the evidence to be disclosed, no further action is needed. However, if the parties cannot agree, a party may request

20 NOU 2001: 32 *Rett på sak* 716 and 947; See the Norwegian Code of Civil Procedure section 20-3 on cost sanctions and Magne Strandberg, 'Standards of Evidence in Scandinavia' in Lubos Tichý (ed), *Standard of Proof in Europe* (Mohr Siebeck 2019) 154.

21 HR-2020-2469-A section 42.

22 Gomard and Kistrup (n 1) 566–568.

23 Gomard and Kistrup (n 1) 566–568; Strandberg, 'Standards of Evidence in Scandinavia' (n 20) 157–158.

24 The Danish Code of Procedure section 318.

25 Such a duty was analyzed and to some degree suggested by Peter Westberg, *Anskaffning av bevisning i dispositiva tvistemål* (Norstedts Juridik 2010) 123–152.

26 Lars Heuman, *Bevisbörda och beviskrav i tvistemål* (2nd edn, Norstedts Juridik 2022) 115–128 and 238 ff; Strandberg, 'Standards of Evidence in Scandinavia' (n 20) 144–145.

27 The Swedish Code of Procedure section 35:6.

28 Henry John Mæland, 'Fremleggelse av dokumentbevis i tvistemål' (1990) 25 (1) Jussens Venner 4, 10; Gomard and Kistrup (n 1) 611.

an access to evidence court order.[29] As a main rule, such requests should be made as soon as possible during the preparatory stage.[30] If the legal conditions for access to evidence are met, the court may issue an order, but only after giving the opposing party an opportunity to be heard.[31] The requesting party has the burden of assertion concerning the main requirements for access to evidence, while the opposing party responsible for asserting defenses based on privileges or inadmissibility. These orders may be appealed.[32]

Whenever a court decides whether to approve a request for an access to evidence order, two questions are decisive: (1) Is the evidence in question within the scope of application of the rules on *edisjonsplikt*? (2) Are the criteria for *edisjonsplikt* fulfilled? **7.016**

2. Applicability: means of evidence and evidence stored abroad

While the rather vague and soft principles mentioned in Section B apply generally to evidence law, the more effective rules on *edisjonsplikt* have a narrower scope. In all Scandinavian countries, *edisjonsplikt* applies to real evidence or physical evidence, including documents and digitally stored information of any kind. Descriptive for Scandinavian law in general, the Norwegian CCP section 26-1 contain a wide and technologically neutral definition of real evidence: **7.017**

> Real evidence consists of individuals and objects (real property, movable property, documents, electronically stored information, etc.) where the person or object as such, or its properties, state, or content, contains information that may be important to the factual basis for the ruling in the case.

Although Sweden and Denmark do not have similar explicit definitions, their legal systems align with this concept, including its application to digitally stored information.[33] Moreover, individuals may be regulated under *edisjonsplikt* when their role resembles that of real evidence rather than witnesses, see the Norwegian CCP section 26-4: **7.018**

> Individuals are obligated to make themselves available for examination to the extent that this can be done without undue strain and without causing offence.

---

29 The Norwegian Code of Civil Procedure section 19-1 (2); The Swedish Code of Procedure sections 38:4 (1) and 38:5; The Danish Code of Procedure sections 298 (1) and 299 (1).

30 The Norwegian Code of Civil Procedure section 9-4 (2) f. New requests for access to evidence can be put forward during appellate proceedings in Norway, but not in Sweden, see NJA 2001 404.

31 The Norwegian Code of Civil Procedure section 9-6 (1); The Swedish Code of Procedure section 38:4 (2); The Danish Code of Procedure section 300 (2).

32 The Norwegian Code of Civil Procedure section 29-2 (1); The Swedish Code of Procedure section 49:5 (3); compare The Danish Code of Procedure section 389 (1) and 389a (1).

33 The Danish appeals court decision U 2011 2; the Swedish Supreme Court decisions NJA 1998 829 and NJA 2020 373.

7.019 The provision may be applied in cases involving personal injuries or where a person's body or health is directly relevant. Moreover, the rule may be applied when there is doubt concerning whether a witness has problems with his sight, his hearing, or any other aspect which may affect the evidential value of his testimony.[34]

7.020 For real estate property and other objects which cannot easily be brought into a courtroom, special rules for visual inspection apply. In Denmark and Sweden these rules are called *syn*.[35] The court manages the inspection, which may involve one or several experts, and all parties are allowed to participate. These inspections typically occur during the main hearing but may be conducted during the preparatory stage if necessary to preserve evidence or for practical or economic reasons.[36] Although these rules are special means of taking of evidence, they function as equivalents, enabling parties to request access to evidence they do not possess.

7.021 Even though the concept of real evidence is rather broad, Scandinavian access-to-evidence rules do not extend to all forms of evidence. For instance, they do not apply to witnesses, and there is no equivalent to American-style depositions or pre-trial witness examinations.[37] Furthermore, the Scandinavian tradition does not entail anything similar to American rules on interrogations or other mechanisms for pre-trial examination of other parties.[38]

7.022 None of the Scandinavian countries have special provisions for access to evidence stored abroad. The provisions on *edisjonsplikt* do not distinguish between evidence located domestically and evidence stored in foreign jurisdictions, implying that they also apply to evidence stored abroad. When applying these provisions, the sovereignty of the jurisdiction where the evidence is located must be respected and some access to evidence orders may require a formal letter of request in accordance with the Hague Convention on taking of evidence or the EU Regulation on taking of evidence abroad.[39] However, the national courts' competence to order access to evidence

34 NOU 2001: 32 *Rett på sak* 978.

35 The Danish Code of Procedure chapter 19; The Swedish Code of Procedure section 39:1. Norway used to have *syn* as a category of evidence, but in the 2005 reform *syn* was replaced by Code of Civil Procedure section 26-3 making courts competent to decide how real evidence shall be presented, for example by visual inspection.

36 The Danish Code of Procedure section 340; The Swedish Code of Procedure sections 35:8 and 39:2; The Norwegian Code of Civil Procedure Chapter 27 and section 21-11 (1).

37 Westberg, *Anskaffning av bevisning i dispositiva tvistemål* (n 25) 507–510.

38 Westberg, *Anskaffning av bevisning i dispositiva tvistemål* (n 25) 516–518.

39 The Hague Convention on the Taking of Evidence Abroad in Civil and Commercial Matters of 18 March 1970, Regulation (EU) 2020/1783 of the European Parliament and of the Council of 25 Nov 2020 on cooperation between the courts of the Member States in the taking of evidence in civil and commercial matters. Both Denmark, Sweden, and Norway are parties to the Hague Convention while Sweden is also bound by the EU Regulation.

without involvement of the courts of another country has not yet been clarified by decisions from the Supreme Courts[40] or other legal sources, and the issue has not been much debated by legal scholars. In line with Swedish professor Peter Westberg,[41] I would suggest that rules on *edisjonsplikt* apply to evidence stored abroad without letters of request:

Firstly, this conclusion aligns with the fundamental purposes of Scandinavian rules on access to evidence. Both the purpose of achieving a sound evidential basis for a judgment and the purpose of reducing the benefit for a party who has evidence in his possession suggest that evidence should be disclosed regardless of where the evidence is stored. Secondly, distinguishing between domestically stored and foreign-stored evidence is particularly impractical in the context of digital information. Scandinavian courts likely issue orders for evidence stored in cloud systems or on servers with foreign IP addresses. Thirdly, most problems concerning requests for access to evidence orders for information stored abroad should be handled under the general criteria for providing such orders. If obtaining such evidence proves excessively difficult or disproportionate, courts can deny the request under the criteria of accessibility and proportionality.[42] **7.023**

However, certain limits must guide the application of these rules in order to respect the sovereignty of the country where the evidence is stored. Non-compliance with an access to evidence order must be dealt with by sanctions within the procedural *lex fori* competence. Hence, the alternatives for sanctions are procedural sanctions, such as default judgments, cost sanctions, or a reversal of the burden of proof. Direct enforcement of orders concerning foreign evidence remains beyond the forum court's jurisdiction. Since any duty under these rules applies to evidence in the possession of the party, ordering disclosure abroad should not be much of a problem. Moreover, orders for evidence disclosure can only be directed at individuals or entities under the court's jurisdiction. While such orders apply to parties involved in the lawsuit, they can only extend to third parties who fall within the court's authority. **7.024**

40 See, however, the Norwegian Supreme Court decision HR-2019-610-A concerning a criminal proceeding where the prosecutor was allowed to search for information contained in servers abroad. The use of force had a legal basis in the Norwegian Code of Criminal Procedure and was not regarded a breach of another country's sovereignty because all actions were taken from Norway, and the information would be intact at the server. The decision is relevant to civil cases as well, see Skoghøy (n 1) 843.

41 Westberg, *Anskaffning av bevisning i dispositiva tvistemål* (n 25) 733–734.

42 See n 7.033 et seq.

3. The criteria for *edisjonsplikt*

(a) Relevance

7.025 A basic criterion for *edisjonsplikt* is that the requested evidence must be relevant for a pending lawsuit.[43] The required evidence must pertain to a fact that is relevant under the substantive law, pleaded by a party, and contested by the opposing party.[44] Importantly, this requirement excludes access to documents that solely contain legal information or reasoning as these do not meet the standard of evidential relevance.[45] When requesting access to evidence, the requesting party must concretize the contested fact which the evidence is relevant for, see for instance this reasoning from the Norwegian Supreme Court:

> An order to present evidence may, as demonstrated in the case at hand, imply an extensive and resource-demanding obligation to present internal documents. It thus seems reasonable that the requesting party specifies what the evidence is meant to prove, and that this must also be reflected in the court's ruling. Such a requirement may also be necessary for the issue to be reviewable by way of appeal.[46]

7.026 In order to prevent US-style fishing expeditions, the requested evidence must be relevant in itself for the contested fact. A party cannot seek access to information purely in the hope that it might lead to the discovery of relevant evidence.[47]

7.027 However, the requirement of relevance is relatively relaxed. Evidence may be indirectly relevant if it supports an evidentiary fact that, in turn, bears on the material fact. The required evidence is also considered relevant if it affects the evidential value of other evidence, for example when a party requires access to information concerning the skills or experience of a person who is presented as an expert.[48] Additionally, since access to evidence is normally requested before the court has examined the evidence, its relevance may be uncertain. The Supreme Courts have underlined that the requesting party only needs to demonstrate that there is reason to believe that the evidence will possess at least minimum evidential value.[49]

---

43 The Norwegian Code of Civil Procedure section 21-5; The Danish Code of Procedure section 300 (1); The Swedish Code of Procedure section 38:1 (1).

44 e.g. The Swedish decisions NJA 2002 41; NJA 2014 651; NJA 2022 199.

45 e.g. The Danish decisions UfR 2014 138; UfR 2014 899.

46 HR-2019-997-A section 60; the Swedish Supreme Court's decision NJA 1998 590; the Danish Supreme Court's decision UfR 2015 3319 H.

47 UfR 1997 p. 837 H; UfR 2011 p. 431 H; Lindell (n 1) 577.

48 Ragnhild Haugen, 'Bevistilgang til sakkyndigbevisets underliggende materiale – særlig om sakkyndigbevis i personskadesaker' (2022) 19 (1–2) Tidsskrift for Erstatningsrett 7.

49 NJA 1998 590 I; NJA 2014 651; UfR 1985 549 H; UfR 1993 169 H; Per Olof Ekelöf, Henrik Edelstam and Lars Heuman, *Rättegång IV* (6th edn, Norstedts Juridik 2009) 265; Robert Nordh, *Praktisk process VI: Bevisrätt A* (Iustus 2009) 104; Lindell (n 1) 576; Peter Bang, 'Partsedition' UfR 1997 B 268 (1997) 131, 271; Astrup Hjort, *Tilgang til bevis i sivile saker* (n 5) 113–116.

(b) Specification

A characteristic feature of Scandinavian access to evidence rules is that a party cannot simply ask for all relevant evidence in the opposing party's possession; the requested evidence must be specifically identified.[50] Even though specification was not explicitly required in the civil procedure codes, such a requirement has been acknowledged since the rules on *edisjonsplikt* were established approximately a hundred years ago. Probably inspired by German law, the requirement of specification was traditionally regarded as extremely strict. A party could not ask for a group or category of evidence but had to specify each piece more or less uniquely. Due to the strict requirement of specification, rules on *edisjonsplikt* had little practical significance.[51] **7.028**

From the early 1990s, however, the Supreme Courts began to adopt a more flexible approach,[52] permitting access to evidence orders based on broader and more general descriptions of evidence.[53] For instance, the Norwegian Supreme Court allowed a request for 'all invoices in the period 16 August 1986 – 16 August 1989 that the plaintiff has issued to its principals, and which relate to the assignments that the respondents have performed for the plaintiff in the same period'.[54] Similarly, the Swedish Supreme Court granted an order for all documents in a bank's possession related to a disputed loan agreement.[55] This development opened access to masses of evidence based on a single request, which enhanced the practical importance of the rules on *edisjonsplikt* and prepared the ground for further development when digitally stored information became increasingly important. Access to evidence orders became even more potent as parties were permitted to submit multiple requests or combine various aspects into a single request. In a case decided by the Norwegian Supreme Court in 2019, the requested party protested against 18 different requests which they regarded too unspecified: **7.029**

> Felleskjøpet has emphasised 18 items which it considers not to be adequately specified. Several items are generally formulated, such as the request to access to 'any written document', 'all internal communication', 'emails', 'all documentation' and 'internal minutes/memoranda/minutes of meetings'.[56]

Even after the liberalization of the requirement on specification, some specification is still necessary. A party cannot simply ask for any relevant document in the possession of the opposing party, which is an essential difference to Anglo-American law and a **7.030**

50 The Danish Code of Procedure section 298; The Norwegian Code of Civil Procedure section 26-6.
51 Astrup Hjort, *Tilgang til bevis i sivile saker* (n 5) 41–43.
52 Astrup Hjort, *Tilgang til bevis i sivile saker* (n 5) 43–46; Westberg, *Civilrättskipning I* (n 8) 307.
53 NJA 1998 590 II; Nordh (n 49) 106; Ekelöf, Edelstam and Heuman (n 49) 263–264.
54 Rt. 1991 183, 184.
55 NJA 1998 590 II; NJA 2002 41.
56 HR-2019-997-A para 70.

hindrance towards general disclosure or discovery. An example of the Scandinavian attitude towards Anglo-American discovery or disclosure was seen in the Norwegian 2005 reform. After having considered the rules on discovery found in US law and the modified rules on disclosure found in English law after the Woolf reform,[57] the law commission underlined that those rules were based on important purposes that were relevant also under Norwegian law. However, the commission found the Anglo-American rules too radical and too costly and suggested further development of existing rules on *edisjonsplikt* instead of copying American or English law. The commission suggested that the ongoing liberalisation concerning specification should continue and should be further liberalised under the new code.[58] The wording of the new Norwegian CCP section 26-6 (1):

> A request for access to or questions concerning real evidence shall be specified in such detail that it is clear as to which item of evidence the application relates.

7.031 The Swedish and Danish codes lack explicit definitions of specification, but the Norwegian wording is descriptive also for these countries. Ultimately, the critical factor is that the party subject to the request must be able to clearly understand which documents they are required to disclose to fulfill their obligation.[59] Consistent with this principle, it has been emphasised that only sufficiently specific court orders can be effectively enforced.[60]

7.032 If a request could be further specified without excluding any relevant evidence, such a refinement should be made. However, a request should not be narrowed if doing so would exclude pertinent evidence, even if compliance entails significant costs. In principle, the number of documents or the amount of information is not relevant as long as the scope of the requested evidence is clearly defined. While cost considerations are undoubtedly important, proportionality, accessibility, and admissibility serve as more practical and appropriate criteria for assessing the reasonableness of a request than the requirement of specification alone.

(c) Proportionality or balance of interests

7.033 Throughout the last decades, Scandinavian civil procedure has developed from a rather strictly rule-based, non-flexible paradigm to allowing flexibility in order to make proceedings fit with the peculiarities of each case.[61] The rules on access to evidence have seen a similar development. As the traditional criteria of relevance and

---

57 NOU 2001: 32 *Rett på sak* 460–465.

58 NOU 2001: 32 *Rett på sak* 977.

59 Ekelöf, Edelstam and Heuman (n 49) 264.

60 Nordh (n 49) 106.

61 F ex Nylund (n 12) 61; Bellander, *Rättegångskostnader* (Iustus 2017) 130–143.

specificity have been softened, a new criterion – proportionality or balancing of interests – has emerged to prevent access to evidence orders that impose undue expense or burden relative to their justification in a given case. This proportionality test weighs the evidential benefits of granting access against the costs and other disadvantages related to disclosing the evidence. However, the specifics of the test vary among the Scandinavian countries.

In Norway, the 1915 code did not entail a proportionality test, though aspects of such a test may have been implied within the requirement of specification. With the 2005 reform, proportionality was codified in section 26-5 (3) of the CPP: **7.034**

> The court may refuse access to evidence pursuant to subsections (1) or (2) if such access would incur expenses that are not reasonably proportionate to the dispute and the potential value of the evidence.

The proportionality assessment involves balancing the costs of granting access against the value of the disputed claims and the expected evidential value of the evidence. While the costs and the claim value are typically straightforward to determine, the evidential value is more difficult to assess because the court has not yet seen the evidence. Furthermore, the court must consider the potential added value of the requested evidence in comparison to the evidence already submitted. This includes determining whether the evidence is relevant to a substantive, potentially decisive issue or merely to a matter of indirect significance. Although the proportionality test has been applied by the Supreme Court,[62] its practical application remains as ambiguous as the legislative provision itself. **7.035**

A proportionality test for access to evidence does not follow from the Swedish procedural code. However, the Supreme Court has developed and applied a test that balances the costs and other disadvantages for the requested party against the expected evidential value of the evidence.[63] Notably, the value of the disputed claim is not explicitly involved in the Supreme Court's test, though its significance has been highlighted by others.[64] Hence, a proportionality test similar to the test found in Norwegian law seems to be a condition for imposing an access to evidence order. Scholars generally emphasize that parties are obliged to disclose evidence in their possession if it is relevant.[65] As a result, disclosure is considered disproportionate only under extraordinary circumstances. The Supreme Court has upheld access to evidence orders that entail **7.036**

62 HR-2018-2403-A; HR-2019-997-A; HR-2022-1981-U.
63 NJA 1977 254; NJA 1998 829; NJA 2014 651.
64 Lindell (n 1) 575–576.
65 Lindell (n 1) 575; Nordh (n 49) 105; Ekelöf, Edelstam and Heuman (n 49) 269.

substantial effort, such as one requiring approximately one month of full-time work as a single individual.[66]

7.037 Although the Danish code of procedure does not explicitly require proportionality for access to evidence, courts have paid attention to the workload imposed by such requests.[67] A balance between the expected evidential value of the evidence and the costs or disadvantages faced by the requested party is typically conducted as part of a broader normative assessment.[68] Although Danish case law does not explicitly operate a proportionality test, legal scholars suggest that such a test is de facto applied and should be regarded as an element of Danish law.[69]

7.038 If the court finds an access to evidence request disproportionate, it usually does not reject the entire request. Instead, it narrows the scope of evidence to be disclosed. Both parties have the right to be heard regarding which evidence will be disclosed and the methods for disclosure. The Norwegian CCP section 26-5 (3), second sentence, permits access to evidence orders to be made 'conditional upon an advance of the expenses involved from the person having requested access'. However, these costs may be shifted at the end of proceedings if the requesting party happens to win the lawsuit. In Sweden, payment in advance may be ordered only when evidence is requested from third parties.[70]

(d) Possession, accessibility, and existence

7.039 A request based on *edisjonsplikt* will only be approved if a relationship or connection exists between the required party and the evidence in question. In general, a party may demand access only to evidence that is accessible to the required party. This requirement mirrors the purpose of Scandinavian disclosure rules, which aim to eliminate the advantage of exclusive access to evidence rather than to facilitate discovery or broader investigations. However, the nature of the required connection between the party and the evidence varies across Scandinavian countries.

7.040 In Denmark, a party may claim disclosure only of evidence within the required party's possession.[71] Similarly, in Sweden, a party must disclose evidence only if he is 'holding a written document',[72] meaning the requested party must be in possession of the

66 NJA 1998 829.

67 UfR 1957 761; UfR 1962 104 H; UfR 1995 670 H.

68 Gomard and Kistrup (n 1) 614; Ulrik Rammeskow Bang-Pedersen, Lasse Højlund Christensen and Clement Salung Petersen, *Den civile retspleje* (5th edn, Hans Reizels 2020) 574–575.

69 Lars Lindencrone and Erik Werlauff, *Dansk retspleje* (9th edn, Karnov Group 2023) 320.

70 The Swedish Code of Procedure section 38:7.

71 The Danish Code of Procedure section 298 (1).

72 The Swedish Code of Procedure section 38:2 (1).

document.[73] Both jurisdictions have faced disputes over whether a parent company must disclose evidence controlled by a subsidiary company.[74] In contrast, Norway's 2005 procedural code more broadly requires disclosure of evidence 'in their possession or which they can obtain possession of'.[75]

A request for access to evidence will not be granted if the requesting party could reasonably obtain the evidence through other means. For example, the Norwegian CCP section 26-5 (3) stipulates that a request for access to evidence shall be refused '... if the party has approximately the same possibility of obtaining access to such evidence'. Such a situation does not regularly occur in practice but could, for instance, be when the requesting party could have found the information accessible online instead of claiming the evidence from the opposing party. In line with this, the Danish Supreme Court held that a party cannot require access to evidence which he can more easily present to the court by other means.[76] **7.041**

The rules on *edisjonsplikt* apply only to existing evidence. In accordance with prevalent view, a party is not obliged to produce new evidence.[77] *Edisjonsplikt* shall ensure equal access to existing and known evidence rather than supporting the creation or development of new evidence.[78] That said, any distinction between existing and non-existing evidence can be unclear, especially in a digitalized society. For instance, creating a screenshot may involve minimal effort and could be regarded as either generating new evidence or simply securing existing information. Under Norwegian law, a party must produce such a screenshot or a web history printout, even if this requires some development effort. There are also some straightforward exceptions. Under the Swedish CP section 42:8 (1), a party may request the opposing party to specify what additional items evidence they hold. Similarly, Norwegian CCP section 26-5 (2) provides that parties 'may also be ordered to prepare comparisons, extracts or other reviews of information that may be gathered from items of evidence'. **7.042**

In practice, orders granting access to evidence based on *edisjonsplikt* may involve the creation of new evidence. For example, a court may require a party to allow its production facility to be inspected, enabling the opposing party to generate new evidence based on the access provided. In one case, the Norwegian Supreme Court ordered a producer of artificial fertilizer to allow the opposing party access to the production **7.043**

73 Ekelöf, Edelstam and Heuman (n 49) 266.
74 Bang-Pedersen, Christensen and Petersen (n 68) 573; Ekelöf, Edelstam and Heuman (n 49) 267.
75 The Norwegian Code of Civil Procedure section 26-5 (1).
76 UfR 1982 p. 171 H; Gomard and Kistrup (n 1) 612.
77 Lindencrone and Werlauff (n 69) 318.
78 Westberg, *Civilrättskipning I* (n 8) 305.

area in order to provide tests of the fertilizer.[79] These tests were relevant because the fertilizer, according to the insurance company in a tort case, was suspected of having caused smoke and toxic gasses developed in a shipload.

(e) Admissibility

7.044 In Scandinavian law, a party is obliged to give access to evidence only if the evidence can be presented to court and can serve as a basis for the judgment. Scandinavian legal systems do not differentiate between admissibility and discoverability. If a party can lawfully refuse to present certain evidence or if consent is required for its presentation, that same evidence can also be withheld from disclosure.

7.045 In Sweden and Denmark, the obligation of parties and non-parties to disclose documents is limited by the same constraints that apply to the duty to testify or respond to questions as a witness.[80] In Norway, evidential privileges are comprehensively outlined in chapter 22 of the CCP, which governs both the presentation and access to evidence.[81] In Sweden and Denmark, most of these privileges are codified in their procedural laws, although some are derived from judicial precedent. Across all Scandinavian jurisdictions, contractual arrangements, such as non-disclosure agreements, cannot create new evidential privileges. This ensures that such agreements do not override the obligation to provide access to relevant evidence.[82]

7.046 While the specifics of evidential privileges differ slightly across jurisdictions, the most significant privileges – those for information entrusted to attorneys, healthcare professionals, and priests in their professional capacities – are universally recognized in Denmark, Sweden, and Norway.[83] These privileges safeguard confidential relationships, such as those between attorneys and clients or doctors and patients. Information covered by these privileges may be disclosed if the person who has a right to secrecy consents.[84] Although courts formally require clear consent, in practice, implied or tacit consent is sometimes recognized. Moreover, a party cannot selectively disclose certain pieces of evidence while withholding related evidence.[85]

---

79 HR-2020-2469-A.

80 The Danish Code of Procedure section 298 (1); The Swedish Code of Procedure section 38:2 (2).

81 The Norwegian Code of Civil Procedure section 21-5.

82 Westberg, *Anskaffning av bevisning i dispositiva tvistemål* (n 25) 680; Strandberg, 'Evidentiary Contracts in Civil Proceedings' (n 18) 49–50.

83 The Danish Code of Procedure section 170; The Swedish Code of Procedure section 36:5 (2) and (4); The Norwegian Code of Civil Procedure section 22-5.

84 The Swedish Code of Procedure section 36:5 (3); The Norwegian Code of Civil Procedure section 22-5 (3); compare The Danish Code of Procedure section 170 (2).

85 Rt. 2001 1113; Rt. 2009 1204; Rt. 2012 608 A; HR-2017-2262-A.

In the context of *edisjonsplikt*, close relatives of a party are exempt from the duty to testify but are generally not exempt from disclosing documents. The exemption applies only to evidence entrusted to them by the party, not to other documents or items they might possess.[86] 7.047

A more important exemption is that a party is not obliged to disclose documents or other evidence containing trade secrets, see for instance the Norwegian CCP section 22-10:[87] 7.048

> A party or witness may refuse to provide access to evidence that cannot be made available without revealing trade or business secrets. The court may nevertheless order such evidence to be made available if, after balancing the relevant interests, the court finds this to be necessary.

While the general rule is that trade secrets are protected from disclosure, courts have the authority to order their release when deemed essential.[88] In practice, courts frequently mandate disclosure of such evidence, often imposing measures like redacting sensitive parts or issuing confidentiality orders for the requesting party.[89] When there is a need for fading out trade secrets, the costs for doing so will be relevant under the proportionality test.[90] Trade secrets do not seem to be explicitly exempted from disclosure under Danish law, but the existence of such secrets will be factored into the broader proportionality analysis undertaken by the courts, as discussed in Section C.4. 7.049

4. *Edisjonsplikt* for third parties

In Scandinavian law, the duty of disclosure extends to third parties.[91] In general, any physical or legal person who is in possession of information of relevance to an ongoing litigation may be ordered to disclose that information. This obligation includes administrative bodies, and it is common for parties to request access to evidence from tax authorities or social security bodies under the principles of *edisjonsplikt*. As a general rule, a party may request evidence from a third party rather than from the opposing party, and such requests are not formally considered secondary or subsidiary to those made between the parties. 7.050

In general, the criteria for requiring disclosure by third parties largely mirror those applicable to parties involved in the litigation. However, some requirements may be 7.051

86 The Danish Code of Procedure section 171; The Swedish Code of Procedure 38:2 (2); The Norwegian Code of Civil Procedure section 22-8.

87 See also The Swedish Code of Procedure 38:2 (2), cf section 36:6 second meaning.

88 The Swedish Code of Procedure 36:6 (3).

89 The Norwegian Code of Civil Procedure section 22-12 (3).

90 e.g. HR-2019-997-A.

91 The Danish Code of Procedure section 299; The Swedish Code of Procedure section 38:2; The Norwegian Code of Civil Procedure sections 21-5 and 26-1.

applied stricter when access to evidence is required from a third party. In particular, factors that involve balancing the evidential benefits against the burdens placed on the required party may be weighed more heavily in favor of the third party. Consequently, a request for evidence may be denied when directed at a third party, even if the same request would have been granted if made against a party to the case.

5. Choice of disclosure method

7.052 In light of the ongoing digitalisation, methods for providing access to evidence have been somewhat debated in Scandinavian countries over the past two decades.[92] While these issues are not comprehensively regulated, some foundational principles were established in Norway's 2005 legal reform, which probably reflects practices in Denmark and Sweden as well. In Norway, orders granting access to evidence must concretise the evidence that shall be disclosed, the timing of disclosure, and the location where it is to take place. The order may also define the method for granting access, see for instance the Norwegian CCP section 26-7 (3):

> The court shall determine in more detail and to the extent necessary how the evidence shall be made available, how it shall be stored and other issues of relevance to the presentation of such evidence.

7.053 The court has a wide margin of appreciation in determining the methods for implementing evidence access, and the parties have the right to be heard on these matters. Throughout the last years, methods for disclosure have been a matter of dispute in quite a few cases, often requiring courts to issue multiple orders to resolve procedural disagreements.

7.054 One recurring issue concerns access to real property, where it is frequently disputed whether such access should be provided directly between the parties or towards the court as evidence taken by visual inspection. Under Article 8 of the European Convention on Human Rights (ECHR), a party cannot be compelled to allow the opposing party or a party-appointed expert direct access to their private home or residence. Access in such cases must be facilitated through a court-led inspection.[93] However, in a case decided in 2020, the Norwegian Supreme Court ordered access to evidence between the parties without the court's involvement.[94] This case did not involve access to a private home, but to the place of production for a specific kind of artificial fertilizer. The court stipulated that both parties must be present during the testing of the fertilizer and emphasized that the rules on evidence access generally

---

92 Westberg, *Anskaffning av bevisning i dispositiva tvistemål* (n 25) 455–604; Astrup Hjort, *Tilgang til bevis i sivile saker* (n 5) 124–133.

93 Rt. 2014 1084.

94 HR-2020-2469-A.

govern rights and obligations between the parties. Furthermore, it stated that the parties have an obligation to cooperate for realizing the right to access evidence, and that the court's role is to decide on matters which the parties cannot agree on.[95]

Another significant area of contention relates to access to digitally stored information, which raises specific technical and procedural challenges. Often, evidence is preserved before being made available to the requesting party, ensuring no disclosure occurs until disputes over access are conclusively resolved by the court.[96] Various methods for sorting relevant and admissible evidence from the information that is irrelevant or inadmissible have been developed. While many of these approaches, such as technology-assisted review, originate in American e-discovery practices,[97] they are increasingly proposed and debated within Scandinavian legal contexts.[98] 7.055

6. Remedies and consequences of non-compliance

In Sweden, the enforcement of a disclosure order can be carried out either through the rules governing witnesses or by issuing an enforcement declaration.[99] In contrast, in Denmark and Norway, only disclosure orders directed at third parties are subject to enforcement mechanisms.[100] In Denmark, a party failing to comply with a disclosure order may be sanctioned under the assessment of the evidence. The Danish CP section 344 (2) allows the court to favor the opposing party if a party's disclosure or presentation of evidence is incomplete or unclear.[101] 7.056

The Norwegian code does not entail such a provision, but sanctioning under the evaluation of the evidence is well-known and was recognized by the law commission when preparing the 2005 code.[102] However, this approach is sometimes deemed inadequate in certain situations. To address this, the 2005 Norwegian reforms provided courts with the competence to issue follow-up orders, allowing them to declare that the non-disclosing party will be regarded as absent if the required evidence is not disclosed 7.057

95 HR-2020-2469-A para 42-47.

96 The Norwegian Code of Civil Procedure section 26-7 (3) last sentence.

97 Maura R Grossman and Gordon V Cormack, 'Technology-Assisted Review in E-Discovery Can Be More Effective and More Efficient Than Exhaustive Manual Review' (2011) 17 (5) Richmond Journal of Law and Technology 1; Gideon Christian, 'Predictive Coding: Adopting and Adapting Artificial Intelligence in Civil Litigation' (2019) 97 The Canadian Bar Review 486.

98 Magne Strandberg, 'The Justice System Takes Account of the (Social, Economic) Digital Revolution: Evidence Law Adjusted to Digitally Stored Information' in B Hess, M Woo, L Cadiet, S Menétrey and E García (eds), *Comparative Procedural Law and Justice* (Part IX Chapter 2, CPJL 2024).

99 The Swedish Code of Procedure section 38:5 last sentence.

100 The Danish Code of Procedure section 299 (2) and section 178; The Norwegian Code of Civil Procedure section 26-8.

101 This sanction is important in Denmark, see Bang (n 49) 271; Gomard and Kistrup (n 1) 615.

102 NOU 2001: 32 *Rett på sak* 982; Ot.prp. no 51 (2004–2005) *Om lov om mekling og rettergang i sivile tvister* 468.

within a defined timeframe.[103] In such cases, a default judgment may be issued against the non-compliant party. Non-compliance with access to evidence orders may also be sanctioned under cost-shifting rules if the non-compliance caused unnecessary expenses.[104]

D. ACCESS TO EVIDENCE PRE-COMMENCEMENT

1. General starting points

7.058 The main legal mechanisms for requiring access to evidence in Scandinavia, *edisjonsplikt*, apply after commencement of pleadings. However, Scandinavian law entails a number of rules that are applicable before a lawsuit is formally initiated. In contrast to rules applicable post-commencement, the rules applicable pre-commencement vary significantly from one country to another. Consequently, the laws of Denmark, Sweden, and Norway must be addressed separately to understand their distinct approaches.

7.059 Despite these differences, the countries share a foundational principle: as a main rule, parties cannot demand access to evidence before initiating legal proceedings. This restriction extends to prohibiting access to the evidence of potential future parties for the purpose of conducting investigations assessing the risk of litigation. In general, the exceptions to this principle typically arise when there is a risk of destruction or manipulation of evidence that may become relevant for a future lawsuit.

7.060The The discussion is divided into two main sections: Section D outlines the general rules applicable to civil proceedings, while Section E focuses on specific provisions for intellectual property rights and Section F focuses on the provisions for competition cases. In all Scandinavian countries, parties may be obliged to disclose evidence due to a general duty of cooperation, see section B. However, before the commencement of proceedings, this duty is far less stringent and more ambiguous compared to the rules governing disclosure during active litigation.

2. Sweden

7.061 In Sweden, potential parties may apply to secure evidence for use in a future lawsuit if there is a risk that the evidence might be lost or lose quality. The rule applies to all civil proceedings and to most sources of evidence which can be preserved prior to proceedings. The legal basis is the Swedish CP section 41:1:

---

103 The Norwegian Code of Civil Procedure section 16-7 (2).

104 The Norwegian Code of Civil Procedure section 20-2 (3) and section 20-4 letter c.

> If there is a risk that evidence concerning a circumstance of importance to a person's legal rights may be lost or difficult to obtain and no trial concerning the rights is pending, a district court may take and preserve for the future evidence in the form of witness examination, expert opinion, view, or written evidence.

To invoke this rule, there must be a demonstrable risk that evidence relevant to a specific legal right could be lost or become inaccessible. The evidence must be of direct or indirect importance for a material fact,[105] and the requesting party must specify the material facts to which the evidence is relevant.[106] Most scholars argue that the party applying for securing of evidence has a burden of proof and must substantiate and justify the claimed risk.[107] Diverging views are held on whether these rules are applicable for identification of a future or potential counterparty.[108] **7.062**

If the criteria for preservation of evidence are met, the court 'may' take evidence and is thereby not obliged to order preservations of evidence. This discretion allows the court to balance the interests of all parties involved before making a decision.[109] **7.063**

While section 41:1 of the Swedish PC primarily addresses the preservation of evidence, it does not explicitly grant the requesting party access to the preserved evidence. In practice, it may still resolve difficulties or problems which otherwise would have been solved by access to evidence rules. One of the main issues with unequal access is that one party may control the existence or availability of critical evidence. A court order under section CP section 41:1 may reduce or set aside that risk of asymmetrical access. Furthermore, the purpose of securing evidence may be to get information in order to assess the prospects of winning a potential future trial. **7.064**

3. Denmark

In Denmark, a general statutory provision for isolated evidence-taking (*isoleret bevisoptagelse*), allowing the collection of evidence prior to the commencement of a lawsuit or independent of a pending case, was established in 1980 following a recommendation made in 1973.[110] This provision enables evidence to be gathered through a written request from a party, with no other formal requirements.[111] As suggested in the recommendation, the court was provided a very broad competence, as outlined in the Danish CP section 343 (1), first sentence: **7.065**

---

105 Nordh (n 49) 114; Lindell (n 1) 583.
106 Nordh (n 49) 115.
107 Nordh (n 49) 115–116 and Lindell (n 1) 582.
108 NJA 1982 650; NJA 1984 47; Nordh (n 49) 115; Lindell (n 1) 583–584.
109 Lindell (n 1) 584.
110 Betænkning om behandling af borgerlige sager, no 698/1973.
111 UfR 2000 3228 Ø; Bang-Pedersen, Christensen and Petersen (n 68) 543.

The court may allow taking of evidence even when such evidence taking is not for use in a pending lawsuit.

7.066 The main purpose of this broad and general rule on evidence-taking is to avoid unnecessary proceedings.[112] While section 343 explicitly mentions isolated evidence-taking in the form of visual inspection, the rule applies to other means of evidence as well. However, a party is not obliged to give access to privileged or inadmissible evidence.[113] The court can permit evidence-taking whenever deemed appropriate and will do so unless it finds the evidence irrelevant to the matter at hand.[114] This rule shares similarities with rules on *edisjonsplikt* and may provide a party access to evidence that was not previously within their control.

7.067 Isolated evidence-taking can be ordered against both parties and third parties.[115] The practical application of section 343 in cases involving third parties is illustrated by two notable cases related to access to IP addresses in intellectual property rights disputes.[116] In both cases, the claimants were not able to identify the infringers and therefore encouraged the internet providers to disclose the information necessary to identify names and addresses of the infringers. Getting access to the identification from the internet providers was the only available mechanism for the claimants, which implied that these access to evidence requests were within the scope of application of the rules on isolated evidence-taking.

7.068 Unless the parties have agreed otherwise, the party requiring isolated taking of evidence shall cover the costs incurred and the court may order security for costs as well.[117] However, the costs incurred may be shifted in a later lawsuit concerning the substantive issues which the evidence was secured for.[118]

4. Norway

7.069 Compared to Sweden and Denmark, the Norwegian CCP chapter 28 contains more demanding rules on access to evidence prior to commencement. Although chapter 28 has obvious similarities with rules found in the code of 1915, the practical role of the rules has changed dramatically. The code of 1915 contained an entire chapter dedicated to securing evidence outside of pending lawsuits, and while it offered

112 Lindecrone Petersen and Djurhuus (n 4) 296.
113 UfR 2005 3053 Ø; UfR 2011 406 Ø.
114 Lindecrone Petersen and Djurhuus (n 4) 295.
115 UfR 2003 2264 Ø.
116 UfR 2003 2264 Ø; UfR 2005 1410 V.
117 Danish Code of Procedure section 343 (2) and (3).
118 Gomard and Kistrup (n 1) 423.

generous provisions for requiring parties, the rules were rarely applied in practice.[119] An important amendment to those rules was established in 2004: After the Supreme Court underlined that ex parte securing of evidence was not allowed under Norwegian law,[120] such rules were established by a new section 271a of the 1915 code in order to get Norwegian law in accordance with the TRIPS-agreement.[121] While securing of evidence ex parte was supposed to be an exceptional measure for extraordinary situations, in practice the mechanism has been applied frequently and probably more frequent than proceeding with notification of the required party. Importantly, these provisions were given a broader scope of application, extending beyond the scope of intellectual property rights covered by the TRIPS Agreement. Chapter 28 of the current CCP replaced these rules and maintained the general scope of application. Chapter 28 has become an important tool for access to evidence, much more influential than what was expected. Even though 'securing of evidence' suggests that these rules are applicable only for avoiding future damage to evidence, the purposes of these rules are broader. As underlined by the law commission and the Supreme Court, the rules shall provide a potential party with access to evidence in order to clarify whether there is a substantial basis for a claim and to prepare the ground for well-informed settlements.[122]

Access to evidence prior to commencement shall be ordered by the court upon application if the conditions for giving such an order is fulfilled. Most of the conditions follow from chapter 28, others from analogical application of rules on *edisjonsplikt*. The main requirements are found in the CCP section 28-2: **7.070**

> Evidence may be secured if it can be of significance in a dispute to which the applicant may become a party or intervener, and there is either a clear risk that the evidence will be lost or considerably weakened, or there are other reasons why it is particularly important to obtain access to the evidence before legal proceedings are instigated.

Firstly, some requirements limit the persons who may be parties to securing of evidence proceedings. It must be possible for the requesting party to become a party or an intervener of a future litigation in which the requested evidence may be relevant. While the requested party is often a potential future party to the litigation, this is not a prerequisite for applying for securing evidence. Like the rules on *edisjonsplikt*, the provisions apply to third parties as well. Secondly, one of two basic grounds must be fulfilled. The most common is the 'clear risk that the evidence will be lost or considerably **7.071**

119 Astrup Hjort, *Tilgang til bevis i sivile saker* (n 5) 50 found only 18 cases for the approximately six decades the provision was in force.

120 Rt. 2000 1261.

121 NOU 2001: 32 *Rett på sak* 989–990; Ot prp no 33 (2003–2004) *Om lov om endringer i tvistemålsloven (bevisopptak utenfor rettssak)*.

122 NOU 2001: 32 *Rett på sak* 987–988; Rt. 2010 774 section 30.

weakened', such as when evidence is prone to decay, damage, or digital data is at risk of deletion or alteration.[123] The alternative ground, 'other reasons why it is particularly important to obtain access to the evidence before legal proceedings are instigated', is more open-ended and is typically applied only under exceptional circumstances where securing evidence is justified, even without a clear risk of loss or damage.[124]

7.072 Thirdly, the requested evidence must be relevant to a future dispute. This criterion of relevance is similar to the requirement found in the rules on *edisjonsplikt*. Since the securing of evidence proceeding is prior to commencement, the relevance-test will be more abstract. Chapter 28 applies to all forms of evidence, but documents – in particular electronically stored information – are by far the most important evidence to be accessed under these rules.

7.073 Fourthly, the requested evidence must be sufficiently specified. While section 28-2 does not explicitly state this requirement, it has been emphasized by both the law commission and the Supreme Court.[125] Specification is understood based on practical considerations and the purpose of securing evidence.[126] A gradual or two-step approach to specification is often used, particularly in cases concerning securing of evidence ex parte. In a number of cases, an initial broad request may lead to more detailed specifications before the evidence is made available.[127]

7.074 Fifthly, the application for securing of evidence must be proportionate. This criterion, although not explicitly mentioned in section 28-2, is a general principle under the 2005 code and has been applied by the Supreme Court in securing evidence cases.[128] The principle of proportionality applies throughout the process and has a content very similar to section 26-5 (3) concerning *edisjonsplikt*.[129] However, the application of the criterion is more difficult since the content of future disputes is less specified, and the need to protect the required party from unnecessary undue burdens and privacy invasions becomes even more significant.[130] While the substantive claim does not need to be fully substantiated nor probable, the potential evidential support is a relevant factor in the proportionality assessment.[131] Courts must also ensure compliance with

123 NOU 2001: 32 *Rett på sak* 987; Astrup Hjort, *Tilgang til bevis i sivile saker* (n 5) 248–249.
124 Astrup Hjort, *Tilgang til bevis i sivile saker* (n 5) 257–264.
125 NOU 2001: 32 *Rett på sak* 990.
126 Rt. 2006 626 para 36.
127 Rt. 2006 626 para 37.
128 HR-2014-962-U.
129 See n 7.033 et seq.
130 HR-2014-962-U.
131 HR-2014-962-U.

Article 8 of the ECHR and section 102 of the Constitution, which protect the privacy of individuals.[132]

Finally, rules on admissibility limit the application of securing of evidence.[133] Professional privileges and trade secrets may restrict access to certain evidence. While it is possible to request the securing of inadmissible evidence, such evidence must be separated from admissible evidence during the sorting phase. **7.075**

As a main rule, the required party must be notified before securing of evidence is ordered. However, if there is reason to believe that notification could obstruct the securing of evidence, a request for access to evidence prior to commencement may be fronted without notice.[134] The requesting party cannot access the evidence 'until the ruling is final if it may be important for the opposite party to prevent such access', and the requested party has a right to be heard in a court hearing before the court makes its decision.[135] **7.076**

Securing of evidence proceedings are complex, costly, and time-consuming. The costs shall be covered by the requiring part unless the other party has not cooperated or has contested the request without reasonable cause.[136] These costs may, however, be recoverable in subsequent litigation related to the substantive issues for which the evidence was secured.[137] Although most cases concerning securing of evidence do not lead to a lawsuit, the potential for cost recovery plays a significant role in settlement negotiations. **7.077**

The 2005 code's law commission did not see the need for additional rules regarding the implementation of securing evidence.[138] The courts were given a general competence to decide on the methods for securing evidence, with the authority to include specific criteria or requirements for implementation, see CCP sections 28-4 and 26-7 (3). The court may, for instance, set up time limits for access to evidence and for when it shall be returned.[139] The court may also appoint an expert to assist with the securing and sorting of evidence and may define the expert's mandate. However, issues related to the implementation of securing of evidence have led to practical challenges **7.078**

---

132 Rt. 2010 774 para 55 ff.

133 Rt. 2010 774 para 37.

134 Code of Civil Procedure section 28-4 (3) first sentence.

135 Code of Civil Procedure section 28-4 (3) third and fourth sentence.

136 Code of Civil Procedure section 28-5; The requested party may require security for costs if the requesting party is not resident in an EEA country, see the Code of Civil Procedure section 22-11; HR-2018-2164-U.

137 Magne Strandberg, 'Bevissikring og sakskostnader' (2019) 56 (3) LoR 2017 159, 173–177.

138 NOU 2001: 32 *Rett på sak* 990; Ot prp no 50 (2004–2005) *Om lov om mekling og rettergang i sivile tvister* 471.

139 HR-2021-69-U.

and criticism from both the Supreme Court and academics due to the lack of detailed rules and guidelines.[140]

E. CASES CONCERNING INFRINGEMENTS OF INTELLECTUAL PROPERTY RIGHTS

7.079 In order to implement Articles 6, 7, and 8 of Directive 2004/48/EF on enforcement of intellectual property rights, Sweden and Denmark established special rules governing access to evidence in cases concerning infringements of intellectual property rights. Denmark implemented these provisions into its procedural code by creating dedicated chapters,[141] while Sweden implemented the rules into Acts governing substantive rules on the intellectual rights.[142] Both countries' frameworks include two distinct mechanisms for accessing evidence: rules on information orders, reflecting Article 8 of the Directive,[143] and rules on securing of evidence, corresponding to Article 7.[144] The requirements and effects of these mechanisms align closely with those outlined in the Directive. The rules apply both before and after the commencement of legal proceedings,[145] though pre-commencement applications are more common in practice.[146] A requesting party must present evidence providing reasonable ground to believe that his intellectual property rights have been or will be infringed.[147] If the requested access to information is regarded proportionate after having considered the evidential value of the required evidence compared to the harm caused to the required party,[148] the court shall normally approve the application.

7.080 Norway took a different approach, initially asserting that the procedural nature of the Directive's provisions placed them outside the scope of the EEA Agreement.

140 HR-2017-111-A section 48; Maria Astrup Hjort, 'Behov for reformering av tvistelovens bevissikringsregler' (2017) 56 (3) LoR 131, 141–144; Maria Astrup Hjort, 'Mandat til å sortere digitalt materiale' (2019) 19 (2) LoR 209, 233–234.

141 Danish Code of Procedure chapters 29a and 57a.

142 Act on trademark of 9 Dec 2010 no 1877 (*Varumärkeslagen*) chapter 9; Act on copyright of 30 Dec 1960 no 729 (*upphovsrättslagen*) sections 53c-53f and 56a to 56h; Act on patents of 1 Dec 1967 no 837 (*patentlagen*) sections 57 c til 57 g §§ and 59a to 59h §§; Act on Design Protection of 29 June 1970 no 485 (*mönsterskyddslagen*) sections 35c to 35g and 37a to 37h; Act on Companies of 29 March 1974 no 156 (*firmalagen*) sections 18b to 18f and 20a to 20h; Act on circuit design of 17 Dec 1992 no 1685 (*kretsmönsterlagen*) sections 9c to 9g and 12a to 12h; Act on Plant Variety Rights of 29 May 1997 no 306 (*växtförädlarrättslagen*) sections 5a to 5e and 9:7a to 9:7h.

143 Danish Code of Procedure chapter 29a; The Swedish Varumärkeslagen of 9 Dec 2010 no 1877 sections 9:1 to 9:4 (identically in other Acts listed in fn XX).

144 Danish Code of Procedure chapter 57a; The Swedish Varumärkeslagen of 9 Dec 2010 no 1877 sections 9:5 to 9:13 (identically in other Acts listed in fn 143).

145 The Norwegian Code of Civil Procedure section 28A-3 (1).

146 Bang-Pedersen, Christensen and Petersen (n 68).

147 Danish Code of Procedure section 653 (1); The Norwegian Code of Civil Procedure section 28A-1.

148 Danish Code of Procedure section 653 (4); The Norwegian Code of Civil Procedure section 28A-2.

However, Norwegian businesses should not face disadvantages compared to their European competitors.[149] Therefore, a set of rules based on the Directive was included in the Code of Civil Procedure. The CCP chapter 28A has a scope of application similar to the Directive and contains rules on information orders, in line with Article 8 of the Directive. However, the chapter does not address securing of evidence, presumably leaving such matters to the general provisions in CCP chapter 28.

One may wonder why a separate set of rules on information orders was necessary. Since Norway has broad rules on access to evidence before and after commencement, the justification for special rules for intellectual property cases seems unclear. The government found the rules in the Directive better suited for the typical need for access to evidence and information in cases concerning intellectual properties. However, in practice, the Norwegian rules under Chapter 28A have been rarely utilized. **7.081**

F. CASES CONCERNING DAMAGES FOLLOWING FROM INFRINGEMENTS OF COMPETITION LAW

In order to implement the EU Directive 1014/104/EU, Sweden established a special Act for damages following from infringements of competition law.[150] According to the Swedish government, establishing a new Act for the private law matters following from infringements of competition law was the best option. Incorporating these private law provisions into the predominantly public-law-focused Competition Act would, according to the government, overly complicate the legislation.[151] The Swedish government also determined that the Directive's requirements regarding national rules on access to evidence were already met by the provisions on *edisjonsplikt* in Chapter 38 of the Swedish CP.[152] Therefore, section 5:4 first sentence simply refers to the CP chapter 38. However, the Act includes special provisions regarding access to information held by competition authorities. Section 5:5 includes provisions limiting the duty to give access to evidence under the rules on *edisjonsplikt*. Section 5:7 extends these provisions to apply before the commencement of legal proceedings, specifying that sections 4 to 6 also apply in pre-commencement contexts. **7.082**

149 Prop. 81 L (2012–2013), *Endringer i lovgivningen om industrielt rettsvern m.m. (styrking av håndhevingsreglene)* 13; Halvard Haukeland Fredriksen and Magne Strandberg, 'Norwegian Civil Procedure Under the Influence of EU Law' in Alan Uzelac and C H van Rhee (eds), *Transformation of Civil Justice. Unity and Diversity* (Springer 2018); Maria Astrup Hjort, 'The EU's Influence on Norwegian Civil Procedure Through National Substantive Law' in Anna Nylund and Magne Strandberg (eds), *Civil Procedure and the Harmonisation of Law* (Intersentia 2019) 116–117.

150 The Swedish Konkurrensskadelag of 3 Nov 2016 no 964.

151 Prop. 2016/17:9 *Konkurrensskadelag* p. 24.

152 Prop. 2016/17:9 *Konkurrensskadelag* p. 65.

7.083 Denmark took a similar approach. A separate Act was established for the substantive private law claims covered by the Directive, with the procedural rules also included in this legislation.[153] Like Sweden, Denmark relied on its existing *edisjonsplikt* rules to meet the Directive's requirements on access to evidence. Section 4 of the Act directly refers to *edisjonsplikt* provisions in the Danish Code of Procedure, but it also restates key aspects of Article 5 of the Directive. This rephrasing likely served to ensure full compliance, even if the considerations and limitations mentioned in the Directive were already inherent in *edisjonsplikt* framework.

7.084 Sections 5 and 6 of the Act implement Articles 6 and 7 on access to and presentation of evidence in possession of the competition authorities. These sections were necessary because the Danish CP lacked equivalent provisions for handling such information. The Act has been applied in one case.[154] The request for disclosure was rejected and the arguments were in line with the criterion of specification and relevance under the well-established rules on *edisjonsplikt*.

7.085 In contrast, Directive 1014/104/EU has not had any influence on Norwegian law. That is due to a dispute between Norway (in particular) and the EU on whether the Directive is within the scope of the EEA Agreement.[155] Since the purpose of the Directive was to provide a more level playing field for competitors in the European market, the Commission marked the Directive as 'Text with EEA Relevance'. The Norwegian government saw both pros and cons of including the Directive in the EEA Agreement, but in the end concluded that the Directive was outside the scope of the Agreement due to the rules' procedural nature.[156] The dispute has not found a solution, which means that the Directive is not (yet) a part of the EEA Agreement.

G. SOME CONCLUDING REMARKS

7.086 Access to evidence rules have become far more important in Scandinavian civil litigation from the 1990s onwards. While Sweden, Denmark, and Norway historically based their rules of civil procedure on German and Austrian influences, recent developments show a clear shift toward Anglo-American legal principles. The traditionally very strict criteria of the rules on *edisjonsplikt* have been made far more flexible and generous for the party who requests access to evidence. This change allows parties to access large volumes of information through a single broad request, multiple targeted

153 The Danish *Lov om behandling af erstatningssager vedrørende overtrædelser af konkurrenceretten* of 13 Dec 2016 no 1541.

154 UfR 2022 4676.

155 Fredriksen and Strandberg (n 149).

156 Forslag til endringer i konkurranseloven – gjennomføring i norsk rett av direktiv 2014/104/EU om privat håndheving av EU/EØS-konkurransereglene 12–14.

requests, or requests encompassing various categories of evidence. At least for physical evidence, including documents and digitally stored information, modern Scandinavian proceedings have similarities to English disclosure and American discovery. On the other hand, a fear of fishing expeditions and other aspects of American extremism is still present, and arguments based on contrasts to Anglo-American are recognized both in law commissions,[157] court practice,[158] and academic writings.[159] The modern *edisjonsplikt* is a middle-ground solution which provides parties with rich opportunities to gain access to evidence while at the same time not opening up broad and totally unspecified requests for such access. Despite some differences in specific criteria and applications across the Scandinavian countries, the fundamental principles and effects of *edisjonsplikt* are largely consistent across Sweden, Denmark, and Norway.

The increasing significance of *edisjonsplikt* has influenced the structure of civil litigation in Scandinavia, particularly in the preparatory stages of proceedings. Traditionally, Scandinavian litigation featured a brief preparatory stage, with the main hearing as the obvious center spot. In contrast, modern proceedings devote more attention to evidence access requests, making the preparatory phase a more critical component of the process. Although to a lesser degree, this Scandinavian development is similar to Anglo-American proceedings where the 'pre-trial' stage has become much more important than the trial or main hearing which it was supposed to prepare for. With similarities to Anglo-American disclosure or discovery proceedings, the conceptual distinction between access to evidence and presentation of evidence has become clearer and more important during the last decades. **7.087**

While the rules on *edisjonsplikt* provide a genuine Scandinavian model for access to evidence after commencement, a common model does not exist for access to evidence prior to commencement. Separate sets of rules have been developed in Sweden, Denmark, and Norway for access to evidence in this very early phase of proceedings. Both the content of the rules and the outcome of the rules vary quite a lot from one Scandinavian country to another. **7.088**

Due to the influence of EU law, special rules on access to evidence are found for cases concerning infringements of intellectual property rights and for damages following from infringements of competition law. Although these EU rules do not bind Norway, the country has voluntarily adopted similar provisions for intellectual property rights infringements, aligning itself with its Scandinavian counterparts in this specific area. **7.089**

---

157 NOU 2001: 32 *Rett på sak* 460–465.

158 HR-2019-997-A para 30, 35 and 73.

159 e.g. Per Magne Ristvedt og Amund Tørum, 'Provokasjoner, begjæringer om bevistilgang og edisjonsplikt; tvistelovens modifiserte discovery' (2016) 21 (2) Tidsskrift for forretningsjus 105.

8

THE APPLICATION OF U.S. DISCOVERY FOR EUROPEAN DISPUTES

Nicolò Trocker

A. INTRODUCTION – DISCOVERING U.S. DISCOVERY

8.001 One of the more intriguing phenomenon generated in the context of international civil litigation is to see parties that used to contest and strongly oppose U.S.-style discovery when they are involved in litigation before U.S. courts, reaching out to the same discovery tools to secure information and evidence located in the United States to support their cases actually pending or in preparation in their home country.

Viewed as a potential source of cost and delay, U.S. discovery has been banned in significant part from the official route of cross-border assistance in the gathering of information and evidence established by the multilateral treaty negotiated at The Hague. Article 23 of that treaty allows Signatories to either flatly decline incoming American requests for the production of documents in the pretrial stage or to severely limit their receptivity if the requests do not comply with the standards unilaterally established by the Signatory's own internal law.[1] When U.S. courts, vested with *in personam* jurisdiction over foreign parties, rely on the regulatory framework of the Federal Rules of Civil Procedure to secure evidentiary material located in foreign countries for the resolution of transnational disputes brought before them, their orders are often questioned in relation to their pertinence to the claims or defenses asserted in the action or because of their overbroad, burdensome and intrusive nature.[2] **8.002**

In contrast to the facets of persisting tensions and conflicts between the United States and other countries around the world on this paradigmatic subject of transnational litigation, over the last decades or so we have noticed persons and entities involved in, or simply contemplating, litigation in their home country arising out of cross-border transactions, turning to American-style discovery as a valuable resource for furthering their claims. Shopping for the powerful tools such discovery provides has become common under a long time neglected provision – Section 1782 of Title 28 of the U.S. Code – which allows, among others, "any interested person" in a proceeding in a foreign or international tribunal to seek discovery in the form of testimony or statements or production of documents, including electronic files or other tangible evidence, from persons or entities that reside or can be "found" in the United States by way of a direct request to a Federal district court, without first having to apply to the foreign tribunal for letters rogatory. Parties from around the world increasingly seem to have **8.003**

1 Article 23 of the Hague Evidence Convention provides that: "A Contracting State may at the time of signature, ratification or accession, declare that it will not execute Letters of Request issued for the purpose of obtaining pretrial discovery of documents as known in Common Law countries". It was the British delegation that insisted on the insertion in the Convention of this provision. The phrase "pretrial discovery of documents as known in Common Law countries" cleverly obscured the significant differences between the procedures available in England and the United States. As to the continental European countries, Germany joined the Hague Convention in 1997 and for nearly half a century – until 2022 – maintained its flat declaration under Article 23 that: "The Federal Republic of Germany will not, in its territory, execute, Letters of Request issued for the purpose of obtaining pretrial discovery of documents as known in common law countries". Under the new Section 14 of the amended Implementing Act which entered into force on July 1, 2022 German courts will execute request for mutual assistance in pretrial discovery of documents only if a series of detailed and extensive requirements are met, including: "(1) the documents to be produced are specified in detail; (2) the documents to be produced are of direct and clearly identifiable importance for the proceedings in question and their outcome; (3) the documents to be produced are in the possession of a party involved in the proceedings". Third-party pretrial discovery is simply excluded.

2 Well-reflected in the Reporters' Note 1 to § 442 of the Restatement (Third) of the Foreign Relations Law of the United States (1987): "No aspect of the extension of the American legal system beyond the territorial frontier of the United States has given rise to so much friction as the application of U.S. discovery rules to the taking of evidentiary material located in foreign countries for investigation and litigation in the United States".

discovered the intrinsic virtues of American fact and evidence finding devices for the resolution of their civil disputes with international elements.

8.004 In a wide range of areas, from labor cases in Brazil[3] to probate disputes in Hong Kong,[4] from antitrust litigation in Korea[5] to divorce proceedings in Austria,[6] from bankruptcy matters in Italy[7] to shareholder disputes linked to the Russian Federation,[8] from trademark infringement claims in Germany[9] to breach of contract actions in the United Kingdom,[10] from investment related proceedings in the Netherlands[11] to securities fraud claims in Denmark,[12] environmental controversies in Ecuador[13] and merely contemplated trials in Singapore,[14] as well as in many other cases in between, parties seek discovery aid from United States Federal courts through the § 1782 path in order to reach information and/or evidence which appears necessary to successfully plead or defend their cases in courts on their home turf.

8.005 In some cases, to make § 1782 procedure an attractive device it may be the simple fact that the information or evidence, like documents in the traditional form of hard copies or, more importantly, electronically stored information, are with entities in the United States or in their control, not in the country where litigation is ongoing. Multinational companies trade with their U.S. counterparties; financial transactions clear through Wall Street; electronic data are accessible from the United States.

8.006 But there are also deeper reasons involved. In most civil law jurisdictions around the world, from continental Europe to Latin America and large parts of Asia, including Japan and the People's Republic of China, where procedural systems are based on a rigid fact-pleading rule and stringent substantiation requirements are set at the filing stage, parties may see § 1782 of Title 28 of the U.S. Code as a welcomed device to get access to information and evidentiary material necessary to prepare certain legal disputes and to calculate their risk, prior to the commencement of proceedings, before

3 *In re Application for an Order for Judicial assistance in a Foreign Proceeding in the Labour Courts of Brazil*, 466 F. Supp. 2d 1020 (N.D. Ill. Dec. 6, 2006).

4 *In re Application of Esses*, 101 F. 3d 873 (2d Cir. 1996).

5 *In re Cathode Ray Tube (CRT) Anti-trust Litigation* (N.D.Cal. 2013).

6 *Glock v. Glock Inc.*, 797 F. 3d 1002 (11th Cir. 2015): Austrian ex-wife filed the § 1782 proceeding to obtain discovery for use in her Austrian divorce proceeding; *In re Reiko Aso* (S.D.N.Y. June 3, 2019): 1782 discovery assistance for use in divorce proceedings in Japan.

7 *Lancaster Factory Co. Ldt v. Mangone*, 90 F.3d 38 (2nd Cir. 1996).

8 *In re Application for an Order pursuant to 28 USC § 1782 to conduct discovery for use in a foreign proceeding* (D.D.C. Aug. 18, 2017). The request was for use in proceedings in the Netherlands.

9 *Heraeus Kulzer GmbH v. Biomet Inc.*, 633 F. 3d 591 (7th Cir. 2011).

10 *In re BM Brazil 1 Fundo de Investimento em Participacoes Multistratgia* (S.D.N.Y. Jan. 18, 2024).

11 *In re Ex Parte Upper Brook Companies* (S.D.N.Y. Dec. 29, 2022).

12 *In re Ex Parte Application of CI Investments Inc & others* (S.D.N.Y. Dec. 14, 2023).

13 *In Re Republic of Ecuador*, 735 F. 3d 1179 (10th Cir. 2010).

14 *In re Ex Parte DNG FZE* (S.D.N.Y. Jan. 11, 2024).

coming to the determination as to whether to initiate a suit and against whom or to seek an out of court settlement.[15]

In the same jurisdictions, once proceedings are instituted, the § 1782 discovery route becomes a welcomed and needed complement to the domestic limitations surrounding document disclosure which require parties to identify with heightened particularity the documents they seek before a court will grant an order, and where non-compliance with a court order to provide documents or other evidentiary material does not trigger contempt-type sanctions.[16] **8.007**

Section 1782, as early applications show, is an attractive device also for litigants in common law countries outside the United States which have limited disclosure with no pretrial depositions and only limited third party discovery. The scope of documents which fall to be disclosed in English proceedings on the standard order are more limited than those accessible under the broad general U.S. standard of Rule 26(b)(1) of the Federal Rules of Civil Procedure, as routinely interpreted by American courts. Even more importantly, while U.S. law allows lawyers to take wide-ranging depositions exploring what a witness may say under cross-examination as well as investigating what relevant documents may exist, under the English Civil Procedure Rules 1998 there is no deposition process or opportunity to cross-examine witnesses on their evidence as part of the pretrial stage and the types of documents which non-parties can be compelled to produce are clearly limited.[17] **8.008**

Then there is the "leverage" that under § 1782 an application for discovery assistance can be made in two ways, either: indirectly, "pursuant to a letter rogatory issued or request made by a foreign or international tribunal"; or directly, upon application of any "interested person". Parties may choose whichever of these alternatives they prefer, **8.009**

---

15 Pre-litigation discovery is limited under Federal Rule of Civil Procedure 27(a)(1). Therefore, depending on the circumstances of the case, prospective European litigants may be in a better position at home relying on Article 145 (*référé probatoire*) of the Code of Civil Procedure in France, or "preliminary expert reporting" under Article 696 *bis* of the Italian Code of Civil Procedure, or Article 168 (preliminary hearing of witnesses) of the Dutch Code of Civil Procedure in the Netherlands. Still, in *Kiobel v. Cravath, Swaine & Moore LLP*, 895 F. 3d 238 (2d Cir. 2018), because Dutch law requires high factual and evidentiary showing at the filing stage, petitioner Esther Kiobel sought to obtain discovery via Section 1782 in the U.S. in order to prepare her claims against Shell in the Netherlands, Shell's home country, for its tortious human rights violating conduct in the Niger Delta, asking for the production of the documents Shell had previously disclosed to the petitioner in the class-action lawsuit filed in the U.S.

16 The foreign proof-gathering restrictions are frequently mentioned and emphasized in § 1782 proceedings before U.S. courts. See e.g. *Illumina Cambridge Ltd v. Complete Genomics, Ltd.* (N.D. Cal. April 20, 2020).

17 On the restrictions under the "mere witness rule", see Leonard Hoffmann, *Changing Perspectives in Civil Litigation,* 56 *Mod. L. Rev.*, 1993, 297, 300. Pursuant to the new Section 34 of the 1999 Amended Senior Court Act 1981 there is a possibility for a party to litigation to in effect obtain disclosure of documents in the hands of non-parties to litigation, and Civil Procedure Rules, CPR, r. 31.17 (3) allows limited document disclosure against non-parties. Worth mentioning also the new jurisdictional gateway (effective Oct. 1, 2022) under PD 6B para. 3.1(25) on service out of jurisdiction of information orders on foreign third parties.

but the strategic advantages of the latter are clear. Not surprisingly, "demand from foreign parties now overshadow demand from foreign tribunals in both number and complexity".[18] Making an application under § 1782 directly to the U.S. court may turn out to be the only way of securing information or evidence a court in the home country could not ask for via the traditional judicial assistance channels either because litigation has not yet started or because the forum court, in framing the request for assistance, cannot reach out to information and evidence which is not discoverable under the domestic law. A skillful direct cross-border strategy further avoids the often time-consuming and cumbersome medium of a letter of request under the Hague Evidence Convention if the State where the proceeding is pending is a party to the Convention, or the otherwise even more troublesome route of a letter rogatory to be transmitted to the foreign authorities through the traditional diplomatic channels. Direct applications also allow to secure in one stroke depositions and document production to be used in multiple proceedings, actual or merely contemplated, before different jurisdictions.[19]

B. THE PECULIAR FEATURES OF U.S. DISCOVERY AND ITS ROLE IN AMERICAN LITIGATION CULTURE

8.010 Before offering guidance through the complex picture and the key terms of the 28 U.S.C. § 1782 mechanism, it seems appropriate to shed some light on the peculiar features of U.S. discovery, briefly illustrate how they relate to distinctive aspects of the procedural system, and point to the role discovery plays in American litigation culture.

8.011 In procedural systems of civil law tradition around the world strict requirements limit the scope of the fact-finding process at a relatively early stage of the dispute. Civil procedure codes of continental Europe generally require the assertion of detailed facts and the proffer of specified means of evidence during the pleading phase of the proceedings. Even in typical common law countries, parties are expected not to embark on litigation unless they already have a clear concept of their cause of action. Under the English Civil Procedure Rules 1998, for instance, a party has to assert sufficiently detailed facts in the statement of the case capable of disclosing reasonable grounds for bringing a case.[20]

---

18 See Yanbai Andrea Wang, *Exporting American Discovery*, 87 *Univ. Chicago L. Rev.*, 2020, 2089–2174. For an overall picture see also Nicholas J. Boyle, *The Long Arm of the Law: The Availability of U.S. Discovery in Non-U.S. Cases*, 29 *Civ. J. Q.*, 2010, 73 ff.; and the line of cases discussed in the *Brief of Petitioners-Appellee Ester Kiobel in the U.S. Court of Appeal for the Second Circuit* No.17-424-CV, Document 79, May 18, 2017.

19 See *infra* Section 5, text and footnotes 54–56.

20 Pertinent references in Oscar G. Chase – Helen Hershkoff (eds.) *Civil Litigation in Comparative Context*, West 2017, 226–230, 258–262.

In contrast, one of the distinctive aspects of the American Federal Rules of Civil Procedure is not to impose a straitjacket on the original pleadings to get a case underway. Federal Rule of Civil Procedure 8(a)(2) – traditionally associated with the concept of "notice pleading" – requires only a "*short* and *plain* statement of the claim showing that the pleader is entitled to relief" (emphasis added). The relaxed pleading requirements have been partly reshaped under two U.S. Supreme Court decisions: *Bell Atlantic Corp. v. Twombly (2007)* and *Ashcroft v. Iqbal (2009).*[21] The discrete changes directing the Federal courts to engage in more vigorous ("plausibility") scrutiny of complaints before allowing the plaintiff to proceed to discovery, however, do not reflect a deeper and broader change to American pleading.[22] Compared to foreign models, the pleading stage of an American lawsuit has a limited role to play in the ultimate framing of issues in the litigation.[23] **8.012**

Since claimants in Federal courts are not expected to have particularly comprehensive command on the relevant facts at the time they file suit, the investigation and uncovering of facts and information potentially relevant to define the case takes place between the completion of the pleadings – i.e. the submission of complaint and answer or counterclaim – and the beginning of trial: this is the period of *pretrial discovery*. **8.013**

Under the heading "Scope and limits of discovery", the paradigm provision of *Rule 26(b)(1)* of the Federal Rules of Civil Procedure first makes clear that parties have a duty to disclose information and evidence to each other, without awaiting a discovery request and without any court order; then it specifies that "parties may obtain discovery regarding any matter *relevant* to the claim or defense of any party" (emphasis added), and that "information within the scope of discovery need not be admissible in evidence to be discoverable". **8.014**

Two key points are to be taken from these provisions: (i) the system embraces a duty to disclose to each other in terms unknown anywhere else; (ii) "discovery" is different from "evidence". **8.015**

The standard of *relevance* required under Rule 26 for discovery is substantially different from the one which applies to evidence. Only if the "material", including facts and information that the parties are required to disclose to each other, bears no conceivable **8.016**

21 *Bell Atlantic Corp. v. Twombly* 550 US 544 (2007); *Ashcroft v. Iqbal* 129 S.Ct. 1937 (2009).

22 Scott Dodson, *Comparative Convergences in Pleading Standards*, 158 *Univ. Penn. L. Rev*, 2010, 441, 443, 463; Adam N. Steinman, *The Rise and Fall of Plausibility Pleading?*, 69 *Vand. L. Rev.*, 2016, 333–391.

23 "The later stages of the pretrial process (...) do a more robust job in illuminating the nature of the dispute between the parties". Linda J. Silberman, *Contrasting Procedural Systems* in Chase – Hershkoff, *Civil Litigation*, note 20 at 28.

relationship to the claim or defense does the concept of relevance limit the scope of the discovery process.[24]

8.017 In clear contrast, where a *strict fact pleading rule* is applied, as it is the case in most systems of the civil law as well as of the common law world outside the United States, once the case (a lawsuit) is started, there is little room for the parties to go around searching (critics would say: "fishing") for facts and information to build the case; there is need for *evidence*. Evidence is probative material that supports, contradicts or weakens a fact at issue in the proceeding. And a court will order testimony or the production of documents only where a party can describe the facts that the evidence is intended to prove.[25]

8.018 Misunderstandings arise when "foreigners" forget to properly consider U.S. discovery's dual purpose: first, the purpose to allow the gathering of extensive amounts of unspecified and detailed *information* "relevant" for its pertinence to the ultimate framing of issues in the litigation, and second, the purpose of making it possible to obtain *evidence* in a technical sense "relevant to the issues in the proceedings", which will then be used at trial.[26]

8.019 Strictly related to the differences in the treatment of fact or information gathering are the differences between American procedure and the procedure of most (if not all) other countries, as to the scope of the obligations to disclose "information", particularly in the context of the production of documents or electronically stored data.

8.020 Under Federal Rule of Civil Procedure 34(a)(1), courts commonly hold that a requesting party is not required to have actual knowledge of the existence and location of each and every responsive document. Documents and objects relevant to the action and in the responding party's possession, custody or control need not be identified with precision (specificity) to be subject to discovery. It is quite standard that requests are made for documents by entire categories, general description or simply for "any" or "all" documents regarding a given subject in a certain time period. In the seminal *Aérospatiale* case, a product liability and wrongful death action arising out of an air crash on U.S. soil, the French corporate defendants were targeted with a request to produce "all of the design specifications, line drawings and engineering plans and all engineering change orders and plans and all drawings concerning the leading edge slots for the

24 Richard L. Marcus, *Retooling American Discovery for the Twenty-First Century: Toward a New World Order?*, 7 *Tul. J. Int'l & Comp. L.*, 1999, 153, discussing America's unique discovery apparatus.

25 Michele Taruffo, *Rethinking the Standards of Proof*, 51 *Am. J. Comp. L.*, 2003, 675.

26 Stephen N. Subrin, *Fishing Expeditions Allowed: The Historical Background of the 1938 Federal Discovery Rules*, 39 *Boston College L. Rev.*, 1998, 691–745.

Rallye type aircraft manufactured by the defendants and involved in the accident".[27] The obligation to disclose documents that are "relevant" to the case includes those that are not admissible themselves but could potentially lead to the discovery of admissible evidence.

Furthermore, discovery is not limited to the parties. Anyone with discoverable infor- **8.021**
mation can be requested and, if necessary, required, to make it available (under the threat of contempt sanctions), either by way of an oral deposition under oath or by the production of documents or other evidence (Rule 45 of the Federal Rules of Civil Procedure).[28]

Things are significantly different elsewhere. In continental Europe the principle that **8.022**
each party has to make its own case and no party has to help her opponent in their inquiry into the facts – is still very much alive and continues to have a strong impact on the parties' access to documentary evidence. Where courts have been vested with (new) powers to order parties or third parties to disclose documents in their possession or to which one of the litigants has made reference, the *relevance* and *specificity* standards required for the taking of evidence tend to preclude court orders without detailed factual or evidentiary contentions. This means that there is no way where a litigant can apply for the production of a document the existence of which has not somehow independently come to his attention.[29]

Under the English Civil Procedure Rules, CPR r.31.6, "standard disclosure" requires **8.023**
a party to disclose those documents they intend to rely upon, those adverse to their case, those adverse to and those that support their opponent's case and those required to be disclosed by any relevant Practice Direction. In contrast to the wide range of

27 *S.N.I.Aérospatiale v. District Court*, 483 U.S. 522, 545 (1987) and see the bitterly fought *Taishan Drywall* case *In re Chinese-Manufactured Drywall Products Liability Litigation* (E.D. La., Sept. 26, 2014). Discussion in Ray W. Campbell – Ellen C. Campbell, *Clash of Systems: Discovery in U.S. Litigation Involving Foreign Defendants*, 4 *Peking Univ. Trans'l L. Rev.*, 2016, 157–166.

28 Analytical discussion in *Universiy of Montreal Pension Plan v. Bank of America Securities*, 685 F. Supp. 2d 456, 469 ff. (S.D.N.Y. 2010).

29 An attitude well-reflected in the requirements set forth in Section 424 of the German Code of Civil Procedure. Specificity requirements are set in Article 213 of the Italian Code of Civil Procedure and Article 94 of the Provisions for the Implementation of the Code, in Article 843a if the Dutch Code of Civil Procedure and are read into Article 138 of the French Code of Civil Procedure: the application for the production of documents "*doit permettre d'identifier les piecés*". On the EU side, innovative steps in matters of access to information and evidence have been taken by the Directive 2004/48 on the enforcement of intellectual property rights and the Directive 2014/104 on antitrust damages actions. But, as the precision test in Article 5(2) of (and Recital 16 to) the Directive 2014/104 emblematically shows, disclosure remains limited to "specified items of evidence or relevant categories of evidence identified as precisely and narrowly possible" and the traditional relevance standard applies to the new provisions. There is a certain "vigilance" by the European lawmakers and by the European courts, both at the supranational and the national level, to prevent an "Americanization" of the disclosure rules in the EU. For an overall view, our *From Access to the Courts to the Right to an Effective Remedy: A European Perspective of Modern Procedural Challenges*, 47 *Revista de Direito do Trabalho e Seguridade Social*, 2021, 38, 49.

American discovery, English pretrial requests for documents are limited to those directly relevant to facts alleged by the statement of claims or directly material to an issue in the action. English law has always set its face against so-called "fishing expeditions" and courts have been vigilant not to allow disclosure or disclosure related devices like Norwich Pharmacal orders to be used for "wide roving inquisitions".[30]

8.024 Legal systems provide confidentiality protection and confidentiality restrictions on the scope of information which can be subjected to the litigation process and have traditionally been a source of major conflicts between European countries and the United States in the area of business related information (e.g. information on research development, marketing, enterprise strategy and the like). In recent years, issues of confidentiality have given rise to new challenges because of the inherent tension between cross-border discovery – today mainly electronic discovery – and data privacy interests, a tension rooted in different cultures of privacy, with different sensibilities that have produced significantly different laws in the U.S. and in Europe, in particular with the EU's General Data Protection Regulation.[31]

8.025 One final point needs to be emphasized. Liberal discovery is not a mere procedural rule, nor a mere step in the adjudication process. Liberal discovery is a hallmark of American litigation practice and culture reflected also in other features like aggressive lawyering, contingent fee agreements, jury trials, punitive or treble damages designed to enhance deterrence, and routine aggregation of plaintiffs into class actions. More than other legal systems, the United States entrust civil litigation with roles far more general than just resolving disputes between parties.[32] Broad discovery is an essential instrument of policy implementation critical in many situations in which civil litigation is used to enforce civil rights, provide consumer protection, implement trade related aspects of intellectual property law, enforce products liability rules, environmental

30 *Zuckerman on Civil Procedure: Principles of Practice*, 4th edn., Sweet & Maxwell, 2021, ch. 15. Under the disclosure regime of PD 57 AD (effective Oct. 1, 2022) there are five models of "extended disclosure" that can be ordered by the court in addition to, or as alternative to, initial disclosure of key documents a party has to provide when serving a statement of case. The key differences to discovery in U.S. federal courts remain. See *AQR Capital Management, LLC & others v. The London Metal Exchange & anor* [2022] EWHC 3313 (Comm.): *Norwich Pharmacal* orders should not be used for "fishing expeditions". At the time the Hague Evidence Convention was drafted, the United Kingdom was the only country that had some experience with the American-style pretrial discovery. Lord Goddard in *Radio Corporation of America v. Rauland Corporation* [1956] 1 Q.B. 618, 649 already called it a "fishing proceeding which is never allowed in the English courts".

31 On the diverging approaches to privacy and their underlying philosophy in Europe and the United States, James Q. Whitman, *The Two Western Cultures of Privacy: Dignity v. Liberty*, 113 *Yale L. J.*, 2004, 1151–1221.

32 The classical essay by Abram Chayes, *The Role of the Judge in Pubic Law Litigation*, 89 *Harv. L. Rev.*, 1976, 1282. Samuel Issacharoff, *Regulating After the Fact*, 56 *DePaul L. Rev.*, 2007, 375, 377, 382: "The idea that a sufficient level of state or federal regulation could effectively displace private litigation is almost inconceivable". Erica Gorga – Michael Halberstam, *Litigation Discovery and Corporate Governance: The Missing Story About the "Genius of American Corporate Law"*, 63 *Emory L. J.*, 2014, 1384, 1394. An increasingly conservative Supreme Court has made enforcement of rights through lawsuits less friendly.

provisions, securities, and antitrust statutes. It took the resources of pretrial discovery to uncover concealed information in the battled asbestos and tobacco litigation and modern discovery has had a profound impact on the evolution of shareholder litigation, corporate governance and the culture of corporate disclosure in the United States. "There are situations," Stephen Subrin forcefully argues, "when discovery restraint will not make sense".[33]

Amendments to the Federal discovery rules during the last several decades have been in the direction of narrowing discovery. The commitment to advance goals of cooperation, proportionality and active judicial case management has been at the heart of the 2015 Amendments. In the aggregate "these changes have clipped the wings of unconstrained party-driven discovery", but liberal discovery remains a way of life in American litigation.[34] **8.026**

C. UNILATERALISM INSTEAD OF TREATY-BUILDING: THE BACKGROUND OF 28 U.S.C. § 1782 AND ITS TWIN AIMS

The survey should have raised some awareness of what it means to authorize U.S. Federal courts to assist in the production of information and evidence for use in foreign courts through 28 U.S. Code § 1782 which, as relevant to this analysis, in its current form provides as follows: **8.027**

> (a) The district court of the district in which a person resides or is found may order him to give his testimony or statement or to produce a document or other thing for use in a proceeding in foreign or international tribunal (...). The order may be made pursuant to a letter rogatory issued or request made, by a foreign or international tribunal or upon application of any interested person and may direct that the testimony or statement be given, or the document or other thing be produced before a person appointed by the court. By virtue of this appointment, the person appointed has power to administrate any necessary oath and take the testimony or statement. The order may prescribe the practice and procedure, which may be in whole or in part the practice and procedure of the foreign country or the international tribunal, for taking the testimony or statement or producing the document or other thing. To the extent that the order does not prescribe otherwise, the testimony or statement shall be taken, and the document or other thing produced, in accordance with the Federal Rules of Civil Procedure.
>
> A person may not be compelled to give his testimony or statement or to produce a document or other thing in violation of any legally applicable privilege.

---

33 Stephen N. Subrin, *Discovery in Global Perspective: Are We Nuts?*, 52 *DePaul L. Rev.*, 2002, 309, 317–318. Europe is not particularly at "ease" with similar challenges and in crucial fields relies on the role of public bodies (in some countries called "independent agencies") vested with broad investigatory powers and using special procedures.

34 Richard L. Marcus, *The Magnetic Pull of American Discovery: Second Thoughts About American Exceptionalism?*, in Augusto Chizzini et al (eds.) *Processo civile e Costituzione. Omaggio a Nicolò Trocker*, Giuffrè, 2023, 529–546.

8.028 The central point of this provision is well-illustrated in Judge Posner's statement in *Heraeus Kulzer v. Biomet* (2011) – a document discovery request from a German company suing its American competitor in Germany for alleged misappropriation of trade secrets: "A party to litigation in a foreign country can seek [through § 1782] discovery relating to that litigation in a U.S. Federal district court, and, in the discretion of that court, can obtain as much discovery as it could if the lawsuit had been brought in that court rather than abroad".[35] The reasons behind this generous "hospitality" and its basic aims deserve to be briefly explained.[36]

8.029 When U.S. Congress, in view of the significant changes that were occurring in international commerce, created the "Commission on International Rules and Judicial Procedure" instructing its members to "investigate and recommend improvements to existing practices of judicial assistance and cooperation between the United States and foreign countries", the Commission entered the far reaching determination that rather than "laying the groundwork for international agreements or treaties which require negotiations with foreign governments by the Department of State", it would first concentrate on "unilateral improvements of relevant provisions of Unites States Codes and the Federal Rules of Civil Procedure". The Commission on that basis transmitted a proposed bill which, in language essentially identical to that used by the Commission, was presented by the Senate Judiciary Committee with the following observations:

> The enactment of the bill into law will constitute a major step in bringing the United States to the forefront of nations adjusting their procedures to those of sister nations and thereby providing equitable and efficacious procedures for the benefit of tribunals and litigants involved in litigation with international aspects.
>
> It is hoped that the initiative taken by the United States in improving its procedures will invite foreign countries similarly to adjust their procedures.

8.030 With unilateral lawmaking instead of treaty-building as the preferred course, Congress agreed to adopt without change the proposals for the new version of the statute.

8.031 Concerns about the lawmaking prerogatives of the states might have contributed to favor unilateralism, but the animating force to introduce a device like § 1782 was a strong preference for domestic solutions. The objective of obtaining "more enlightened views from other countries" reveals the expectation that the virtues of the American model of discovery assistance eventually would be emulated by other legal systems.

---

35 *Heraeus Kulzer*, note 9 at 594. The discovery request was for "all documents" referring or relating to various matters, defined in very broad terms.

36 See the contributions of one of the major architects of the present version of Section 1782, Hans Smit, *Assistance Rendered by the United States in Proceedings Before International Tribunals*, 62 *Colum. L. Rev.*, 1962, 1264; Id., *American Assistance to Litigation in Foreign and International Tribunals: Section 1782 of Title 28 of the U.S.C. Revisited*, 25 *Syracuse J. Int'l L. & Com.*, 1998, 1 ff.

Some might consider this a naive view. But grants of unilateral assistance are matched with claims of unilateral power.[37]

D. THE "FOREIGN-DISCOVERABILITY" ISSUE AND THE SUPREME COURT'S POLICY ORIENTED RULING IN *ADVANCED MICRO DEVICES, INC. V. INTEL CORPORATION* (2004)

For quite some time § 1782 had been a largely neglected provision. When resorting to U.S. discovery assistance became more popular among "interested persons", individuals and corporate entities in Europe and other parts of the world, the "twin aims" of the statute were the dominant factors to persuade Federal courts to be comfortable with a wide latitude in accepting foreign requests and allowing parties to foreign litigation to obtain access to information and evidence across the Atlantic they could not obtain under the substantive or procedural laws of the country where the action was being heard.[38] **8.032**

In the influential *Euromepa* (1995)[39] opinion rendered on appeal from a French insurance brokerage firm against the district court's denial of a discovery request from the American opponent for use in a pending French litigation, the Second Circuit emphasized that the plain language of the statute and the effort to liberalize the assistance provided by American courts to foreign and international tribunals exclude to engraft a "quasi-exhaustion requirement" onto § 1782 that would force litigants to seek "information through the foreign or international tribunal before requesting discovery from the district", and that there is no room for "any general requirement that the evidence sought in the United States pursuant to § 1782 be discoverable under the laws of the foreign country that is the locus of the underlying proceeding". For foreign litigants to obtain evidence from parties in the United States for use in the foreign jurisdiction it should be enough to determine that "the material sought was pertinent to the subject matter and that the testimony and the documents asked for, on their face, appeared to have a bearing on the issues the parties were disputing in the foreign jurisdiction". Concern about "possible offense" to a foreign nation whose procedures include limited pretrial discovery could be adequately addressed as a factor that informs the court's **8.033**

---

37 See the insightful account by Stephen B. Burbank, *The Reluctant Partner: Making Procedural Law for International Civil Litigation*, 57 *Law & Cont. Problems*, Summer 1994, 103, 107–110, 136–138. See also Paul R. Dubinsky, *Is Transnational Litigation a Distinct Field? The Persistence of Exceptionalism in American Procedural Law*, 44 *Stan. J. Int'l L.*, 2008, 301, 315.

38 For some time, there was a split between the Circuits surrounding the "discoverability" requirement. See for the different views, on the one hand *In re Application of Asta Medica* 981 F 2d 1 (1st Cir. 1992), and on the other *In re Malev Hungarian Airlines* 964 F. 2d 97, 99–100 (2d Cir. 1994).

39 *Euromepa S.A. v. Esmerian*, 51 F 3d 1095 (2d Cir. 1995).

discretion to impose reasonable limitations and conditions upon discovery, rather than "by simply denying relief outright".[40]

8.034 At the turn of the millennium, authoritative approval on the specific issue came from the Supreme Court's opinion in the high profile case *Advanced Micro Devices, Inc. v Intel Corporation,* a document disclosure dispute between arch rivals in the microprocessor business linked to an antitrust complaint (by AMD that Intel monopolized the market in Windows-capable microprocessors) filed with the Directorate-General for Competition of the Commission of the European Communities.[41]

8.035 The 7–1 majority opinion authored by Justice Ruth Bader Ginsburg – the first and still the only thorough review of Section 1782 since the 1964 amendments[42] – offered a broad policy-oriented ruling on the proper construction of § 1782's mandatory requirements, and equipped Federal courts with a set of discretionary factors to guide the application of § 1782, disposing of virtually all the limitations and qualifications lower courts had read into the provision. *Intel* remains the key benchmark for discovery assistance practice.

8.036 First, the Court explained that the text of § 1782 with its formulation "upon the application of any interested person" plainly reaches beyond the universe of parties to an actual foreign proceeding. No doubt, litigants are included among, and may be the most common example of, the "interested persons" who may invoke § 1782. A potential future litigant may qualify as an "interested person" under § 1782.

8.037 The Court then turned to the specification in § 1782 "for use in a foreign or international tribunal" and cited with approval the broad definition of the term "tribunal" as including "investigation magistrates, administrative and arbitral tribunals, and quasi-judicial agencies, as well as conventional civil, commercial, criminal and administrative courts".[43]

---

40 *Euromepa* at 1099–1100.

41 *Advanced Micro Devices Inc. v. Intel Corp.*, 124 S. Ct. 2466 (2004). For analysis and comment Marat A. Massen, *Discovery for Foreign Proceedings after "Intel v. Advanced Micro Devices": A Critical Analysis of 28 U.S.C. § 1782 Jurisprudence*, 83 *S. Cal. L. Rev.*, 2009–2010, 875; Gabriela B. Clark, *Interpretative Challenges of 28 U.S.C. § 1782 in the Aftermath of Intel Corp. v. Advanced Micro Devices Inc.*, 53 *Vand. J. Trans'l L.*, 2020, 1378–1426. The only question dealt with twice by the Supreme Court relates to what is a "tribunal" for the purposes of Section 1782. On June 13, 2022 in *ZF Automotive US, Inc. v. Luxshare Ltd,* 596 U.S.619 (2022) the Supreme Court ruled that privately-constituted international arbitration tribunals are not "foreign or international tribunals" for purposes of the statute, ending a lengthy circuit split. Recent cases discuss the availability of Section 1782 discovery in aid of investor-state arbitration under the ICSID Convention. See *Webuild Spa. v. WSP USA, Inc.* (2d Cir. July 19, 2024).

42 At 2478. For the Court, "with significant participation rights in Commission proceedings the complainant AMD qualifies as an "interested person" within "any fair construction of that term".

43 At 2479. The Court found that the term "encompassed" an investigation into alleged violation of competition laws by the European Commission's Directorate General for competition. Adopting a very broad reading of the statute's language, the Court also found that the European Commission, although not a court in the classic sense, represents

The Court also clarified that § 1782 does not limit the provision of judicial assistance to "pending" foreign proceedings. § 1782 requires only that the proceeding be "within reasonable contemplation".[44] **8.038**

In dealing with the "foreign discoverability", the Court noted that "beyond shielding material safeguarded by an applicable privilege, nothing in the text of § 1782 limits a district court's production-order authority to materials that could be discovered in the foreign jurisdiction if the material were located there". "A foreign nation may limit discovery within its domain for reasons peculiar to its own legal practices, culture, or traditions" – Justice Ginsburg wrote – yet, there is "no reason to assume that because a country has not adopted a particular discovery procedure, it would take offense at its use".[45] **8.039**

Then, the Court emphasized the flexibility imagined by the statute and defined the "two-step inquiry" which, once the mandatory requirements are satisfied, allows to tailor discovery assistance to the specific needs and the individual circumstances of the case. The Court outlined four factors, which courts should take into account when ruling on a § 1782 request.[46] **8.040**

a) First, the Court cautioned that "when the person from whom the discovery is sought is a party to the foreign proceeding (…) the need for § 1782 aid generally is not as apparent as it ordinarily is when evidence is sought from a nonparticipant in the matter arising abroad". The foreign tribunal can order the parties before it to produce documents or carry other pretrial discovery as it sees fit. On the other hand, "nonparticipants in the foreign proceeding may be outside the foreign tribunal's jurisdictional reach; hence, their evidence, available in the United States, may be unobtainable absent § 1782 aid".
b) Second, it advised courts to take into account "the nature of the foreign tribunal, the character of the proceedings underway abroad and the receptivity of the foreign government or the court or agency abroad to U.S. Federal-court judicial assistance".
c) Third, although it had made clear that the material sought need not be discoverable under the relevant foreign law for the U.S. court to render assistance under § 1782, the Supreme Court warned that the § 1782 request could "conceal an attempt to circumvent foreign proof-gathering restrictions or other policies of a foreign country or the United States".
d) Fourth, it directed Federal courts confronted with foreign assistance applications to examine whether discovery requests are otherwise "unduly intrusive or burdensome".

---

a kind of tribunal as it acts as a first-instance decision-maker in antitrust proceedings, and therefore qualified as a foreign tribunal within the meaning of Section 1782.

44 At 2480: "we reject the view (…) that § 1782 comes into play only when adjudicative proceedings are "pending or imminent".

45 At 2481. Justice Ginsburg also noted that the drafters of § 1782 were quite aware of the circumstance that civil law systems generally do not have American type pretrial discovery.

46 At 2481–82.

8.041 The Court saw no need for categorical limitations with respect to the interpretation of the statute and declined to adopt supervisory rules. In its view, the listed factors provided adequate guidance in determining whether an application should be granted and an order issued in a particular case, and offered safeguards against abusive use of § 1782 and undue interference with foreign proceedings.[47]

E. THE RESORT TO § 1782 DISCOVERY FOR USE IN JURISDICTIONS OF CIVIL LAW TRADITION AND THE NEED OF COMPLEX LAWSUITS FOR WIDE-RANGING FACTUAL INVESTIGATION

8.042 To build up a picture of § 1782's operation, we start with a fairly typical case: a party involved in proceedings in a country of civil law tradition – as a European continental country would be – applies to a U.S. district court to obtain information or evidence for use against the adverse party in the proceeding at home which is not available under the domestic disclosure provisions. The issues raised in such a context and the reaction from a U.S. court to the foreign applicant's discovery request are well-illustrated in the opinion rendered in *In re Servicio Panamericano.*[48]

8.043 In that case, the § 1782 discovery application was for the production of "all documents" concerning any insurance claim, and any insurance payment received, by HSBC bank for the loss of more than ten million dollars arising from non-delivery of currency to two Venezuelan banks at issue in the foreign proceedings. Under Venezuelan Rules of Civil Procedure, defendant *Servicio* could not obtain them through domestic disclosure mechanisms by way of court order unless it had evidence that *specific* documents existed and he had reason to believe that the target (person or entity) possessed the documents.[49]

8.044 In granting the § 1782 application, the United States court emphasized that the inability of the foreign tribunal to order itself the production of the requested evidence made the exercise of its power under § 1782 "necessary". The foreign party's step "did not appear to conceal an attempt to circumvent foreign proof-gathering restrictions or policies", it rather had to be understood "as a reasonable effort to overcome a *technical* limitation of foreign discovery rules". Application of a foreign discoverability rule

---

47 Justice Breyer, in his dissenting opinion, proposed categorical limits on the scope of § 1782 arguing that they would lead to more predictable results than the majority's balancing tests and presumably unnecessary litigation. He also found that "a court should not permit discovery when a private person seeking discovery would not be entitled to that discovery under foreign law".

48 354 F. Supp. 2d 269 (S.D.N.Y. Dec. 6, 2004).

49 The relevant provision is Article 436 of the Venezuelan Code of Civil Procedure. Similar provisions in various European Codes of Civil Procedure. *Supra* note 29.

in this case would have been "senseless", the court continued, pointing to the facts that the documents were "directly relevant" (if not "central") to the requesting party's defense in the foreign action and that granting the application would have "facilitated" judicial efficiency by enabling the foreign tribunal to hear the claims "to determine quickly if the suit could be disposed of, or if the scope of litigation could be limited".[50]

The reasoning in *In re Servicio Panamericano* is significant in many respects: it illustrates the court's perception of foreign evidence rules (as "technical" limitations of the truth-finding process); shows the importance and purpose the court assigns to the U.S. discovery device and the concept of fair play it embodies; and evidences the role the court is willing to play in relation to the proof-taking stage of an action pending abroad.[51] **8.045**

Close similarities in regard to intent, purpose and prospective outcome can be found in European cases like the one of *Pfaff v. Deutsche Bank & others* (2020) where applicant Pfaff resorted to § 1782 discovery assistance in order to get access to information related to Silver and Silver derivatives transactions operated by defendant Deutsche Bank on the Commodity Exchange (COMEX) in New York relevant to the threshold issues in the German investment lawsuit.[52] Pfaff's discovery application targeted (among others) Deutsche Bank, party to the German action and directly within the tribunal's jurisdictional reach, but he would have been met with serious difficulties to obtain the sought information on home turf where the *nemo tenetur edere contra se* dogma is still well and alive and the provisions of Sections 142, 422–430 of the domestic *Zivilprozessordnung* severely limit court-ordered document production. The same can be said and was well-captured by the U.S. district court in relation to the § 1782 discovery petition *In re ex Parte Porsche Automobil Holding SE* (2016) arising out of a string of securities fraud actions brought against Porsche in Germany by a large group of investors claiming that Porsche had made misrepresentations and engaged in market manipulation in connection with its 2008 investment in Volkswagen. To bolster its limitations defense in the German action, Porsche sought to obtain from plaintiffs and affiliates of plaintiffs "evidentiary production of a type and scope in the United States that the German court could not and, in any case, would not order". Evidence far broader than available at home "where Porsche would also have to specify **8.046**

50 Id. at 273, 275. Whether HSBC was insured was "central" to *Servicio*'s defenses, in that under Venezuelan law a party whose loss is compensated by insurance lacks standing to sue.

51 For comment and critical remarks Massen, *Discovery* note 41 at 905–907. The author points out that the court's reference to Venezuela's discovery laws as mere "technical limitations" downplays the importance of foreign policy choices and evidences the effort of the court to present as "a reasonable effort to overcome a technical limitation" what in reality was a strategy to "circumvent" restrictive foreign evidence rules.

52 S.D.N.Y July 15, 2020.

with considerable precision the particular documents it wants in order to get document production".[53]

8.047 U.S. courts have been quite forthcoming also with requests that through a single § 1782 application ask for disclosure of information and evidence for use in multiple proceedings, ongoing or reasonably contemplated, on the same subject matter (e.g. patent infringement) in different foreign jurisdictions.[54] "It is more efficient for a court located in the United States to order discovery from persons located in the U.S. than to force the applicant to seek the same discovery in as many as foreign actions in five different jurisdictions [France, Germany, The Netherlands, United Kingdom and Japan in that case] and return to this court if its efforts abroad fail", the court emphasized in *In re Procter and Gamble Company*.[55] The applicant is considered an "interested party" in the contemplated foreign proceeding because it is a party to the pending lawsuit, and material obtained for the ongoing proceedings is assumed to be used also for the contemplated ones.[56] However, courts would not permit discovery in a patent infringement action relating to damages if the foreign court has not yet ruled on the infringement issue and the foreign action's damage phase, bifurcated from the infringement stage under the law of the foreign jurisdiction, has not yet begun.[57]

8.048 With the Federal Rules of Civil Procedure serving as the default standards, there should be no surprise to find § 1782 requests of a typical breath for U.S. litigation reflecting the basic philosophy of U.S. discovery famously expounded in the Supreme Court's landmark opinion of *Hickman v. Taylor*.[58] At the same time, it is the need for wide-ranging factual information typical of certain cases (say: in the field of

53 S.D.N.Y. Feb. 18, 2016. The quoted parts are at 15, 17. See also *In re ex Parte Porsche Automobil Holding S.E. v. John Hancock Life Insurance Company* arising out of one of a separate string of securities fraud actions brought against Porsche in Germany alleging Porsche's malfeasance in connection with the Volkswagen emission scandal. Porsche sought to gain insights on the trading activities and strategies employed by certain affiliates of three John Hancock Funds, investment managers for various plaintiff's in the German securities fraud litigation. 985 F.3d 115 (1st Cir. 2021). For references the decision of Magistrate Judge Page Kelley in *In re Porsche Automobil Holding SE* (D. Mass. Nov. 6, 2019).

54 Among the many possible examples *In re ex Parte Application of Caterpillar Inc.* (M.D.Tenn. April 21, 2020) where the applicant's request for discovery from entities "found" in the United States was for use in proceedings in different courts in Italy and Germany. In *Illumina Cambridge Ltd. v. Complete Genomics, Inc.*, (*supra* note 16) application to obtain discovery – documents and testimony – from respondents, affiliates of BGI Group, a Chinese biotech conglomerate, in connection with four separate patent infringement proceedings in four foreign jurisdictions: Germany, Switzerland, Turkey and Denmark.

55 334 F. Supp. 2d 1112,1116 (E.D. Wisc. Sept. 1, 2004).

56 See on the issue of non-pending litigation, *Caterpillar*, note 54 at 5–6.

57 See *In re Lufthansa Technik AG* (W.D. Wash. July 22, 2011): discovery allowed in relation to infringement allegations but denied in relation to the damage phase not yet begun.

58 "Mutual knowledge of all relevant facts gathered by both parties is essential to proper litigation. To that end either party may compel the other to disgorge whatever facts he has in his possession". *Hickman v. Taylor* 329 U.S. 495 (1947).

intellectual property) filed before European courts that most naturally generate broad discovery applications.[59]

When the patent infringement battle between *Lufthansa Technik AG* and *Astronics Advanced Electronic Systems Corp. (AES)* (the American competitor of power supply systems used in aircraft cabins) fought in various European jurisdictions – Germany, France and the United Kingdom – reached the damages stage in the German action, Lufthansa applied for discovery assistance from Panasonic Avionics Corporation, a U.S. customer of AES, who incorporates AES's "infringing" product in its in-flight entertainment units, many of which are installed on Airbus aircrafts in Europe. The district court granted the requests for a broad range of "information" – documents and testimony – regarding Panasonic's "purchase and use of the AES product, where the AES product was installed, and the distribution chain for this product, including indirect deliveries"; found that Panasonic is "uniquely positioned to provide this information" and noted that it was "convinced by Lufthansa's assertion that the information sought is useful for identifying all deliveries into Germany, establishing AES's knowledge regarding the destination of the product and otherwise calculating damages".[60] Without attempting to conduct an in-depth analysis of the foreign jurisdiction's laws, the court had no problem to consider the sought information "relevant" and "for use" in the foreign proceedings. At the same time, the court, using its supervising powers, required Lufthansa to limit the temporal scope of the requests to documents that fell within the relevant statute of limitation for patent suits in the target country and determined that Lufthansa's request from Panasonic regarding "AES direct sales outside the United States or communications between AES and Airbus are more appropriately sought from AES".[61] **8.049**

59 Illustrative also the broad discovery requests in *Caterpillar*, note 54.

60 See the details of the discovery order in the concluding section of *Lufthansa Technik AG v. Panasonic Avionics Corp.* (W.D. Wash. Dec. 11, 2017).

61 The decision was followed by *In re Matter of Lufthansa AG* (W.D. Wash. Jan. 22, 2019) denying in part discovery from Panasonic because some of the discovery sought was more likely in Astronics control who had intervened in the discovery proceeding, by *In re Matter of Lufthansa AG* (W.D. Wash. Jan. 25, 2019) compelling Astronics to produce documents updating prior discovery granted to Lufthansa for use in foreign litigation actual and contemplated, and by *In re Lufthansa Technik AG* (W.D. Wash. June 22, 2021) on Astronic's objections concerning in part the existence and in part the relevance of certain requested information. See also the account of the discovery battle between Lufthansa Technik and Thales Avionics Inc., a California-based customer of AES's power systems in *Lufthansa Technik AG v. Thales Avionics Inc.* (C.D. Cal., March 31, 2023) with references to the 2019 order granting Lufthansa's § 1782 application. The discovery dispute over the years between Lufthansa and Astronics shows that in highly controversial areas Section 1782 applications may set the stage for prolonged satellite litigation that is likely to prove expensive. Under U.S. rules, if discovery is granted (as it is frequently the case) the party providing the discovery will typically bear the costs of providing it. Complying with discovery subpoenas is considered a normal obligation even for non-parties and fee-shifting is not likely to occur. See the limited protection in Rule 45(d)(29)(B).

8.050 "Fishing expeditions" is the catch word popular among foreign observers who are not particularly at "ease" with American fact investigation and evidence gathering practice in civil litigation.[62] "Prevention of fishing expeditions" is a common argument by foreign courts that routinely reject or narrow U.S.-style document requests made pursuant the Hague Evidence Convention, as being overly broad and thus incompatible with local discovery rules. But discovery is not an unconstrained party-driven venture. Courts are vested with important powers to shape the discovery process.[63]

F. THE ROADS TO SUCCESSFUL APPLICATIONS UNDER *INTEL'S* DISCRETIONARY FACTORS

8.051 Applications for discovery assistance under Section 1782 presented by parties involved in litigation before European courts are subject to a two-step test: first, the U.S. district court will examine whether certain mandatory factors required in the face of the statute – "interested person", "found", "for use" and "foreign tribunal" – have been satisfied; second, it will consider a number of discretionary factors in deciding whether to exercise its discretion to permit § 1782 discovery, in particular it will consider the four discretionary factors articulated by the Supreme Court in *Intel* to aid the reviewing court in deciding whether a discovery request has been correctly applied and supports the discovery sought.[64]

---

62 See the breadth of discovery orders directing the production of documents by categories and general description without detailed specification or reference to individual pieces of evidence in *In Imanagement Services v. Bank of New York (BNY)* (E.D.N.Y. Aug. 16, 2005); in *Minatec Finance S.A.R.L. v. SI Group Inc.* (N.D.N.Y. Aug. 18, 2008) and *In re Schottdorf* (S.D.N.Y. Dec. 29, 2006).

63 See the detailed schedule the court prepared for the parties to address and clear up the controversial discovery points in *Caterpillar*, note 54 at 32.

64 Applications under § 1782 are often submitted *ex parte*. If a court grants such an *ex parte* application, it will be without prejudice for the respondent to present a motion to reconsider the decision and invalidate the discovery order or quash the subpoena issued. A motion to vacate or reconsider *ex parte* orders opens the way to an adversarial testing of whether the underlying application has met § 1782's statutory requirements and discretionary standards. *Ex parte* applications are subject to the duty of candor. *In re WinNet R CJSC* (S.D.N.Y. April 13, 2017); and importance is placed on the fact that § 1782 applications submit supporting materials, e.g. the complaint or other pleadings providing knowledge about the terms of the case and information about the underlying foreign dispute to help the court analyze and evaluate the merit of the discovery request. See *In re ex Parte Application of Nokia* (N.D. Cal. Nov. 8, 2013) at 6. Some scholars are very critical about the *ex parte* practice under § 1782. See Edward D. Cavanagh, *Discovery in Federal Courts in Support of Foreign Litigation: Lending a Helping Hand or Legal Imperialism?*, 13 *Fed. Courts L. Rev.*, 2021, 86, 101–102: "*ex parte* proceedings undermine the adversary system"; "the potential unfairness is clear". But courts appear to be well aware of potential risks and "when applicants articulate no compelling need to proceed *ex parte*, they will direct the applicants to serve respondents with a copy of the application and supporting materials, and set a briefing schedule". Illustrative the discussion *In re Hansainvest*, note 84 at 248. Courts have also underscored the importance of the due process principles protecting the rights of respondents resisting *ex parte* discovery orders. *Banca Pueyo S.A. et al. v. Lone Star Fund et al.* (5th Cir. Dec. 13, 2012). On the other hand, see *In re Application of Deposit Guarantee Fund Ukraine* (S.D.N.Y. April 21, 2021) at 3–4: notice could provide the potential defendants (in the UK) with opportunity to conceal or destroy evidence". If the district court denies a Section 1782 request, the person making the application may appeal. The appellate court will only reverse the previous decision if it finds that the judge

Under the first *Intel* factor – discovery sought in the United States from a party to the foreign litigation subject to the foreign tribunal's jurisdiction – § 1782 applications may be denied where the applicant has already requested the foreign tribunal to compel the production of the disputed document and the document sought appears to be within the tribunal's jurisdictional reach, as well as in cases where the application is for evidence from a person in the U.S. but the foreign court, under the applicable procedural rules, could order the defendant to produce the relevant documentary evidence held by a third party as "document custodian".[65] On the other hand, courts do point out that "participation in the foreign proceedings does not automatically foreclose § 1782 aid" and emphasize that "practical assessment of whether the evidence is available to the foreign tribunal" is required, "not a formalistic analysis of whether the respondent is a participant in the foreign proceeding".[66] This is a clear expansion of the applicant's remedies. **8.052**

A frequent challenge of § 1782 orders is their non-compliance with the third *Intel* factor. U.S. courts do caution applicants that "a party's failure to invoke local discovery procedures remains significant and may be considered", and that "a perception that an applicant has side-stepped less-than-favorable discovery rules [applicable in the foreign proceeding] by resorting immediately to § 1782 can be a factor in a court's analysis".[67] However, the general trend is that the "circumvention argument" hardly ever deserves a favorable response because "a Section 1782 applicant does not circumvent a foreign court's purview merely by seeking discovery that would not be available in that jurisdiction" and that it is well within a district court's authority to grant broader discovery under section 1782 than might be permitted in the foreign tribunal.[68] Opposing parties are also reminded that the Federal statute exists precisely **8.053**

---

made a serious error, such as applying the wrong legal standard to evaluate the request or has abused its discretion. Critical about the (deferential) standard appellate review, Dubinsky, *Transnational*, note 37 at 338–339.

65 *In re Application of Nokia Corp.* (W.D. Mich. June 13, 2007) at 7–8; *Frasers Group PLC v. Novick* (D.N.J. Jan. 12, 2024) at 10.

66 *Pfaff*, note 52 at 22–23 Focusing on the "availability" issue in *In re Porsche*, note 53 at 15 the court remarked: "the evidence Porsche seeks (through its discovery application) is far broader than the German court could order". In similar terms, in respect to a Dutch discovery request, *In re Upper Brook Companies*, note 11 at 16. *Gorsoan Ltd. v. Bullock*, 652 F. App'x 7, 9 (2d Cir. 2016); *In re Batbold* (S.D.N.Y. Feb. 17, 2023).

67 See *Frasers*, note 65 at 7.

68 For some examples, among many others, see *Illumina Cambridge*, note 16 at 6; *In re Joint Stock Co.* (N.D. Cal. Nov. 2, 2016); *In re Biomet Orthopaedics Switzerland GmbH*, 742 F. App'x 690, 694 (3d Cir. 2018): "the applicant could use German procedures to request specific documents, it could not request a broader set of documents pertinent to its defense". *In re BM Brazil*, note 10 at 27, 31: the fact that English courts would not approve of document demands for broad classes or categories of documents is not an impediment *per se* to use § 1782 discovery. *Caterpillar*, note 54 at 24–25, finding the respondents' argument that limited discovery is available in Italian patent cases "unavailing". But see *In re Application of Digitechnic* (W.D. Wash. May 8, 2007) at 6: the court questioned the failure of petitioner to attempt any discovery means in France, and gave credit to the evidence presented by respondent Microsoft of a quite general discovery order it obtained in France under the French disclosure rules. In *Eli Lilly v. Novartis Pharma AG* (E.D. Va. 2022) the district court vacated the discovery order granted by the Magistrate judge having Eli Lilly

for the purpose "to provide efficient assistance to participants in foreign litigation"[69] and that it is the lack of effective discovery mechanism available to the applicant in the pertinent foreign jurisdiction that "weighs in favor of allowing applicants to obtain the discovery material (documents or testimony) via § 1782".[70]

8.054 When opponents to a § 1782 request claim that the discovery sought is "unduly intrusive or burdensome" or directed to marginally relevant subject matter, Federal courts' first and most prominent reaction is to remind parties that assessment of the fourth *Intel* factor is governed by the Federal Rules of Civil Procedure; that the scope of a § 1782 subpoena is the same as applicable to Rule 34 and the other discovery rules, that under Rule 26(b)(1) a party is entitled to discovery of "any non-privileged matter that is relevant to any party's claim or defense", and that information within the scope of discovery need not be admissible in evidence to be discoverable.[71]

8.055 Applications under § 1782 are denied where the information sought is "vague" and "not even moderately relevant" to the subject matter as it was the case in *Hulley Enterprises Ltd.* (2017) with the request for evidence of the Russian Federation's alleged manipulation of Armenian court proceedings in 2010 and 2011 presented in the course of the multi-front litigation concerning the seizure of the Yukos Oil Company's assets.[72] In a similar vein, in *In re Effecten-Spiegel AG* (2018) the New York court denied the motion of a German private equity firm to take § 1782 discovery of Merrill Lynch NY serving a subpoena upon its former Chairman and Chief Executive Officer to "appear for a deposition and produce any document in his possession related to the financial relationship between any Merrill Lynch entity and Porsche and documents related to the financing and structuring of Porsche's investment in Volkswagen securities". The petitioners had not made a showing that the person targeted had "any unique personal knowledge relevant to the German (securities) litigation".[73] *In re Digitechnic* the U.S.

---

already requested this information in Novartis' European suit. This appeared to be "circumvention of foreign discovery procedures".

69 *Diedenhofen-Lennartz v. Diedenhofen* 931 A 2d 439, 449 (Del. Chan. 2007): the court also remarked that § 1782 would be rendered largely superfluous if it could be invoked only where a foreign discovery mechanism was already available.

70 *In re AIS GmbH Aachen Innovative Solutions* (N.D. Cal. July 21, 2017).

71 *Caterpillar,* note 54 at 26*; In re Upper Brook Companies,* note 11 at 17.

72 *Hulley Enterprises, Ltd. v. Baker Botts LLP,* 286 F. Supp. 3d 1 (D. D.C. Dec. 9, 2017) discussing also "unduly burdensome" discovery and the role of privileges. *In re Akhmedova* (W.D. Tex. Oct. 30, 2020) at 8: document request found "overbroad"; *Minatec Finance S.A.R.L. v. SI Group Inc.* (N.D.N.Y. Aug. 18, 2008): "the primary issue for us is whether Minatec is pursuing this discovery in bad faith".

73 *In re Effecten-Spiegel AG* (S.D.N.Y. Aug. 10, 2018): "petitioners are not allowed to pursue a fishing expedition through the files of Merrill Lynch NY entities". *In re Ex Parte Saul Klein* (S.D.N.Y. Dec. 21, 2023): "the subpoenas pursued material with little apparent or likely relevance to the subject matter of the foreign proceeding". *In re Qualcomm* the Section 1782 application to subpoena a host of U.S. technology giants – Apple, Intel, Broadcom, Texas Instruments etc. – was not tailored temporally, geographically or in its subject matter. 162 F. Supp. 3d 1029, 1043 (N.D. Cal. 2016).

district court rejected the French computer manufacturer's application for discovery to be used in an unfair competition claim against Microsoft's French subsidiary because the request was for a vast swath of documents ("involving hundreds of thousands if not millions of pages") spanning over a seven-year period, and was presented after years of foreign litigation.[74]

At the same time, parties objecting to discovery requests as "overly broad, burdensome or oppressive", are admonished that they cannot rely on simple cursory assertions. Persons opposing § 1782 discovery orders, Judge Posner pointedly stated in *Heraeus Kulzer* (2011), have to demonstrate "by more than angry rhetoric" or "vague arguments of burdensomeness" that allowing the discovery sought would "disserve the statutory objectives".[75] And lack of "proportionality" of the discovery request cannot be demonstrated "by using boiler plate language".[76] **8.056**

Perhaps most instructive is the clear option against an "all-or-nothing approach", outlined by the Second Circuit back in its *Euromepa* opinion: "it is far preferable for a district court to reconcile whatever misgivings it may have about the impact of its participation in the foreign litigation, by using a closely tailored discovery order rather than by simply denying relief outright".[77] Finding § 1782 requests for "all documents" on certain topics overly broad, the court in *In re Eni S.p.a.* (2021) used its authority to modify the subpoenas accordingly.[78] Requests prefaced by words such as "including" or "including but not limited to", if found overly broad and unduly burdensome (also in terms of costs), may prompt a court to "roll up its sleeves" and "trim" these requests to something more reasonable.[79] Courts often direct parties to take steps to negotiate the proper scope of discovery, and may eventually rely on the parties' own agreement to modify previous discovery orders. Overall, because issues of "overbreadth" can be remedied in various ways, this factor is unlikely to be decisive in favor of opponents to discovery orders. **8.057**

74 Actually, after twelve years of litigation with the most recent case pending at the appellate level (W.D. Wash. May 8, 2007).

75 *Heraeus Kulzer,* note 9 at 594.

76 *Consorcio Ecuatoriano de Telecomunicaciones S.A. v. JAS Forwarding (USA)* 747 F. 3d 1262, 1269 (11th Cir. 2014).

77 *Euromepa*, note 39 at 1109.

78 D. Del. March 19, 2021 at 12. *In re Porsche*, note 53 at 3.

79 *Pfaff,* note 52 at 26. Not so in *Financial Right GmbH v. Robert Bosch LLC,* 294 F. Supp. 3d 721, 739 (E.D. Mich. 2018) where the court was not inclined to "trim" the requests to something more reasonable.

G. "EXTERNAL FACTORS" SHAPING § 1782 DISCOVERY ORDERS: FORUM SELECTION CLAUSES, CONFIDENTIALITY INTERESTS AND CHOICE OF LAW ISSUES IN DISPUTES OVER PRIVILEGES

8.058 Attention has to be drawn to "external factors" that can have a serious impact on the § 1782 discovery route, starting with forum selection clauses.

8.059 When parties in their contractual dealings decide to confer exclusive jurisdiction over future disputes to, say, German, Swiss, French or English courts – in their intention it could well be to avoid the intricacies and the unpredictability of American jurisdiction law – they should be aware that their choice (intended to secure benefits) could have the effect of making access to U.S. style discovery for use in the pertinent proceedings unavailable. Some Federal courts tend to share the line of reasoning that signing up for a forum selection clause which provides for exclusive jurisdiction over any dispute between the parties in a foreign country, implies signing up for the procedural law of that jurisdiction including the rules governing discovery. And giving conclusive weight to the forum clause referring disputes to the foreign tribunal, they find that a party seeking discovery in the U.S. under § 1782 is side-stepping the contractual bargain and using § 1782 as a vehicle to avoid unfavorable discovery decisions. Thus, their applications should be denied.[80] A more flexible approach considers the forum selection clause a factor that bears on the *Intel* analysis in a given § 1782 case having regard to the language and scope of the clause, the relationship between the subpoenaed party and the parties in the case and the nature of the discovery sought. To avoid denial of a § 1782 application, credit is given to the argument that the forum selection clause "prohibits the bringing of substantive disputes in a foreign jurisdiction", not applications seeking evidence in support of substantive proceedings brought in the chosen court, especially when sought from a non-party. For the purpose of § 1782, a forum clause should not be enforced against a non-signatory who is not closely related to another signatory.[81]

8.060 Another main factor to consider in shaping discovery requests are proposed *confidentiality* concerns, be it commercial confidentiality (i.e. trade secrets) or sensitive private information. Rule 26 (c) of the Federal Rules of Civil Procedure generously permits "for good cause shown" the making of protective orders governing discovery, considering various factors that have to be balanced against the relevance of the sought information and the interest of justice in bringing about a fair result in the proceeding. In the context of § 1782 procedures, "sealing orders" can limit, and indeed have limited,

80 *In re Alghanim* (S.D.N.Y. May 5, 2022); *Aventis Pharma v. Wyeth* 2009 WL 3754191 (S.D.N.Y. Nov. 9, 2009); *Venequip S.A. v. Caterpillar, Inc.* 83 F. 4th 1048 (7th Cir. 2023).

81 See the discussion in *In re BM Brazil,* note 10 at 28–34.

the circulation and use of the discovered material for a specified case.[82] Parties may be directed to negotiate an appropriate confidentiality agreement to be converted into a protective order. In *Illumina Cambridge,* the court gave due weight to the commitment of the applicant to cooperate in requesting the tribunals in the foreign jurisdictions (Danish, German, Swiss and Turkish jurisdiction involved in that case) to ensure the confidentiality of information obtained through the U.S. discovery device.[83] In *In re Hansainvest Hanseatische Investment GmbH* (2018) the court granted the foreign private parties the discovery requested in its entirety with respect to documents held by U.S. custodians, but with respect to the documents held by foreign custodians only to the extent that applicants "(1) assume the costs of the document production including the costs of compliance with the EU's General Data Protection Regulation or other applicable European data privacy laws, and (2) indemnify respondents against any potential breaches of European data privacy laws".[84] In *In re AIS GmbH Aachen Innovative Solutions* a protective order was entered holding the "Highly Confidential-Attorney's Eyes Only" designation for the controversial cardiac support device (Heart Made PHP), not yet commercialized in Europe, that respondent Thoratec, the U.S. competitor of AIS, had produced pursuant a § 1782 discovery order in connection with the patent infringement litigation in Germany.[85]

8.061 In the course of document production it is not uncommon that parties raise issues of *privilege* and with them issues of choice of law combined with the question whether it is for the U.S. court or for the foreign tribunal, where the main action is pending, to resolve the privilege dispute. It is fairly settled that the language "any legally applicable privilege" in § 1782 has an expansive meaning and that the legislative history makes clear that this language "provides for the recognition of all privileges to which a person may be entitled, including privileges recognized by foreign law".[86] Thus, different laws may come into play for purposes of determining which privileges are "legally applicable" in the § 1782 context. And due to the different attitudes and cultures involved in this highly sensitive area, competing national laws may provide different results. To tackle the choice of law issue, the courts in the Second Circuit apply to claims of privilege the "touch base" test – a traditional choice of law contact analysis – which directs courts to identify "the law of the country that has the predominant or the most direct and compelling interest in whether communications should remain

82 *Gambale v. Deutsche Bank AG,* 377 F. 3d 133, 140–142 (2d Cir. 2004); *In re Lufthansa Technik AG* (W.D. Wash. Sep. 13, 2024).

83 Discussion in *In re Hulley Enterprises Ltd.,* 400 F. Supp. 3d 62 (S.D.N.Y. 2019). In *Illumina Cambridge,* note 16 at 20.

84 364 F. Supp. 3d 243, 252 (S.D.N.Y. 2018). In *Pfaff,* note 52 at 28; *In re Okean B.V.,* 60 F. Supp. 3d 419 (S.D.N.Y. Sept. 4, 2013).

85 N.D. Cal. Jan. 28, 2021.

86 As the Second Circuit has long recognized in *In re Erato* 2 F. 3d 11, 14 (2d Cir. 1993).

confidential, unless that foreign law is contrary to the public policy of the forum". The country with the predominant interest is either the place "where the alleged privileged relationship was entered into" or "the place in which that relationship was entered at the time the communication was sent".[87] As a flexible balancing of interest device, the "touch base" test can be a powerful instrument to conduct § 1782 requests in different directions: compelling discovery over assertion of foreign privileges, applying foreign privileges to limit disclosure of certain documents, or applying U.S. privilege law to preclude foreign applicants access to evidentiary material in the United States.

8.062 In *In re BM Brazil,* the New York court under the "touch base" test found that certain documents withheld by the § 1782 subpoenaed investment bank in New York, who had served as financial advisor in the disputed share purchase agreements at issue in the English proceeding, were protected by the "legal advice privilege" under English law, and decided that it was for the court, not the foreign tribunal where the main action was pending, to resolve the privilege issue applying English law. The court noted that the parties agreed on the relevant principles of English privilege law and that it would be inefficient for the parties to present their privilege dispute to a UK court when the issue was already before a U.S. court. Most importantly, the court found that "the United States did not have the predominant, or even significant interest in the parties' privilege dispute". Many of the documents found privileged under English law would not have been protected under U.S. privilege law.

8.063 The "touch base" test dispensed a less favorable result to the European consumers (car owners), potential litigants in German courts, who in *In re ex parte Application of Financialright GmbH* via § 1782 sought to obtain from the law firm, Jones Day, for use in the proceedings they planned to file at home against Volkswagen, a report and documents related to an investigation that Jones Day had conducted for Volkswagen in the U.S. and Germany under a legal services agreement. The documents requested were found to be covered under the U.S. attorney client privilege, and because the court found no "privilege waiver" under U.S. law when Jones Day disclosed the privileged information to the U.S. Department of Justice, the German discovery request was denied.[88] Of course, if the "touch base" test leads to compelling discovery over

---

87 The "touch base" test was approved by the Second Circuit in *Mangouras v. Boggs*, 980 F. 3d 88, 98–100 (2d Cir. 2020). There is the rather uncompromising statement that: "a foreign country [Spain in that case] cannot short-circuit our choice of law analysis via submissions asserting that the foreign country's privilege law is applicable". If the "touch base" test points to the application of American, rather than foreign privilege law, "the foreign countries' submissions are irrelevant on the privilege question". In *In re Polygon Global Partners* (D. R.I. Jan. 12, 2022) a Section 1782 discovery request in connection with a lawsuit in Spain the district court in Rhode Island found that "because the scope of Spanish professional secrecy remains contested, the law of the U.S. should apply".

88 On the pertinent points in the two cases, see the third decision of the New York district court in *In re BM Brazil 1 Fundo de Investimento Em Participacoes Multistratgia* (S.D.N.Y. May 7, 2024) and the opinion and order in *In re ex parte application of Financialright GmbH* (S.D.N.Y. June 23, 2017).

assertions of foreign privileges, the foreign court as the prospective end-user of the material obtained in the U.S. will be free to decide whether or not to "use" it: at all times, the foreign courts are the masters of their domain.

H. THE CONTOURS OF SECTION 1782'S "FOR USE" REQUIREMENT AND THE LIMITS OF PRE-ACTION DISCOVERY ASSISTANCE

This leads us to § 1782's statutory requirement that information and evidence sought in the U.S. must be "for use" in a proceeding in a foreign tribunal. Absent guidance from the Supreme Court in *Intel*, application of the "for use" requirement can become a contentious issue. **8.064**

Brandi-Dohrn, acting for a group of German shareholders, applied under § 1782 for a discovery order against three non-parties on U.S. soil – IKB Capital Corporation, Lord Securities Corporation and William O'Brien – to obtain documents and depositions for use in the securities fraud action filed in Germany against IKB Deutsche Industriebank for alleged failure of the bank to disclose the extent of its exposure to collateralized debt obligations backed by U.S. subprime mortgages. Judge Paul Crotty at the New York Southern District Court was confronted with what can be considered a fairly routine application: a request by an "interested party" of information and evidence from entities "found" in the district and for use in a foreign proceeding displaying complex factual and economic issues. The deposition from third parties was likely beyond the German court's jurisdictional reach, and the documents requested seemingly non-"discoverable" under German procedural law. Judge Crotty granted the discovery *ex parte*, as it is not unusual, and the relevant subpoenas were issued. Before any discovery was produced, *IKB* moved to vacate the discovery order and quash the subpoenas. **8.065**

In view of the rather firmly settled case law, for IKB's lawyers there was little room for successfully claiming non-compliance of the discovery order with one or more of the four discretionary *Intel* factors. They opted to focus the challenges upon the failure of Brandi-Dohrn's § 1782 application to meet the "for use" requirement. At issue were the facts that the German proceeding had progressed to the appellate stage (before the Higher Regional Court) and that Brandi-Dohrn had filed the application in New York more than a year after the case was dismissed in the first instance. Moreover, domestic law in Germany did not allow for new evidence to be introduced on appeal except in limited circumstances, which could be thought unlikely to apply to the sought-after evidence. The district court found the respondent's arguments persuasive and quashed **8.066** the subpoenas concluding: "the likelihood of use has not been shown" because the evidence was unlikely to be admitted in the German proceedings.[89]

8.067 On appeal, the Second Circuit reversed the ruling. For the Court it was conclusive to note that the Supreme Court had rejected the insertion of a generally applicable "foreign discoverability" rule into the text of § 1782, and there was no reason why a "foreign admissibility rule" should not suffer the same fate. "For use" does not require that the foreign tribunal admits the requested discovery; it is free to exclude the evidence obtained through a § 1782 request or place conditions on its admission. The Court also indicated that an admissibility requirement would require difficult interpretation and analysis of foreign law making the provision of U.S. judicial assistance less efficient, and could ultimately impede the statute's objective of helping foreign litigants and foreign tribunals obtain information that would otherwise be outside their reach.[90]

8.068 Federal courts rather consistently find that the "for use" test is met when the applicant makes a *prima facie* showing that the (information or) evidence obtained through the § 1782 discovery assistance can be "offered" by the applicant to the foreign tribunal, "can serve some use at some stage of a foreign proceeding", or can be "employed with some advantage in the proceedings abroad".[91] In *In re Catalist Managerial Services (CMS)* the court authorized discovery from sixteen banks for use in a wrongful contract-termination action brought in the United Kingdom by CMS against Lybia Africa Investment Portfolio (LAP) and explained that "the documents showing the wire transfer made by and to LAP and its affiliates through U.S. banks *could be used* to establish the extent of CSM's lost profits following termination of the contract".[92] In *Caterpillar,* relying on the status of the patent infringement proceedings before the Italian courts, illustrated in the applicant's brief, the court noted that the discovery granted pursuant to § 1782 "could impact a final technical report", "support the applicant's request for additional fact discovery", bolster "a motion to reopen the record" or "any combination of these possibilities" in the claims pending in the Italian courts.[93] Testimony or documents obtained may never get to influence the foreign tribunal's

---

89 References to the procedural history in *Brandi-Dohrn v. IKB Industriebank* 673 F. 3d 76 (2d Cir. 2012).

90 *Brandi-Dohrn,* note 89 at 81–82. The case law on the "for use" requirement is thoroughly analyzed in Andrew Scappaticci Brickfield, *Use or Abuse of § 1782 Discovery in Less -Developed Legal Systems*, 57 *Columbia J. Trans'l Law*, 2019, 357, 382–393.

91 *Mees v. Buiter,* 793 F. 3d 291, 298 (2d Cir. July 17, 2015). In *In re Reis Veiga* the court noted it is not supposed to "assess the weight of individual pieces of evidence in excruciating details, and then attempt to discern the precise nexus between such evidence and the claims and defenses raised in the foreign proceedings". 746 F. Supp. 2d 8, 11 (D. D.C. Oct. 20, 2010). *In re Application of Eni Spa* (D.Del. July 15, 2021): § 1782 only requires that the court finds that "the information will be employed with some advantage or serve some use in the proceeding".

92 2d Cir. Feb. 23, 2017.

93 *Caterpillar,* note 54 at 16. *Weber v. Finker,* 554 F. 3d 1379,1384 (11th Cir. 2009); *In re Imanagement Services Ltd.* (E.D.N.Y. 2005).

definition,[94] but the fact-and-evidence-revealing material secured may create the conditions to reach out for an out-of-court solution of the dispute. There is some evidence that large settlements reached in European jurisdictions have profited from American § 1782 discovery assistance.[95]

What might come as a surprise to foreign observers, and has been reason for serious disappointment among European prospective litigants, like Esther Kiobel attempting to adequately prepare her tort case against Shell in the Netherlands, whose laws require high factual and evidentiary showing at the filing stage,[96] as well as for German consumers seeking collective relief in German courts in connection with Volkswagen's "clean diesel" fraud,[97] is that the liberal reading of the "for use" requirement has not inspired U.S. courts to build upon the statute's often emphasized aim a solid basis to develop § 1782's strategic potential in providing discovery assistance at the pre-action stage. There are various reasons to that. One is that Federal Rule of Civil Procedure 27(a)(1) severely limits the availability of pre-filing discovery in domestic cases, giving credit to argue that broader discovery should not be provided for foreign cases as such discovery would be a "drastic departure from the underpinnings of the U.S. legal system". Another somewhat related reason is that the familiar Federal Rules model, which links discovery to proceedings already instituted, has brought courts, in the context of § 1782 applications, to look for some "discernible procedural mechanisms" by which the material sought can be used, or to require a showing of "participation rights" on the part of the applicant for the availability of the discovery assistance path. While courts have been open to grant discovery requests jointly for use in ongoing and contemplated proceedings on the same substantive matter in different jurisdictions, they have struggled to offer an autonomous determination of what qualifies as proceeding "within reasonable contemplation" when discovery assistance was sought for the pre-action stage in foreign jurisdictions.[98] **8.069**

---

94 *In re Biomet*, note 68 at 696: "the German court retains the authority to disregard irrelevant or cumulative evidence, or even to conclude that it will not admit any of the submissions". The determination of admissibility is "more appropriately left to the foreign courts".

95 Cleary Gottlieb, *U.S. Discovery für den deutschen Ziviprozess – eine unterschätzte Option*, Alert Memorandum, Feb. 19, 2019, mentions the impact that resort to § 1782 discovery had on the settlement reached in the *HSH Nordbank* investor suit.

96 *Kiobel*, note 15. Judge Hellerstein at the New York district court granted Kiobel's request, but the Second Circuit reversed on various (questionable) grounds arguing, *inter alia*, that Kiobel's lawyers were attempting "an end run around limitations on discovery in the Netherlands" and that, despite the negotiated confidentiality order, there was no guarantee that the Dutch court would treat the documents as confidential in the Dutch proceeding.

97 See *Financialright GmbH v. Robert Bosch LLC*, 294 F. Supp. 3d 721 (E.D. Mich. Feb. 12, 2018) finding that the documents requested in the United States from Bosch hardly "could have any meaningful effect" in the contemplated German litigation.

98 Under Federal Rule of Civil Procedure 27(a)(1), pre-litigation discovery is only available to a litigant who is unable to file suit presently and only to preserve specified information that is shown to be likely to be unavailable after suit is ultimately filed, but not to uncover evidence to support the filing of a lawsuit. The Supreme Court's inclusion of

I. THE STATUTE'S GEOGRAPHIC REACH: DOES U.S. LOCATION OF THE EVIDENCE MATTER? THE MOVE FROM PAPER TO ELECTRONIC WORLD AND ITS EFFECT ON CROSS-BORDER DATA GOVERNANCE

8.070 A critical question that over the years has surrounded the operation of § 1782 is whether the evidence sought through the discovery motion must be physically present in the United States or whether the statute's reach extends to evidence that is located abroad as well. The question was not addressed by the Supreme Court in its *Intel* decision notwithstanding the various nuances, and in part pervasive disagreements, Federal courts had already shown regarding the complex issue.

8.071 For quite some time, Federal courts showed sympathy for the argument that § 1782 was not intended to provide discovery of evidence maintained within a foreign jurisdiction.[99] In *In Re Sarrio S.A.* a subtle reasoning supported that result.

8.072 There, the Spanish company Sarrio started suit in Spain for breach of contract against three other Spanish companies and the Kuwait Investment Authority. Sarrio applied to the Southern District of New York for an order compelling production of documents related to a transaction handled by one of Chase Manhattan's European Branches. The European Branch had sent the documents to New York for review by Chase's American legal counsel. This very circumstance provided a foothold to argue that documents that are only present in the U.S. for an attorney review and could not have been in the U.S. otherwise are not subject to a subpoena seeking documents "located within the United States". The Court treated the documents as if they were located abroad and denied the discovery request.[100]

8.073 The issue remained largely unsettled. While some courts took the view that § 1782 "permits the discovery of documents held outside the United States so long as the person who is the target of the subpoena is within the jurisdiction of the court",[101] others denied discovery for documents located abroad but foreshadowed situations where

the term "reasonable" in the "within contemplation" formulation was designed to indicate that proceedings cannot be merely speculative. What more precisely is needed to obtain pre-litigation discovery pursuant to § 1782 remains not well-defined.

99 Strongly proposed by Hans Smit, the primary architect of the revised version of § 1782, in *American Assistance*, note 36 at 11–12. In a subsequent contribution, in part revisited, *The Supreme Court Rules on the Proper Interpretation of Section 1782: Its Potential Significance for International Arbitration,* 14 *Am. Rev. Int'l Arb.*, 2004, 328.

100 *In re Sarrio S.A.* (S.D.N.Y., Oct. 10, 1995). On appeal, the Second Circuit reversed on the ground that the bank that was asked to produce the evidence did not object to doing so. Therefore, the case became one involving application of subsection (b) of § 1782. 199 F. 3d 143 (2d Cir. 1997).

101 See the decision of the Magistrate Judge reversed on other grounds in *Norex Petroleum Ltd. v. Chubb Insurance Co. of Canada et al.* 384 F. Supp. 2d 45 (D.C. Cir. 2005). In *Kestrel Coal Pty Ltd. v. Joy Global Inc.*, the discovery request was denied on the ground that under corporate law principles a holding company cannot be compelled to produce documents held by its subsidiaries. 362 F.3d 401 (7th Cir. 2004).

extraterritorial discovery might be justified, i.e.: (1) documents are located in a foreign country that is not the location of the foreign litigation; and (2) documents formerly located in the U.S. "spirited out of the United States" to evade discovery.[102] A strong (but controversial) statement came in *In re Gemeinschaftspraxis Dr. med. Schottdorf & Partners*, where Judge Jones held that § 1782 discovery of a report and the related documents McKinsey had prepared for a German professional association could be ordered even though the material was located in the country (Germany) where the foreign litigation was underway, and the German courts had previously denied the production of the documents. The foreign party's application, "a last resort to acquire discovery that it had been unable to obtain abroad", could not be considered an "impermissible" use of § 1782. "In some respects", he argued, "that is precisely the type of assistance that the statute was designed to offer".[103]

A new chapter was brought forth when courts began to give effect to the complementary reach of the Federal Rules of Civil Procedure and § 1782, identifying the determinant under the latter not in the physical location of the documents, but in the "possession, custody or control" when, rather than documents in the traditional paper form, the materials sought through the discovery action were electronically stored information. **8.074**

Under the Federal Rules there is no restriction on the location of the document [or other tangible evidence]. Rule 34(a) and Rule 45(a)(1)(C) combined allow courts to compel parties as well as non-parties subject to their jurisdiction to produce documents or other tangible evidence in "their *possession, custody or control*".[104] The phrase is in the disjunctive and only one of the numerated requirements needs to be met. Moreover, "control" is broadly construed as including, along with "the legal right to obtain documents upon demand", the "practical ability to obtain" the material sought which may be established "where affiliated corporate entities have actually shared responsive information and documents in the normal course of their business dealings".[105] **8.075**

The move from paper to the electronic world has not changed the fundamentals of discovery: the documents and information still have to be relevant and not privileged, but its impact on discovery is far-reaching when data cross borders rendering notions **8.076**

102 *Four Pillars Enterprises Company v. Avery Dennison Corp.* 308 F. 3d 1075 (9th Cir. 2002).

103 *In re Schottdorf*, note 62 at 15, 19.

104 Cavanagh, *Discovery*, note 64 at 94 finds that "it is somewhat anomalous that U.S. courts are making the discovery process under section 1782 available to foreign persons and tribunals, while at the same time barring claims for substantive relief by foreign plaintiffs purporting to sue under American law on claims that arise outside the United States".

105 See *In re Application of Republic of Kazakhstan* order granting leave to obtain discovery from an international law firm in New York although the materia was located in the firm's London office. 110 F. Supp. 3d 512, 518 (S.D.N.Y. June 22, 2015).

of location or accessibility quaint.[106] "Respondents' concerns about producing documents located outside the United States are largely anachronistic – the district court of the Northern District of California emphasized in *Illumina Cambridge Ltd v. Complete Genomics* (2020) – when documents and information are located in electronic storage, which can be accessed with equal effort from any location".[107] And in *Pfaff*, dismissing the respondent's objection based on the physical location of the requested documents, the court commented ironically "where applicants seek e-discovery there is no shipping back and forth across the Atlantic Ocean".[108] This makes § 1782 an increasingly powerful tool for participants in legal proceedings outside the United States.

J. THE DISCOVERY TARGETS: PERSONS "RESIDING" OR "FOUND" IN THE DISTRICT OF A U.S. DISTRICT COURT

8.077 Who are the targets of discovery requests? Under § 1782 assistance for use in European proceedings can be sought from a "person" – regardless of whether an individual or business entity – who *resides* or *is found* in the district of the district court to which the application is made. Absent any statutory definition, the question how these two terms translate into the district court's jurisdiction to compel a person "to give testimony or statement or to produce a document or other thing" is key to understanding the statute's potentially long reach.[109]

8.078 Looking at the type of physical presence that satisfies the "is found" language, some courts have adopted a relaxed reading of the statute and have been willing to exercise

106 Embracing the Federal Rules' focus on "control", and the co-extensiveness of the court's power under § 1782 with the Federal Rules, the Eleventh Circuit in *Sergeeva v. Tripleton Int'l Ltd.* (2016) found that the district court had applied the correct legal standard ordering Trident Atlanta, a U.S. based company, to produce evidence held by affiliates in the Bahamas. 834 F.3d 1194, 1200 (11th Cir. Aug. 2016). Citing *Sergeeva*, in *In re del Valle Ruiz* (2019) the Second Circuit held that an American affiliate of the Spanish bank Santander based in New York, Santander Investment Securities Inc., had to turn over documents located abroad concerning the financial status of Banco Popular Espanol, requested by Mexican investors contrasting in various European proceedings the legality of the forced sale of Banco Popular Espanol to Banco Santander. (2d Cir. Oct. 7, 2019). *In re The Liverpool Ltd. Partnership* (D. Del. Aug. 26, 2021) ordering the Bank of America Corp. to produce documents held by its Japanese subsidiary that served as an advisor in the going-private transaction at issue in the Japanese appraisal proceeding.

107 (N.D. Cal. Feb. 19, 2020) at 13–14. Problematic in several aspects are § 1782 discovery requests from U.S. based electronic communication service providers. *Rainsy v. Facebook*, 311 F. Supp. 3d 1101 (N.D. Cal. 2019); *In re Application of West Face Capital Inc.* (N.D. Cal. March 22, 2020).

108 *Pfaff*, note 52 at 27. The move from boxes of hardcopy documents to electronically stored information (ESI) has brought about new challenges and problems in several aspects. In particular, with the explosion of technology the average amount of information stored by companies has increased exponentially. And with the large volume of data stored, discovery (i.e. production of ESI) in complex litigation has become a very costly and time-consuming process.

109 391 F. 3d 120, 125 (2d Cir. 2004). For analysis of the circumstances that may meet the "resides or is found" requirement for purposes of § 1782, see *In re Godfrey*, 526 F. Supp. 2d 417 (S.D.N.Y. 2007); *In re Oxus Gold Plc Co.* (N.J. Oct. 11, 2006); *In re Lloreda*, 323 F. Supp. 3d 552 (S.D.N.Y. 2018); *Frasers Group Plc v. Novick* (D. N.J. Jan. 12, 2024).

their authority for purposes of a § 1782 application to reach individuals, residing in a foreign (viz. European) country, who are "found" in the district on a *temporary visit.*

In the case of *In re Edelman*,[110] Claude Taittinger – the well-known owner of the French champagne label – received discovery order pursuant to § 1782 while visiting the Gagosian Art Gallery in New York. Taittinger's family's own enterprise (*Société du Louvre*) had entered securities litigation in Paris against Asher Edelman, an American corporate raider, and five investment funds controlled by him. Taittinger was not personally a party to the French lawsuit. Edelman's lawyers, by serving the *subpoena*, demanded that Taittinger acts as non-party witness in the dispute by returning to the Southern District of New York for a deposition and surrendering documents he allegedly had created and stored in France.[111] **8.079**

The targeted individual moved to quash the *subpoena*, but the courts found "no basis to conclude that the target was in any way privileged or immunized from § 1782's personal reach whether on account of the transient nature of his visit to New York or the purpose for which he made the trip". "If the State could properly exercise jurisdiction over a foreigner who is just passing through [under the Supreme Court's ruling in *Burnham*], there is no reason why service of a *subpoena* under Rule 45(b)(2), which is simply a discovery mechanism and does not subject a person to liability, should require more".[112] **8.080**

The question when a *corporation* can be a discovery target has become tricky because of the split between the Fourth Circuit's holding in *Eli Lilly & Co* (2022)[113] that the "found" language in § 1782 has a definite connotation of physical presence, which requires a corporation to be "physically present by its officers and agents carrying on the corporation's business" in the judicial district[114] and the line of cases adhering to the contact-based theory of personal jurisdiction articulated in the Supreme Court's landmark decision in *International Shoe v. Washington.* However, the latter, entangled in the evolving tests for "general personal jurisdiction" – traditionally equated with **8.081**

110 *In re Edelman*, 295 F. 3d 171, 174 (2d Cir. 2002).

111 In the instant case *Société* had already availed itself of the § 1782 mechanism to gain information for use in the French litigation securing documentary evidence from Edelman and some of its companies. In response Edelman sought his own order for issuance of subpoenas under the authority of § 1782. Without providing any specific analysis courts continue *Edelman*'s "is found" approach. *Sandra Holding Ltd. v. Fawzi Musaed Al Saleh* (D. Mass. July, 15, 2019) *In re Fourworld Event Opportunities Fund* (S.D.N.Y. April 12, 2023).

112 *Edelman*, note 110 at 179. Protection is provided under Federal Rule 45(c)(3) to a foreigner who is served with a subpoena during a short visit to the U.S. and then returns home. See *In re Microsoft* 428 F. Supp. 2d 188, 193 (S.D.N.Y. 2006): "even where respondent were found in the District, he could not be compelled to appear because he is outside the 100 mile territorial limit".

113 37 F. 4th 160 (4th Cir. 2022).

114 At 165.

"systematic and continuous activities" in the forum[115] – has, following the Supreme Court's decision in *Daimler* (2014),[116] which imposed the more exacting "at home" standard, favored rulings that brought foreign corporations not "incorporated" in the U.S. – including foreign banks with branches, agencies or representatives offices there – simply beyond the reach of § 1782:[117] an implication hardly in line with the statute's often celebrated aim to liberalize the assistance to litigants in foreign proceedings with international aspects.[118] Courts started to envisage the need of a § 1782 application resting on a *specific* jurisdictional predicate.[119] The idea materialized in *In re del Valle Ruiz* (2019),[120] where the Second Circuit concluded that the Spanish Bank Santander's New York-based affiliate, Santander Investment Securities Inc., was clearly "found" in the district because the discovery materials sought under § 1782 "*proximately* resulted from the respondent's forum contacts".[121] The standard of specific jurisdiction for § 1782 purposes which links "contacts" (for purposes of due process) to the actual discovery sought rather than to the underlying cause of action translates into § 1782's expanded *in personam* reach over foreign corporations or entities. Transactions on U.S. exchanges, such as the New York Commodities Exchange (COMEX), may provide a jurisdictional basis for § 1782 aid, the court ruled in *Pfaff v. Deutsche Bank & others* (2020).[122] Entities that are not subject to general jurisdiction in the U.S. should understand that they may be subject to a district court's specific jurisdiction for purposes of § 1782 where discovery materials are closely tied to their activity in the forum.

K. THE "RECEPTIVITY" CONCERNS AND THE "AUTHORITATIVE PROOF" STANDARD TO DECLINE FOREIGN DISCOVERY REQUESTS

8.082 Notwithstanding its reluctance to impose categorical limitations with respect to the interpretation of § 1782, the Supreme Court in *Intel* did not dismiss concerns about interference with foreign proceedings. Rather it clearly indicated that one of the

115 *In re Application of Nokia* (W.D. Mich. Jun. 13, 2007) in a § 1782 request in connection with a German patent infringement proceeding, the court ruled that the contacts of subsidiaries do not satisfy the "resides or found" requirement.

116 *Daimler AG v. Bauman et al.*, 571 U.S. 117 (2014).

117 *In re Sargeant,* 278 F. Supp. 3d 814-821 (S.D.N.Y. Oct. 10, 2017).

118 *New Zealand Banking Group v. APR Energy Holding Ltd.* 2017 WL 3841874 (S.D.N.Y. Sept. 1, 2017).

119 *In re Fornaciari* (S.D.N.Y. Jan. 29, 2018).

120 939 F. 3d 520, 526–528 (2d Cir. 2019).

121 The Second Circuit remarked that, although it could not exercise jurisdiction over the Spanish Bank Santander itself, the New York-based affiliate, Santander Investment Securities Inc., was clearly "found" in the district. It was sufficient for purposes of due process that the non-party's contacts with the forum go to the actual discovery sought rather than the underlying cause of action. See the discussion in Part III(B)(2) of the decision.

122 *Pfaff,* note 52 at 8–21, following *del Valle Cruz,* found that respondents' trading activity at COMEX in New York provides a sufficient basis to exercise specific personal jurisdiction for the purposes of § 1782: "the trades for which petitioner seeks discovery occurred largely through COMEX which operates in New York".

factors that "bear consideration" when a court rules on a § 1782 request is the "receptivity" of the foreign government or the court or agency abroad to U.S. Federal court assistance.[123] The purpose of the statute's use had to be support, not imposition, upon foreign proceedings.

Federal courts tend to frame the inquiry on the receptivity to U.S. judicial assistance generally, not whether the specific foreign tribunal would admit each specific piece of evidence sought via the assistance device. Admissibility and receptivity should not be conflated.[124] A more articulated view on how receptivity should be determined and what role it had to play in the foreign discovery setting, has come from the Second Circuit's opinion in *Euromepa* (1995), where Judge Calabresi, writing for the majority, elaborated what has since been the leading approach: "A district court's inquiry into the discoverability of requested materials should consider only authoritative proof that a foreign tribunal would reject the evidence obtained with the aid of Section 1782. Such proof, as embodied in a forum country's judicial, executive or legislative declarations that specifically address the use of evidence gathered under foreign procedures, would provide helpful and appropriate guidance to a district court in the exercise of its discretion". Absent this type of clear objection, a court's ruling should be informed by § 1782's overarching interest in "providing equitable and efficacious procedures for the benefit of tribunals and litigants involved in litigation with international aspects".[125] **8.083**

As a clear case of "non-receptivity" the New York courts treated *Schmitz et al v. Bernstein, Liebhard & Lifshitz* (2004), where the German Ministry of Justice and the German prosecutor presented their opposition to the German plaintiff's attempt to secure via § 1782 for their securities fraud action filed against Deutsche Telekom in Germany, access to the documents that Deutsche Telekom had already been compelled to produce in the American class action lawsuit instituted by American purchasers of Deutsche Telekom American depository shares.[126] The German authorities contentions that the discovery would "jeopardize" an ongoing German criminal investigation on the same matter – where access to documents held in "official custody" by the German Prosecutor had already been denied to the plaintiffs in the German civil action – and that "disclosure of the documents sought could jeopardize German **8.084**

123 124 S. Ct. 2466, 2483 (2004).

124 See the discussion in *In re BM Brazil,* note 10 at 23–25.

125 *Euromepa,* note 39, 1100.

126 *Schmitz et al v. Bernstein Liebhard & Lifshitz LLP*, 376 F. 3d 79 (2d Cir. 2004). The civil action in Germany alleged that Deutsche Telekom misled investors by overstating the value of its real estate assets. Similar allegations of fraud were also the focus of a criminal investigation of former Deutsche Telekom employees and others. Approximately 300.000 documents were produced by the German company in the American action.

sovereign rights"[127] warranted denial of the German plaintiff's petition for discovery assistance, even though their request satisfied the statutory requirements.[128]

8.085 "Authoritative proof" came also from the Korean Fair-Trade Commission in *Ex Parte Application of Qualcomm, Inc.*, where the Agency presented letters to the U.S. court stating that it had "no need or use" for U.S. discovery related to disputes between Qualcomm and Apple. As authority in charge of enforcing compliance with the Republic of Korea's Monopoly Regulation and Fair Trade Act, it was not at all open to U.S. Federal court assistance in this matter.[129]

8.086 Closely related is the field where "receptivity" has been playing a crucial role in relation to Europe: § 1782 discovery requests interfering with Europe's reliance on "leniency programs" in the antitrust regulatory context.

8.087 In *Intel* the European Commission filed an *amicus curiae* brief before the U.S. Supreme Court explaining that granting *Advanced Micro System's* § 1782 discovery of documents request in the U.S. for use in the European antitrust investigation would be a "direct interference" with the Commission's own "orderly process"; would "undermine its policies and divert its enforcement resources" linked to the "leniency program". Based on the factors set out by the Supreme Court, on remand the Northern District of California denied AMD's discovery request and complied with the European Commission's expressed objection to U.S. § 1782 discovery assistance.[130]

8.088 *In re Microsoft Corp.* – probably the most significant case – the New York District Court granted the respondents' motion to quash subpoenas and vacate the prior discovery order under the "receptivity" factor finding that Microsoft's resort to § 1782 in the course of a European antitrust investigation was an attempt to circumvent specific restrictions the European Commission had imposed upon Microsoft; namely, that certain information the Commission had gathered through its leniency program and used to monitor Microsoft's compliance with European competition rules had been deemed confidential by the Commission, and could be disclosed to Microsoft only in compliance with the Commission's procedures. "A decision by this court upholding Microsoft's discovery request would contravene the purpose of § 1782 by pitting this court against the Commission rather than fostering cooperation between them".[131]

---

127 At 81.

128 At 84. Compare with *In re Application of Chevron Corp.*, (S.D.N.Y. May 6, 2010).

129 *In re Qualcomm Inc.*, 162 F. Supp. 3d 1029 (N.D. Cal. 2016). An Examiner Report from the Korean Fair Trade Commission (KFTC) charged Qualcomm and its licensing of standard essential patents with violating South Korean anti-trust law.

130 *Advanced Micro Devices, Inc v. Intel Corp.* (N.D. Cal., Oct. 4, 2004). References in Wang, *Exporting*, note 18 at 2095–2096.

131 *In re Microsoft Corp.*, 428 F. Supp. 2d 188 (S.D.N.Y. April 20, 2006) at 190.

§ 1782's basic aim returns to the forefront where there is no "authoritative proof" or dispositive foreign authority objecting to Federal court ordering discovery. The default position is to permit the discovery sought. Courts repeat that objections by a foreign tribunal should not be presumed from the fact that a country has not adopted a particular discovery procedure. Parties that apply for discovery under § 1782 enjoy a presumption in favor of a foreign tribunal's receptivity that can only be offset "by reliable evidence that the foreign jurisdiction rejected outright Federal assistance from the United States".[132] Expert opinions on foreign law produced by disputing parties may and at times are taken into account when Federal courts declare that "courts in the United Kingdom are receptive to section 1782",[133] that "no evidence suggests that a German court would be unreceptive to section 1782 assistance",[134] or that "no specific direction indicates a lack of receptivity of Italian courts to section 1782 discovery".[135] On occasion, foreign law experts may get a less friendly reception. "The cannonade of legal affidavits, both parties leveled, with a spiraling array of competing legal pontification, among other things, as to whether the German court would be receptive to Federal court assistance has not changed our attitude", the court noted in *Minatec Finance*, a § 1782 application from a Luxembourg corporation. "Since we are not presented with authoritative declarations addressing the use of evidence that may be gathered by this court, we will rely on the statute's overarching interest in providing equitable and efficacious procedures for the benefit of tribunals and litigants involved in litigation".[136] Absent clear and unequivocal indication that the foreign tribunal would not be receptive to the evidence, "we are not expected to declare a winner in a battle-by-affidavit of international experts", the court noted in *Schottdorf*.[137] **8.089**

L. SECTION 1782 DISCOVERY AID BEFORE EUROPEAN TRIBUNALS: A WELCOME BENEFIT? THE SOUTH CAROLINA INSURANCE CO. CASE AND THE PRAGMATIC ATTITUDE OF ENGLISH COURTS

So far, the purpose of the present contribution was to provide a comprehensive account of the constructions given to § 1782 by the Federal courts and the main issues involved **8.090**

---

132 *Illumina Cambridge*, note 16 at 8; *Financial Right GmbH*, note 79; *In re Babcock Borsing AG*, 583 F. Supp. 2d at 241 (D. Mass. 2008): in the present case, the court somewhat equivocally required "affirmative indication of the foreign tribunal's receptivity to the materials requested". *In re Majed Amir Al-Attabi* (S.D.N.Y. Jan. 26, 2022) at 8 *In re Batbold* (S.D.N.Y. Feb. 17, 2023) at 12: only "authoritative proof" weighs against permitting discovery under § 1782.

133 Examples are *In re BM Brazil*, note 10 at 24; *In re Akhmedova* (W.D.Tex. Oct. 30, 2020): finding that English courts would likely by receptive of the assistance granted.

134 *Pfaff*, note 52 at 23; *Cryolife, Inc. v. Tenaxis Medical, Inc.* (N.D. Cal. Jan. 13, 2009).

135 *Caterpillar*, note 54 at 24; *In re Mariani* (S.D.N.Y. April 16, 2020): "petitioner produced evidence that an Italian court would be receptive to materials produced pursuant to a Section 1782 application".

136 *Minatec Finance*, note 45 at 22, 24.

137 *Schottdorf*, note 103 at 21 and 23.

in the provision's practical application. But what about the role ultimately played by the provision in relation to proceedings brought before European courts (as well as before courts of other jurisdictions outside the United States): judicial assistance or judicial interference?

8.091 Some might argue that by opening up the possibility of broad American discovery U.S. courts encourage parties engaged in foreign litigation to bypass the practices and procedures of the foreign court and possibly supplant narrow discovery laws in foreign jurisdictions with a view to shift the focus of foreign litigation to the United States without the intervention or the involvement of the court having jurisdiction over the main action. The question, obviously, is not one of "offending" foreign tribunals. It is a question of interfering with or of disrupting the process of adjudication before the foreign tribunal. Do American courts underestimate the risk when they note that the receiving court can protect itself from the effects of any unwarranted discovery by simply refusing to admit the evidence? Some scholars and commentators across the Atlantic opt for a critical answer and point at the § 1782 device as "injection of American discovery procedures into foreign proceedings" or represent its operation as "American interference, chauvinism or legal imperialism".[138] There are various reasons not to share similar views.

---

138 The statements come mainly from American commentators and are not based on a rigorous analysis of reactions and views taken by foreign courts and legal scholars on the § 1782 discovery assistance experience. See for the quoted expressions, Molly W. Lien, *The Cooperative and Integrative Models of International Judicial Comity: Two Illustrations Using International Discovery and Breard Scenarios*, 50 *Cath. Univ. L. Rev.*, 2001, 591, 624. Vivian Grosswald Curran, *Federal Rule 44.1: Foreign Law and US Courts Today*, 30 *Minn. J. Int'l. L.*, 2020, 60, citing a single French source writes: "Section 1782 and U.S. discovery in general often are characterized by serious commentators as part of a U.S. hegemonic drive to force its system on Europe to the detriment of European economic interests". It is also highly questionable to point to Section 1782 "as undermining the vital international cooperation the Hague Evidence Convention embodies" Id at 62. The Hague Convention suffers on its own shortcomings and defects, in particular its inability to bridge the differences between the procedural systems of the Signatory States. For a more articulate critical perspective Wang, *Exporting*, note 18 at 2126, 2145. Clark, *Interpretative Challenges*, note 41 at 1409 critically notes that interpretation of the statute has been confronted mostly by practitioners with little consideration from law school professors and non-practicing researchers. The authors, due to the nature of their work and their professional interests, tend to focus on a single issue, as opposed to engaging in a comprehensive review of § 1782. Dubinsky, *Transnational*, note 37 at 337: the author's main criticism is that "American courts rarely tailor their discovery orders to be compatible with the discovery norms in the foreign legal system in which the main action is pending" and, more generally, that the "attitude toward transnational discovery (...) continues to be shaped by domestic precedents". Lauren Ann Ross, *A Comparative Critique to U.S. Courts' Approach to E-Discovery In Foreign Tribunals*, 11 *Duke Law & Technology Rev.*, 2012, 314, 328, also argues that § 1782 should not be treated like a normal request under the Federal Rules in domestic litigation and suggests a comparative approach to the balancing test set forth in *Intel*. For Cavanagh, *Discovery*, note 64 at 107 among the principal shortcomings of Section 1782 is "the lack of coordination between U.S. courts and foreign tribunals". In clear contrast, Federal courts tend to be proud of their "hospitable view of applications to compel the production of evidence by persons found or residing in the United States for use in foreign litigation", and emphasize that "the hospitality derives from Congress's desire to make the United States a helpful world citizen". *In re Porsche*, note 53 at 3. On the European continent, German scholars and commentators – Germany is the country where the instrument of § 1782 has been and continues to be used in a broad range of legal proceedings – without ignoring risks and shortcomings, predominantly consider U.S. discovery assistance as

First, the United States Supreme Court in *Intel* did not dismiss concerns about interference with foreign proceedings. Accordingly, the Court specifically listed a series of factors as standards for the district courts' exercise of discretion that, when satisfied, contribute to the likely absence of foreign objections to the use of § 1782, namely: the receptivity of the courts abroad to U.S. judicial assistance; the reduced need for § 1782 aid when the person from whom discovery is sought is a participant in the foreign proceeding; the consideration whether the request for discovery conceals an attempt to circumvent policies of a foreign country; the notice that unduly intrusive or burdensome requests may be rejected or trimmed; the reminder that discovery can be conditioned upon reciprocity; and the district court's discretion to consider appropriate measures, if needed, to protect the confidentiality of materials. **8.092**

Second, the kind of aid U.S. courts provide to parties involved in foreign litigation via § 1782 in matters of fact and evidence gathering is not an isolated phenomenon in the wider spectrum of disputes spanning across multiple legal systems. There are close similarities, in purpose and underlying reasons, to what we have been witnessing in recent times in a related field of transnational litigation: courts in one country ready to lend their support to litigants in foreign proceedings through the issuance of provisional or protective measures not available or unknown in the foreign forum. When the English Mareva injunction (now "freezing order") entered the scene, it became clear that the legal nature and the practical usefulness of the newly created device were quite different from the characteristics of an *Arrest*, a *saisie conservatoire* or a *sequestro*. Litigants on the Continent consequently learned to take advantage oof the revised Section 25 of the Civil Jurisdiction and Judgment Act 1982, which empowered English courts to grant Mareva injunctions and related ancillary orders in support of proceedings on the merits in Brussels or Lugano Contracting States. And when parties sought to challenge such orders arguing that England was not the jurisdiction where the substantive proceedings were taking place, and claimed that the issuance of such orders amounted to an unwarranted interference with the jurisdiction of the court trying the substantive dispute, Millett L.J., in one of the prominent cases, promptly replied – and his arguments echo those recurring in the § 1782 discovery assistance context – that the target of the order is properly amenable to the jurisdiction of the English court for the purpose of Section 25 of the Jurisdiction and Judgment Act's assistance to foreign jurisdictions, and that the terms of the order granted will not allow it to be directly enforced in the foreign jurisdiction without approval from **8.093**

an opportunity for courts and litigants. See among the earlier contributions Eike Dirk Eschenfelder, *Möglichkeiten deutscher Unternehmen, US-amerikanische Discovery auch vor deutschen Gerichten zu nutzen*, in *IPRax*, 2006, 89; Oliver Rieckers, *Europäisches Wettbewerbverfahren und US-amerikanische Discovery*, in *RIW*, 2005, 19. Fabian Klein, *Die Verwertbarkeit gem. 28 U.S.C. § 1782 (a) erlangter Beweismittel im deutschen Zivilprozess*, Tübingen, 2019. The author suggests a more restrictive solution if the Section 1782 target is the defendant to the proceeding in the forum.

the foreign court. "We do not seek to force our cooperation on those who do not welcome it".[139]

8.094 Third, as to the attitude of the courts – the proposed end users of the material obtained or sought to be obtained through the § 1782 procedure – judicial experience cautions against the understanding that assistance to parties in obtaining information and evidence non-discoverable under the law of the forum is perceived as inherently intrusive or offensive by foreign tribunals. Courts of continental Europe have shown in various ways not to be hostile at all to discovery aid requested, gathered or found across the Atlantic by parties fighting their case in the forum. The evidence available is manifold.

8.095 There are instances where European courts have declined to restrain a party from presenting a U.S. discovery request or to direct a party to withdraw its application for discovery assistance under Section 1782;[140] cases where courts have set deadlines to allow a party to proceed with the § 1782 discovery procedure initiated in the United States, and cases where deadlines were set to allow the evidence gathered abroad to be introduced in the proceedings on the main action.[141] There are also examples where courts have explicitly signaled their receptiveness to the information sought in the United States,[142] have actively defined the scope of the evidence they expected applicants to obtain via the foreign assistance device[143] and examples where, in rendering

139 *Credit Suisse Fides Trust SA v. Cuoghi* [1997] All E.R. 724, 730 (C.A.). For the broader picture, our contribution, *Provisional Remedies in Transnational Litigation: A Comparative Outline of Forms of Judicial Cooperation*, in Rolf Stürner – Masanori Kawano (eds.) *Comparative Studies on Enforcement and Provisional Measures*, Mohr, 2011, 271–308.

140 See *Convex c.s. v. Duizendstraal c.s.*, Utrecht District court, April 9, 1996, KG 1996, 158; the decision was upheld by the Amsterdam Court of Appeals, Oct. 24, 1996, NIPR, 1997, 120. See generally, Kasper J. Krzeminski, *U.S. Discovery for use in Dutch Civil Proceedings, Tjdschrift vour Civiele Rechtspleging*, 2002, 48–55; Annet J. van Hooft, *Effective Use of Discovery Obtained Pursuant to 28 U.S.C. § 1782 in Proceedings Before Dutch Courts*, in *Jones Day Commentary*, Sept. 2000.

141 In *Kulzer v. Esschem Inc.*, 390 F. App.'x 88, 92 (3d Cir. 2010) the German court not only expressed receptivity of evidence secured in the United States which it could not order a third party to produce, but postponed its own hearing specifically for the purpose of permitting a litigant extra time to pursue its Section 1782 discovery requests in Indiana and in Pennsylvania. In *Digitechnic*, note 68 at 3, the Paris Court of Appeals granted an extension of the brief deadline to allow applicant to proceed with the U.S. discovery.

142 In *In ex Parte Porsche Automobil Holding SE, supra* note 53, the German tribunal signaled its receptiveness of the information concerning the type of trading activity and strategy used by U.S. affiliates relevant in the German investor action, which the defendant sought to secure via the Section 1782 procedure. In *Schmitz*, note 126: the Presiding Judge of the Frankfurt District court where the case against Deutsche Telekom was pending, first stated that the court will take notice of the documents from American proceeding, but later changed his mind after finding out that the German Ministry of Justice had opposed it. In *Polygon*, note 87 at 6 the Spanish court where the main proceedings were pending declared its receptiveness "to some measures of assistance".

143 In the discovery battle between Pfaff and the Deutsche Bank, the German court knew about the discovery the claimant was seeking via Section 1782. Indeed, it also stepped in defining the scope of evidence it expected the petitioner to obtain and refrained from setting a trial date, thus indicating its interest in receiving the evidence to be obtained through Section 1782. *Pfaff*, note 52 at 3.

their ruling, courts have relied on documents that one of the parties in litigation has produced through the § 1782 request.[144]

Moreover, there are important statements of principles like the one rendered by the Dutch Supreme Court that evidence could not be considered unlawful (and thus inadmissible) because obtained through procedural means, like the § 1782 discovery device, unknown to Dutch law,[145] and the one coming from the German Federal Court that the conduct of U.S. discovery does not in itself constitute sufficient ground for violation of the country's *ordre public*.[146] Not less significant the far-reaching declaration that a Contracting State's reservation under Article 23 of the Hague Evidence Convention that it would not execute U.S. requests of pretrial discovery of documents, should not be intended as barring a party from using § 1782 aid to gather documentary evidence in the United States for use in proceedings before a court of that Contracting State.[147] **8.096**

Of great interest, finally, is the balanced approach of the courts across the channel, elaborated in the decision of the House of Lords in *South Carolina Ins. Co. v. Assurantie Maatschapij "De Zeven Provincien" N.V.* v. *Al Ahlia Insurance Co. & another* (1986).[148] **8.097**

South Carolina, an American insurance company, brought suit in the Commercial Court in London against a Dutch insurance company and others claiming substantial sums due under contracts of reinsurance. Before the defense was served, the reinsurers, to bolster their defenses, initiated proceedings in the U.S. under § 1782 in order to secure production and inspection of documents in the possession of third parties in the United States, "necessary, material and relevant to the litigation in England". Rather than responding to the application in the U.S. court, South Carolina moved in **8.098**

144 *In re Biomet*, note 68 at 696: "*In* rendering its ruling, the German court relied on some documents that Biomet produced to Heraeus through the § 1782 request". See also *In re Schlich*, note 62 at 52 referring to an instance where evidence obtained pursuant to a § 1782 order was submitted to the European Patent Office in an opposition proceeding, and the European Patent Office admitted and relied upon the evidence obtained with the U.S. court assistance; and the indications in *Polygon*, note 87 at 5: "Spanish court admitted into evidence documents obtained from Providence in Rhode Island and from a member of the consortium in New York, postponed proceedings so as to grant parties additional time to make use of 1782 discovery".

145 *Alfred Mol v. Kinetics Technology Int'l B.V.*, Hoge Raad, Feb. 6, 1998, N.J.1999, 479. On the Dutch "receptiveness" see also, *In re Judicial Assistance Pursuant to 28 U.S.C. § 1782 by Macquarie Bank Ltd*, 2015 U.S. Dist. Lexis 72544 (D. Nev. May 28, 2015); *In re Upper Brook Companies*, note 11 at 13.

146 For analytical comment of the decision of June 4, 1992 see Peter Hay, *The Recognition and Enforcement of American Money–Judgments in Germany*, 40 *Am. J. Comp. L.*, 1992, 1001.

147 The Utrecht District court in *Convex*, note 140, referring to the Netherlands' declaration under Article 23 of the Hague Evidence Convention.

148 [1986] 3 WLR 398; [1987] AC 24 (H.L.). For the broader picture Lord Lawrence Collins, *The Use and Abuse of 28 U.S.C. § 1782 Litigation in England*, 56 *N.Y.U. Int.'l L. & Politics*, 2024, 151, 155: "the emphasis on § 1782 in discussion of the English cases has tended to be on its potential abuse, but the evidence of published judgments is that often the use of § 1782 for the purposes of English litigation is entirely uncontroversial". See the examples at 155, text and notes 12–15.

London for an order directing defendants to withdraw their application for discovery in the U.S. district court on the ground that the defendants' action was an "abuse of process" of the English court. The point was that the documents sought in the United States through the § 1782 proceeding could not be obtained under England's disclosure rules because they were not in the possession of plaintiffs. The High Court issued an injunction restraining the defendants from pursuing the § 1782 application in the U.S. and the Court of Appeal affirmed finding that once parties had submitted to the jurisdiction of the English court, it was a fundamental principle that the applicable procedural rules were those of the English court, and it was for that court to control the proceedings and ensure that litigation was conducted in accordance with its procedure.[149]

8.099 The House of Lords in an insightful opinion by Lord Brandon rejected the lower courts' reasoning and dissolved the injunction.

8.100 Three propositions are at the core of Lord Brandon's reasoning: (1) civil procedure of U.S. courts differs essentially from that of the English High Court in that it allows parties to an action to compel, against non-parties, a full measure of pretrial discovery; (2) such third-party discovery in the U.S. does not constitute a violation of English procedural law; and (3) English courts generally do not exercise any control over the manner in which a party obtains the evidence which it needs to support its case. The basic principle underlying the preparation and presentation of a party's case in the High Court in England is that it is for that party to obtain and present the evidence which it needs by its own means, provided that such means are lawful in the country in which they are used.[150]

8.101 A stringent *sequitur* is the answers to the specific issues raised in regard to the re-reinsurers' application for discovery assistance in the United States. Lord Brandon noted:

> I cannot see that the re-reinsurers by seeking to exercise a right potentially available to them under the Federal law of the United States have in any way departed from, or interfered with, the procedure of the English Court. All they have done is what any party preparing his case in the High Court here is entitled to do, namely, to try to obtain in a foreign country, by means lawful in that country, documentary evidence which they believe that they need in order to prepare and present their case.
>
> I can see no good reason why the re-reinsurers should not have chosen whichever of the two available options – application for a letter of request to issue to the proper judicial authorities in the United States or direct application – they preferred.

149 [1985] 2 *Lloyd's Rep.* 147 (Court of Appeal).
150 *South Carolina*, note 148 at 35–38, 41.

The application by the defendants to the U.S. district court did not amount to "unconscionable conduct" on their part, and so could not justify the exercise of the court's power to grant injunctions against them.[151] **8.102**

The effect of the decision in *South Carolina* was felt in subsequent cases, like the hard-fought patent revocation proceedings between *Nokia Corp.* and *Interdigital Technology Corp.* (2004), where Interdigital applied for an injunction to prevent Nokia from pursuing § 1782 applications in Texas for documents and other evidence from Ericsson and Sony-Ericsson, or for a declaration that such evidence, if the application succeeded, would not be considered as relevant by the court. Following the ruling of the House of Lords, the High Court refused to give the injunction, and found that there had been no abusive behavior on the part of Nokia which had prejudiced the defendants.[152] **8.103**

On some occasions English courts have "baulked" at the use of § 1782 but it has not been because of any hostility to the use of the procedure *per se*.[153] Courts have objected to the use of the procedure when the § 1782 application was pursued in a manner considered "disruptive" to the conduct of the English proceedings to the point of arising to an abuse of process. Probably the most notable example in the UK where the court objected to the use of the procedure is *Bankers Trust Int'l Plc. (BTI). v. PT Dharmala Sakti Sejahtera (DSS)* (1995):[154] a complex dispute arising out of transactions in derivatives which BTI had entered with DSS, an Indonesian company, through the Singapore office of Bankers Trust Company (BTCo). In that case the English court (per Mance J.) restrained the defendants (DSS) from enforcing a § 1782 order for disclosure directed to BTCo and its parent and associated company they had obtained from the U.S. district court under § 1782, and from proceeding with further applications. This did not come as a surprise, given that the § 1782 discovery in the U.S. had **8.104**

---

151 *South Carolina*, note 148 at 42, 44. Lord Lawrence Collins, *The Use and Abuse*, note 148 at 159: "the effect of the decision in the *South Carolina* case was for most practical purposes to remove obstacles in England to the use of § 1782 for English proceedings. Following the decision, applications for injunctions to restrain the use of § 1782 have failed in several cases". Among the more recent cases he refers to *Soriano v. Forensic News LLC* [2023] EWCA Civ. 223 refusing an injunction to restrain the § 1782 proceedings.

152 [2004] EWHC 2920 (Pat). Subsequently, a district court of the Eastern District of North Carolina refused to make a § 1782 order in favor of Nokia against Sony-Ericsson, finding that Nokia's request concealed an attempt to circumvent foreign proof-gathering restrictions and was overbroad and unduly burdensome. *In re Nokia Corp.* 2005 WL 8159342 (E.D. N.C. March 16, 2005).

153 *Omega Group Holdings Ldt v. Kozeny* [2002] C.L.C. 132, 135 (Q.B.2001). A complex dispute involving allegations of fraudulent misrepresentation in connection with an investment in the privatization process in the Republic of Azerbaijan. The court held that it was "unconscionable for a defendant party to pursue orders in the U.S. under § 1782 for testimony and production of documents in respect of individuals that the claimant intended to call to give oral evidence at the trial of the English proceedings". For a similar concern *Benfield Holdings Ltd. v. Elliott Richardson* [2007] EWHC 171 (QB).

154 *Banker's Trust Int.'l PLC,* C.L.C. 252, 254 (Q.B. 1995).

been sought and obtained *ex parte* after the trial in England of the claim and counterclaim had taken place, and judgment was reserved; that many of the categories of documents had already been the subject of unsuccessful disclosure applications in the English proceedings; and that the judge considered the further evidence gathering exercise as speculative, with the potential to blow out in a large-scale investigation. The applications made under § 1782 were abusive and oppressive. The Court was not prepared to allow such an exercise to derail conclusion of the proceedings, noting that "there must be some end to litigation" and the trial in the action had taken place.[155]

8.105 In *Dreymoor Fertilisers Overseas Pte Ltd. v. EuroChem Trading GmbH* (2018) the Commercial Court reaffirmed that English courts will only restrain, via injunction, the resort to U.S. discovery procedures in support of, or in the course of, English proceedings where it would lead to "unconscionable" interference with the local proceedings.[156] A § 1782 order is not in itself unconscionable conduct. A foreign lawful procedure is not carried into the realm of unconscionability simply because it is unfamiliar to a jurisdiction. Although the attitude of English courts towards disclosure is regulated by the English Civil Procedure Rules and the scope of disclosure is essentially circumscribed by the pleaded issues, it is open to a litigant in English proceedings to make use of foreign discovery procedures to ascertain facts and obtain documents of which he might be unaware, and deploy the information in the English proceedings, if necessary, after appropriate amendment.

155 *Banker's Trust*, at 256.

156 *Dreymoor Fertilisers Overseas PTE Ltd v. Eurochem Trading GmbH* [2018] EWHC (Comm.) 2267 at 59–60. Dreymoor applied for an injunction restraining Eurochem from enforcing a U.S. § 1782 discovery order. Bryan J. granted the injunction but Males J., sitting in the English commercial court, discharged it finding that, on the facts of the case, the "unconscionability" was not met because: 1) the U.S. court had granted the discovery order for use in the British Virgin Island and Cyprus proceedings; 2) it was not the English court's role to police the conduct of foreign litigation; 3) it was left to the foreign tribunals to decide whether the evidence so obtained in the U.S. should be admissible in the London arbitration.

9

ACCESS TO EVIDENCE IN COMMERCIAL ARBITRATION

Michael Stürner and Johannes Landbrecht

A. INTRODUCTION

The present volume focusses on access to evidence, rather than on administration of evidence more generally. Accordingly, this chapter deals with access to evidence in the context of arbitration, touching upon the wider topic of the administration of evidence by arbitral tribunals only in passing. Furthermore, the discussion in this chapter is limited to commercial arbitration proceedings, as arbitration involving public law elements may create additional and quite distinct concerns with respect to access to evidence.[1] **9.001**

State courts are usually themselves in a position to ensure a party's access to evidence as per the applicable procedural rules, for instance through compelling witnesses to **9.002**

1 Similarly, the other chapters of this publication limit themselves to access to evidence in civil (and commercial) proceedings as opposed to public law proceedings, e.g. in administrative matters.

testify or through ordering the opposing side to produce documents. Uncooperative individuals or entities will meet the corresponding state's *imperium*, i.e. application of its coercive power. If evidence remains unattainable within a state court's jurisdiction, such court may seek judicial assistance from foreign state courts under their civil procedure rules and the relevant conventions or supranational rules in place.

9.003 Arbitral tribunals, however, as private decision-makers not integrated into a state's judiciary, have no coercive power and thus more limited means of ensuring themselves access to evidence (below B.). Notwithstanding that, arbitral tribunals also have at their disposal the tool of 'judicial assistance'. Namely, if evidence is to be gathered from uncooperative (third) individuals or entities, state courts may support arbitral proceedings according to their own domestic procedural rules (below C.).

B. ACCESS TO EVIDENCE IN ARBITRAL PROCEEDINGS

9.004 Domestic arbitration laws and institutional arbitration rules remain largely silent on evidentiary issues, leaving their determination to the parties' agreement (if any) and the arbitral tribunals' discretion. This includes the issue of whether and to what extent to grant access to relevant evidence (below B.1.). To further guide the parties in their agreement (if any) and arbitral tribunals in exercising their discretion in evidentiary matters, the International Bar Association (the 'IBA') has drafted a soft law instrument, the 'IBA Rules on the Taking of Evidence' (the 'IBA Rules'), that has gained considerable importance in arbitral practice worldwide. The IBA Rules are meant to provide a model for supplementary rules on the taking of evidence, including access to evidence, that may then be adapted flexibly to the needs of individual parties and their respective proceedings (below B.2.). Beyond the usefulness in individual arbitral proceedings, the IBA Rules have contributed to a fruitful debate about evidentiary matters across jurisdictions worldwide (below B.3.).

9.005 This Section B will thereby deal primarily with access to *documentary* evidence[2] rather than to witness and expert testimony. Since arbitral proceedings most often deal with contractual disputes, relevant documents are usually in the possession, custody, or control of one of the parties to the proceedings, i.e. a party has at least the possibility to obtain such documents, for instance from another group company, even if it is not currently itself in possession of them. While parties may be reluctant to provide access to documents that are detrimental to their case, arbitral tribunals are able, even without direct access to a state's coercive power, to influence the parties' behaviour within

2 'Documents' are defined in the IBA Rules as 'a writing, communication, picture, drawing, program or data of any kind, whether recorded or maintained on paper or by electronic, audio, visual or any other means'.

the proceedings. This is because tribunals may, and will, draw adverse inferences from a party not complying with a tribunal's order to provide access to documents in said party's possession, custody, or control.[3] By contrast, witnesses and experts are, but for parties testifying themselves, exclusively third parties over which the tribunal has no coercive power. Access to such witnesses and experts in arbitral proceedings thus depends on them testifying voluntarily, unless 'judicial assistance' can be obtained from state courts in support of arbitral proceedings as discussed in the subsequent Section C.[4] The same would apply in the (probably rare) cases where access to documentary evidence is required that is not in the possession, custody, or even mere control of a party to the arbitral proceedings.

1. Discretion of arbitral tribunals

Many domestic arbitration laws[5] and institutional arbitration rules[6] confer, subject to the parties agreeing otherwise, wide discretion on arbitral tribunals to determine issues of procedure,[7] including[8] issues of the taking of and granting access to evidence. **9.006**

---

3 For further details, see below Section B.3.

4 We will thus not deal with Article 4 (witnesses of fact), Article 5 (party-appointed experts), and Article 6 (tribunal-appointed experts) IBA Rules. Accordingly, we will also not deal with Article 8 (evidentiary hearing) as evidentiary hearings are primarily used for the tribunal to hear fact witnesses and experts rather than to investigate documents (on the possibility of an inspection 'of any site, property, machinery or any other goods, samples, systems, processes or Documents', see however Article 7 IBA Rules). Yet we note that the IBA Rules specifically refer to 'judicial assistance' from state courts regarding witness testimony, providing a mechanism for a party to ask the tribunal 'to take whatever steps are legally available to obtain the testimony' of a recalcitrant witness or to 'seek leave from the Arbitral Tribunal to take such steps itself' (Article 4(9) IBA Rules).

5 Statutory rules (as opposed to case law) regulating evidentiary issues in any detail are almost entirely inexistent. Cf. e.g. sec. 1042(4) German Code of Civil Procedure: 'Failing an agreement by the parties, and in the absence of provisions in this Book, the arbitral tribunal shall conduct the arbitration in such manner as it considers appropriate. The arbitral tribunal is empowered to determine the admissibility of taking evidence, to take evidence and assess freely such evidence.' Sec. 34(1) English Arbitration Act 1996: 'It shall be for the tribunal to decide all procedural and evidential matters, subject to the right of the parties to agree any matter.' Article 1509(2) French Code of Civil Procedure: 'Unless the arbitration agreement provides otherwise, the arbitral tribunal shall define the procedure as required, either directly or by reference to arbitration rules or to procedural rules.' Article 182(2) Swiss Private International Law Act: 'If the parties have not determined the procedure, the arbitral tribunal shall determine it to the extent necessary, either directly or by reference to a law or to arbitration rules.'

6 Cf. e.g. Article 21.3 DIS Rules 2018: 'When the Rules are silent as to the procedure to be applied in the proceedings before the arbitral tribunal, such procedure shall be determined by agreement of the parties, in the absence of which the arbitral tribunal in its discretion shall decide upon the procedure, after consultation with the parties.' Article 19 ICC Rules 2021: 'The proceedings before the arbitral tribunal shall be governed by the Rules and, where the Rules are silent, by any rules which the parties or, failing them, the arbitral tribunal may settle on [...].' Article 19(1) Swiss Rules 2021: 'Subject to these Rules, the arbitral tribunal may conduct the arbitration in such manner as it considers appropriate, including by adopting measures for the efficiency of the arbitration proceedings, provided that it ensures equal treatment of the parties and their right to be heard.' A well-known exception are the relatively detailed provisions in Articles 50 to 57 WIPO Arbitration Rules 2021.

7 Bernhard Berger and Franz Kellerhals, *International and Domestic Arbitration in Switzerland* (5th edn, Stämpfli ea 2025) N 1312; Reto Marghitola, *Document Production in International Arbitration* (Wolters Kluwer 2015) Ch 4.

8 For sec. 1042 German Code of Civil Procedure, see e.g. Joachim Münch in *Münchener Kommentar zur ZPO* (6th edn, CH Beck 2022) § 1042 N 96; for Article 182 Swiss Private International Law Act, see e.g. Bernhard Berger and

9.007 Issues of the taking of evidence include, as the English Arbitration Act 1996 specifies, 'whether any and if so which documents or classes of documents should be disclosed between and produced by the parties and at what stage',[9] 'whether to apply strict rules of evidence (or any other rules) as to the admissibility, relevance or weight of any material (oral, written or other) sought to be tendered on any matters of fact or opinion, and the time, manner and form in which such material should be exchanged and presented',[10] or 'whether and to what extent there should be oral or written evidence or submissions'.[11]

9.008 These statutory and arbitration rules that expressly confer discretion on arbitral tribunals to determine issues of procedure, absent any party-agreement or rule in the respective arbitration law or rules, indirectly also clarify that arbitral tribunals are not bound by provisions of domestic civil procedure laws applied in state courts,[12] whether applied in state courts at the seat of the arbitral tribunal or elsewhere. None of the domestic civil procedure rules serve as 'default' rules in arbitral proceedings, although arbitrators may use such laws as 'sources of inspiration' when exercising their discretion in procedural matters. Indeed, as a matter of fact, and although this is often not what the parties expected or what is otherwise suitable in arbitral proceedings, some arbitrators tend to turn to procedural solutions similar to those adopted in state court proceedings in the jurisdiction in which the respective arbitrators received their professional training (which may have no connection whatsoever with the parties or their dispute). Those procedural solutions adopted by the corresponding state courts are possibly the rules that the respective arbitrators are most familiar with, in particular if they have limited experience in international arbitration.

9.009 As will be explained in more detail below (at C.6), it follows from the scarcity of statutory and arbitration rules on evidentiary matters, including on the issue of granting access to evidence, that state courts will rarely review, at the set-aside or enforcement stage, an arbitral tribunal's exercise of its direction on evidentiary matters.

9.010 The foregoing clarifies what arbitral tribunals are (not) obliged to take into account when regulating evidentiary issues, including the access to evidence. The question remains how arbitral tribunals will actually go about regulating such issues. A need for regulation of some kind will arise in virtually all proceedings. Such need may be

---

Franz Kellerhals, *International and Domestic Arbitration in Switzerland* (5th edn, Stämpfli ea 2025) N 1311.

9 Sec. 34(2)(d) English Arbitration Act 1996.

10 Sec. 34(2)(f) English Arbitration Act 1996.

11 Sec. 34(2)(h) English Arbitration Act 1996.

12 See e.g. Simon Gabriel and Andreas Schregenberger in *Berner Kommentar IPRG* (Stämpfli 2023), Art 182 IPRG N 2; Joachim Münch in *Münchener Kommentar zur ZPO* (6th edn, CH Beck 2022) § 1042 N 93; Ana Serra e Moura in *Arbitration in Portugal* (Kluwer 2020), § 7.04[A].

visible already at the beginning of the proceedings. At this stage, the tribunal can still discuss the issue with the parties. The parties might then come to an agreement on the respective issue. At least, the tribunal will be able to take into account the parties' expectations when exercising its procedural discretion. Such need for regulation may also arise throughout the further course of the proceedings. In either scenario, if arbitration statutes and rules provide only limited guidance,[13] and the parties fail to agree, the arbitral tribunal must develop a solution *ad hoc*.

Developing *ad hoc* solutions has its benefits. In particular, *ad hoc* solutions can be tailored to the specific needs of each case. *Ad hoc* solutions can make good use of arbitration's flexibility when compared to domestic civil procedure rules. **9.011**

The downside of *ad hoc* solutions is that inexperienced arbitrators may have difficulty developing a suitable solution in the first place and then take recourse to the domestic civil procedure rules they are accustomed to—without regard for the needs of arbitral proceedings and the parties' expectations. And even for experienced arbitrators, developing procedural solutions *ad hoc* can be a considerable burden. To the extent that *ad hoc* solutions are difficult for the parties to predict, relying on them may furthermore lead to inefficiencies.[14] In any event, solutions 'imposed' on the parties *ad hoc* have the potential of frustrating at least one of them if the parties had diverging expectations as to the suitable regulation of a particular evidentiary issue, or if they are simply inexperienced.[15] Diverging expectations will occur in particular if the parties and their representatives have differing legal backgrounds. Accordingly, with respect to evidentiary issues including the access to evidence, considerable divergences in approach and expectations have been observed namely between 'civil law countries' and 'common law countries'.[16] **9.012**

2. The IBA Rules on the Taking of Evidence 2020

To address and hopefully remedy the above-mentioned concerns about the use of *ad hoc* solutions to evidentiary issues, international arbitral practice has developed, over the past forty years, what has been described as a 'generally accepted code of principles **9.013**

13 E.g. the ICC Rules provide rudimentary additional guidance on how to regulate the issue of the production of documentary evidence, see Appendix IV to the ICC Rules 2021 ('Case Management Techniques'), lit d.

14 On the interplay of flexibility, predictability, and efficiency, see in detail Johannes Landbrecht, 'Recalibrating Arbitration's Efficiency Debate with Luhmann—Forget Tech, Embrace Law, and Motivate!' in b-Arbitra 2021/1, 7, N 104–113.

15 This is highlighted by the IBA Commentary on the revised text of the 2020 IBA Rules on the Taking of Evidence in International Arbitration, 2021, p. 2.

16 See e.g. Alan Redfern and Martin Hunter, *On International Arbitration* (7th edn, Oxford University Press 2022) N 6.79 et seq.

for the taking of evidence in international arbitration',[17] namely the 'IBA Rules on the Taking of Evidence in International Arbitration'. The first edition of the IBA Rules was published in 1983 as the 'Supplementary Rules Governing the Presentation and Reception of Evidence in International Commercial Arbitration'. Major revisions took place in 1999 and 2010.[18] Their latest version was adopted by the IBA Council on 17 December 2020. A commentary to the IBA Rules, aimed at assisting parties and arbitral tribunals in their application and interpretation of the IBA Rules, followed in January 2021.[19]

9.014 The IBA Rules are sometimes criticised for being too 'common law style', in particular allowing document production too freely. In reaction thereto, the so-called 'Prague Rules'[20] were published in 2018.[21] In the following, we will nevertheless focus on the IBA Rules as they appear to remain, at present, more relevant in practice.[22]

9.015 Aiming at reflecting a 'transnational consensus',[23] the IBA Rules are 'intended to provide an efficient, economical and fair process for the taking of evidence in international arbitrations, particularly those between Parties from different legal traditions' (Preamble, paragraph 1).

9.016 The IBA Rules are 'designed to supplement the legal provisions and the institutional, ad hoc or other rules that apply to the conduct of the arbitration' (Preamble, paragraph 1). This demonstrates that the IBA Rules consider themselves to be (mere) suggestions. While parties and arbitral tribunals may adopt the IBA Rules in their entirety, they are invited to modify them or to use them as mere guidelines when determining the procedure for their respective arbitral proceedings if that better serves their purpose. Thus, paragraph 2 of the Preamble emphasises that the IBA Rules 'are not intended to limit the flexibility that is inherent in, and an advantage of, international arbitration'.

---

17 Bernhard Berger and Franz Kellerhals, *International and Domestic Arbitration in Switzerland* (5th edn, Stämpfli ea 2025) N 1313.

18 See Tobias Zuberbühler, Dieter Hofmann, Christian Oetiker and Thomas Rohner, *IBA Rules of Evidence* (2nd edn, Schulthess Verlag 2022) V.

19 The relevant texts are available at https://www.ibanet.org/resources.

20 'Rules on the Efficient Conduct of Proceedings in International Arbitration (Prague Rules)', see https://www.praguerules.com.

21 Cf. Alan Redfern and Martin Hunter, *On International Arbitration* (7th edn, Oxford University Press 2022) N 6.106.

22 Same approach in Alan Redfern and Martin Hunter, *On International Arbitration* (7th edn, Oxford University Press 2022) N 6.106.

23 Bernhard Berger and Franz Kellerhals, *International and Domestic Arbitration in Switzerland* (5th edn, Stämpfli ea 2025) N 1313. Similarly, Alan Redfern and Martin Hunter, *On International Arbitration* (7th edn, Oxford University Press 2022) N 6.112: 'current version of the IBA Rules, by which many tribunals will today be guided in the exercise of their discretion'.

In accordance with this general approach, the IBA Rules define their scope of application primarily by reference to the parties' agreement. The IBA Rules may also 'apply' by determination of an arbitral tribunal (Article 1(1)). The latter is not surprising, nor problematic, considering that arbitral tribunals enjoy wide discretion when determining issues of procedure, as demonstrated above. To give an example, if a tribunal determines that the application of, or reference to, the IBA Rules is 'appropriate' pursuant to sec. 1042(4) German Code of Civil Procedure, it is legitimate for such tribunal to 'apply' the IBA Rules. All this is in any event subject to mandatory provisions. The IBA Rules in their Article 1(1) expressly reserve the application of these mandatory provisions. **9.017**

Yet to further 'strengthen' the role of the parties when it comes to determining issues of evidence, as well as to assess and potentially take into account the parties' respective interests and expectations, to establish a good atmosphere,[24] and to avoid unpleasant surprises, Article 2(1) IBA Rules first and foremost instructs the arbitral tribunal to 'consult the Parties at the earliest appropriate time in the proceedings'. The parties should also be invited to 'consult each other with a view to agreeing on an efficient, economical and fair process for the taking of evidence'. This has also been dubbed a 'meet and consult' approach of the IBA Rules.[25] In practice, such consultation will often be combined with what is referred to, for instance, as organisational, preparatory, or case management conferences and prescribed by various arbitration rules.[26] **9.018**

Article 3 ('Documents'[27]) is then the IBA Rules' core provision on how to deal with and how to obtain access to documentary evidence. **9.019**

Article 3(1) IBA Rules establishes the principle that parties are required to submit all documents on which they themselves rely and that are available to them. While unsurprising in and of itself,[28] this provision has the additional benefit of clarifying *a contrario* that a party is *not* obliged to submit documents *adverse* to its case.[29] Parties may submit additional documents later in accordance with Article 3(11). **9.020**

---

24 Cf. Tobias Zuberbühler, Dieter Hofmann, Christian Oetiker and Thomas Rohner, *IBA Rules of Evidence* (2nd edn, Schulthess Verlag 2022) Article 2 N 3.

25 Cf. IBA Commentary on the revised text of the 2020 IBA Rules on the Taking of Evidence in International Arbitration, 2021, p. 6.

26 See e.g. Art 24(1) ICC Rules 2021 ('case management conference'); Art 19(2) Swiss Rules 2021 ('initial conference').

27 On the IBA Rules' definition of 'Documents' see above note 2.

28 Similarly, Tobias Zuberbühler, Dieter Hofmann, Christian Oetiker and Thomas Rohner, *IBA Rules of Evidence* (2nd edn, Schulthess Verlag 2022) Article 3 N 65: 'in line with the general principle that the parties have a burden to introduce the evidence supporting their case'.

29 Reto Marghitola, *Document Production in International Arbitration* (Wolters Kluwer 2015) § 5.16; Tobias Zuberbühler, Dieter Hofmann, Christian Oetiker and Thomas Rohner, *IBA Rules of Evidence* (2nd edn, Schulthess Verlag 2022) Article 3 N 66.

9.021 These principles relating to the *submission* of documents that are available to a party are uncontroversial. More debated is the further issue of whether, to what extent, and under what conditions a party may request the other side, or a third party, to make available, i.e. to *produce*, certain documents that are unavailable to the party who wishes to rely on them.[30] This topic is labelled 'document production'[31] and is regulated in much detail in Article 3(2)-(9) IBA Rules. We will set out the relevant details in the following.

9.022 Pursuant to the principle established in Article 3(2) IBA Rules, any party to the proceedings *may* submit requests for the production of documents. It must do so within the time limit granted by the tribunal. Legal commentators consequently observe that there appears to be a consensus that at least some level of document production is appropriate in international arbitral proceedings.[32]

9.023 Article 3(3) IBA Rules further specifies the content of such document production request. Article 3(3) is one of the key provisions of the IBA Rules. It is meant to strike a balance between the wide approach to discovery and disclosure in common law jurisdictions—widely considered inappropriate in international arbitral proceedings[33]—and the more restrictive approach in civil law jurisdictions.[34] The approach of the IBA Rules is to allow document production in principle, but then to strictly police its scope. The following limits are to be observed.

---

30 For an overview and on key aspects of the debate see e.g. Tobias Zuberbühler, Dieter Hofmann, Christian Oetiker and Thomas Rohner, *IBA Rules of Evidence* (2nd edn, Schulthess Verlag 2022) Article 3 N 19-32.

31 We follow Tobias Zuberbühler, Dieter Hofmann, Christian Oetiker and Thomas Rohner, *IBA Rules of Evidence* (2nd edn, Schulthess Verlag 2022) Article 3 N 14-17, in avoiding the terms 'discovery' and 'disclosure' as the latter have no specific meaning in many jurisdictions but have a very specific and technical meaning in US and English litigation, respectively. US-style discovery, in particular, has a much broader meaning than envisaged for 'document production' by Article 3 IBA Rules in that discovery refers not only to the production of documents but also includes depositions of potential witnesses and experts as well as the inspection of factual matters in dispute.

32 Cf. IBA Commentary on the revised text of the 2020 IBA Rules on the Taking of Evidence in International Arbitration, 2021, p. 8; Tobias Zuberbühler, Dieter Hofmann, Christian Oetiker and Thomas Rohner, *IBA Rules of Evidence* (2nd edn, Schulthess Verlag 2022) Article 3 N 77(b).

33 Cf. IBA Commentary on the revised text of the 2020 IBA Rules on the Taking of Evidence in International Arbitration, 2021, p. 8; Tobias Zuberbühler, Dieter Hofmann, Christian Oetiker and Thomas Rohner, *IBA Rules of Evidence* (2nd edn, Schulthess Verlag 2022) Article 3 N 77(a); ASA User Council, '"Taming the Beast"—A Whitepaper on Document Production' in Matthias Scherer (ed), (43 ASA Bulletin 3/2025) p. 555.

34 A compromise solution, for civil and commercial proceedings before state courts, has been proposed also by the 2020 Model European Rules of Civil Procedure (ELI/UNIDROIT Model European Rules of Civil Procedure. From Transnational Principles to European Rules of Civil Procedure, OUP 2021). In drafting Part VII, in particular the Access to Evidence Orders, as laid down in Rules 100 to 110 of the Model European Rules of Civil Procedure, account has been taken of the IBA Rules (cf. Introduction to Part VII; see generally Fernando Gascón Inchausti and Michael Stürner, 'Access to Information and Evidence in the ELI/UNIDROIT European Rules on Civil Procedure: Some Fundamental Aspects' (2019) 24 Uniform Law Review 14, as well as Astrid Stadler and Magne Strandberg, General and procedural issues, in Astrid Stadler, Vincent Smith and Fernando Gascón Inchausti (eds), *European Rules of Civil Procedure. A Commentary on the ELI/UNIDROIT Model Rules* (Edward Elgar 2023) Ch. 12).

First, the requesting party must specifically identify the document requested. At the very least, it must describe a 'narrow and specific' category of documents (Article 3(3)(a)).[35] While the notion of a 'category of documents' remains somewhat vague, the qualifiers 'narrow and specific' are meant to avoid far-reaching fishing expeditions,[36] unnecessary 'hassling' of the opposing party, and an overly costly and burdensome document production process.[37] **9.024**

Second, the requesting party must explain how the requested documents or category of documents are 'relevant to the case and material to its outcome' (Article 3(3)(b)).[38] The precise meaning of this part of the requirements of document production is also unclear. The better view, it is submitted, may be that materiality to the outcome of the case is a stricter test than relevance to the case. A document may serve to prove a fact that is relevant to the case, but producing the document may not be material to the outcome of the case to the extent that said fact is already proven or can be proven by other means.[39] The requirements of document production may then vary from one arbitration to the next depending on how the proceedings are structured and at what stage requests for the production of documents are permitted. **9.025**

It is furthermore disputed whether the burden of proof shall play a role in assessing whether the production of a specific document is 'relevant to the case and material to its outcome'. While some argue that a party may request the production of a document only to prove a fact for which this party bears the burden of proof, others highlight that a party may need documents to complement the other party's potentially misleading and selective presentation of evidence on a point for which such other party bears the burden of proof (counter-evidence or '*Gegenbeweis*'). A more nuanced approach requires that the requesting party at least point to a 'specific factual allegation'[40] that this party intends to prove with the requested document(s).[41] **9.026**

Third, the documents must generally not be in the possession, custody, or control of the requesting party but in the possession, custody, or control of the requested party **9.027**

35 For details see Reto Marghitola, *Document Production in International Arbitration* (Wolters Kluwer 2015) § 5.05.

36 IBA Commentary on the revised text of the 2020 IBA Rules on the Taking of Evidence in International Arbitration, 2021, pp. 9–10.

37 Cf. Tobias Zuberbühler, Dieter Hofmann, Christian Oetiker and Thomas Rohner, *IBA Rules of Evidence* (2nd edn, Schulthess Verlag 2022) Article 3 N 99.

38 For details see Reto Marghitola, *Document Production in International Arbitration* (Wolters Kluwer 2015) § 5.06.

39 For this reading, see also Tobias Zuberbühler, Dieter Hofmann, Christian Oetiker and Thomas Rohner, *IBA Rules of Evidence* (2nd edn, Schulthess Verlag 2022) Article 3 N 129.

40 Tobias Zuberbühler, Dieter Hofmann, Christian Oetiker and Thomas Rohner, *IBA Rules of Evidence* (2nd edn, Schulthess Verlag 2022) Article 3 N 133.

41 For details and further references, see Tobias Zuberbühler, Dieter Hofmann, Christian Oetiker and Thomas Rohner, *IBA Rules of Evidence* (2nd edn, Schulthess Verlag 2022) Article 3 N 130-135.

(Article 3(3)(c) IBA Rules).[42] Issues sometimes arise in practice where a specific entity is not itself in possession, custody, or control of a particular document but would not have great difficulty obtaining such document from another group company.

9.028 According to Article 3(4) IBA Rules, the requested party shall then transmit the documents to the production of which it does not object.

9.029 Yet to the extent that the requested party objects to the document production requests pursuant to Article 3(5) IBA Rules, the 'reasons for such objection shall be any of those set forth in Articles 9.2 or 9.3, or a failure to satisfy any of the requirements of Article 3.3'.

9.030 Article 9.3 IBA Rules provides that the arbitral tribunal may 'exclude evidence obtained illegally'.

9.031 According to Article 9.2 IBA Rules, an arbitral tribunal 'shall, at the request of a Party or on its own motion, exclude from evidence or production any Document, statement, oral testimony or inspection, in whole or in part, for any of the following reasons':

> (a) lack of sufficient relevance to the case or materiality to its outcome;
> (b) legal impediment or privilege under the legal or ethical rules determined by the Arbitral Tribunal to be applicable (see Article 9.4 below);
> (c) unreasonable burden to produce the requested evidence;
> (d) loss or destruction of the Document that has been shown with reasonable likelihood to have occurred;
> (e) grounds of commercial or technical confidentiality that the Arbitral Tribunal determines to be compelling;
> (f) grounds of special political or institutional sensitivity (including evidence that has been classified as secret by a government or a public international institution) that the Arbitral Tribunal determines to be compelling; or
> (g) considerations of procedural economy, proportionality, fairness or equality of the Parties that the Arbitral Tribunal determines to be compelling.

9.032 This enumeration is not exclusive. For instance, a production request must also be rejected if a certain document does not exist.[43]

9.033 The most controversial element in the above list of reasons to reject a document production request is the 'legal impediment or privilege' under Article 9.2(b) IBA Rules,[44] further addressed in Article 9(4) as follows:

---

42 For details, see Reto Marghitola, *Document Production in International Arbitration* (Wolters Kluwer 2015) § 5.08.

43 Cf. Tobias Zuberbühler, Dieter Hofmann, Christian Oetiker and Thomas Rohner, *IBA Rules of Evidence* (2nd edn, Schulthess Verlag 2022) Article 3 N 167.

44 For details, see Reto Marghitola, *Document Production in International Arbitration* (Wolters Kluwer 2015) § 5.09 and § 5.10.

> In considering issues of legal impediment or privilege under Article 9.2(b), and insofar as permitted by any mandatory legal or ethical rules that are determined by it to be applicable, the Arbitral Tribunal may take into account:
> (a) any need to protect the confidentiality of a Document created or statement or oral communication made in connection with and for the purpose of providing or obtaining legal advice;
> (b) any need to protect the confidentiality of a Document created or statement or oral communication made in connection with and for the purpose of settlement negotiations;
> (c) the expectations of the Parties and their advisors at the time the legal impediment or privilege is said to have arisen;
> (d) any possible waiver of any applicable legal impediment or privilege by virtue of consent, earlier disclosure, affirmative use of the Document, statement, oral communication or advice contained therein, or otherwise; and
> (e) the need to maintain fairness and equality as between the Parties, particularly if they are subject to different legal or ethical rules.

Issues of evidentiary privilege are difficult to handle in a cross-border situation because the corresponding concepts differ across jurisdictions, in particular between common law (attorney-client privilege) and civil law jurisdictions (duty of professional secrecy).[45] It is already unclear whether privileges are matters of procedure or matters of substance, which is in turn only one reason why it is difficult to determine the law applicable to evidentiary privileges in international arbitral proceedings.[46] Particular difficulties arise, in view of the obligation of arbitral tribunals to treat parties equally,[47] if the standards and concepts of evidentiary privileges differ for the different parties and their counsel involved. The approach adopted most frequently in practice is probably to apply the strictest standard of privilege/duty of secrecy to all concerned. Thereby, no party is required to disclose what it expected to remain secret—at the price of granting everyone else the same 'privilege' and protecting others more than they might have expected. **9.034**

The requesting party may have an opportunity to respond to the objections raised by the requested party (Article 3(5), third sentence, IBA Rules). Upon 'receipt of any such objection and response', the arbitral tribunal may invite the parties to further consult 'with a view to resolving the objection' (Article 3(6) IBA Rules). If such consultation yields no result, or if the arbitral tribunal has not asked for a consultation, it will rule on any remaining objections if so requested (Article 3(7)). **9.035**

45 Cf. IBA Commentary on the revised text of the 2020 IBA Rules on the Taking of Evidence in International Arbitration, 2021, p. 28.

46 Cf. Tobias Zuberbühler, Dieter Hofmann, Christian Oetiker and Thomas Rohner, *IBA Rules of Evidence* (2nd edn, Schulthess Verlag 2022) Article 9 N 19.

47 See e.g. Article 182(3) Swiss Private International Law Act: 'Regardless of the chosen procedure, the arbitral tribunal shall ensure equal treatment of the parties and their right to be heard in adversarial proceedings.'

9.036 Should it be impossible to determine the 'propriety of an objection' without looking at the document, the arbitral tribunal may decide not to review the document itself but to 'appoint an independent and impartial expert, bound to confidentiality, to review any such Document and to report on the objection' (Article 3(8) IBA Rules).

9.037 Furthermore, Article 3(9) IBA Rules addresses the scenario where a party seeks to obtain documents 'from a person or organisation who is not a Party to the arbitration and from whom the Party cannot obtain the Documents on its own'. As arbitral tribunals have no power over parties outside the respective proceedings, obtaining documents from such third parties is difficult in practice. The only solution will often be the seeking of assistance from state courts.

9.038 Finally, Article 3(10) IBA Rules clarifies that the arbitral tribunal itself may request the production of documents on its own motion. The existence of such power seems to be generally accepted in principle.[48]

3. Critical assessment

9.039 Following this account of the rules and principles on access to evidence in arbitral proceedings, we shall briefly reflect on how effective they are in practice, in particular how effectively the above provisions on document production ensure access to relevant evidence.

9.040 As mentioned, arbitral tribunals lack coercive powers, including when it comes to ordering a party to produce documents. Yet Article 9(6) IBA Rules mentions another, and possibly equally effective, measure when it comes to ensuring compliance with document production orders, namely the drawing of adverse inferences:[49]

> If a Party fails without satisfactory explanation to produce any Document requested in a Request to Produce to which it has not objected in due time or fails to produce any Document ordered to be produced by the Arbitral Tribunal, the Arbitral Tribunal may infer that such document would be adverse to the interests of that Party.

9.041 To discipline parties in connection with evidentiary matters more generally, Article 9(8) IBA Rules furthermore provides for cost consequences if 'the Arbitral Tribunal determines that a Party has failed to conduct itself in good faith in the taking of evidence'.

---

48 Cf. Tobias Zuberbühler, Dieter Hofmann, Christian Oetiker and Thomas Rohner, *IBA Rules of Evidence* (2nd edn, Schulthess Verlag 2022) Article 3 N 222.

49 For further details, see e.g. Tobias Zuberbühler, Dieter Hofmann, Christian Oetiker and Thomas Rohner, *IBA Rules of Evidence* (2nd edn, Schulthess Verlag 2022) Article 9 N 59-75.

Despite all the criticism levelled at the IBA Rules, it is probably safe to say that most observers consider the IBA Rules to provide at least suitable guidelines, or at the very least a suitable starting point for dealing with evidentiary matters in arbitral proceedings. In any event, a lot of the criticism voiced may not concern the content of the IBA Rules themselves but the way they are handled by an arbitral tribunal in a particular case. 9.042

In any event, it is submitted that the key contribution of the IBA Rules to the practice of arbitration transcends the suitability of their individual provisions, provisions that the parties and arbitral tribunals can in any event adapt to the specificities and requirements of their respective cases. Namely, the text of the IBA Rules has provided a crystallisation point for the debate about evidentiary matters that enabled the arbitration community to fully understand the issues at stake.[50] A uniform text was available, could be discussed, and had to be applied—by individuals from many different backgrounds. It quickly became apparent that these individuals interpreted and applied this very same text very differently. This may have frustrated some. Yet this uniform text, and the visibility of the differences in approach and interpretation, provided the opportunity to discuss those differences. It was sometimes possible to find common ground. Sometimes an insurmountable disagreement remained. Still, the reasons for this disagreement, and why it was insurmountable, were detected. Consequently, experienced participants are now able to navigate more safely even the most entrenched differences in the handling of evidentiary matters, including access to evidence—if only by negotiating *ad hoc* solutions for a specific case that all participants can plan for. 9.043

C. ACCESS TO EVIDENCE THROUGH STATE COURTS

As mentioned, arbitral tribunals, as private decision-makers, do not have the power to compel a claimant or respondent, and even less so third parties, to provide documents, appear as witnesses, grant access to premises, etc. Arbitral tribunals owe their existence to a contract. Therefore, their power to enforce their own orders is at the outset limited to private law mechanisms. While these mechanisms often provide suitable sanctions in case of non-compliance by the parties, e.g. with respect to the failure to produce documents within their sphere of influence,[51] things are fundamentally different when it comes to, for instance, witness evidence or documents in the custody of third parties. Consequently, to ensure an effective procedure, in particular effective access to evidence, a need may arise for arbitral tribunals to ask state courts for support. 9.044

50 On the following see Johannes Landbrecht, *Rechtssprachliche Kommunikation* (Mohr Siebeck 2023) p. 250.
51 Cf. above, at B.3.

9.045 In this section, the role of state courts will thus be analysed with regard to the gathering of evidence in arbitral proceedings (e.g. sec. 1050 dZPO) ('juge d'appui'). We do not aim at providing a complete picture, but select four major European jurisdictions—England (below C.1.), France (below C.2.), Germany (below C.3.), and Switzerland (below C.4.)—representing different traditions and attitudes towards arbitration. The US approach is referred to in a concluding comparative assessment (below C.5.). The latter reveals that these differences in tradition and attitude are indeed mirrored in the scope of assistance the respective state courts offer when it comes to supporting the access to evidence in arbitral proceedings.

9.046 In this context, one must also not forget that state courts have an important indirect influence on shaping access to evidence in arbitral proceedings, namely through their role in the context of annulment and enforcement proceedings with respect to arbitral awards. State courts review, albeit to a limited extent, how access to evidence has been granted by an arbitral tribunal in a particular case. If a state court considers that access to evidence was insufficient, it will annul the award or refuse its enforcement. Interested in avoiding both, an arbitral tribunal will try to anticipate how relevant state courts will react, and the tribunal will exercise its discretion with respect to the granting of evidence accordingly (below C.6.).

1. England

9.047 The English law rules applicable to private arbitration proceedings seated in England are contained in the 1996 Arbitration Act. Sec. 42 to 45 Arbitration Act 1996 spell out a number of rules relating to the powers of the state courts in relation to arbitral proceedings.

9.048 Recently, the Arbitration Act was subject to a revision.[52] The English Law Commission has been asked in 2021 by the Ministry of Justice to conduct a report with a view to ensuring the high quality and international standing of England as venue for arbitration. On the basis of a public consultation process, the Law Commission has issued its Final Report and Draft Bill in July 2023.[53] The Final Report also addresses court powers in support of arbitral proceedings.[54] However, the modifications proposed therein are not fundamental in nature. On 1 August 2025, the Arbitration Act 2025 entered in force. It brings a number of amendments to the Arbitration Act 1996, but leaves its structure and main content unchanged. In particular, the reform brings amendments to sec. 44 Arbitration Act. Moreover, a new sec. 41a was inserted, dealing with emergency arbitrators and their powers during arbitral proceedings. All the references

52 Cf. Johannes Landbrecht, 'Revision des English Arbitration Act 1996' in Matthias Scherer (ed), (41 ASA Bulletin 4/2023) p. 812.

53 Law Commission, *Review of the Arbitration Act 1996: Final Report and Bill* (Law Com No 413, 5 July 2023).

54 Final Report (previous note) Ch 7.

made hereinafter to the Arbitration Act 1996 pertain to the said Act in its present form, as modified by the Arbitration Act 2025.

Sec. 43 Arbitration Act 1996 is concerned with securing the attendance of witnesses, while sec. 44(2)(a) concerns the taking of the evidence of witnesses. To a certain extent, sec. 43 Arbitration Act draws on Article 27 UNCITRAL Model Law. However, unlike in German law, which has chosen to follow the Model Law rather strictly,[55] there are significant differences in the approach. **9.049**

Sec. 43 Arbitration Act 1996. Securing the attendance of witnesses

(1) A party to arbitral proceedings may use the same court procedures as are available in relation to legal proceedings to secure the attendance before the tribunal of a witness in order to give oral testimony or to produce documents or other material evidence.
(2) This may only be done with the permission of the tribunal or the agreement of the other parties.
(3) The court procedures may only be used if—
    (a) the witness is in the United Kingdom, and
    (b) the arbitral proceedings are being conducted in England and Wales or, as the case may be, Northern Ireland.
(4) A person shall not be compelled by virtue of this section to produce any document or other material evidence which he could not be compelled to produce in legal proceedings.

Sec. 44 Arbitration Act 1996. Court powers exercisable in support of arbitral proceedings

(1) Unless otherwise agreed by the parties, the court has for the purposes of and in relation to arbitral proceedings the same power of making orders (whether in relation to a party or any other person) about the matters listed below as it has for the purposes of and in relation to legal proceedings.
(2) Those matters are—
    (a) the taking of the evidence of witnesses;
    (b) the preservation of evidence;
    (c) making orders relating to property which is the subject of the proceedings or as to which any question arises in the proceedings—
        (i) for the inspection, photographing, preservation, custody or detention of the property, or
        (ii) ordering that samples be taken from, or any observation be made of or experiment conducted upon, the property;

    and for that purpose authorising any person to enter any premises in the possession or control of a party to the arbitration;
    (d) the sale of any goods the subject of the proceedings;
    (e) the granting of an interim injunction or the appointment of a receiver.
(3) If the case is one of urgency, the court may, on the application of a party or proposed party to the arbitral proceedings, make such orders as it thinks necessary for the purpose of preserving evidence or assets.
(4) If the case is not one of urgency, the court may act only on the application of a party to the arbitral proceedings made with—(a) the permission of the tribunal or (as the case may be) the emergency arbitrator, or (b) the agreement in writing of the other parties.

55 See below at B.3.

(4A) An application under subsection (4) may be made only upon notice to the other parties and to the tribunal or the emergency arbitrator.

(5) In any case the court shall act only if or to the extent that the arbitral tribunal or the emergency arbitrator, and any arbitral or other institution or person vested by the parties with power in that regard, has no power or is unable for the time being to act effectively.

(6) If the court so orders, an order made by it under this section shall cease to have effect in whole or in part on the order of the tribunal, the emergency arbitrator or of any such arbitral or other institution or person having power to act in relation to the subject-matter of the order.

(6A) Subject to subsection (7), an appeal lies from a decision of the court under this section.

(7) The leave of the court is required for any such appeal by a party or proposed party to the arbitral proceedings.

(a) General remarks

9.050 Requests for assistance by state courts in evidentiary matters will only be granted in cases where the arbitral tribunal, or indeed the emergency arbitrator, does not have any power to take action. Such principle of subsidiarity is enshrined in sec. 44(5) and also in sec. 44(6) Arbitration Act 1996. The parties may derogate from sec. 44 Arbitration Act 1996, as this provision works entirely in their interest. This includes a partial derogation.[56] By contrast, sec. 43 Arbitration Act 1996, dealing with securing the attendance of witnesses, is mandatory, as transpires from Article 4(1) with Schedule 1. While it is true that sec. 44(2)(a) seems to be wide enough to encompass both securing the attendance of witnesses, regulated by sec. 43, and taking of witness evidence, this mandatory nature of sec. 43 is a strong argument that sec. 43 is not redundant.[57]

(b) Support in the taking of evidence

9.051 Pursuant to sec. 43(1) Arbitration Act 1996, a party may use ordinary evidentiary proceedings, e.g. disclosure and inspection, or the questioning of a witness. But the other party must consent, or otherwise the tribunal must grant permission, sec. 43(2) Arbitration Act 1996. While the arbitral tribunal is not compelled to grant such permission, it will not lightly refuse it either, as sec. 33(1) Arbitration Act 1996 requires the tribunal to give each party a reasonable opportunity of putting its case. By contrast, the rule in sec. 44(4), as amended by the Arbitration Act 2025, is more party-driven, as it operates 'on the application of a party' with the consent of the arbitral tribunal or the emergency arbitrator. In practical terms, the questioning of witnesses is by far more prone to judicial support than disclosure and inspection of documents.

9.052 In cases of urgency, pursuant to sec. 44(3) Arbitration Act 1996, the court may make such orders as it thinks necessary for the purpose of preserving evidence or assets. It

---

56 Bruce Harris, Rowan Planterose and Jonathan Tecks, *The Arbitration Act 1996. A Commentary* (4th edn, Wiley Blackwell 2007) at note 44C.

57 Cf. the discussion in the Final Report (note 53 above), at paras 7.45 and 7.49.

has a fairly wide discretion. However, it will come into play only on application of a party or proposed party to the arbitral proceedings.

9.053 Under sec. 43 Arbitration Act 1996, no order may be sought to obtain disclosure from a third party. Any such request for judicial assistance must clearly state which documents are to be produced.[58] The normal rules on privilege apply also in the context of judicial assistance (sec. 43(4) Arbitration Act 1996, which points to rule 34.2(5) of the Civil Procedure Rules). This provision operates in domestic proceedings only, sec. 43(3)(b) Arbitration Act 1996, or when the witness is in the United Kingdom, sec. 43(3)(a).

9.054 As sec. 93 Arbitration Act 1996 clarifies, a judge at the High Court may accept an appointment as sole arbitrator or umpire (but not in another capacity).[59] Should the arbitral tribunal consist of one or more judge-arbitrators, the tribunal itself may exercise the court's power under sec. 43 Arbitration Act 1996 concurrently with the High Court.[60] Schedule 2 to the Arbitration Act 1996 spells out in more detail the powers of the judge-arbitrator within the meaning of sec. 93. Para 4, which deals with the exercise of court powers in support of arbitration, provides as follows:

> (1) Where the arbitral tribunal consists of or includes a judge-arbitrator the powers of the court under sections 42 to 44 (enforcement of peremptory orders, summoning witnesses, and other court powers) are exercisable by the High Court and also by the judge-arbitrator himself.
> (2) Anything done by a judge-arbitrator in the exercise of those powers shall be regarded as done by him in his capacity as judge of the High Court and have effect as if done by that court.
>
> Nothing in this sub-paragraph prejudices any power vested in him as arbitrator or umpire.

Should the court refuse support, an appeal against this decision lies only with leave of the court, cf. sec. 44(6A),(7) Arbitration Act 1996.

(c) Applicable procedural rules

9.055 As to the procedure in carrying out the request, the normal rules apply, e.g. part 34 of the 1999 Civil Procedure Rules.[61]

9.056 Pursuant to sec. 43(4) Arbitration Act 1996, a person shall not be compelled by virtue of this section to produce any document or other material evidence which such person could not be compelled to produce in legal proceedings.

---

58 Cf. *Tajik Aluminium Plant v Hydro Aluminium AS* [2006] 1 Lloyd's Rep. 155

59 This is subject to the consent of the Lord Chief Justice, sec. 93(2) AA.

60 Bruce Harris, Rowan Planterose and Jonathan Tecks, *The Arbitration Act 1996. A Commentary* (4th edn, Wiley Blackwell 2007) at notes 42E and 43G.

61 Bruce Harris, Rowan Planterose and Jonathan Tecks, *The Arbitration Act 1996. A Commentary* (4th edn, Wiley Blackwell 2007) at note 43D.

2. France

9.057 The French rules governing arbitration proceedings seated in France are to be found in Articles 1442 to 1527 of the French Code of Civil Procedure (Code de Procédure Civile, CPC). French arbitration law is not based on the UNCITRAL Model Law. Articles 1460 and 1469 CPC deal with the 'juge d'appui' and its role in support of the arbitral proceedings.

> Article 1460
> A dispute shall be referred to the juge d'appui either by a party or by the Arbitral Tribunal or one of its members.
> The judge shall rule in accordance with the accelerated procedure on the merits.
> The juge d'appui shall give a judgment that is not subject to appeal. However, this judgment may be appealed if the judge declares that there are no grounds for appointment for one of the reasons set out in Article 1455.

> Article 1469
> If a party to the arbitral proceedings intends to rely on an authentic instrument or a private document to which he was not a party or on a document held by a third party, he may, at the request of the Arbitral Tribunal, summon such third party before the President of the Tribunal in order to obtain a copy of the instrument or document or the production thereof.
> The territorial jurisdiction of the President of the Tribunal shall be determined in accordance with Articles 42 to 48.
> The application shall be lodged, investigated and judged in accordance with the accelerated procedure on the merits.
> If the President deems the application to be well-founded, he shall order that the original, copy or extract, as the case may be, of the document be issued or produced under the conditions and subject to the guarantees that he shall determine, if necessary subject to a fine.
> This decision is not automatically enforceable.
> It may be appealed within fifteen days of service of the decision.

(a) General remarks

9.058 The 2011 reform of the rules on arbitration have increased the power of the 'juge d'appui' in arbitration, e.g. when it comes to solving procedural disputes relating to arbitration proceedings seated in France, such as the appointment of the arbitral tribunal or challenges to arbitrators. This will be of particular importance for *ad hoc* arbitration. The powers of the 'juge d'appui' are exercised by the President of the Paris Court of First Instance (Article 1459 CPC). The decisions of the 'juge d'appui' are final (Article 1460(3) CPC), safe in exceptional cases (Articles 1460(3) and 1469(6) CPC).

(b) Support in the taking of evidence

9.059 The role of the 'juge d'appui' before or during arbitration is rather limited. He may assist the parties to an arbitration agreement in gathering evidence before or during the arbitration. Prior to the commencement of the proceedings, the parties may apply to the French courts in order to seek discovery orders for evidence located in France. Such proceedings are conducted *ex parte*.

During the arbitration, the parties may, with the authorisation of the arbitral tribunal, apply for a judicial disclosure order to compel the production of documents held by third parties (Article 1469 CPC). **9.060**

(c) Applicable procedural rules

The procedure before the 'juge d'appui' is governed by the rules on the accelerated procedure on the merits (Articles 839 and 481-1 CPC). **9.061**

3. Germany

Under German law, arbitral tribunals do not exercise sovereign power. Article 92 of the German constitution confers judicative power exclusively on the judiciary. By the same token, arbitral tribunals do not have coercive means at their disposal. As a substitute, sec. 1025 of the German Code of Civil Procedure (*Zivilprozessordnung*, dZPO) contains rules on judicial support in the taking of evidence and other judicial acts. Sec. 1050 dZPO provides as follows: **9.062**

> [1]The arbitral tribunal or a party with the consent of the arbitral tribunal may request the court to assist in the taking of evidence or to perform other judicial acts which the arbitral tribunal is not authorised to perform. [2]The court shall, unless it considers it inadmissible, carry out the request in accordance with its procedural rules applicable to the taking of evidence or other judicial act. [3]The arbitrators shall be entitled to participate in the taking of evidence and to ask questions.

This rule applies to domestic arbitral proceedings. As to foreign arbitral proceedings, i.e. where the seat of the arbitral tribunal is outside of Germany or not yet designated, sec. 1025(2) dZPO provides that sec. 1050 dZPO shall nonetheless apply. **9.063**

As opposed to the other jurisdictions examined, sec. 1050 dZPO follows Article 27 of the 2006 UNCITRAL Model Law. That provision provides as follows: **9.064**

> Article 27. Court assistance in taking evidence
> The arbitral tribunal or a party with the approval of the arbitral tribunal may request from a competent court of this state assistance in taking evidence. The court may execute the request within its competence and according to its rules on taking evidence.

(a) General remarks

Sec. 1050 dZPO operates only in cases where the arbitral tribunal lacks the necessary coercive powers to act itself. According to the prevailing opinion, the request for assistance can only be considered if the arbitral tribunal has exhausted its own possibilities in **9.065** this respect.[62] Hence, the principle of subsidiarity applies.[63] Assistance of state courts is needed mostly where steps have to be taken which require the use of state power, e.g. if the appearance of a witness or expert witness must be compelled or an examination under oath appears necessary. It is a question of degree, however, to assess where the arbitral tribunal in all likelihood has no possibility to act or has a possibility to act but, in all likelihood, will fail. Insofar, the court has a certain margin of appreciation.[64] It is safe to say that the arbitral tribunal does not need to have attempted what is clearly a hopeless endeavour.[65] On the other hand, one commentator has suggested that requests of the arbitral tribunal may be struck out on the grounds of abuse of process where it is obvious that the tribunal is in a position to take the necessary step itself (e.g. where a witness is to be examined who would voluntarily appear before the arbitral tribunal and there is no need to swear an oath).[66]

9.066 Even though sec. 1050 dZPO is silent on the issue, it may be derogated by the parties. As arbitration is a private matter, and the assistance by the state courts is provided purely to help the parties to the arbitral proceedings, not to realise some higher public goal, the parties may waive this right.[67] By the same token, they must be in a position to limit the right of the arbitral tribunal to call upon the competent state court for assistance.[68]

9.067 By contrast, it seems questionable whether or not the state court may be called for assistance in cases where the arbitral tribunal has possibilities to act (legally) but such action would cause unreasonable expenses. Some authors argue for an application by analogy of sec. 1050 dZPO.[69] However, given the function of that provision to serve

62 Cf. Bundesgerichtshof in SchiedsVZ 2021, 43 at para 28 with further references.

63 Cf. Joachim Münch in *Münchener Kommentar zur ZPO* (6th edn, CH Beck 2022) § 1050 ZPO paras 4 and 26.

64 Joachim Münch in *Münchener Kommentar zur ZPO* (6th edn, CH Beck 2022) § 1050 ZPO para 26.

65 Peter Schlosser in *Stein and Jonas Kommentar zur Zivilprozessordnung* (23rd edn, Mohr Siebeck 2014) § 1050 ZPO para 11.

66 Peter Schlosser in *Stein and Jonas Kommentar zur Zivilprozessordnung* (23rd edn, Mohr Siebeck 2014) § 1050 ZPO para 11.

67 Joachim Münch in *Münchener Kommentar zur ZPO* (6th edn, CH Beck 2022) § 1050 ZPO para 12; Stephan Wilske and Lars Markert in Volkert Vorwerk and Christian Wolf (eds), *BeckOK ZPO* (58th edn, CH Beck 2025) § 1050 ZPO para 2. See, however, the diverging approach taken by Peter Schlosser in *Stein and Jonas Kommentar zur Zivilprozessordnung* (23rd edn, Mohr Siebeck 2014) § 1050 ZPO para 3.

68 This is (probably) also the position of the Bundesgerichtshof in SchiedsVZ 2016, 328, at 333.

69 Wolfgang Kühn, 'Die Bedeutung der Gerichte bei der Durchführung von Schiedsverfahren' in Karl-Heinz Böckstiegel (ed), *Schiedsgerichtsbarkeit im Umfeld von Politik, Wirtschaft und Gerichtsbarkeit* (Carl Heymanns 1992) p. 65; Peter Schlosser in *Stein and Jonas Kommentar zur Zivilprozessordnung* (23rd edn, Mohr Siebeck 2014) § 1050 ZPO para 12; Ben Steinbrück, *Die Unterstützung ausländischer Schiedsverfahren durch staatliche Gerichte* (Mohr Siebeck 2009) p. 417; Stephan Wilske and Lars Markert in Volkert Vorwerk and Christian Wolf (eds), *BeckOK ZPO* (58th edn, CH Beck 2025) § 1050 ZPO para 3; cf also Christoph Althammer in *Zöller ZPO* (36th edn, Otto Schmidt 2026) § 1050 ZPO para 8.

as a substitute in cases where the arbitral tribunal does not have the *possibility* to act, questions of economic viability are not covered from the outset.[70]

(b) Support in the taking of evidence

Pursuant to sec. 1050(1) dZPO, the arbitral tribunal may request a state court to assist. Likewise, the application may also be made by the parties, but only with the consent of the arbitral tribunal. This is meant to prevent frivolous and vexatious applications with the only goal to protract and procrastinate. However, if both parties put the request before the arbitral tribunal, it may reject the application only if it is totally outside the realm of sec. 1050 dZPO.[71] The state court assesses the admissibility of the application in its own discretion even if the arbitral tribunal has refused to accept the mutual application of the parties. **9.068**

Pursuant to sec. 1025(2) dZPO, judicial assistance under sec. 1050 dZPO may also be requested if the place of arbitration is outside Germany.[72] Hence, the German courts support foreign arbitral proceedings just as they support domestic ones. In doing so, the competent court has at its disposal all the means of the taking of evidence as in ordinary civil proceedings (cf. sec. 1050(2) dZPO). Consequently, a request by the arbitral tribunal to order third parties to produce several unspecified documents will be refused. The same is true for requests to support cross-examination. It should be noted, however, that in such cases, pursuant to the case management powers under sec. 139 dZPO, the court may not simply refuse a request for assistance but will have to ensure that the request is drafted in a way that enables the court to fulfil the request.[73] **9.069**

Sec. 1050 dZPO draws on Article 27 of the UNCITRAL Model Law but goes well beyond it in that it covers not only the gathering of evidence but extends to other judicial activity. Consequently, as the legislative materials make clear,[74] e.g. a request to an authority to produce a document in its possession, a request for service of documents, or the obtaining of authorisation to give evidence for the questioning of officials and judges also fall within the scope of application of the (German) provision. **9.070**

The application must be submitted to the competent court, which is the local court (*Amtsgericht*) in the district of which the judicial act is to be carried out (sec. 1062(4) dZPO). That court has a limited power to check if the conditions of sec. 1050 dZPO **9.071**

70 Joachim Münch in *Münchener Kommentar zur ZPO* (6th edn, CH Beck 2022) § 1050 ZPO para 8.

71 Stephan Wilske and Lars Markert in Volkert Vorwerk and Christian Wolf (eds), *BeckOK ZPO* (58th edn, CH Beck 2025) § 1050 ZPO para 7.

72 Cf. amply Markus Wirth and Urs Hoffmann-Nowotny, 'Rechtshilfe deutscher Gerichte zugunsten ausländischer Schiedsgerichte bei der Beweisaufnahme – ein Erfahrungsbericht' in SchiedsVZ 2005, 66.

73 Peter Schlosser in *Stein and Jonas Kommentar zur Zivilprozessordnung* (23rd edn, Mohr Siebeck 2014) § 1050 ZPO para 28.

74 Bundestags-Drucksache No 13/5274, p. 51.

have been met. It may refuse the application only if (1) there is no approval of the application by the arbitral tribunal, (2) the arbitral tribunal would be in a position to carry out the requested measure itself, and (3) if there are general grounds for inadmissibility of the requested measure under procedural law. The latter may be the case if the request amounts to a US style discovery of documents.[75] By contrast, the requested court may not question the necessity of the requested measure, as this would interfere with the competence of the arbitral tribunal. Likewise, any doubts as to the validity of the arbitration agreement on the basis of which the respective arbitral tribunal acts must not be raised during the proceedings. Separate proceedings exist to address such issues (cf. sec. 1032(2), 1040(3) dZPO). An exception is discussed for very blatant cases,[76] but this seems to be a fairly theoretical point.[77]

9.072 The decision of the court may be appealed pursuant to the general rules (i.e. sec. 567 dZPO).[78]

(c) Applicable procedural rules

9.073 There are no specific rules for the taking of evidence under sec. 1050 dZPO. Instead, the usual procedure concerning the taking of evidence applies (sec. 1050(2) dZPO). Pursuant to the general rules of procedure (sec. 357 dZPO), the parties to the arbitral proceedings are summoned to the evidentiary hearing, and they are allowed e.g. to ask questions to the witness. Moreover, the arbitrators have an explicit 'right to be heard' (sec. 1050(3) dZPO). This is meant to give them the complete picture of the taking of evidence. Clearly, the German law principle of the immediacy of the taking of evidence, central to proceedings before state courts (cf. sec. 355(2) dZPO), has influenced this extension.[79]

9.074 The parties receive a certified copy of the protocol of the taking of evidence. Moreover, the arbitral tribunal may also request such a copy, even in cases where judicial assistance was sought by the parties.[80] It is entirely up to the arbitral tribunal to evaluate the result of the taking of evidence.[81]

---

75 Bundestags-Drucksache No 13/5274, p. 51.

76 Wolfgang Voit in Hans-Joachim Musielak and Wolfgang Voit (eds), *ZPO* (22nd edn, Vahlen 2025) § 1050 ZPO Rn 5.

77 Against any power of control of the requested court even in very obvious cases Joachim Münch in *Münchener Kommentar zur ZPO* (6th edn, CH Beck 2022) § 1050 ZPO para 21.

78 Bundesgerichtshof in SchiedsVZ 2021, 43 para 11.

79 Cf. Joachim Münch in *Münchener Kommentar zur ZPO* (6th edn, CH Beck 2022) § 1050 ZPO para 31 and 34.

80 Christoph Althammer in *Zöller ZPO* (36th edn, Otto Schmidt 2026) § 1050 para 6.

81 Wolfgang Voit in Hans-Joachim Musielak and Wolfgang Voit (eds), *ZPO* (22nd edn, Vahlen 2025) § 1050 ZPO Rn 8.

4. Switzerland

Under Swiss law, Part 3 of the Code of Civil Procedure (chZPO) regulates Swiss domestic arbitral proceedings. For Swiss international arbitral proceedings, the Act on Private International Law (*Bundesgesetz über das Internationale Privatrecht*, IPRG) contains specific rules in its Chapter 12. One may thus distinguish three categories of arbitration under Swiss law: Swiss domestic arbitration (seated in Switzerland, governed by the chZPO), Swiss international arbitration (seated in Switzerland, governed by the IPRG), and foreign arbitration (seated abroad). The latest reform of the IPRG, which entered into force on 1 January 2021, has expanded the power of the Swiss courts explicitly to provide assistance in the latter cases (Article 185a IPRG). For Swiss international arbitral proceedings, Articles 184, 185 and 185a IPRG provide as follows: 9.075

> Article 184 IPRG
> 1. The arbitral tribunal shall take the evidence itself.
> 2. If state legal assistance is required for the conduct of the evidentiary proceedings, the arbitral tribunal or a party may, with the consent of the arbitral tribunal, request the assistance of the state court at the seat of the arbitral tribunal.
> 3. The state court shall apply its own law. Upon request, it may apply or consider other forms of procedure.
>
> Article 185 IPRG
> If further involvement of the state court is required, the judge at the seat of the arbitration tribunal shall have jurisdiction.
>
> Article 185a IPRG
> 1. An arbitral tribunal with its seat abroad or a party to foreign arbitration proceedings may request the co-operation of the state court at the place where a precautionary or protective measure is to be enforced. Article 183 paragraphs 2 and 3 apply by analogy.
> 2. An arbitral tribunal with its seat abroad or a party to foreign arbitration proceedings with the consent of the arbitral tribunal may request the co-operation of the state court at the place where the taking of evidence is to take place. Article 184 paragraphs 2 and 3 apply mutatis mutandis.

(a) General remarks

As in other systems, Swiss law is based on the principle of subsidiarity when it comes to state court assistance in arbitral proceedings. Consequently, pursuant to Article 184(1) IPRG,[82] the arbitral tribunal shall take evidence itself. 9.076

(b) Support in the taking of evidence

Support of a state court may be provided on application of the arbitral tribunal, Article 375(2),(1) chZPO, Article 184(2) IPRG and Article 185a(2) IPRG. The parties to the arbitral proceedings may also apply to the state court, but their application must 9.077

82 Article 375(1) chZPO is to the same effect.

be backed by the consent of the arbitral tribunal, Article 375(2),(2) chZPO, Article 184(2) IPRG and Article 185a(2) IPRG. The competence lies with the judge at the seat of the arbitral tribunal (Articles 184(2) and 185 IPRG).

9.078 In the context of foreign arbitral proceedings, i.e. where the application is made by an arbitral tribunal seated abroad or by a party to foreign arbitral proceedings, Article 185a(1) IPRG provides that such request for support by Swiss state courts must be addressed to the court at the place where a precautionary or protective measure is to be enforced. When it comes to the taking of evidence, Article 185(2) IPRG provides that an arbitral tribunal seated abroad or a party to foreign arbitral proceedings, with the consent of the arbitral tribunal, must address the request for support by Swiss courts to the state court at the place (in Switzerland) where the evidence is to be taken.

9.079 From the subsidiarity principle enshrined in Article 184(1) IPRG it transpires that the support of Swiss state courts can only be requested with respect to such evidentiary measures that cannot be taken by the arbitral tribunal itself.

(c) Applicable procedural rules

9.080 Pursuant to Article 184(3) IPRG, the state court requested to assist in Swiss international arbitral proceedings shall apply its own law. The same applies to assistance to foreign arbitral proceedings, Article 185a(2) IPRG. However, upon request (by the arbitral tribunal or the parties to the arbitral proceedings, cf. Article 184(2) IPRG), the Swiss state court may also apply or consider other forms of procedure. This helps build a bridge between the foreign arbitral procedural rules, where certain types of the taking of evidence may be permissible, and the Swiss rules on the taking of evidence. These provisions were introduced in a 2018 reform and entered in force on 1 January 2021. Insofar, Swiss law is more generous than e.g. German law, the latter explicitly limiting the court's assistance to those mechanisms that would be available in ordinary civil proceedings.[83] The official explanatory memorandum to the 2018 reform remains silent as to the limits of this power of the Swiss courts to use 'foreign' approaches to the taking of evidence.[84] It would seem plausible, in light of the general intention of the reform to make Swiss arbitral proceedings more attractive,[85] that the Swiss legislator granted the Swiss courts wide discretion, limited only by general overarching principles of Swiss law.

83 See above at C.3 (b).

84 *Botschaft zur Änderung des Bundesgesetzes über das Internationale Privatrecht*, BBl 2018, 7198.

85 Cf. e.g. *Botschaft zur Änderung des Bundesgesetzes über das Internationale Privatrecht*, BBl 2018, 7171.

5. Comparative assessment

In a nutshell, all domestic arbitration laws discussed above start from the assumption that arbitral tribunals deal with evidentiary matters primarily themselves. This reflects the principle of party autonomy as well as the respect for the arbitration agreement, which derogates the competence of state courts. Consequently, the parties may (mostly) agree on limiting or indeed excluding the possibility to ask state courts for assistance in evidentiary matters. **9.081**

All the (recent and less recent) reforms of the pertinent rules have been (or will be, as the case may be) implemented with a view to bolstering the attractiveness of the respective venue for international arbitration. If the power of state courts to assist in the taking of evidence has been enlarged, as this has been the case e.g. in Switzerland, the primary goal of this was to enhance efficiency in the taking of evidence. Basically, there should be no difference regarding access to information and evidence whether the parties choose to litigate before state courts or before arbitral tribunals. **9.082**

While the pertinent rules cover all types of evidence, in practice, at least in Europe, arbitral tribunals and parties are probably unlikely to request state court assistance other than to compel witnesses to testify. All other types of evidence can normally be substituted, e.g. by drawing adverse inferences from the lack of production of a document. **9.083**

The openness of domestic laws to requests for support made by foreign arbitral tribunals also bears witness to the growing acceptance and importance of arbitration as an independent dispute settlement mechanism. However, such mechanisms may also invite 'judicial assistance shopping', to make allusions to a well-known procedural phenomenon. To avoid such assistance shopping, state courts may interpret the respective rules in a restrictive manner, as recent developments in the USA demonstrate. **9.084**

US courts must provide assistance to foreign and international tribunals and to litigants before such tribunals under 28 U.S.C. § 1782. This opens the door to US style discovery, a means of access to information and evidence unknown in most other systems, also in proceedings before certain foreign and international tribunals. To limit the scope of § 1782, the US Supreme Court, in *Intel Corp. v. Advanced Micro Devices, Inc.*,[86] held that once the prima facie requirements of § 1782 are met, district courts must further consider a series of discretionary factors, e.g. 'the nature of the foreign tribunal, the character of the proceedings underway abroad, and the receptivity **9.085**

86 *Intel Corp v Advanced Micro Devices, Inc* 2004 542 US 241.

of the foreign government or the court or agency abroad to US federal-court judicial assistance'; 'whether the sec. 1782(a) request conceals an attempt to circumvent foreign proof-gathering restrictions or other policies of a foreign country or the US'; and whether the request is otherwise 'unduly intrusive or burdensome'. Still, some lower instance courts considered that commercial arbitration tribunals could qualify as 'foreign and international tribunals' under § 1782.

9.086 More recently, however, in June 2022, in *ZF Automotive US, Inc. v Luxshare, Ltd.*,[87] the Supreme Court held that § 1782 does not apply to international commercial arbitration or *ad hoc* UNCITRAL investor-state arbitration. The court concluded:

> In sum, only a governmental or intergovernmental adjudicative body constitutes a 'foreign or international tribunal' under § 1782. Such bodies are those that exercise governmental authority conferred by one nation or multiple nations. Neither the private commercial arbitral panel in the first case nor the *ad hoc* arbitration panel in the second case qualifies.

6. The role of state courts as a safety net with respect to access to evidence

9.087 We have so far focussed on the state courts' direct role when it comes to ensuring access to evidence in arbitral proceedings through assisting arbitral tribunals with the taking of evidence in circumstances where the arbitral tribunals' powers are (too) limited. Yet state courts also have an important indirect influence when it comes to shaping access to evidence in arbitral proceedings, namely through their role in the context of annulment and enforcement proceedings with respect to arbitral awards.

9.088 There is no binding instrument that would harmonise transnationally the rules about the annulment of arbitral awards, although the UNCITRAL Model Law on International Commercial Arbitration of 1985 (the 'Model Law', with amendments as adopted in 2006) provides some guidance and direction. Namely, Article 34(2)(a)(iv) of the Model Law stipulates that an arbitral award may be set aside if 'the arbitral procedure was not in accordance with the agreement of the parties, unless such agreement was in conflict with a provision of this Law from which the parties cannot derogate, or, failing such agreement, was not in accordance with this Law'. The extent to which an arbitral tribunal's granting of access to evidence is reviewed in the context of annulment proceedings otherwise depends on the corresponding domestic arbitration law. The same is true for the recognition and enforcement of *domestic* arbitral awards. A detailed assessment of the relevant rules would go beyond the scope of this contribution.

---

87 *ZF Automotive US, Inc v Luxshare, Ltd* 2022 596 US 16–17.

However, some harmonisation is provided transnationally with respect to the recognition and enforcement of *foreign* arbitral awards through the 1958 New York Convention on the Recognition and Enforcement of Foreign Arbitral Awards (the New York Convention), in particular because the New York Convention today enjoys almost universal recognition. When requested to recognise and enforce a foreign arbitral award, state courts may thereby control, at least to a limited extent, how an arbitral tribunal has granted access to evidence in a particular case. **9.089**

Pursuant to Article V(1)(d) of the New York Convention, recognition and enforcement of an award may be refused if 'the arbitral procedure was not in accordance with the agreement of the parties, or, failing such agreement, was not in accordance with the law of the country where the arbitration took place'. The applicability of this provision thus requires a party agreement or a statutory rule, the latter largely missing on evidentiary matters in most arbitration laws. Consequently, without an agreement of the parties that may have been violated, a tribunal's determination of evidentiary matters, and how it granted access to evidence in a particular case, will rarely be reviewed by a recognising state court. **9.090**

On the other hand, Article V(1)(b) of the New York Convention concerns more broadly certain categories of violations of the right to be heard. Such violations of the right to be heard might also constitute violations of public policy as enshrined in Article V(2)(b) of the New York Convention. Recognition and enforcement of foreign arbitral awards could be refused if an arbitral tribunal has not complied with these (minimum) standards of procedural fairness. **9.091**

As the granting of effective access to evidence may be seen as a facet of the general principle of a right to a fair trial, and, with similar justification, of the overarching right to be heard,[88] state courts may sanction with non-recognition of the arbitral award any undue restrictions by arbitral tribunals of access to relevant evidence.[89] Notwithstanding the arbitral tribunals' wide discretion when it comes to dealing with evidentiary matters, state courts thus have a certain role to play as a safety net when it comes to ensuring access to evidence in commercial arbitration. **9.092**

88 Cf. e.g. Reinhold Geimer, *Internationales Zivilprozessrecht* (9th edn, Otto Schmidt 2024) at para 2351.
89 Cf. Reinhold Geimer and Gottfried Hammer in Walter Eberl (ed), *Beweis im Schiedsverfahren* (Nomos 2015) § 10 at paras 55 and 86.

10

COMPARATIVE ANALYSIS AND CONCLUDING REMARKS

Fernando Gascón Inchausti, Astrid Stadler and Magne Strandberg

A. INTRODUCTION

10.001 Modern civil procedure law tends to be party-driven systems based on key principles of party autonomy: it is for the parties to plead facts and to produce evidence in order to prove those facts.[1] Although the court may have powers and duties to take evidence *ex officio* and may encourage parties to plead new facts and produce new evidence, the main initiative is left to the parties and the main role of the courts is to fill in the gaps when the parties have not taken adequate initiatives in order to produce a sound

1 See e.g. European Law Institute and UNIDROIT, *ELI-UNIDROIT Model European Rules of Civil Procedure. From Transnational Principles to European Rules of Civil Procedure* (ERCP) (OUP 2021) rr 24–25.

factual and evidential basis. In line with the basic principles of party initiative and autonomy, a party is entitled to offer whatever evidence to the court and evidence shall be admitted when it is relevant and not covered by a privilege or another special ground for inadmissibility. A party is also entitled to produce any counterevidence to any evidence suggested by the opposing party and is allowed to comment on any weakness in the evidence offered by the opposing party. In theory, party-driven systems gather results in balanced and well-founded evidential situations because at least one party has an interest in the production of any evidence as long as the evidence supports one of the parties' factual assertions.

However, party-driven systems face difficulties when one party has significantly better access to evidence than the opposing party. Although a party formally has the right to offer whatever relevant evidence, making effect of such a formal right is impossible if the party lacks access to the evidence. While the basic principles of party autonomy may suggest that a party is free to choose which evidence shall be produced or given access to, other basic goals or purposes of modern civil procedure law may suffer. A goal of truth-finding and realisation of substantive rights may suffer if the information-controlling party is free to decide which evidence shall be presented to court. Since that party will not have any incentive to produce any other evidence than that which is positive to his or her case, there is a real risk of producing evidential situations which are tilted, biased or dominated by evidence in favour of the evidence-controlling party. Furthermore, imbalance in access to evidence may result in other unreasonable advantages for the controlling party: The information asymmetry may lead to a strategical imbalance in favour of the evidence-controlling party in the form of a better informational basis to decide on matters such as whether a law suit shall be initiated, which claims shall be presented, which facts could be asserted and indirectly the choice of legal strategy in order to find the most persuasive and effective way to succeed. Imbalance of information may also be a strategical imbalance during negotiations for settlement before or after initiation of proceedings. **10.002**

On the other hand, obliging evidence-controlling parties to disclose information may cause trouble for basic goals such as respect for private life and the need to keep sensitive information secret. Furthermore, while rights of access to evidence may primarily be established in order to adjust procedural advantages and inequalities, they may give rise to new inequalities and disadvantages. In a modern information-based society, broad and general rights to access evidence may lead to costly and time-consuming proceedings which may cause delay, misuse and obstruction. Broad and general duties to disclose evidence may, to an unreasonable degree, favour strong and wealthy parties. **10.003**

Arguably, the problem of access to evidence is more or less universal as the inherent characteristics of the problem are recognisable over time and between procedural **10.004** traditions.[2] Whenever a party has better access to evidence than the opposing party, the problem is whether the evidence-controlling party has a right to pick and choose within the available evidence or whether that party must disclose the evidence to the other party or to the court. Historically, very different approaches to that problem have been found. Many procedural traditions have been characterised by the old Latin phrase *nemo tenetur contra se edere*. An example is the German ZPO of 1887, which contained very few and very limited rules obliging a party to disclose evidence regardless of whether the evidence was asked for by the opposing party or not.[3] Similar traditions are found in other European jurisdictions, such as Italy and Spain.[4] The common law tradition, on the other hand, developed an approach based on a goal of equal access to evidence. In the landmark case *Peruvian Guano* from 1882, the English Court of Appeal strongly emphasised the need for broad and general access to evidence between the parties based on a reluctant criterion of evidential relevance. Later, the common law jurisdictions moved in different directions.[5] While the US rules on discovery found in the FRCP from its origin back in 1938 further strengthened the parties' mutual obligation to provide access to all types of potentially relevant evidence,[6] English law developed more moderate access to evidence obligations which first and foremost apply to documents and tangible evidence.[7]

10.005 These historical-traditional contrasts between procedural families are well-known and especially the contrast between US law and other traditions has been thoroughly analysed by numerous scholars.[8] However, at least some of the previous studies have taken a too general approach where all so-called "civil law jurisdictions" are regarded as one common figure. In order to shed light on the nuances of civil law jurisdictions and the differences between them, we will in this Chapter dig deeper into a comparison within a European context. Based on the previous Chapters of this book, which

---

2 T Einhorn, "Evidence-Gathering Techniques" in B Hess, M Woo, L Cadiet, S Menétrey and E Vallines García (eds), *Comparative Procedural Law and Justice* (Part VII Chapter 2), cplj.org/a/7-2, accessed May 8, 2025; L Kahl, "Limits on Disclosure and Discovery" in B Hess, M Woo, L Cadiet, S Menétrey and E Vallines García (eds), *Comparative Procedural Law and Justice* (Part VII Chapter 3), cplj.org/a/7-3, accessed May 8, 2025.

3 Germany, n 1.011.

4 Italy, n 4.003; Spain, n 5.021.

5 *Compagnie Financiere du Pacifique v Peruvian Guano Company* (1882) 11 QBD 55; see n 2.022.

6 See nn 8.010 et seq.

7 See nn 2.021 et seq.

8 SN Subrin, "Discovery in Global Perspective: Are We Nuts?" (2002) 52 DePaul Law Review 299–318; R Verkerk, *Fact-Finding in Civil Litigation: A Comparative Perspective* (Intersentia 2010); RL Marcus, "Putting American Procedural Exceptionalism into a Globalized Context" (2005) 53 The American Journal of Comparative Law 709–740; M Strandberg, "Access to Evidence in US, Germany, and Norway" in M Woo and CH van Rhee (eds), *Comparative Civil Procedure* (Edward Elgar 2025); RL Marcus, "Extremism in the Pursuit of Truth is Our Virtue: The American Infatuation with Broad Discovery" in CH van Rhee and A Uzelac (eds), *Truth and Efficiency in Civil Litigation. Fundamental Aspects of Fact-Finding and Evidence-Taking in a Comparative Context* (Intersentia 2012) 165–188.

provide insight into the particularities of access to evidence law in leading European jurisdictions, this Chapter will examine whether the historical differences between traditions of civil procedure law still prevail or whether the differences have faded away or diminished. We will address access to evidence issues on a European and national level, but at the heart of our analysis is the comparative perspective on differences and similarities between European countries. Our analysis addresses commercial litigation and regular civil lawsuits, which means that administrative proceedings, family proceedings and insolvency proceedings are left aside. Since quite a lot of the commercial cases are handled by arbitration, and such proceedings are dominated by international agreements, we will include that as well as proceedings before state courts.

B. THE EUROPEAN DIMENSION

The way in which the challenges associated with information asymmetry and access to evidence held by the opposing party and third parties have been addressed has been strongly affected by European Union law. The gateway to this influence, however, have not been the Union's powers in cross-border litigation, to build a European Area of Justice, but something much more prosaic, the consolidation of the internal market. **10.006**

As is well known, Articles 67 and 81 TFEU confer competence on the European Union in matters of cross-border litigation to ensure the cooperation of national courts in civil and commercial matters. In the development of this competence, the EU has regulated its own cooperation mechanisms for the taking of evidence in civil matters between Member States, first with the 2001 Regulation, replaced in 2020 by the one currently in force.[9] None of these texts, however, have directly addressed the issue of access to sources of evidence held by the other party or third parties. They regulate the way in which a court in one Member State may request the assistance of a court in another Member State in order to obtain existing evidence already in that Member State (e.g. documents) or to have a certain evidentiary activity carried out in that Member State (e.g. to have a witness heard or an expert witness carry out all or part of his operations). Such a request for cooperation may have been triggered by the court of origin as a result of a request received from a (prospective or actual) claimant who has activated the existing mechanisms in the law of the State of origin to gain access to such evidence. But this "prior step" is not regulated in these instruments. To what extent these domestic mechanisms are conditioned by European law depends, in turn, **10.007**

9 Council Regulation (EC) No 1206/2001 of May 28, 2001 on cooperation between the courts of the Member States in the taking of evidence in civil or commercial matters [2001] OJ L 174/1; Regulation (EU) 2020/1783 of the European Parliament and of the Council of November 25, 2020 on cooperation between the courts of the Member States in the taking of evidence in civil or commercial matters (taking of evidence) (recast) [2020] OJ L 405/1.

on whether the dispute concerns a matter whose regulation has been harmonised by the European legislator.

10.008 Article 114 TFEU, as is well known, provides for the approximation of legislation for the construction of the internal market, and is to be read in conjunction with Article 26 establishing the priority objective of the proper functioning of the internal market, a goal which is also referred to in Article 81(2) TFEU. Backing on these provisions, Directives have been adopted to harmonise certain aspects of national procedural law with regard to certain substantive matters, normally associated with the field of consumer and business activity. In these cases, the European rules are not limited to cross-border litigation, but their aim is to force changes in national procedural laws, because harmonisation is necessary for the proper functioning of the internal market and for the correct regulation and defence of substantive rights that are also regulated in a harmonised manner by the European legislator – this is what some call "vertical harmonisation."[10]

10.009 In some of these sectors, the European legislator has included among the "procedural regulatory needs" the provision of mechanisms to compensate for information asymmetry: they require national legislators to provide legal operators with effective instruments to get access to information and sources of evidence that are in the possession of the opponent or of a third party. More specifically, the 2004 IP Directive[11] and the 2014 Directive on competition damages claims[12] opened the door to harmonise this specific area,[13] more recently followed by the 2020 Directive on representative actions[14] and the brand new 2024 Directives on corporate sustainability due diligence[15] and on liability for defective products.[16]

---

10 G Wagner, "Harmonisation of Civil Procedure: Policy Perspectives" in XE Kramer and CH van Rhee (eds), *Civil Litigation in a Globalising World* (Asser Press 2012) 93–119, 101.

11 Directive 2004/48/EC of the European Parliament and of the Council of April 29, 2004 on the enforcement of intellectual property rights [2004] OJ L 157/45.

12 Directive 2014/104/EU of the European Parliament and of the Council of November 26, 2014 on certain rules governing actions for damages under national law for infringements of the competition law provisions of the Member States and of the European Union [2014] OJ L 349/1.

13 On this, see E Vallines García, "Harmonising Access to Information and Evidence: The Directives on Intellectual Property and Competition Damages" in F Gascón Inchausti and B Hess (eds), *The Future of the European Law of Civil Procedure: Coordination or Harmonisation?* (Intersentia 2020) 123 ff.

14 Directive (EU) 2020/1828 of the European Parliament and of the Council of November 25, 2020 on representative actions for the protection of the collective interests of consumers and repealing Directive 2009/22/EC [2020] OJ L 409/1.

15 Directive (EU) 2024/1760 of the European Parliament and of the Council of June 13, 2024 on corporate sustainability due diligence and amending Directive (EU) 2019/1937 and Regulation (EU) 2023/2859 [2024] OJ L 2024/1760 (amended by Directive (EU) 2025/794 as regards the dates from which Member States are to apply certain corporate sustainability reporting and due diligence requirements [2025] OJ L 2025/794, April 16, 2025).

16 Directive (EU) 2024/2853 of the European Parliament and of the Council of October 23, 2024 on liability for defective products and repealing Council Directive 85/374/EEC [2024] OJ L 2853/1, November 18, 2024. It should be

The common core and motivation of these rules is the need for national procedural laws to provide for mechanisms of access to sources of evidence held by the opposing party or a third party. Their progressive adoption has allowed the European legislator to gradually refine the "European standards" on this point. **10.010**

The starting point is to be found in Article 6 of the 2004 IP Directive, inspired by the 1995 TRIPS Agreement,[17] which laid the foundations for a "European way to disclosure" which aims to move away from "US-style discovery" and the evils associated with it (abuses in the form of fishing expeditions, high costs and delays). The standards that can be deduced from this first European regulation are as follows: (i) prior appearance of plausibility of the claim, i.e. the existence of a kind of *fumus boni iuris*, which prevents its use in support of frivolous claims; (ii) the existence of judicial control or filter, as it must be the judge who orders disclosure, after analysing the applicant's request; (iii) the speciality or specificity of the request, which must refer to specific evidence or categories of evidence, susceptible to prior identification, as a way of avoiding the feared fishing expeditions; (iv) proportionality as a criterion for deciding on the request itself and on the scope to be given to the measures, which requires weighing up the legitimate interests of all parties and third parties concerned; and (v) concern for the protection of confidentiality. Article 7 of the Directive, for its part, establishes a clear link between access to evidence and the preservation of the evidence accessed. **10.011**

In 2014, Article 5.5 of the Competition Damages Directive incorporated a "symbolic" novelty, with a sort of "official abandonment" of the *nemo tenetur* principle which, as has already been pointed out, was the premise from which many national jurisdictions approached this issue: "The interest of undertakings to avoid actions for damages following an infringement of competition law shall not constitute an interest that warrants protection." In addition, a new standard was added: (vi) access to evidence instruments must be available not only to the plaintiff but also to the defendant, which means that they can be activated not only prior to litigation but also during the course of litigation. **10.012**

In 2020, Article 18 of the Representative Actions Directive assumes the previous acquis, but makes a relevant clarification: evidence shall be disclosed by order of the court (or, where appropriate, the administrative authority) "in accordance with national procedural law." This provision can be seen as a reminder of the procedural autonomy **10.013**

---

stressed that this Directive is an update of the previous 1985 legislation; at that time, the European legislator did not say anything about disclosure of evidence, but subsequent developments have made the inclusion of a standard on access to sources of evidence unavoidable.

17 Agreement on Trade-Related Aspects of Intellectual Property Rights (adopted April 15, 1994, entered into force January 1, 1995) 1869 UNTS 299 (TRIPS Agreement).

of the Member States and, perhaps, as a concession to each Member State's procedural tradition and culture. However, it should not be interpreted as a kind of "going backwards," i.e. it does not allow those Member States that do not have mechanisms for accessing sources of evidence held by the other party or third parties, or that have ineffective tools, to be released from this obligation, as this would call into question the principle of the effectiveness of Union law.

10.014 This development crystallised twice in 2024. On the one hand, in Article 29(3)(e) of the Directive on corporate sustainability due diligence;[18] on the other hand, in Article 9 of the Directive on liability for defective products.[19] The European legislator

---

18 Article 29(3)(e) of the Corporate Sustainability Due Diligence Directive reads as follows:
(e) when a claim is brought, and a claimant presents a reasoned justification containing reasonably available facts and evidence sufficient to support the plausibility of their claim for damages and has indicated that additional evidence lies in the control of the company, courts are able to order that such evidence be disclosed by the company in accordance with national procedural law; national courts shall limit the disclosure of the evidence sought to that which is necessary and proportionate to support a potential claim or a claim for damages and the preservation of evidence to that which is necessary and proportionate to support such a claim for damages; in determining whether an order for the disclosure or preservation of evidence is proportionate, national courts shall consider the extent to which the claim or defence is supported by available facts and evidence justifying the request to disclose evidence; the scope and cost of disclosure as well as the legitimate interests of all parties, including any third parties concerned, including preventing non-specific searches for information which is unlikely to be of relevance for the parties in the procedure; whether the evidence the disclosure of which is sought contains confidential information, especially concerning any third parties, and what arrangements are in place for protecting such confidential information; Member States shall ensure that national courts have the power to order the disclosure of evidence containing confidential information where they consider it relevant to the action for damages; Member States shall ensure that, when ordering the disclosure of such information, national courts have at their disposal effective measures to protect such information."

19 Article 9 of the Defective Product Liability Directive is expressed in the following terms:
1. Member States shall ensure that, at the request of a person who is claiming compensation in proceedings before a national court for damage caused by a defective product (the 'claimant') and who has presented facts and evidence sufficient to support the plausibility of the claim for compensation, the defendant is required to disclose relevant evidence that is at the defendant's disposal, subject to the conditions set out in this Article.
2. Member States shall ensure that, at the request of a defendant that has presented facts and evidence sufficient to demonstrate the defendant's need for evidence for the purposes of countering a claim for compensation, the claimant is required, in accordance with national law, to disclose relevant evidence that is at the claimant's disposal.
3. Member States shall ensure that the disclosure of evidence pursuant to paragraphs 1 and 2, and in accordance with national law, is limited to what is necessary and proportionate.
4. Member States shall ensure that, when determining whether the disclosure of evidence requested by a party is necessary and proportionate, national courts consider the legitimate interests of all parties concerned, including third parties, in particular in relation to the protection of confidential information and trade secrets.
5. Member States shall ensure that, where a defendant is required to disclose information that is a trade secret or an alleged trade secret, national courts are empowered, upon a duly reasoned request of a party or on their own initiative, to take the specific measures necessary to preserve the confidentiality of that information when it is used or referred to in the course of or after the legal proceedings.
6. Member States shall ensure that, where a party is required to disclose evidence, national courts are empowered, upon a duly reasoned request of the opposing party or where the national court concerned deems it appropriate and in accordance with national law, to require such evidence to be presented in an easily accessible and easily understandable manner, if such presentation is deemed proportionate by the national court in terms of costs and effort for the required party.
7. This Article does not affect national rules relating to the pre-trial disclosure of evidence, where such rules exist.

does not introduce new standards in these Articles in terms of the content of access to evidence, but a different "form" of expression can be detected in them, as they are particularly careful in their wording to convey the message that balance, prudence and proportionality must be the basis on which these rules must operate in civil liability proceedings for infringement of the requirements imposed on companies by both Directives. In short, the European legislator wants to make clear that this is a delicate instrument which must be handled with great care by legal operators and administered with prudence by judges.

The impact of the European regulations on national legal systems has been evident, **10.015**
especially on those that had a previous reluctant attitude to require access to evidence. The Directives show that the European legislator, at least in certain sectors of legal traffic, considers that the right to evidence must prevail – always in a proportionate manner – over other interests, as a way of guaranteeing the principle of effectiveness of EU law. For the protection of rights and interests to be real, the mechanisms of judicial protection must be effective (Article 47 CFREU); and, without evidence, judicial protection is not possible. This message is generally valid, although the European legislator has, for the time being, only sent it with regard to certain matters.

The transposition of the 2004 and 2014 Directives has been the basis for significant **10.016**
regulatory changes in most Member States, and this is evident in all Chapters.[20] In the vast majority of cases, however, the changes have been sectoral, i.e. they have not been used to introduce general rules – noteworthy is the situation described with respect to Spain,[21] where an attempt was made to use the transposition of the 2014 Directive to make a general regulation of access to sources of evidence, but it was finally reduced to the field of antitrust damages. However, it is worth trusting in the expansive force that European law tends to have in the long term: legal operators who see the advantages of a reasonable regulation of access to sources of evidence in intellectual and industrial property, competition damages claims, representative/collective actions, corporate sustainability due diligence or – even more clearly – defective product liability will tend to demand them for other areas of litigation as well. The European legislator himself, in fact, seems to be caught up in this same spiral: the 2024 Directives show that the harmonisation of national procedural laws on disclosure of evidence has become increasingly commonplace.

20 See for Germany, nn 1.018–1.039; for Austria, nn 1.051–1.052; for France, nn 3.045–3.054; for Italy, nn 4.017–4.019; for Spain, nn 5.086–5.096; for The Netherlands, nn 6.058–6.095; and for Denmark, Norway and Sweden, nn 7.079–7.085.

21 See nn 5.087–5.088.

10.017 The existence of European standards in this area and their transfer to the level of national legislation through the transposition of the Directives also makes it possible to predict a general harmonisation of this part of the national procedural systems in the future: it is to be expected that a general regulation of access to evidence, where it only exists in a sectoral way, will be made taking as a starting point this sectoral regulation, which is already harmonised and which, moreover, is "well"-harmonised, in the sense that the European standards are clear, without variations or divergences from one Directive to another. This hypothetical harmonisation must be seen as something very positive for the reinforcement of legal certainty and effective judicial protection. This is suggested, in fact, by the regulation proposed for this sector by the ERCP Rules 100 to 110, which establish a general mechanism for access to information and evidence held by the opposing party and third parties that is fully consistent with the standards deriving from the European Directives and which is designed to be applied in any area of litigation.[22]

10.018 The European dimension of the regulation of access to sources of evidence offers the system an additional potential: it opens a space for action by the Court of Justice, which is called upon to interpret the Directives that are at the origin of national rules and whose decisions also have a strong harmonising impact on the interpretation of national rules. We already have, in fact, two important examples in relation to measures of access to sources of evidence in competition damages claims:

10.019 In the *PACCAR* case,[23] the court gave an expansive interpretation of what is to be understood by disclosure related to the 2014 Directive: it also includes "those documents which the party to whom the request to disclose evidence is addressed must create *ex novo* by compiling or classifying information, knowledge or data in its possession." In addition, the court underlined that the duty of disclosure is limited by requirements of relevance, proportionality and necessity which the national courts must apply when "taking into account the legitimate interest and fundamental rights" of the disclosing party. A generalisation of this solution could have very significant consequences, especially in terms of the cost of implementing the measures.

22 On this see F Gascón Inchausti and M Stürner, "Access to Information and Evidence in the ELI/UNIDROIT European Rules on Civil Procedure: Some Fundamental Aspects" (2019) 24 (1) *Uniform Law Review* 14–41; M Stürner, "The ELI/UNIDROIT European Rules of Civil Procedure: Access to Information and Evidence" in F Gascón Inchausti and B Hess (eds), *The Future of the European Law of Civil Procedure: Coordination or Harmonisation?* (Intersentia 2020), 205 ff; A Stadler and M Strandberg, in A Stadler, V Smith and F Gascón Inchausti (eds), *ERCP Commentary* (Beck 2022) para 12.066 ff; F Gascón Inchausti, "The Approach of the Model European Rules to Access to Information and Evidence" (2024) 29 (4) *Uniform Law Review* 33.

23 Case C-163/21 ECLI:EU:C:2022:863, Judgment of November 10, 2022.

And in the *Tráficos Manuel Ferrer* case,[24] for its part, the CJEU highlights the significance that the existence of measures of access to sources of evidence has for the procedural system as a whole. Specifically, in respect of antitrust damages claims, the court emphasises two things: (i) that the tools of access to sources of evidence serve to correct the balance of power between the parties to the dispute (§§ 45 and 46); and (ii) its influence on the judicial power to estimate the damage. In § 56 the judgment highlights "the need to undertake a judicial estimation of the harm may depend, in particular, on the result obtained by the claimant following a request for the disclosure of evidence" and (§ 57) "to determine whether the claimant has made use of it. If the practical impossibility of assessing the harm is the result of inaction on the part of the claimant, it is not for the national court to take the place of the latter or to remedy its shortcomings." **10.020**

The existence of such measures therefore affects many other dimensions of civil litigation and burden-sharing among parties. The ERCP, for example, include them in the discussion about the possibility of using illegally obtained evidence: any use will be more justified where there is no legitimate way of accessing decisive evidence held by the other party or a third party.[25] **10.021**

Potentially, the CJEU may establish duties of disclosure directly on the principle of effectiveness, which has been addressed within EU anti-discrimination law. Rules on reversed burden of proof have been established in order to make the anti-discrimination law more effective. When a person claiming to be a victim of discrimination has provided evidence that prima facie suggests that he or she may have been discriminated, it is for the opposing party to prove that it is still a case of non-discrimination.[26] The shift of the burden of proof may be regarded as a means to reduce the asymmetrical access to evidence which is characteristic of these cases. Following up on that line of reasoning, the CJEU has been asked whether the Directives on anti-discrimination law, read in conjunction with the principle of effectiveness, entitle alleged victims of discrimination a right of access to relevant information controlled by the opposing party. While the CJEU acknowledged the victim's need for having such access in **10.022**

24 Case C-312/21 ECLI:EU:C:2023:99, Judgment of February 16, 2023.

25 See ERCP Rule 90, cmt 3: "Exceptions to the general rule, under Rule 90(2), should be rare. They should only be permitted by the court carrying out a careful balancing exercise, which considers all relevant interests, including the right of access to evidence, fundamental rights' protection, especially, those connected to privacy, good faith and fair play."

26 Council Directive 2000/43/EC of June 29, 2000 implementing the principle of equal treatment between persons irrespective of racial or ethnical origin [2000] OJ L 180/22, Article 8; Council Directive 2000/78/EC of November 27, 2000 establishing a general framework for equal treatment in employment and occupation [2000] OJ L 303/16, Article 10(1); Directive 2006/54/EC of the European Parliament and of the Council of July 5, 2006 on the implementation of the principle of equal opportunities and equal treatment of men and women in matters of employment and occupation [2006] OJ L 204/23, Article 19(1).

order to provide prima facie evidence, the court still concluded that the Directives do not entail obligations to disclose evidence.[27] On the other hand, the court stressed that the national courts must ensure that the procedural rules are within the requirements established by the principle of effectiveness in particular by taking a refusal to disclose evidence into account when assessing whether sufficient evidence has been presented.[28]

10.023 In the referred cases, the CJEU has been reluctant to establish obligations to disclose evidence directly on the principle of effectiveness in the area of anti-discrimination. This approach, however, may change as a result of the recent developments mentioned above. A new momentum to expand the potential of the principle of effectiveness may be the result of the requirements of disclosure set up in the newest Directives on corporate sustainability and product liability, and the general rules suggested by the European Model Rules. It remains to be seen whether the CJEU will develop minimum requirements for access to evidence directly based on the principle of effectiveness, but such a development would be in line with current trends of civil procedural law.

C. GRANTING ACCESS TO INFORMATION AND EVIDENCE – GENERAL PRINCIPLES AND REQUIREMENTS

1. The starting point

10.024 In principle, all procedural systems assume that a civil judgment should be based on the true facts of the case and, at the same time, leave it to the parties to establish the facts. As a consequence, a "duty of truth" of the parties to the litigation is explicitly mentioned in some codes of procedure.[29] In the end, however, it is a duty or truthfulness more than a duty of truth. The parties must be allowed to submit mere assumptions where they have no certain knowledge. Ultimately, the obligation to present facts truthfully can only be used to prevent parties from knowingly lie.[30] Moreover, no one seriously disputes that in adversarial civil proceedings without an *ex officio*

---

27 Case C-104/10 *Kelly* ECLI:EU:C:2011:506, paras 33–34; and Case C-415/10 *Meister* ECLI:EU:C:2012:217, paras 37–40.

28 Case C-415/10 *Meister*, para 42.

29 Austria, Code of Civil Procedure (Zivilprozessordnung, ZPO) s 178; Germany, Code of Civil Procedure (Zivilprozessordnung, ZPO) s 138; Netherlands, Code of Civil Procedure (Wetboek van Burgerlijke Rechtsvordering) Article 21; for details see Chapter 6, nn 7 et seq; Norway, Code of Civil Procedure (Lov om mekling og rettergang i sivile tvister, tvisteloven) s 21–4; for Italy see A Piekenbrock, *Der italienische Zivilprozeß im europäischen Umfeld* (Duncker & Humblot 1998) 227. The ERCP do not mention a duty of truth explicitly, but a duty to act in good faith (r 3 (e)).

30 Krans and Zondag, nn 6.007–6.013. The same conclusion is drawn in German civil procedure law: Bundesgerichtshof, Judgement of September 19, 1985 – IX ZR 138/84, NJW 1986, 246 (247); also published in BeckRS 1985, 31071259;

investigation, there is a direct link between establishing the truth as the basis for the court's judgment and the parties' access to evidence. Nevertheless, the best possible fact-finding must always be balanced against the protection of the legitimate interests of parties and third parties, the principles of fairness and reasonable limits to cooperation. The idea of the proportionality of measures granting access to information and evidence is also becoming increasingly accepted across Europe. However, the analysis of the legal systems examined here shows that, despite certain convergences, the rules on the parties' access to relevant evidence still vary greatly.

2. Constitutional law and substantive law as legal basis for access to information and evidence

In quite a few jurisdictions, the right to evidence is enshrined in the constitution.[31] The European Court of Human Rights (ECtHR) is also inclined to consider the right to evidence as part of the right to be heard as guaranteed by Article 6 ECHR.[32] However, this does not mean unfettered access to any evidence not already in the possession of a party.[33] As a matter of fact, jurisdictions having a right to evidence contained in their constitution tend to have less extensive rights to access evidence in practice. **10.025**

Many jurisdictions provide access to information and evidence by rules in substantive law. These rules can be grounded in public or private law. Particularly, freedom of information acts give broad access to information in the hands of administrative bodies and public regulators.[34] In many cases, this helps in the preparation of civil proceedings, just as it can be helpful in some cases to inspect files of the public prosecutor in criminal investigations that run parallel to or before civil proceedings, e.g. traffic accidents or capital market disputes. In principle, the criminal prosecution authorities have more extensive possibilities of obtaining evidence than parties in civil proceedings. They can **10.026**

J Braun, "Wahrheitspflicht im Zivilprozess" (2021) 76 *JuristenZeitung* 53, 58; L Rosenberg, K Schwab and P Gottwald, *Zivilprozessrecht* (18th edn, CH Beck 2018) § 65 n 66.

31 For example, in Italy Article 111(1) of the constitution grants a right to evidence as part of the due process principle; in Germany the constitutional right to be heard (Article 103 of the German Constitution) includes the right to present evidence to the court and the court's obligation to take it into account. In Switzerland a right to present evidence is part of the CPC Article 152. The ERCP Rule 11 also includes a comprehensive right to be heard that covers the right to present evidence.

32 *Mantovanelli v France* App no 21497/93 (ECtHR, March 18, 1997); *Dombo Beheer BV v Netherlands* App no 14448/88 (ECtHR, October 27, 1993); *LL v. France* App no 7508/02 (ECtHR, October 10, 2006); see also nn 3.031 et seq for French case law since 2012.

33 In France, there is a debate on whether the right to evidence as accepted by the Cour de cassation may require the judge to take investigative measures. There seems to be tendency in recent case law to interpret Article 145 of the French Code of Civil Procedure (Code de procedure civile) as giving a party a right that the judge requests the production of relevant documents, n 3.041.

34 For example in Scandinavia, see Strandberg n 7.008.

easily confiscate documents and other evidence that may also be important for civil litigation against the defendant. Nevertheless, the rules on access to criminal files vary from country to country. For example, German criminal procedural law only grants a right of access to the file after the investigation has been completed.[35] This may come too late for use in civil proceedings or for their preparation if the civil claims are about to become time-barred and an action has to be brought.

10.027 Some procedural codes, like the German and Austrian, combine procedural rules with those from substantive law and grant a right to the presentation of documents and inspection of objects in civil proceedings particularly if the party seeking evidence has a substantive claim for the production of documents and things against the opponent or a third party.[36] Claims for information and disclosure under substantive law, however, are a broad field. Therefore, the focus of this analysis is on procedural rules.

3. Strict or limited obligations of the parties to the proceedings to grant access to evidence?

10.028 It is hardly surprising that the procedural codes of some European jurisdictions are generous when it comes to access to evidence in the hands of the opposing party or third parties while other codes take a far more restrictive approach. As was explained in the introduction, this is part of a long-lasting legal and cultural tradition,[37] and procedural rules rarely change overnight. While a cautious tendency to facilitate access to evidence before and during litigation is emerging, most jurisdictions are even today dominated by the attitudes and starting points formed by their historical traditions. In many jurisdictions, the broad and expensive US pre-trial discovery is apparently "the elephant in the room" when it comes to reform efforts and a fear of fishing expeditions has a deterrent effect also to suggested reforms that are much more modest than the US system. Access to evidence is, generally speaking, easier where an overarching principle of cooperation for the parties, as suggested by Article 2 and 3 of the ERCP, applied in civil proceedings. This is, however, the case only in a small albeit growing number of jurisdictions. In France, the principle of cooperation came into force with the 1976 reform of civil procedure rules accompanied by greater case management powers for the court.[38] In some jurisdictions, it is only a general postulate of fairness that does not immediately lead to a claim to gain access to evidence in the hands of the opponent.[39] Other jurisdictions, like Germany or Spain, are not ready for a paradigm

35 German Code of Criminal Procedure (Strafprozessordnung, StPO) s 406e(2).

36 For Austria, nn 1.046–1.047; Germany, nn 1.012–1.013; Sweden, Code of Judicial Procedure (Rättegångsbalken) Chapter 38.

37 See above n I.002.

38 France, nn 3.017–3.018.

39 For Italy, n 4.005 referring to Article 88 of the Italian Code of Civil Procedure (Codice di procedura civile).

shift towards a general rule on cooperation of (prospective) parties to a civil litigation, whereas the new Swiss Code of Civil Procedure (2011) has established rules on cooperation at least for the taking of evidence.

Assuming that a party can sufficiently substantiate the facts to be proven and the desired evidence (for details on this cf. C.6., C.7.), in principle two systems can be distinguished with regard to the opponent's obligation to cooperate. The procedural systems in Germany and Italy are traditionally restrained and adhere to the principle that a party does not have to present material that is likely to adversely affect their own case and only supports the opponent's case.[40] There is no general procedural obligation of a party to disclose or present evidence in his or her possession. The English and Welsh CPR, by contrast, explicitly include to the scope of standard disclosure documents which adversely affect a party's own case, adversely affect another party's case or support another party's case.[41] Some other countries today also have a general obligation to provide evidence, in particular relevant documents and other sorts of tangible evidence, in the interest of establishing the truth.[42] This is also the starting point of the ERCP in Rule 25, which was based on a comparative law analysis and a best-practice approach. **10.029**

Where there is a general obligation of the parties to cooperate, an important balancing mechanism lies in the application of the principle of proportionality. Based on English law, it has been adopted in the ERCP.[43] However, it is also applied in the Nordic countries to avoid burdensome and costly production of evidence.[44] As a general approach the expenses incurred by disclosure must be reasonably proportionate to the dispute or the potential value of the evidence.[45] **10.030**

---

40 For Italy, n 4.003 (an exception to this rule are formal examinations of a party on the opponent's request, the purpose of which is to induce the party to acknowledge the truth of facts that are favourable for the opponent); Germany, nn 1.010–1.013: under German procedural rules documents and other things for inspection must be produced only if the requesting party is entitled to under substantive law or if the opponent himself has relied on these documents or objects as means of evidence.

41 Civil Procedure Rules 1998, r 31.6(b)(i)–(iii); See also the Norwegian CPC ss 5–3 (pre-commencement) and 21–4 (post-commencement) obliging any party to inform any opposing party on any important evidence that the opposing party is probably not aware of "irrespectively of whether such evidence favours the case of the party or that of the opposite party." Along the same lines ERCP r 25(2): "It is not a basis of objection to such disclosure by a party that disclosure may favour the opponent or other parties."

42 French CPC Article 10 (documents); in Austria, such an obligation is not explicitly stated in the CPC, but based on case law, nn 1.048–1.050; for Switzerland nn 1.056–1.060 (art 160 of the Swiss CPC (Zivilprozessordnung, ZPO)); Norwegian CPC, ss 21–4 and 21–5.

43 See e.g. ERCP r 5 as an overarching principle, rr 7, 28, 104 (proportionality of sanctions) and 8 (proportionality of costs).

44 See nn 7.033–7.038.

45 Norwegian CPC s 26–5(3). In Sweden the proportionality test has been developed by the Supreme Court, but disclosure is considered to be disproportionate only in extraordinary situations.

10.031 In England and Wales, the 1999 reform introduced case tracks and court-controlled case management. These new principles, together with the principle of proportionality, were intended to put an end to excessive documentary disclosure with high costs and delay but was not overall successful.[46] Upon a court order for compulsory disclosure the recipient must first provide a list with documents that come within the scope of the order, confirm their existence and identity, and evidentiary privileges if applicable. Only in a second step, the applicant has a right to inspect the documents.[47] No other procedural system provides for such a gradation of the scope of the document submission according to the applicable procedural track (fast track, intermediate and multitrack) which are in general related to the amount in dispute[48] as in England and Wales.[49]

4. Proactive information on evidence

10.032 At first glance self-initiated disclosure of evidence seems to be a key element when it comes to promoting procedural fairness, transparency and the search for truth as the basis of the court's decision. Such an obligation may, however, be considered to be in conflict with the principle of party autonomy and the idea of adversarial proceedings that is fundamentally based on each party pursuing their own interests. In any case, the adversarial element alone does not lead to a fair result if it is not simultaneously ensured that each party must provide material relevant to the proceedings. Today, most procedural systems achieve a balancing of interests by requiring disclosure only when requested by a party, very often, only upon the issuance of a court order. English law tends to rely on voluntary and self-initiated disclosure of all relevant information at least in the pre-action stage of proceedings.

10.033 But here, too, the rules are currently changing to some extent. Norway, Denmark[50] and Spain have implemented rules similar to those applicable in England and Wales. As in England, in the Nordic countries the first step of disclosure is limited to revealing the existence of evidence. It does not include the party's presentation of the evidence nor the opposing party's access to the evidence. The English and Welsh CPR even define "disclosure" as the mere statement that a document exists or has existed.[51] A recent reform in the Netherlands goes one step further. Article 195 CPC as of 2025 provides a right to inspection of documents for the parties without court

46 See nn 2.024–2.025.

47 See n 2.026.

48 Claims allocated to the fast track are between the value of £ 10.000 and £ 25.000.

49 In fast track cases, the parties are required to try to agree on the scope of disclosure; in intermediate and multi-track cases standard disclosure according to CPR r. 31.6 applies; see nn 2.026–2.027.

50 See nn 7.010–7.014, s 5-3 Norwegian CPC. In Denmark, court practice tends to establish a similar duty.

51 CPR r 31.2. From disclosure follows a right to inspection that is subject to the exceptions listed in CPR r. 31.3.

intervention.[52] This can be a role model at least for non-complex cases in which the parties may assess for themselves when they are entitled to certain information and when they must comply with the opponent's request.

In Spain, pre-existing evidence, like documents, audio and video records, reports prepared by party-appointed experts,[53] electronically stored information, etc. must be introduced and presented by both parties with their written statements.[54] "Personal evidence" such as witness statements, the examination of the parties or reports by court-appointed experts will appear typically at later stages of the proceedings and need not be mentioned in the written statements of claim and defence.[55] 10.034

5. *Ex officio* evidence-gathering

Civil proceedings are generally adversarial in nature and the parties are primarily responsible for presenting facts and evidence.[56] In all the jurisdictions examined, the starting point is that the parties are responsible not only for stating facts, but also for providing the necessary evidence to support them in order to comply with their burden of proof. Civil courts are traditionally not supposed to play a central role in obtaining evidence. In this respect, civil proceedings differ from criminal and administrative proceedings, in which the principle of *ex officio* investigation normally applies. 10.035

However, the role of judges has changed considerably, particularly in England where it has become more like the continental model. The simply facilitative role of the judge was particularly important in England and Wales until the Woolf reforms of 1999. The idea of a managing judge, widespread on the Continent, had been rejected there for a long time. "The court had no power to either require evidence to be adduced nor did it have any power to control the nature and amount of evidence adduced."[57] The English Civil Procedure Rules 1999 stick to the principle of party autonomy, but it is now subject to court control over evidence. Courts must ensure that the gathering and presentation of documents is consistent with the overarching commitment to procedural proportionality. 10.036

---

52 Netherlands, n 6.050.

53 For exceptions see Spain, Code of Civil Procedure (Ley de Enjuiciamiento Civil, LEC), Article 337.

54 Spain, nn 5.022–5.023; Article 265 Spanish CPC.

55 Spain, nn 5.028–5.030.

56 The *iura novit curia* principle applies to a different extent in the jurisdictions analysed here. While in the German system there are practically no exceptions to the principle, in France and Spain it is the responsibility of the parties to also present the legal basis, and the court may not change this *ex officio*, Spain, n 5.005; France, nn 3.018 et seq – the *da mihi factum, dabo tibi ius* – principle comes with various modifications in French law.

57 See n 2.001.

10.037 Our analysis looked primarily at the parties' ability to obtain information and evidence. In most jurisdictions,[58] however, the court may – in addition to party activities – take evidence *ex officio* in principle.[59] The court's power may be limited to certain types of evidence.[60] Very often the court has a discretionary power to at least demand explanations from the parties and also ask for the disclosure of documents or things for inspection.[61] Particularly, in legal systems where the parties themselves have very limited access to information and evidence, they are dependent on the courts to the extent that the judges have further possibilities to make use of them.[62] This is the case in Italy and Germany, but apparently judges there are traditionally not inclined to use that power. It seems that courts in the Netherlands are more ready to use this power.[63] Moreover, in Austria, the court's *ex officio* powers to ask questions and to take evidence (although not much used in practice) were the basis for developing a general obligation of the parties to give access to evidence.[64] Interestingly, the tendency in some States to set up special panels or chambers for international disputes can also be accompanied by granting more judicial power with regard to *ex officio* evidence in order to increase the attractiveness of these panels.[65]

6. The necessity to obtain a court order and requirements of direct relevancy and substantiated fact pleading

10.038 In many jurisdictions, an obligation to give access to or to present evidence still arises only from a court order,[66] which in some jurisdictions is even subject to appeal.[67] This reflects the fundamental difference between the US pre-trial discovery and the continental European system. Another general difference between common law systems and continental jurisdictions is that most of the latter assume that a fact to be proven

---

58 In Switzerland, however, *ex officio* taking of evidence is only allowed if the court has considerable doubts that allegations of a party which were not disputed by the opponent are not true, Swiss CPC, Article 153(2). The rule prevents parties from unanimously telling the untruth and the court from having to base its judgment on this.

59 France, nn 3.018–3.019, 3.025 (French CPC Articles 11 and 146); Germany, n 1.014 (German CPC ss 142–144); Italy, nn 4.006–4.008 (Italian CPC Article 118). In Spain, the court has no power to order the taking of evidence which the parties have not proposed, n 5.006.

60 In Austria, courts can take evidence *ex officio* (Austrian CPC s 183) with the exception of witness testimony and inspection of documents if the parties object, see G Kodek and P Mayr, *Zivilprozessrecht* (6th edn, facultas 2024) n 796. In Germany, the court can take all evidence *ex officio*, except for witnesses that the parties have not relied on, German CPC s 273.

61 French CPC Article 145; German CPC ss 142–144; Dutch CPC Article 22; Netherlands, n 6.018.

62 Germany, nn 1.015–1.016; Italy, n 4.003; for the situation in France see nn 3.018 et seq, 3.025 et seq.

63 Netherlands, nn 6.018–6.020 with reference to the Dutch CPC Article 22.

64 Austria, nn 1.048–1.050.

65 France, nn 3.062 et seq. on the power of the International Chamber of the Paris Commercial Court, International Chamber of the Paris Court of Appeal to order expert opinions and technical experts to be heard.

66 French CPC Article 10, n 3.025; German CPC ss 273, 358, 421 and 428 (documents), 371 (inspection of objects or real property), 450 (formal hearing of a party); Swiss CPC Article 154.

67 Norway, Sweden and Denmark, see n 7.015.

must be directly relevant for the decision of the pending dispute.[68] A court order will be issued only if the requesting party describes in reasonable detail the contested fact which the evidence is relevant for. Relevancy is closely related to the substantive legal basis of a claim or the legal basis of a defence. It is therefore not surprising that legal systems based primarily on case law, not statutory law, apply a less stringent standard of relevancy.

The also often-used rule against US-style fishing expeditions in Europe prohibits a party from seeking access to information or evidence that is not directly relevant for a contested fact and makes an application only in the hope that it might lead to the discovery of further "real" evidence.[69] **10.039**

As a general rule in many jurisdictions, each party must present the facts underlaying her case in reasonable detail.[70] Conversely, the opponent must challenge specific factual allegations made by the other side in a substantiated manner, otherwise these allegations are deemed undisputed, and the judgment can be based on them. If a party is unable to sufficiently substantiate the facts to be proven, procedural rules may reduce the substantiation requirements.[71] This is a concession to grant access to court in cases where the relevant facts took place entirely in one party's sphere (e.g. the behaviour that triggers product liability or the internal knowledge in a company which is crucial in capital market disputes). Another approach to alleviate a claimant's burden to establish his or her case is to reverse the burden of proof for facts to which the party has no access but for which it bears that burden according to general principles. Typical cases for an at least partial reversal of the claimant's burden of proof are anti-discrimination cases,[72] product liability[73] or medical malpractice[74] cases, and there is sometimes a **10.040**

---

68 Austria: HW Fasching, *Lehrbuch des österreichischen Zivilprozessrechts* (2nd edn, Manz 1990) n 837; E-M Bajons, *Zivilverfahren – Grundlehren des Prozesses und der Exekution* (Orac 1991) n 139; Germany, n 1.003; Spain, n 5.063 (documents requested must relate to the subject matter of the proceedings). In Switzerland, Article 150 CPC explicitly states that proof is required (only) for facts that are legally relevant and disputed.

69 Fishing expeditions are not accepted for example in Austria, see n 1.069; Germany, n 1.004; Norway, n 7.026; and in Switzerland, see F Hasenböhler and S Yañez, *Kommentar zur Schweizerischen Zivilprozessordnung* (4th edn, Helbing Lichtenhahn 2025) Article 152 n 28.

70 Austria, see Kodek and Mayr, *Zivilprozessrecht*, n 795; France, see Article 6 of the French CPC; Germany, nn 1.005–1.008. For Switzerland see Hasenböhler and Yañez, *Kommentar zur Schweizerischen Zivilprozessordnung*, Article 152, n 28. This is also the solution of the ERCP r 53.

71 Austria, n 1.044; Germany, nn 1.006–1.007. The ERCP also allow the claimant to amend the statement of claim when more details have come up in the course of the taking of evidence, r 53(3).

72 See the EU Directives mentioned in section B above.

73 In product liability cases that are not subject to the EU Directive 85/374 but dealt with under national law, German courts have established the following rule: The claimant must prove that the product was defect at the time of marketing, any injury and the causality. The manufacturer, however, must prove that there was no breach of duty or fault, for details see Bundesgerichtshof (BGH), NJW 1969, 269; 1988, 2611; 1999, 1029.

74 Netherlands, nn 6.024–6.025; in Germany a partial reversal of the burden of proof had been established case law for many years when the legislator in 2013 provided an explicit rule on the burden of proof in medical malpractice cases,

tendency to extend the idea of a reversal of the burden of proof to other forms of professional liability.[75] However, the broad field of the distribution of the burden of proof is not the focus of this study.

7. Substantiation of the evidence sought (particularly for documents)

10.041 The substantiation of the facts to be proven is to be strictly distinguished from the description of the evidence sought. Due to the great practical importance of documentary evidence, especially in a modern digitalised society,[76] this is to be addressed primarily here. Parties bearing the burden of proof are often in a difficult situation with regard to documents because they can only assume in general terms that certain types of documents must be in the possession of the opposing party, without knowing any details. Three major systems can be distinguished here.

1) An especially generous approach, which we find not only in US pre-trial discovery rules, but also in the UK, requires the parties to disclose all relevant documents. Identification by the party adducing the evidence is not required.[77]
2) At the other end of the scale are particularly strict systems, which are becoming increasingly rare today. The German Code of Civil Procedure and the way it is handled by courts requires, in principle, that documents must be described in great detail, according to content, date of creation, etc. so that they can be easily searched for and identified by the opponent. The submission of entire categories of documents (e.g. "all design documents for product X in period Y") is not permitted.[78] In this regard, German courts also refuse to grant relief when it comes to documents from the opponent's sphere.[79] In France, in regular civil proceedings rather strict rules on the specification of the requested documents apply in order to avoid fishing expeditions US-style. However, Rule 5.1.2 CCIP-CA Protocol of the new French International Commercial Courts of Paris allows parties to seek the production of documents or "precisely identified categories of documents."[80] They thus fall under the next category.
3) A mediating position is adopted by the legal systems in which the documents to be submitted must be designated, but a description by category is sufficient. This is the direction in which case law has developed throughout Scandinavia.[81] France has also adopted a solution that rejects the radical approach of US law but provides some liberalisation.

see German Civil Code s 630h.

75 See nn 6.026–6.033 for the Netherlands; in Germany, the Federal High Court applies a reversal of the burden of proof to some extent if the defendant has grossly neglected or violated a special professional or organisational duty to protect others from danger to life and limb, see BGH, NJW 2018, 301.

76 In French civil proceedings, documents are of utmost importance. Due to Article 1359 Code Civil evidence in contract cases in which the amount in dispute exceeds € 1.500 must be presented in writing. Even witness statements are often presented only in writing, nn 3.006, 3.023.

77 See nn 2.026–2.027.

78 Germany, nn 1.010–1.011.

79 BGH, NJW 2007, 2989 n 16; NJW-RR 2007, 1393 n 10.

80 France, nn 3.063–3.066.

81 See nn 7.028–7.032.

Beyond the legal relevance, the only factor that is considered, and rightly so, is whether the description of a document is sufficient to make clear to which item of evidence the application relates.[82]

Is the gate thus opening too wide? From US pre-trial discovery, we are familiar with the "nuisance value" of broad requests for the production of documents that demand a lot of manpower from the opponent. On the other hand, possible and legal strategy in US lawsuits is to "flood" the requesting party with documents and thus hide relevant material in the mass. Andrews also pointed out that under English law, excessive requests for documents only serve the economic interests of the lawyers on both sides and prolong the process.[83] With moderate substantiation requirements, many European legal systems take a sensible middle course. In any case, the concept of "nuisance value" has lost significance in both directions, since most documents today can be easily found and transmitted electronically but can also be relatively easily searched for litigation-relevant information using search programmes. **10.042**

The restrictive regime of party cooperation has been intensely criticised, especially in Germany. Therefore, parties sometimes resort to arbitration. In international cases, where evidence is located in the United States, there are other options as well. The stricter the substantiation requirements, the greater the practical recourse to the help of US courts under § 1782 US Code if relevant documents are, for example, in the possession of US subsidiaries of the defendant.[84] It is not surprising that many of these requests are made by German litigants. **10.043**

D. THE TEMPORAL DIMENSION

1. The importance of early information

In procedural systems that essentially follow the loser-pays principle, it is particularly important for the plaintiff to be able to assess his or her chances of success before filing the lawsuit. The need for early access to evidence may also depend on how concretely facts that may be unknown in detail to the plaintiff must already be stated in the statement of claim. Pre-action information would be particularly important in procedural systems such as the Spanish one, which requires the parties to present a full statement of facts and pre-existing evidence in their (first and only) written pleadings **10.044**

---

82 France, n 3.022; Norwegian CPC, s 26–6(1); court practice in Sweden and Denmark is similar, see nn 7.028–7.031.

83 Neil Andrews, *English Civil Procedure* (OUP 2003) 597; on the other hand, evidence-gathering can also help to reduce litigation costs by narrowing the issues in dispute. In the ideal case, one of the parties will make concessions or a settlement will be reached, see nn 2.004–2.006.

84 For § 1782 proceedings see Chapter 8.

– without the possibility of later additions and with strict preclusion.[85] Surprisingly, however, the Spanish legislator has not drawn the conclusion from this that pre-litigation cooperation between the parties is necessary. There is no general mechanism to get access to information and evidence. There are, however, some measures that can help the claimant to prepare his case by applying for a court order: preliminary measures to gather a strictly regulated type of information, particularly on the identity of the defendant, respectively the appropriate person to be sued in specific situations, and basic facts of the claim.[86] This may include the production of documents or things. Another instrument that looks good at first sight – requests to parties and third parties to produce documents that relate to the subject matter of the litigation[87] – requires a clear description of those documents or even the production of a copy by the requesting party. Moreover, requests cannot be made prior to the commencement of the proceedings.

10.045 Even in countries which do not apply a strict rule of early presentation of evidence, it is important to be able to assess the evidence if the plaintiff does not already have all the pieces of evidence at his disposal. Ideally, a future claimant would therefore have access to information and evidence in the hands of the defendant even before the action is brought. However, this is not a general procedural standard.

2. Pre-action access to information and evidence

10.046 In the majority of jurisdictions included in this book the rule prevails that requests for access to evidence can only be made after legal action has been taken.[88] English law probably goes the furthest with access to information before a claim has been filed by its pre-action protocols. Pre-action protocol (PAP) disclosure, introduced in 1999, applies to various types of cause of action.[89] PAPs are guidelines for the prospective parties on how to exchange important information prior to an action. Their main purpose is to clearly define the issues in dispute in order to allow better case management. Although compliance is not mandatory, non-compliance may result in adverse procedural consequences or cost orders.[90] Even where there is no relevant pre-action protocol, the parties are expected to exchange correspondence and information.[91] Besides

85 Spain, n 5.010, Article 400 of the Spanish CPC, for an exception see Article 286.

86 Arts 256–263 of the Spanish CPC, nn 5.038 et seq.

87 Arts 328–332 of the Spanish CPC, nn 5.062 et seq.

88 Austria (taking of evidence is restricted to the oral hearing, see Austrian CPC ss 258–259); French CPC Article 10; for Germany, nn 1.001–1.003; for Norway, see nn 7.058–7.059; in Switzerland despite a rather broad rule on pre-action access to evidence in Article 158 of the Swiss CPC, the Federal Court applies very strict requirements, see nn 1.065–1.066.

89 Practice Directions – Pre-Action Conduct and Protocols [2023] para 18: protocols in force (14 all together).

90 See n 2.012.

91 Practice Directions – Pre-Action Conduct and Protocols (2023) para 6, referring to para 3.

pre-action protocol disclosure, a claimant may also apply for a mandatory pre-action disclosure court order in respect of any type of private law or public dispute before proceedings have started.[92] Such orders are deemed to promote access to justice as they enable potential claimants to see if they have a cause of action against the potential defendant.[93] The court may order disclosure of documents if it is likely that both the applicant and the respondent are likely to be parties to subsequent proceedings. It is within the court's discretion to deny orders if there is misuse or an attempt of mere fishing expeditions. English courts have held that applications cannot be successful unless there is a real prospect of success for the applicant's claim, which the applicant must demonstrate e.g. by statements of truth or affidavits.

In the Netherlands, a 2025 reform allows various options for obtaining information **10.047** and access to evidence via the court prior to commencement of the proceedings.[94] European Directives have also begun to provide for pre-litigation access in some sectors.[95] However, the example of Spain also shows how deeply rooted the European aversion to US-style discovery and fishing expeditions is. A Spanish proposal for the implementation of the Cartel Damages Directive, from 2015, which went beyond antitrust law to include general and temporally flexible options for access to "sources of evidence," was met with strong resistance and could not be implemented.[96] Only a few EU Member States have implemented the Directives in a way that goes beyond their narrow scope of application.[97] Even US procedural law should not be seen as too generous when it comes to pre-action access to information. Although there is broad, reciprocal access to evidence in the pre-trial discovery phase, this phase does not take place before the action is brought but between the bringing of the action and the main hearing. However, it should be noted that US law does not place overly strict requirements on the bringing of an action and, with a few exceptions, is still based on the principle of notice pleading, not fact pleading.

Therefore, the ELI/UNIDROIT Model Rules must be regarded as particularly far- **10.048** reaching with respect to pre-litigation access to evidence. ERCP Rules 101 and 106 are very liberal in allowing a potential plaintiff to gain access to evidence in the hands of the defendant even before the lawsuit is filed. The requirements under the English and Welsh pre-action rules on information and the intention to avoid fishing expeditions

92 Civil Procedure Rules 1998, r 3.16. Applications are often made in personal injury or death cases in which the potential defendant has exclusive access to medical records but also in product liability or employment rights case with a similar situation with respect to important documents; for more examples see nn 2.014 et seq.

93 See n 2.012.

94 Netherlands, n 6.043, Article 196 of the Dutch CPC.

95 See section B above.

96 Spain, n 5.088.

97 Paradoxically, one of the States is Norway, to which the Directive is not binding, see n 7.080.

and misuse are very much in line with the ERCP. The latter is not restricted to documents, even though this will be the main area of application. A quite generous access to information before the start of proceedings requires reasonable limitation. In English law, as in the ERCP, pre-litigation access, in particular to documents, is characterised by a broad judicial discretion and the application of the principle of proportionality as a limitation.

3. Preservation of evidence orders for the purpose of information?

10.049 Preservation of evidence orders will be dealt with later in this Chapter. However, a different purpose has now crept into some of the regulations on the preservation of evidence in some States. Some procedural systems allow evidence to be taken even before a lawsuit is filed if this increases the chances of an amicable settlement.[98] In Germany, this is limited to expert opinions,[99] while in other legal systems access to all evidence is granted. In Norway, the rules on the preservation of evidence are also used to give the plaintiff access to information about his claim and the prospects of success. The requested evidence must be sufficiently specified, and the principle of proportionality applies.[100]

E. THE PERSONAL DIMENSION

10.050 Although access to evidence primarily is regarded as a relationship between parties on opposite sides of pending lawsuits, access may also be requested towards third parties. Requests towards third parties could be of interest when the party seeking access could have requested access also from the opposing party to the lawsuit. However, requesting access from third parties is necessary only when neither of the parties to the lawsuit have access to potentially relevant information and that information is controlled by a third party. In contrast to requests for access to evidence between the parties, requests towards third parties are not primarily justified by the need for adjustment of information asymmetry – it is primarily justified by truth-seeking purposes. The parties to the lawsuit may still have divergent opinions on the need for access to evidence orders towards a third party. In general, the disadvantage of mutual non-access is higher for the party carrying the burden of proof, but the practical effect of that burden depends on the standard of evidence and other circumstances.

---

98 In the Netherlands, since January 1, 2025, an act on the simplification and modernisation of the law of evidence allows broad access to information and evidence in order to promote settlements, nn 6.041–6.044. See also Danish Code of Civil Procedure (Retsplejeloven), s 343(1), nn 7.065–7.066, and n 7.069 for Norway.

99 German CPC, s 485(2).

100 See n 7.073.

All jurisdictions covered in this study are open for access to evidence orders towards third parties, but quite some variation is found between different procedural traditions and also from one set of rules to another within a jurisdiction. Some sets of rules which directly or indirectly address problems concerning access to evidence are, due to their legal nature, not applicable towards third parties. Obvious examples are rules derived from general principles concerning the burden of proof or the burden of allegation or special rules governing exceptions or modification of these principles where a party has significantly better access to evidence. Since the burden of proof and the burden of allegation are legal relationships between the parties to a lawsuit, they cannot apply to third parties – for instance, the German rules on secondary burden of allegation are not applicable towards third parties.[101] In the Netherlands, the recently developed requirements of strengthened reasons applied to a party who has better access to evidence are exclusively based on inter-partes reasoning.[102] A non-party cannot provide such reasons and the existence of evidence in the hand of a third party cannot justify the application of such a doctrine. In principle, rules like the German secondary burden of assertion and the Dutch rules on extended reasons could be applicable in some special situations where a third party controls essential evidence – first and foremost if there is a near relationship between a party and a third party, for instance if they are companies belonging to a group of corporations. However, those are exceptions and the paradigmatic situations where these sets of rules apply are asymmetrical access to evidence between the parties to the lawsuit. **10.051**

On the other hand, access to evidence rules which provide the court with competence to order production of evidence, *ex officio* or on application from a party, tend to be applicable both towards parties and third parties. In Germany, Austria and Switzerland, the judge's powers to order production of evidence apply also to third parties and the court's competence for providing such orders depend on the same set of criteria as towards parties.[103] In Italy, the rules on inspection and exhibition of tangible evidence, which allow judges to order taking of evidence *ex officio*, apply to persons and tangible items regardless of whether the evidence is controlled by a party or a third party.[104] However, before ordering exhibition of documents or other tangible evidence towards a third party, the Italian CCP section 210 require the judge to balance the interest of justice against the third party's interest.[105] The court may also order public agencies to disclose evidence that is indispensable for an ongoing lawsuit, cf. the Italian CCP section 213. In Spain, at least one instrument for access to evidence applies both **10.052**

101 Germany, nn 1.006–1.007.
102 Netherlands, n 6.023.
103 German CPC, ss 142–144, see n 1.014.
104 See nn 4.006 et seq referring to the Italian CPC Articles 118 and 210.
105 Italy, n 4.009.

for parties and third parties, that is the duty to disclose documents in accordance with sections 328 to 332 CCP.[106] But the required cooperation is less demanding for third parties, and documents in their possession shall be disclosed only if the documents are of fundamental importance.[107] A third party may also be invited to court in person in order to decide whether he or she shall disclose information.

10.053 Application of *ex officio* powers equally towards parties and third parties makes sense. In general, *ex officio* powers are justified by truth-seeking purposes and realisation of substantive rights more than a need for adjusting asymmetries between the parties. Furthermore, the legal relationship of *ex officio* rules is not an inter-partes relationship, it is a relationship between the court and a party or a third party. In effect, jurisdictions basing their key rules on access to evidence on *ex officio* powers typically handle access to evidence from third parties similarly to access between the parties. The practicing of these powers may still be different for requests towards third parties than for requests between the parties. As emphasised by Gascón Inchausti,[108] the consequences of non-compliance with a court disclosure order cannot be similar to those imposed on parties because a litigant shall not be sanctioned because of unwanted behaviour from a third party unless that third party is closely connected to the party, for instance as two companies within a corporation. In Italy, fines may be imposed on persons who do not comply with a disclosure order. While a fine may be imposed on parties within the range of € 500 to € 3.000, non-parties may be imposed fines from € 150 to € 1.500.[109]

10.054 In contrast, English and Welsh rules on disclosure primarily establish rights and obligations between the parties. The core elements of disclosure, such as the important standard disclosure found in CPR Rules 31.6 and 31.7, only apply to parties. As explained by Sorabji, the inter-partes rules on disclosure are accompanied by rules requiring third persons to attend trial in order to present or produce documents.[110] Compared to the rules on parties, the conditions for ordering disclosure of evidence from third parties are much more restrictive in particular because the requested documents must be strictly specified before a third party must disclose them. CPR Rule 31.17 provides the court with a general competence to order disclosure of evidence from third parties, but the strict requirement of specification applies and the party requesting access must show that a positive effect of the documents is "likely."

---

106 Spain, nn 5.062 et seq.

107 Spain, nn 5.072–5.074.

108 Spain, n 5.073.

109 Italy, n 4.008.

110 See n 2.029 referencing CPR r 34.2.

In Scandinavia, the obligation to disclose evidence applies also towards third parties. The same criterion applies for applications for access to evidence against third parties as towards opposing parties. However, the principle of proportionality and other requirements balancing pros and cons of access to evidence should be applied differently towards third parties, and a party who requests access to evidence from a third party may have the request dismissed due to the fact that a request could have been directed against the opposing party.[111] **10.055**

In our opinion, access to evidence orders should primarily be directed against parties to an ongoing lawsuit. In general, access to evidence orders between the parties is more effective than orders towards third parties. Orders towards third parties are procedurally more complicated because such orders could only be imposed when the third party has had the opportunity to be heard and perhaps also has an opportunity to challenge the court order. Court orders against third parties must be sanctioned separately as well. While parties' non-compliance with access to evidence obligations could be sanctioned within the ongoing lawsuit, for instance by adverse inferences, reversal of the burden of proof or by regarding the opposing party's asserted fact as accepted, such sanctions are not available towards third parties. In our opinion, the balance is fairly well struck in the ERCP where access to evidence orders towards third parties shall be allowed only when necessary.[112] In our opinion, access to evidence orders against third parties shall be regarded under a principle of subsidiarity, which means that such orders are approved only where there are no other available options for having access.[113] **10.056**

F. THE SPACE DIMENSION

Access to sources of evidence held by the opposing party or third parties is intended to provide a tool to circumvent, in a proportionate manner, the disadvantages associated with information asymmetry. This is a problem that also arises in cases of cross-border litigation and where the parties to the dispute have agreed to arbitration. In these two contexts, the challenges that are already created by access to sources of evidence in ordinary cases – domestic litigation – are increased, albeit in different ways and for different reasons. **10.057**

111 See nn 7.050–7.051.
112 ERCP r 100(b).
113 ERCP r 100 Comment 3.

1. Cross-border settings

10.058 A prospective plaintiff or a party to pending proceedings may need access to sources of evidence that are not in his possession or under his control and which, moreover, are located in another State. Even if the litigation is ostensibly domestic, the need for access to information and/or sources of evidence located abroad makes it a matter with a cross-border dimension. This makes it necessary to coordinate the procedural systems of the States involved, which in turn may have different rules on access to sources of evidence, including rules where, for reasons of confidentiality, access may be prohibited or restricted. Possible divergences on this point may become a difficult obstacle to overcome.

10.059 When it comes to access to documents or equivalent information that are apparently in the possession of the opposing party, the fact that they are located abroad may have a secondary impact, at least in some cases: the judge hearing the main proceedings can exercise his powers to compel their production by addressing the party directly and, if necessary, applying the consequences in case of non-production (e.g. sanctions or adverse inferences). If such a solution is sufficient, it will be possible to resolve the problem without involving a foreign judicial authority and without triggering international judicial cooperation mechanisms. But such consequences will not always be appropriate or sufficient, particularly where the information may be necessary to decide whether or not to initiate proceedings, or against whom, or what is sought in the claim. And, in any case, recourse to these cooperation mechanisms will be unavoidable when it comes to obtaining documents and/or information held by third parties located abroad.

10.060 One can imagine two ways of obtaining from the other party or from a third party documents or information that is located abroad.

10.061 (a) First of all, the litigant concerned may apply to the judge already hearing the main proceedings or to a judge of the State with jurisdiction to hear the main proceedings and request access to evidence measures. If the judge grants the request, and after verifying that the measures are to be implemented in another country, he or she will have to activate the relevant international cooperation mechanisms, depending on the rules governing such cooperation.

10.062 In this regard, one of the most relevant legal provisions is Article 23 of the 1970 Hague Evidence Convention: "A Contracting State may at the time of signature, ratification or accession, declare that it will not execute Letters of Request issued for the purpose of obtaining pre-trial discovery of documents as known in Common Law countries." Two things can be deduced from this Article: first, that these cooperation mechanisms may be used for the purpose of helping one of the parties to obtain sources of evidence, and not only for the taking of evidence stricto sensu; second, that this use may not exceed the limits of reasonableness, limits which are associated with the "pre-trial discovery of documents as known in Common Law countries." Many countries made this reservation when acceding to the Convention, as pre-trial discovery was perceived as excessive and contrary to a procedural tradition more associated with *nemo tenetur*, as we have seen above. Developments at the national level and a more reasonable understanding of Article 23 seem to be changing things.

The Special Commission entrusted by the HCCH in 2024 to assess the practical operation of the Convention[114] considered that "the terms of Article 23 continue to be a source of misunderstanding." The SC recommended that Contracting Parties refrain from applying Article 23 to refuse the execution of Letters of Request for the *production of documents that are specified in the request, or otherwise reasonably identified* (emphasis added): As has already been seen, this is the current standard at European level and, to a large extent, in most Member States. The change of position in Germany, analysed by Trocker in his Chapter,[115] or the position adopted by France, explained by Jeuland,[116] are also indicative of an interpretation of the precept in the same sense. **10.063**

At the European level, it did not even seem necessary to resort to a rule equivalent to Article 23 of the Hague Convention: neither the initial 2001 version of the Regulation on the taking of evidence, nor the current 2020 version include a similar caveat. The reason is quite simple: none of the European legal systems provide a mechanism of access to sources of evidence that can be compared to US-type pre-trial discovery. Nor does the European regulation offer a different or specific treatment of requests for cooperation that originate in a prior request for access to sources of evidence: the regulation is not interested in the origin of the need to resort to the cooperation mechanisms of the regulation. As cooperation is only triggered at the request of the judicial authority of the requesting state, the European standard of a judicial filter in any case is ensured, and with it also the control of proportionality and the need to preserve confidential information. **10.064**

(b) The alternative is for the applicant to go directly to the judge of the place where the evidence to which he wants access is located and make a request for access, which that judge may grant or deny according to his own standards: the applicant, in such cases, does not go through the judge of origin and, consequently, is not subject to any control **10.065**

114 Hague Conference on Private International Law (HCCH), *Conclusions & Recommendations of the Special Commission on the Practical Operation of the Service, Evidence, and Access to Justice Conventions* (July 2–5, 2024) 6 https://assets.hcch.net/docs/6aef5b3a-a02c-408f-8277-8c995d56f255.pdf accessed May 8, 2025.

115 Chapter 8, fn 1.

116 See nn 3.057–3.059.

other than that of the judge to whom he goes. This is what § 1782 of Title 28 of the US Code allows, as Trocker's Chapter explains at length: "In a wide range of areas, from labor cases in Brazil to probate disputes in Hong Kong, from antitrust litigation in Korea to divorce proceedings in Austria, from bankruptcy matters in Italy to shareholder disputes linked to the Russian Federation, from trademark infringement claims in Germany, to breach of contract actions in the United Kingdom, from investment related proceedings in the Netherlands to securities fraud claims in Denmark, environmental controversies in Ecuador and merely contemplated trials in Singapore, as well as in many other cases in between, parties seek discovery aid from United States federal courts through the § 1782 path in order to reach information and/or evidence which appears necessary to successfully plead or defend their cases in courts on their home turf."[117] Trocker also highlights how "parties may see § 1782 of Title 28 of the U.S. Code as a welcomed device to get access to information and evidentiary material prior to the commencement of proceedings necessary to prepare certain legal disputes and to calculate their risk before coming to the determination as to whether to initiate a suit and against whom or to seek an out of court settlement."[118]

10.066 This is, in any case, a very special rule, almost unique in the world, which is why it has attracted so much attention. The question arises, however, whether outside the US legal sphere it can be argued that domestic judges have the power to deal with requests for access to sources of evidence made directly to them by a party in support of proceedings already pending abroad or intended to be instituted abroad – without the mediation of another court. At the European level, the only provision with a similar potential is the current Article 35 of the Brussels I bis Regulation, which allows the adoption of provisional and protective measures *lite alibi pendente sive penditura*. The question is therefore whether measures of access to sources of evidence fall within this European notion. The affirmative answer can be inferred from recital 25, which provides as follows:

> The notion of provisional, including protective, measures should include, for example, protective orders aimed at obtaining information or preserving evidence as referred to in Articles 6 and 7 of Directive 2004/48/EC of the European Parliament and of the Council of 29 April 2004 on the enforcement of intellectual property rights. It should not include measures which are not of a protective nature, such as measures ordering the hearing of a witness. This should be without prejudice to the application of Council Regulation (EC) No 1206/2001 of 28 May 2001 on cooperation between the courts of the Member States in the taking of evidence in civil or commercial matters.

10.067 The recital, based in part on the CJEU St. Paul Dairy,[119] excludes those measures that are generically aimed at assessing whether or not legal proceedings should be

---

117 See n 8.004.

118 See n 8.006.

119 Case C-104/03 *St. Paul Dairy* [2005] ECR I-3481, ECLI:EU:C:2005:255.

envisaged. However, it expressly includes measures of access to sources of evidence, in addition to measures for the preservation of evidence, which can more easily be included in the category of protective measures – this is corroborated by ERCP Rules 184 and 198. It can be inferred from this that, at least internally in the European Union – and, by extension, in the Lugano Convention – litigants can use Article 35 BR I bis to apply directly for access to evidence measures where they need them, at least under those European instruments that have provided for them in a harmonised way: In 2012 it was only measures under the Directive on the enforcement of intellectual property rights; but today it would also be measures in antitrust damages, representative actions and, where the respective Directives apply, corporate sustainability due diligence and defective product liability.[120]

Beyond the provisions at the European level, for several of the national legal systems analysed in this book, it is not an obstacle that the documents or information whose disclosure they order are located abroad. Thus, in relation to Scandinavia, it is pointed out that "The provisions on *edisjonsplikt* do not distinguish between evidence located domestically and evidence stored in foreign jurisdictions, implying that they also apply to evidence stored abroad."[121] However, in order to achieve this goal, "the national courts competence to order access to evidence without involvement of the courts of another country has not yet been clarified by decisions from the Supreme Courts."[122] Spanish domestic legislation allows for an equivalent result, in any case using the tools of international judicial cooperation.[123] The International Commercial Courts of Paris also appear to be empowered to order the production of documents or information held abroad.[124] **10.068**

In any case, the use of international cooperation mechanisms also falls within the methods of access to sources of evidence, in some cases autonomously and directly – this is what happens, as we have seen, under US legislation or Article 35 BR I bis – In other cases as a complement to give full effectiveness to the provisions of domestic law. **10.069**

(c) Access to sources of evidence in cross-border settings can also give rise to an additional problem, that of the so-called "blocking statutes," through which it is sought to prevent information that is economically sensitive to the interests of the State in which the requested party is located from being provided in compliance with requests for disclosure or discovery. This is an issue particularly analysed by Jeuland in the **10.070**

120 See above, nn 10.011–10.014.
121 See n 7.022.
122 See n 7.022.
123 See nn 5.097–5.098.
124 See n 3.064.

Chapter on France,[125] which has a law dating from 1980, but which is also dealt with at the European level by Council Regulation (EC) 2271/96 of 22 November 1996 on protection against the effects of the extraterritorial application of legislation adopted by a third country, and against actions based thereon or resulting therefrom.

2. Arbitration

10.071 The need for access to sources of evidence held by the opposing party or a third party may also become apparent where the parties have agreed to arbitration and where arbitral proceedings are already underway. The challenges that arise then are similar to those that arise in cross-border contexts – especially if it is an international arbitration where the seat is in a different place from where the evidence to be accessed is located. In summary, two possible courses of action can be identified.

10.072 (a) On the one hand, the self-sufficiency of arbitration as a dispute resolution mechanism must be enhanced. In this area, this means attributing to arbitrators powers equivalent to those that the legal systems recognise to judges, allowing them to order the parties to produce documents and evidence in their possession at the request of the opposing party. The model here, especially in the context of international commercial arbitration, is Article 3 of the 2020 IBA Rules on the Taking of Evidence, analysed in detail in Chapter 9 by Stürner and Landbrecht. These authors recognise, however, that arbitral tribunals do not always have sufficient coercive powers to achieve the objective of this provision (it is not always feasible to apply sanctions or draw adverse inferences).[126] This deficit is particularly serious when the evidence to which access is sought is in the possession of a third party, since arbitral tribunals lack powers with respect to those who are not party to the arbitration agreement.

10.073 (b) The alternative – or, better, the complement – is judicial support for arbitration so that the parties or the arbitrators themselves turn to the state courts so that they, invested with full power, can try to force the reluctant will of those who have in their possession the evidence necessary for the proper resolution of a dispute submitted to arbitration. In general, domestic arbitration laws contain rules regulating assistance to arbitration in evidentiary matters, including – or not excluding – access to sources of evidence. Article 27 of the Uncitral Model Law has served as a source of inspiration for many of them.[127] In their Chapter, Stürner and Landbrecht analyse the legal

125 See nn 3.057–3.058.

126 See n 9.040.

127 UNCITRAL Model Law on International Commercial Arbitration 1985 (as amended in 2006), Article 27. Court assistance in taking evidence. The arbitral tribunal or a party with the approval of the arbitral tribunal may request from a competent court of this State assistance in taking evidence. The court may execute the request within its competence and according to its rules on taking evidence.

regime in the UK, France, Germany and Switzerland, with different arbitration traditions, not always in line with the Uncitral Model Law. They highlight several, partly contradictory trends. On the one hand, subsidiarity so that the court's help is only called upon when the arbitral tribunal cannot achieve the objective on its own. But at the same time, possible judicial support for arbitration in terms of access to evidence is also seen as a way to make arbitration attractive, especially international arbitration.[128] When the arbitration process has not yet started, it is more frequent that the parties themselves directly ask the judge for support; when the arbitration procedure is underway, on the other hand, the tendency is for judicial assistance to be mediated by the arbitral tribunal. They warn, in any case, that judicial support measures for evidence in arbitration tend to focus primarily on compelling witnesses to testify: "All other types of evidence may be substituted, e.g. by drawing adverse inferences from the lack of production of a document etc."

G. ISSUES WITH CONFIDENTIALITY: PRIVILEGES, TRADE SECRETS AND PRIVACY MATTERS

It has become clear from all the contributions in this book that the protection of confidential information, especially trade secrets, can be a particular challenge in civil proceedings.[129] While the protection of trade secrets of third parties can often be ensured by granting a right to refuse to testify or present documents,[130] the protection of confidential information in the hands of the parties is far more problematic. Very often parties do not have a formal privilege to refuse the production of evidence which includes trade secrets or confidential information.[131] For other information that is worthy of protection there are often privileges and immunities, for example **10.074**

128 See n 9.082.

129 For a comparative overview of the protection of trade secrets before and during proceedings, see also European Commission, *Study on Trade Secrets and Confidential Business Information in the Internal Market* (Final Study, April 2013) https://ec.europa.eu/docsroom/documents/14838/attachments/1/translations/en/renditions/pdf accessed May 27, 2025; and EU Intellectual Property Office, *The Baseline of Trade Secrets Litigation in the EU Member States* (2018) https://euipo.europa.eu/tunnel-web/secure/webdav/guest/document_library/observatory/documents/reports/2018_Baseline_of_Trade_Secrets_Litigations_in_EU_Member_States/2018_Baseline_of_Trade_Secrets_Litigations_in_EU_Member_States_EN.pdf accessed May 27, 2025. More recently, Kahl, "Limits on Disclosure and Discovery" nn 81–86.

130 German CPC ss 142(2), 144(2), 384 no 3; Austria: Austrian CPC s 305 no 4. In Sweden CPC chs 38.2 and 36.6; and Norway CPC s 22–10 protect trade secrets, but the court may order disclosure based on a balancing of interests; see also A Stadler and M Strandberg, in A Stadler, V Smith and F Gascón Inchausti (eds), *European Rules of Civil Procedure, A Commentary on the ELI/UNIDROIT Model Rules* (OUP 2022) r 103 n 12.086. ERCP Rule 91(2)(c) seems to provide evidentiary immunity for trade secrets not only for third parties but also for the parties themselves. However, Rule 91(3) allows the court to consider whether a party's failure to disclose evidence or other information is justified when taking into account to draw adverse inferences. Therefore, it is not an absolute immunity or privilege and the availability of protective measures according to Rule 103 will also be taken into account.

131 In Austria: Austrian CPC s 305 no 4 includes parties to the litigation, witnesses are also privileged by s 321 no 5.

for information held by doctors, lawyers, tax consultants, psychologists, etc. who are obliged by law to maintain confidentiality.[132] Insofar as the confidential information is directly relevant to the decision of the court, there are basically three ways among which a procedural code can choose: 1) absolute protection of the information, which then does not have to be introduced into the litigation against the will of the party concerned.[133] This involves the risk that the judgment is made on an incorrect factual basis. Directly relevant evidence must almost always be disclosed – at least – to the court. If the party whose trade secrets are at issue bears the burden of proof and can only meet this burden if he or she discloses the secrets, the decision lies primarily with that party. 2) A completely opposite answer could be that a legal system does not provide protection for such confidential information at all and requires parties to disclose it if the information is relevant to the court decision. Hardly any procedural system takes this strict approach. 3) As is so often the case, a conciliatory solution has prevailed in most jurisdictions: the parties to the litigation cannot generally refuse to provide relevant but confidential information, but the court can order special protective measures to be taken or encourage the parties to make arrangements for the protection.[134] If it is only a matter of withholding trade secrets from the general public, the exclusion of the public audience from the hearing is a sufficient means and available almost everywhere.[135] It will often be combined with a court order that imposes an obligation to keep the information confidential on all persons present during the

---

132 Whereas in US civil proceedings only a small number of privileges are accepted, including only the privilege against self-incrimination, the attorney-client privilege and a privilege for psychotherapists (*Jafee* v. *Redmond,* 518 US 1 (1996)), European jurisdictions very often grant privileges for spouses, relatives, journalists and all professions that are under a duty of confidentiality (e.g. Austrian CPC s 321, German CPC s 384; Articles 165–166; Norwegian CPC s 22–8; Swiss CPC Articles 165–166; ERCP, r 91).

133 In Austria, s 305 no 4 CPC seems to provide an absolute privilege for parties against the production of document containing business secrets.

134 France: Cour de cassation (Chambre sociale), December 19, 2012, cited in EUIPO, *The Baseline of Trade Secrets Litigation in the EU Member States* (2018) 127 n 1; Germany: CPC s 273a (referring to ss 16–19 of the Act on the Protection of Trade Secrets); German Patent Act (Patentgesetz), s 140d requires the court to take "appropriate" protective measures; Italy: Silvestri sub 3 (referring to intellectual property litigation); Netherlands: Krans and Zondag, sub 9.3.1.; Spain: Gascón Inchausti 2.5. (before 3); Switzerland: Article 156 CPC provides a very general rule, asking the court to take appropriate measures to ensure that taking of evidence does not infringe the legitimate interest of any party or third party. "Confidentiality clubs/rings" are also a measure taken by courts in the UK to restrict access to confidential information, see *IPCom GmbH & Co KG* v *HTC Europe Co Ltd* and *Nokia OYJ (Nokia Corp)* v *IPCom GmbH & Co KG* [2013] EWCH 52 (Pat); EUIPO, *The Baseline of Trade Secrets Litigation in the EU Member States* (2018) 329 n 1. See also the overviews in the World Intellectual Property Organization (WIPO), *WIPO Guide to Trade Secrets,* Part V, ss 6.1–6.4 on Trade Secrets in litigation https://www.wipo.int/web-publications/wipo-guide-to-trade-secrets-and-innovation/en/part-v-trade-secrets-in-litigation.html accessed May 20, 2025.

135 Examples from national law are Austrian CPC s 172; Danish CPC, s 29; Estonian Code of Civil Procedure (Tsiviilkohtumenetluse seadustik) Article 38(1); French CPC Article 435; German Judicature Act (Gerichtsverfassungsgesetz, GVG), s 172 nos 2 and 3; Greek CPC Article 114; Hungarian Code of Civil Procedure (Polgári perrendtartás, Pp) s 5(2); Italian CPC Article 121(3); Latvian Civil Procedure Law (Civilprocesa likums) s 11(3); Lithuanian Code of Civil Procedure (Civilinio proceso kodeksas, CPK) Article 9(1); Dutch CPC Articles 27–29; Spanish CPC Articles 138, 140, 328(3); Swiss CPC Article 54(3).

hearing. Protective measures that prevent the opposing party from learning of the trade secret are more difficult. However, they will often be necessary if the parties are competitors and there is a risk of spying on technical or business information. The basic dilemma in such a situation lies in the conflict between the protection of confidential information on the one hand and the right to be heard on the other. The practice of full *in camera* proceedings sometimes found in US proceedings, in which confidential information or corresponding evidence is only presented to the court and the other party is not granted access,[136] is considered constitutionally problematic in Europe.[137] The solutions provided for these situations in European jurisdictions are still different today, even though the European legislator has provided a solution in Article 9 of Directive (EU) 2016/943 (the "Trade Secrets Directive"). The Directive was designed to protect trade secrets or undisclosed know-how against unlawful acquisition, use and disclosure, but it does not have a focus on general civil proceedings. Article 9 requires Member States to ensure that judicial authorities "take specific measures necessary to preserve the confidentiality of any trade secret or alleged trade secret used or referred to in the course of legal proceedings." This Article, like the whole Trade Secrets Directive, is, however, only directly applicable if the legal proceedings are related to the unlawful acquisition, use or disclosure of a trade secret. If confidential information is used in the context of other civil proceedings, such as patent infringement proceedings or competition law cases, the Directive does not apply directly. Only in some jurisdictions the scope of application was extended when the Directive was transposed into national law.[138] The German legislator, e.g. specified the application in patent litigation from the outset[139] and very recently opened the

136 See n 8.064 with reference to Rule 26 Federal Rules of Civil Procedure; details on protective measures provided by US courts are described by A Stadler, *Der Schutz von Unternehmensgeheimissen im deutschen und US-amerikanischen Zivilprozess und im Rechtshilfeverfahren* (Mohr Siebeck 1989) 219 ff, 223 ff.

137 For the controversial debate in Germany, see A Stadler, 'Geheimnisschutz im Zivilprozess aus deutscher Sicht' [2010] *Zeitschrift für Zivilprozess* 261; Stadler, *Der Schutz von Unternehmensgeheimissen im deutschen und US-amerikanischen Zivilprozess und im Rechtshilfeverfahren*, 239 ff; EJ Melzer, *§ 33g GWB: Offenlegung versus Geheimnisschutz* (Berliner Wissenschaftsverlag 2020); A Götz, *Der Schutz von Betriebs- und Geschäftsgeheimnissen im Zivilverfahren* (Mohr Siebeck 2014); for Austria: J Rassi, *Kooperation und Geheimnisschutz bei Beweisschwierigkeiten im Zivilprozess* (Sramek 2020) 163–171. Swiss courts, only in some situations, also exclude a party from access to confidential information, see S Baumgartner, in P Oberhammer, T Domej and U Haas (eds), *Schweizerische Zivilprozessordnung* (3rd edn, Helbing Lichtenhahn 2021) Article 156 n 5; Hasenböhler and Yañez, *Kommentar zur Schweizerischen Zivilprozessordnung*, Article 156 n 15; for details see G Baumgärtel, "Geheimverfahren im Zivilprozess: Zur Wahrung von Geschäftsgeheimnissen nach Schweizer Vorbild?" in *Liber Amicorum W.J. Habscheid* (Bielefeld 1989) 1 ff; R Stäuber, *Der Schutz von Geschäftsgeheimnissen im Zivilprozess* (St Gallen 2011). In Spain, applicants may be denied access to confidential information in patent infringement proceedings, Gascón Inchausti sub 2.4 (arts. 123 to 126 of the Patent Act).

138 For details on the implementation of the Trade Secrets Directive in the UK, the Nordic countries, Germany, Portugal and Spain, see the contributions in J Schovsbo, T Minssen and T Riis, *The Harmonization and Protection of Trade Secrets in the EU* (Edward Elgar 2020). Very often Article 9 has been implemented only for the narrow scope of application of the Directive.

139 S 145a German Patent Act.

application of protective measures mentioned in Article 9 to all civil proceedings in section 273a CPC.[140] This decision was made under the pressure of a European-wide competition of national courts for major commercial disputes, which are preferably litigated in England or the Netherlands or before arbitration tribunals. Arbitration panels can provide a far greater scope of protective measures than state courts and conduct proceedings behind closed doors as a matter of principle.[141]

10.075 The Directive's solution in Article 9 does not provide for full *in camera* proceedings,[142] but allows the court to restrict access to hearings when trade secrets may be disclosed and to the corresponding record or transcript to a limited number of persons ("confidentiality clubs"). Having in mind that protective measures must ensure compliance with the parties' right to an effective remedy and to a fair trial, at least one natural person from each party and the lawyers must have access to the hearing and the records. It is therefore not an "attorney's-eyes-only" solution.[143] It allows courts to exclude the opponent him- or herself, but it cannot provide absolute protection. Even if non-disclosure court orders are in place, it will be difficult to prove an unauthorised disclosure or use. The party's exclusion from hearings and the taking of evidence requires follow-on protective measures like removing or redacting trade secrets not only from the minutes, but also from the judgment. Article 9(2)(c) allows non-confidential and confidential parts of any judicial decision.[144]

10.076 While the Directive applies in principle to "trade secrets or alleged trade secrets," many jurisdictions are stricter and only allow protective mechanisms if the secrets are genuine and not only "alleged" – depending, of course, on different definitions of trade secrets.[145] In some jurisdictions courts may appoint technical experts, accountants or other trustworthy persons to verify *in camera* whether real trade secrets are at stake and/or whether they are relevant for the case at hand.[146] They are under a duty of confidentiality and will only submit a summary of their inspection to the court

140 Germany, nn 1.026–1.030.

141 Very often the panel appoints "clean teams" or "confidentiality clubs," meaning that only a small number of persons or lawyers have exclusive access to a party's trade secrets.

142 The official comment no 2 to Rule 103 of the ERCP, however, mentions disclosure exclusively to the court, but from the reference made to Article 9 of the Trade Secrets Directive it becomes clear that this is actually not possible as the Directive in any case grants access to relevant trade secrets for a party's lawyer and a representative and does not allow complete *in camera* proceedings.

143 In French pre-trial proceedings access to documents can be restricted to court experts and lawyers, EUIPO, *The Baseline of Trade Secrets Litigation in the EU Member States* (2018) 127 n 1.

144 For similar rules in Switzerland see Baumgartner, *Schweizerische Zivilprozessordnung*, Article 156 n 6.

145 One import feature of trade secrets also highlighted in Article 2(1) of the Trade Secrets Directive is the requirement that the owner of the trade secret must have taken reasonable steps to keep it secret; this has also been emphasised by the English Supreme Court in *Vestergaard Frandsen A/S* v *Bestnet Europe Ltd* [2013] UKSC 31, [2013] 1 WLR 1556.

146 In the Netherlands, the judge him- or herself inspects documents in order to decide whether they contain confidential information and in order to decide to what extent protection is needed, see n 6.021.

("expert-eyes-only"). Depending on the expert's findings, the court can then order certain protective measures or not.[147]

In most jurisdictions, the protection of a party's trade secrets against disclosure (particularly to the opponent) must be determined by courts on a case-by-case basis. The still heterogenous approach taken across Europe might be overcome by national legislators taking into account the ERCP in the future.[148] Rule 103 of the ERCP provides a list of measures which courts should take into consideration when making an order for access to evidence containing confidential information. The list is based on examples from national law and Article 9 of the Trade Secrets Directive. It includes: (a) redacting relevant sensitive passages in documents; (b) conducting hearings *in camera*; (c) restricting the persons allowed to gain access to or inspect the proposed evidence; (d) instructing experts to produce a summary of the information in an aggregated or otherwise non-confidential form; (e) writing a non-confidential version of a judicial decision in which passages containing confidential data are deleted; (f) limiting access to certain sources of evidence to the representatives and lawyers of the parties and to experts who are subject to a duty of confidentiality. In addition, and of utmost importance for the effective protection of confidential information, is the list of sanctions provided for in ERCP Rule 104 if a person beaches any duty of confidentiality.[149] **10.077**

H. PRESERVATION OF EVIDENCE

In addition to access to sources of evidence, national procedural systems also regulate the adoption by the courts of measures aimed at the preservation of evidence.[150] The prerequisite for obtaining measures to preserve evidence is the same in all legal systems and is associated with the risk that the evidence will be lost or destroyed, or that its evidential value will be reduced so that it cannot be produced and/or used at the appropriate procedural moment or so that there is no longer any point in doing so. This risk is stated in some legislations in a generic way (e.g. in Norway or France),[151] while in other legislations this general reference is accompanied, by way of example, by more **10.078**

---

147 For details see Gascón Inchausti and Stürner, "Access to Information and Evidence in the ELI/UNIDROIT European Rules on Civil Procedure: Some Fundamental Aspects" 14, 32.

148 In Spain, the protective measures and sanctions against a breach of confidentiality available in competition law proceedings are already very close to the ELI/UNIDROIT Rules, n 5.094.

149 For details on ERCP rr 103 and 104, see A Stadler and M Strandberg, in Stadler, Smith and Gascón Inchausti, *European Rules of Civil Procedure, A Commentary on the ELI/UNIDROIT Model Rules* (OUP 2022) nn 12.086–12.095.

150 In the field of arbitration, it should be taken into account that UNCITRAL Model Law on International Commercial Arbitration includes, within the power of the arbitral tribunal to order interim measures, an order directed to a party to "Preserve evidence that may be relevant and material to the resolution of the dispute" (Article 17(2)(d)).

151 See nn 3.026–3.027; and n 7.070.

specific circumstances, such as the passage of time (Italy),[152] natural events (Spain) or with the bad faith conduct of the party to whom the evidence would prejudice (again, Spain).[153] Most jurisdictions, moreover, establish similar requirements as to the burdens incumbent on the applicant to obtain the securing of evidence and which, in many cases, are equivalent to those conditioning the measures of access to evidence. Recurrently, it is required to reasonably identify the evidence to be preserved, to provide at least prima facie evidence of the viability of its case and to justify the relevance of the evidence to be preserved to its case, as well as respect for proportionality requirements and the limits arising from the protection of confidential information. In relation to the feasibility of the applicant's action and the relevance of the evidence, the level of rigidity may vary somewhat from one legal system to another (in Switzerland, for example, the standards seem to be very high),[154] although in practice the circumstances of each individual case are always decisive; the control will be more abstract, in any case, if the proceedings have not yet commenced.

10.079 The ERCP, again, provide a good model for regulating these issues. As seen above, the ERCP (Rule 184) evidence preservation measures form part of the more general category of provisional measures so that their general legal regime is the same as that of provisional measures. More specifically, Rule 198 sets out the specific measures that can be adopted[155] and Rule 199 establishes the specific criteria for awarding an Evidence Preservation Measure that must be shown by a party seeking an evidence preservation: "(a) there is a real risk that unless the order is made the evidence will not be available for determining the substantive proceedings on their merits; and (b) if the order requires access to a party's or non-party's property the applicant has a strong prima facie case in respect of the merits of the applicant's claim or proposed claim for relief."[156]

10.080 In principle, access to evidence and securing or preserving evidence are two different concepts pursuing different objectives. However, in practice there can be a clear connection between them. This connection is particularly significant in the case of electronically stored evidence, which is easily manipulated or susceptible to destruction.[157]

---

152 See n 4.029.

153 See n 5.076.

154 See n 1.066.

155 "(a) hearing witness evidence or taking of witness evidence by a third party acting on its behalf; (b) requiring the preservation or protection of evidence by the parties or by requiring it to be placed in the custody of a custodian; (c) appointing an expert to provide expert opinion evidence." With more detail, see T Andersson, *ERCP Commentary* (n.d.) n 18.162 ff.

156 On these criteria, see again Andersson, *ERCP Commentary*, n 18.171 ff.

157 M Strandberg, "The Justice System Takes Account of the (Social, Economic) Digital Revolution: Evidence Law Adjusted to Digitally Stored Information" in B Hess, M Woo, L Cadiet, S Menétrey and E Vallines García (eds), *Comparative Procedural Law and Justice* (Part IX Chapter 2), cplj.org/a/9-2, accessed May 8, 2025, nn 46–59.

In some cases, access measures and preservation measures can be requested and granted in a complementary manner: the evidence is sought and, once the danger has been identified, its preservation is requested so that it can be offered and used at the appropriate procedural moment. In other cases, it may be necessary to secure the evidence while deciding whether or not to grant its disclosure. Finally, the risk to the evidence may also be clear from the outset so that the access measure becomes, in practice, the mechanism to be used in order to make the securing of the evidence effective. These connections, at least in the area of the enforcement of IP rights, result from the interrelationship between Articles 6 and 7 of the 2004 Directive. The ERCP also consider it normal that the request for access to sources of evidence and the adoption of measures for securing that evidence is linked in the same application: according to Rule 101(2), "An application for an order securing access to evidence may include an application for the imposition of measures to protect or preserve evidence, including an application for provisional or protective measures under Part X." And, conversely, pursuant to Rule 198(2), "Evidence preservation orders may, where necessary, authorise access to the evidence. Access may be subject to such conditions as the court considers just."[158] **10.081**

This access/security binomial is also visible in several of the legal systems analysed. In Spain, for example, some preliminary measures – not only in the area of IP rights – can be complemented by protective measures.[159] This interconnection is also found in Italy, where the evidence preservation procedure makes it possible to collect a witness statement, to inspect places or persons and to secure the written report of an expert.[160] The *référé probatoire* of the French Article 145 CCP also allows the preservation of evidence when an item of evidence is threatened with loss or decay, but it can also be used to assess the conditions of existence or even the relevance of a potential action. This obliges the *Cour de cassation* to ensure that Article 145 does not overstep its scope.[161] The legal situation is much clearer in the Netherlands, where the practice on IP rights, thanks to the development of the Supreme Court in the *Molenbeek/Vergeer* case, has been generalised and consolidated by the 2025 reform of the law of evidence, allowing a strong interrelation between access to and securing of evidence.[162] In Sweden, section 41:1 of the Swedish CP allows the court to "take and preserve for the future evidence in the form of witness examination, expert opinion, view, or written evidence." Strandberg points out that this tool does not explicitly grant the requesting party access to the preserved evidence, but notes its usefulness in practice to resolve **10.082**

158 This possible combination is also pointed out by Stadler and Strandberg, *ERCP Commentary*, nn 12.075 and 12.079.
159 See nn 5.041 and 5.078.
160 See n 4.027.
161 See n 3.027.
162 See nn 6.067 et seq.

problems which otherwise would have been solved by access to evidence rules.[163] In Norway, Chapter 28 of the CCP, although it refers to the securing of evidence, has become an important tool for access to evidence, much more influential than what was expected. Even though "securing of evidence" suggests that these rules are applicable only for avoiding future damage to evidence, the rules of that Chapter shall provide a potential party with access to evidence in order to clarify whether there is a substantial basis for a claim and to prepare the ground for well-informed settlements.[164] More generally, and still in Scandinavia, when it comes to *edisjonsplikt* concerning digitally stored information, evidence is often preserved before being made available to the requesting party, ensuring no disclosure occurs until disputes over access are conclusively resolved by the court.[165]

I. EFFECTIVENESS OF THE MEASURES AND CONSEQUENCES IN CASE OF NON-COMPLIANCE: ADVERSE INFERENCES, SANCTIONS, ETC.

10.083 Since a core aspect of access to evidence rules is to oblige the evidence-controlling party to disclose also evidence that is negative to her case, one may not expect such obligations to be fulfilled voluntarily. In order to operate effectively, such obligations must probably be orchestrated by sanctions or other negative effects. All jurisdictions reported allow or expect the court to take different negative consequences or sanctions from non-compliance with access to evidence rules. All jurisdictions allow both direct sanctions, consequences which allow enforcement or the effectivisation of access to evidence rights in itself, and sanctions or consequences which affect the outcome of the pending lawsuit. However, the more exact or detailed features of these consequences vary significantly from one jurisdiction to another:

10.084 Direct consequences or sanctions are any measure taken to make access to evidence obligations effective. The most obvious measures are *court orders* stating and concretising a party's obligations to disclose certain pieces of evidence to the opposing party or the court. In jurisdictions where access to evidence rules primarily take the form of *ex officio* powers for the court, such orders are inherent elements of the system. Such court orders stand to disposal also in systems where access to evidence is primarily regarded as relationships between the parties. Parties to a lawsuit in Scandinavia may request a court order for access to evidence under the rules on *edisjonsplikt*,[166] and parties to English lawsuits may request such orders under the rules on disclosure.[167] However,

163 See nn 7.061–7.064.
164 See nn 7.069–7.078.
165 See n 7.086.
166 See nn 7.016 et seq.
167 See nn 2.018 et seq.

many jurisdictions recognise access to evidence rules which parties cannot request a court order for. That is typical for general and rather vague obligations of loyal cooperation between the parties, such as the rules found in the Norwegian CCP section 5–3 and 21–4 and the unwritten principles found in Austrian law.[168] That is also typical for obligations prior to commencement, such as the English rules on pre-action protocols.[169] Typically, non-compliance with general and vague obligations and obligations pre-commencement are sanctioned by negative inferences or cost sanctions.[170]

Access to evidence court orders are enforceable in some jurisdictions. Preliminary measures for access to evidence under Spanish law are directly enforceable,[171] and an enforcement declaration may be asked for in Swedish law to follow up on a court order based on *edisjonsplikt*.[172] Since enforcement of such orders may lead to a monetary sanction, a comparative functional equivalent may be found in jurisdictions allowing the court to impose a fine on a party or non-party who does not comply with an access to evidence order. Such fines are an important part of Italian law.[173] **10.085**

All jurisdictions analysed in this book open for consequences impacting on the pending lawsuit without directly enforcing the access to evidence obligation. In the English language, such sanctions or consequences are explained under the phrase "negative or adverse inferences." However, very different kinds of sanctions or effects are hidden under this common notion and a genuine comparative analysis must make a more concrete comparison of each form of consequence. **10.086**

First, non-compliance with an access to evidence obligation may be the basis for negative consequences within the evaluation of the evidence. Since most jurisdictions apply a principle of free evaluation of evidence or at least leave the evaluation of the evidence to the judges without any strict rules on the inferences to be made from the evidence, a special legal basis for such inferences is not necessary. All jurisdictions seem to acknowledge such evidential negative inferences made from a party's violation of an obligation to disclose evidence.[174] Such an inference will be taken by the judges in a case-to-case manner where the strength of the inference depends on the evidential value which may be adhered to the fact that a party has not disclosed evidence despite an obligation or expectation of doing so. **10.087**

168 See nn 7.010 and 1.048–1.050.
169 See nn 2.011 et seq.
170 See n 2.012; n 1.050 concerning Austrian law and n 7.012 concerning Norwegian law.
171 Spain, nn 5.056 et seq.
172 See n 7.056. In Danish and Norwegian law, such orders are enforceable only towards third parties.
173 Italy, n 4.008.
174 Spain, n 5.070; Italy, n 4.008; Scandinavia, nn 7.056–7.057.

10.088 Secondly, non-compliance with an access to evidence obligation may lead to a reversal of the burden of proof or an adjustment of the standard of evidence in disadvantage of the party who did not comply. Since the main rules on the burden of proof and to some degree the standard of evidence in most jurisdictions are based on general (non-statutory) principles, most jurisdictions also allow exceptions to be based on non-statutory legal sources, and most jurisdictions do allow such an exception when a party has not disclosed evidence.[175] A reversal of the burden of proof may also be applied not as a sanction against non-compliance, but as a tool in order to benefit a party suffering from information asymmetry.[176] A similar effect is secondary burdens of allegation, which for instance are found in Germany.[177]

10.089 Thirdly, adverse inferences may take the form of acceptance or rejection of claims or factual assertions. In German law, facts may be regarded non-disputed if a party who has better access to those facts does not give sufficient details on the matter.[178] In Dutch law, such effects may be imposed both after non-compliance with the duty of truth, access to evidence orders or the duty of strengthened obligation to state reasons.[179] In Danish law, such an inference may be drawn from the rules on *oplysningspligt*. Pursuant to those rules, a party that does not disclose important evidence which he was obliged to disclose will simply not be successful in the factual issue, or to be more precise: the judgment will be based on the opposing party's alleged fact.[180] In Norwegian law, a similar effect may be based on rules on default judgments: a party may be regarded as absent if he does not comply with an access to evidence order even after having being warned by the judges on the possibility of an default judgment.[181]

10.090 In some jurisdictions, non-compliance with access to evidence orders may lead to a cost sanction. Such an effect is well-known in English law,[182] Dutch law,[183] and Scandinavian law.[184]

10.091 The sanctions available when a party or non-party does not comply with the obligations of making evidence accessible seem to vary quite a lot from one jurisdiction to the other, but all jurisdictions are open for more than one sanction or negative consequence. An important question, then, is whether the courts are left with competence

175 See nn 6.014–6.015, nn 6.034–6.036; also nn 7.056–7.057.
176 Spain, n 5.019; see also nn 10.022–10.023 on EU Directives on anti-discrimination.
177 See nn 1.006 et seq.
178 See n 1.007.
179 See nn 6.013, 6.016, 6.018, 6.034.
180 See n 7.056.
181 See n 7.057.
182 See n 2.012.
183 See nn 6.013, 6.018.
184 See n 7.057.

to choose between available sanctions. In some jurisdictions, the court is left with a wide range of sanctions which may be imposed and the court has a wide margin of appreciation when choosing a suitable sanction. Dutch law is a good example of such a flexible case-to-case approach. Illustratively, the Dutch CCP Article 21 concerning violations of the duty of truth states that "Where the parties fail to comply with this obligation, the court may draw the inference as it deems appropriate." The sanction chosen depends on the seriousness of the violation and may be "for example declaring a party's claim inadmissible, rejecting a claim in its entirety or ordering the party that violates the duty of truth to pay the costs of the proceedings."[185] Italian law is an example from the opposite side of the spectrum, where the system of sanctions is more rigid and leaves less leeway to the courts. Although Italian courts may draw negative inferences from non-compliance with access to evidence orders, such inferences are not regarded effective because the prevailing interpretation of Italian law is that the negative inferences do not carry enough evidential value to establish a fact in itself.[186] Italian courts may impose a fine whenever a party or non-party does not comply with an access to evidence order (inspection or exhibition). However, the fines are not regarded effective because the fines are relatively modest lump sums instead of ongoing monetary punishments. A party may just simply pay the fine and cannot thereafter be obliged to disclose the evidence.[187]

In our opinion, finding an effective set of sanctions and consequences is highly important for the proper functioning of rules on access to evidence. Although the exact content of these effects may reasonably vary to some degree from one jurisdiction to another, a rather flexible system of sanctions and negative consequences seems to be preferable. Violations of obligations to disclose evidence may vary significantly in nature, effect and seriousness and the proper sanctions should reflect those issues. Such a flexible system of sanctions is found in the ERCP. **10.092**

J. COST ISSUES

Any measure for access to evidence held by the opposing party or a third party has a financial cost. In some cases, it may be a very small cost, when the access concerns only a few documents that can be easily located by the requested party. In other cases, it may require a significant investment of material and human resources; it should be recalled in this respect that under the PACCAR judgment of the Court of Justice of **10.093**

185 Netherlands, n 6.013.
186 Italy, n 4.011.
187 Italy, 4, n 4.011.

the EU, the requested party may be obliged to create a document *ex novo* by compiling or classifying information, knowledge or data in its possession.[188]

10.094 The issue of costs is indirectly tackled in most domestic legislations passed to implement the 2014 Directive on competition damages claims, since according to its Article 5(3)(b), the proportionality test that national courts must apply includes considering the [...] "cost of disclosure, especially for any third parties concerned." Many national rules reproduce, more or less literally, this requirement and, at most, establish some specific provision concerning the cost of measures of access to sources of evidence in this specific area (as is the case in Spain).[189]

10.095 The issue, however, is not always directly addressed by national legislation, even less so in a general way. In Norway the costs of securing evidence shall be covered by the requiring party unless the other party has not cooperated or has contested the request without reasonable cause; a security may be requested by the addressee. These costs may, however, be recoverable in subsequent litigation related to the substantive issues for which the evidence was secured; these costs, indeed, seem to play a significant role in settlement negotiations.[190] Similar provisions are applicable in Spain for preliminary measures, i.e. for those that are granted before proceedings are commenced, except for one relevant particular: the applicant will not be entitled to obtain reimbursement of these costs, even if he or she eventually brings a claim and wins the case.[191] In the Netherlands the issue arose in a case decided by the District Court of The Hague under the IP Enforcement Directive between Bacardi and Top Logistics.[192] Among other reasons for opposing a request made by Bacardi, Top Logistics argued that it takes too much time and money to collect and organise all the requested documents. The court recognised this but considered it was not sufficient to outweigh the public interest in preventing counterfeit products; to set a balance, the court ordered Bacardi to reimburse Top Logistics' reasonable and proportionate costs.

10.096 In England and Wales disclosure is considered to trigger costs and delay to the proceedings, which may act as a disincentive to parties to commence proceedings. Despite the Aikens Review (2007)[193] and the Jackson Costs Review (2009)[194] and the attempts in the light of them to more effectively implement a proportionate approach to disclosure, disproportionate cost and delay remained endemic. That in turn led not

---

188 See n 10.019.
189 See n 5.093.
190 See n 7.077.
191 See n 5.052.
192 District Court The Hague, March 29, 2023, ECLI:NL:RBDHA:2023:4857, discussed in nn 6.071 et seq.
193 R Aikens, *Report and Recommendations of the Commercial Court Long Trials Working Party* (Judicial Office 2007).
194 R Jackson, *Review of Civil Litigation Costs: Final Report* (HMSO 2010).

to further reforms of the general scheme concerning disclosure (CPR Pt 31), but rather to the introduction of the special scheme applicable to business and property claims.[195]

A reasonable solution, once again, is offered by the Model European Rules of Civil Procedure, specifically Rule 108 (Costs and Security). **10.097**

(1) The cost of implementing an order for access to evidence shall be borne by the applicant. Where appropriate the court may require the applicant to make an immediate payment of costs to a party or non-party against whom the order is made.
(2) The court may, upon the application of the person against whom an order for access to evidence is made, order security to be given by the party in whose favour the order is made. The order shall be for any predictable expense to be incurred in the implementation of that order.[196] If security is required by the court, it must be provided before any order for access can be given effect.
(3) At the conclusion of the proceedings the court may determine the incidence of costs differently from the general rule.[197]

In the near future, technological issues will probably be higher on the agenda concerning effectivisation of already established duties of disclosure. Experiences from Anglo-American jurisdictions, and to some degree from Scandinavia as well,[198] suggest that solutions from AI or other advanced technologies may be highly helpful in practice. Technologies based on machine-learning and similar techniques have had promising results both concerning accuracy and effectiveness, especially for cases containing disclosure of massive banks of information.[199] **10.098**

K. GENERAL COMPARATIVE FINDINGS

As pointed out in the introduction to this Chapter, at least from the late decades of the 1800s there was a sharp contrast between the attitude towards access to evidence in different procedural traditions or legal cultures. While the Anglo-American legal family required broad disclosure of at least documents and other tangible evidence at an early stage of proceedings, most other legal families in Europe took a far more restrictive approach based on the old Roman slogan *Nemo tenetur contra es eder*. In **10.099**

---

195 See nn 2.018–2.025.

196 According to Stadler and Strandberg, *ERCP Commentary*, n 12.106, in determining the amount of security to be provided the court may also estimate the likelihood of damages for the respondent, if e.g. inspection by an expert requires entering the respondent's premises or the disassembly of things.

197 This provision is consistent with the wide discretionary powers that Rule 241 ERCP proposes granting to the court (on this, V Smith, *ERCP Commentary*, n 21.003 ff).

198 See n 7.055.

199 MR Grossman and GV Cormack, "Technology-Assisted Review in E-Discovery Can Be More Effective and More Efficient Than Exhaustive Manual Review" (2011) 17(5) *Richmond Journal of Law and Technology* 1; G Christian, "Predictive Coding: Adopting and Adapting Artificial Intelligence in Civil Litigation" (2019) 97 *The Canadian Bar Review* 486.

general, these historical differences between procedural traditions still influence the approaches to the problem of access to evidence in Europe. Even today, English and Welsh law are characterised by requirements of pre-trial disclosure of documents and other tangible evidence. German and Italian law, on the other hand, are still characterised by very narrow rules on access to evidence.

10.100 However, a tendency of convergence is clearly seen, especially from the 1990s onwards. After the Woolf reform of 1999 and later reforms, the English and Welsh rules have become less demanding, in particular by restricting duties of disclosure to what is proportionate. Within the German and the Roman procedural traditions, developments towards more demanding access to evidence rules either between the parties or as *ex officio* powers has been seen in most jurisdictions. Although the exact rules vary from one jurisdiction to another and may be more generous in one country than another, in general the development in these two legal families runs in favour of adjusting information asymmetry. Other European jurisdictions, such as the Netherlands and the Scandinavian countries, have developed middle ground solutions where access to evidence can be required if a set of conditions is fulfilled. An element in the development towards proximation or even harmonisation is the access to evidence requirements set up in EU Directives. These Directives, however, apply only for IP cases and cases concerning damages following from infringements of competition law, and most jurisdictions have implemented the Directives only for these two sectors.

10.101 In our opinion, both national legislators and the EU should continue developing access to evidence rules. While acknowledging the potential pitfalls of too broad and general access to evidence, both concerning costs and unnecessary intrusions of private matters, providing such access is instrumental for the effectiveness of many substantive rights and obligations. The fear of American fishing expeditions has had too strong of an impact on the developments in Europe. Even though US-discovery is indeed extreme and somewhat frightening seen from a European perspective, this book underlines the existence of national legal systems which have been able to develop access to evidence rights without ending up with fishing expeditions or other forms of extremism. In our opinion, ERCP provides a middle ground solution which is especially well-suited for further developments either at a European level or a national level.

10.102 Hopefully, the European legislator will expand its efforts on access to evidence issues. As the new Directive on product liability sets up rather broad requirements of disclosure of evidence, there are reasons to hope that the EU will continue setting such requirements also for other fields of law. Since that Directive regards more typical types of cases for civil procedure law than the two previous Directives, national legislators will have a stronger incentive to over-implement the Directive on product liability in order to avoid special rules for just one of several types of claims in the heart of traditional tort law. Hopefully, the entering into force of the product liability Directive also encourages the CJEU to regard disclosure of evidence as a minimum requirement directly based on the principle of effectiveness.

INDEX